D1049728

THE PARTY BATTLES OF THE JACKSON PERIOD

THE PARTY BATTLES OF THE JACKSON PERIOD

BY

CLAUDE G. BOWERS

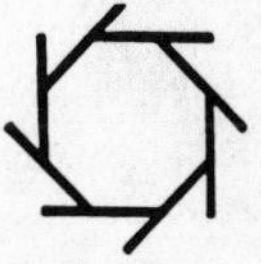

1965

OCTAGON BOOKS, INC.

New York

Reprinted 1965
by special arrangement with Houghton Mifflin Company

OCTAGON BOOKS, INC.
175 Fifth Avenue
New York, N.Y. 10010

Library of Congress Catalog Card Number: 65-25879

Printed in U.S.A. by
NOBLE OFFSET PRINTERS, INC.
NEW YORK 3, N. Y.

PREFACE

It is the purpose of the author to deal, more minutely than is possible in a general history or biography, with the brilliant, dramatic, and epochal party battles and the fascinating personalities of the eight years of Andrew Jackson's Administrations. From the foundation of the Republic to the last two years of the Wilson Administration, the Nation has never known such party acrimony; nor has there been a period when the contending party organizations have been led by such extraordinary politicians and orators. It was, in a large sense, the beginning of party government as we have come to understand it. It was not until the Jacksonian epoch that we became a democracy in fact. The selection of Presidents then passed from the caucus of the politicians in the capital to the plain people of the factories, fields, and marts. The enfranchisement of thousands of the poor, previously excluded from the franchise, and the advent of the practical organization politicians, wrought the change. Our government, as never before, became one of parties, with well-defined, antagonistic principles and policies. Party discipline and continuous propaganda became recognized essentials to party success.

This period witnessed the origin of modern party methods. The spoils system, instead of being a mere manifestation of some viciousness in Jackson, grew out of the assumed necessity for rewarding party service. The recognition of party government brought the national convention. The new power of the masses necessitated compact and drilled party organizations down to the precincts of the most remote sections, and even the card-index system known to-day was part of the plan of the incomparable politicians of the

Kitchen Cabinet. The transfer of authority from the small coterie of politicians to the people in the corn rows imposed upon the leaders the obligation to furnish the rank and file of their followers with political ammunition for the skirmishes at the country stores as well as for the heavy engagements at the polls, and out of this sprang the intense development of the party press, the delivery of congressional speeches for "home consumption," the party platform, and the keynote speech.

The triumph of the Jacksonians over the Clays, the Websters, and the Calhouns was due, in large measure, to their development of the first great practical politicians — that much-depreciated company sneeringly referred to as the Kitchen Cabinet, to whom all politicians since have paid the tribute of imitation.

With the appearance of Democracy in action came some evils that have persisted through the succeeding years — the penalties of the rule of the people. Demagogy then reared its head and licked its tongue. Class consciousness and hatreds were awakened. And, on the part of the great corporations, intimidation, coercion, and the corrupt use of money to control elections were contributed. These evils are a heritage of the bitter party battles of the Jacksonian period — battles as brilliant as they were bitter.

The purpose of this volume is to describe these mad party struggles, and to picture, as they really were, the great historical figures, "warts and all." If Henry Clay is here shown as an unscrupulous, selfish, scheming politician, rather than as the mythical figure who "would rather be right than President"; if John C. Calhoun is here described as petty in his personal hates and spites and in his resentment over the failure of personal ambitions; if Daniel Webster, the most admirable of the three during these eight vivid years, is set forth, not only as the great Nationalist who replied to Hayne and sustained Jackson's Nullification Proclamation, but as the defender of the Bank from which, at the beginning of the fight, he bluntly solicited a "refreshment" of his retainer, it is not through any desire to befoul their fame, but to set down the truth as irrefutably disclosed in the records, and to depict them as they were — intensely human in their moral limitations.

The necessities of history happily call for the featuring of some figures, potent in their generation, attractive in their genius, and necessarily passed over by historians covering much longer periods. No close-up picture of the time can be painted that ignores Edward Livingston, patriot and philosopher; Roger B. Taney, the militant party leader; John Forsyth, the "greatest debater of his time"; John M. Clayton, the real master of both Calhoun and Clay in the Compromise of 1833; George McDuffie, the tempestuous Danton of the Opposition; Hugh Lawson White, the "Cato of the Senate" and the Nemesis of Jacksonian Democracy; William Cabell Preston and Horace Binney, the polished orators, now almost forgotten; Major Lewis, the master of political details; Frank Blair, the slashing journalistic champion of the Administration; and Amos Kendall, the genius of the Kitchen Cabinet.

An analysis of motives and methods has led to some unconventional conclusions. Not only do Clay, Webster, and Calhoun dwindle in moral grandeur, but others, traditionally considered small, loom large. Thus the John Tyler of these eight years stands out in intellectual honesty, courage, and consistency far beyond others to whom history has been more generous.

No apology need be offered for featuring the personalities of the time. They throw light on motives and explain events. The episode of Mrs. Eaton changed the current of political history. The gossip concerning Mrs. White indicates the putridity of political factionalism. The scurrilous biography of Van Buren written by Davie Crockett on the suggestion of Senator White is illuminative of the popular prejudices of the times; and the solemn investigation of the charge that Senator Poindexter had instigated the attempt upon the life of the President at the Capitol discloses the morbidity of the partisan madness. Through the gossip of the drawing-rooms, the jottings of the diaries, the editorial comments of the contemporary press, the social and political intrigues of women, the attempt is made to re-create something of the atmosphere by which the remarkable statesmen and politicians of the Jackson Administrations were affected.

Generations have been taught to respect or reverence the memories of the extraordinary men of the Thirties who rode on the whirlwind to direct the storms; and, their human weaknesses forgotten, their sinister, selfish purposes ignored, their moral or intellectual limitations overlooked, they seem, in the perspective of the years, stern, austere, always sincere, and singularly free from the vices of politicians, as we have come to know them in the leaders of a later day. And yet it would be difficult to find creatures more thoroughly human than these who are usually presented to us as steel engravings, hung high on the wall in a dim light. They move across the page of history scarcely touching or suffering the contamination of the ground. They seem to play their parts upon a stage impressive and imposing, suspended between earth and heaven. That they lived in houses, danced, gambled and drank, flattered and flirted, gossiped and lied, in a Washington of unpaved streets and sticky black mud, made their way to night conferences through dark, treacherous thoroughfares, and played their brilliant parts in a bedraggled, village-like capital, is not apt to occur to one. Thus, in tracing the political drama of this portentous period, an attempt is made to facilitate the realization that they were flesh and blood, and mere men to their contemporaries, not always heroic or even admirable, through the visualization of the daily life they lived in a capital peculiarly crude and filled with grotesque incongruities.

No period in American political history is so susceptible to dramatization. There is grim tragedy in the baffled ambitions of Calhoun and Clay; romance in the rise of Kendall and the fall of Mrs. Eaton; rich comedy, when viewed behind the scenes, in the lugubrious procession of "distress petitioners" trained to tears by the art of Clay and the money of Biddle; and rollicking farce in the early morning flight of a dismissed Cabinet minister, to escape the apprehended chastisement of an erstwhile colleague whose wife's good name had been assailed.

The drama of party politics, with its motives of love, hate, and vaulting ambition — such is the unidealized story of the epochal period when the iron will of the physically feeble Jackson dominated the life of the Nation, and colored the politics of the Republic for a century.

The Drama — its motives — its actors — such the theme of this history.

CLAUDE G. BOWERS

CONTENTS

THE PARTY BATTLES OF THE JACKSON PERIOD

CHAPTER I

THE WASHINGTON OF THE THIRTIES

THE tourist traveling from Philadelphia to Washington in the Thirties anticipated few pleasures and no comforts from the trip that had to be made by coach from Baltimore, over roads intolerably wretched under the best conditions, and all but impassable and not without dangers in inclement weather. The journey from Philadelphia to Baltimore was usually made by boat through the Chesapeake and Delaware Canal, and the entire trip, in winter one of exposure, required the greater part of two days.[1] The fare from Baltimore to Washington was four dollars. Sometimes the ruts in the winter roads would overturn the coach, throwing the passengers into the mire, and occasionally resulting in sprains and broken bones.[2] Later in Jackson's time, the Baltimore & Ohio Railroad was built, with a branch into Washington, and when the first cars, drawn by horses, reached the country-town capital, the enthusiastic statesmen felt that the problem of transportation had been solved. Urging Butler to accept the attorney-generalship, and stressing the fact that acceptance would not preclude his appearance in personal cases in New York and Albany, Van Buren made much of the fact that "to the former place you will next season be able to

[1] *Life of Binney*, 104.

[2] Benton's explanation of the delay of the Bank messenger with the petition for a recharter. *Thirty Years' View.*

go in fifteen hours, and to the latter in a day and a night." [1] Blair, of the "Globe," boasted after the election of 1832 that "in eight days and nights after the closing of the polls in Ohio, the result was known in the city of Washington from all the organized counties except three." This, he declared, "is an instance of rapid communication from the West unparalleled in this country." [2]

The foreigner, expecting a national capital more or less pretentious and compact, was invariably shocked on entering the environs over miserable mud roads, to find only an occasional drab hut or cottage at wide intervals. Usually, until the Capitol attracted his attention, he was wholly unconscious of his arrival at his destination. One of these, who has left a record of his visit, relates that he was "looking from the window of his coach in a sort of brown study, at fields covered with snow," when a fellow passenger startled him with the inquiry as to how he liked Washington.

"I will tell you when I see it," he replied.

"Why, you have been in Washington the last quarter of an hour," was the rejoinder.[3]

Another famous visitor "was taken by surprise" on finding herself within the shadow of the hall of the lawmakers, "so sordid are the enclosures and houses on its very verge." [4]

But as the coach wound round the Capitol, and swung with a merry clatter into Pennsylvania Avenue, the houses at more frequent intervals and connected shops disclosed the town. With a characteristic "clatter and clamp," [5] with a gay cracking of whips, the coach would splash and rumble up to one of the leading hotels, and the cramped and weary tourist would joyously take leave of the conveyance and seek lodgment within.

[1] Van Buren to Butler, *Retrospect of Forty Years*, by Butler, 39–43.
[2] *Washington Globe*, Nov. 17, 1832.
[3] Thomas Hamilton, *Men and Manners in America*, 14.
[4] Harriet Martineau, *Retrospect of Western Travel*, I, 143.
[5] *Retrospect of Forty Years*, 47.

If well advised, he would instruct the coachman to drop him at Gadsby's, then the most popular and comfortable hostelry in town, on the Avenue, a short distance from the Capitol.[1] There he would find, not only a clean bed, but excellent service and a lordly hospitality from the host. Gadsby, for his generation, was a genius at his trade. He moved his small army of negro servants with military precision. "Who that ever knew the hospitalities of this gentlemanly and most liberal Boniface," wrote one who enjoyed them, "can ever forget his urbane manner, his careful attention to his guests, his well-ordered house, his fine old wines, and the princely manner in which he could send his bottle of choice Madeira to some old friend or favored guest at the table?"[2] It was not always, however, that accommodations could be found at Gadsby's, and then the tourist would seek the Indian Queen at the sign of the luridly painted picture of Pocahontas, where he would be met at the curb by Jesse Brown, the landlord.[3] Here, for a dollar and a quarter a day, he could not only find a pleasant room, but a table loaded with decanters of brandy, rum, gin, at short intervals from the head to the foot. If the host of the Indian Queen lacked the lordly elegance of Gadsby, he made up for it in the homely virtues of hospitality. Wearing a large white apron, he met his guests at the door of the dining-room, and then hastened to the head of the table where he personally carved and helped to serve the principal dish.[4] If this, too, was crowded, the tourist would try Fuller's near the White House,[5] where a room would be found for him either in the hotel proper, or in one of the two or three houses adjoining, which had been converted into an annex.[6]

Having rested from his journey and removed the stains of travel, if he were a person of some importance, and especially

[1] The present site of the National Hotel.
[2] Sargent's *Public Men and Events*, I, 53–54.
[3] On the site of the present Metropolitan.
[4] *Perley's Reminiscences*, I, 43.
[5] Present site of the Willard.
[6] *Retrospect of Forty Years*, 48.

a foreigner, he would be speedily deluged with the cards of callers anxious to make his sojourn pleasant. Day by day the hotel registers were eagerly scanned for the names of visiting celebrities, for the Washington of the Thirties loved its lions and lionesses. No possible person was ever neglected, and real personages were fêted, wined, and dined. But not until he set forth to return the calls would he appreciate the Portuguese Minister's description of the capital as "a city of magnificent distances." Inquiring at the hotel how to reach the residences of his callers, he would be not a little puzzled at the nonchalant reply that the coachmen "knew where all the prominent people live." Engaging a coach, he would set forth gayly, in the confident expectation of leaving his card at from thirty to forty houses in the course of the day. A short drive would take him to the end of the macadamized pavement of the Avenue, and thereafter for hours, pitching and plunging, over the ruts and the mud-holes, through miry lanes, and across vacant lots, shaken in body, and sore in spirit, he would find by evening that he had reached six or seven of the forty houses, and was charged by the coachman at a rate "which would keep a chariot and two posters for twice the time in London."[1] In the course of a week he would find that he had spent as much as thirty dollars for coach hire — by odds, the most expensive feature of his Washington sojourn. An English visitor, startled at the cost of travel, contracted with a coachman for services from five o'clock to daylight for twenty dollars, but after having attended five parties on the first evening, the morose driver repudiated his contract, and it was necessary to add five dollars to retain his services.[2] "I should imagine [Washington] to be the very paradise of hackney coachmen," wrote one disgusted visitor. "If these men do not get rich it must be owing to some culpable extravagance, for their vehicles are in continual

[1] N. P. Willis, *American Scenery*, III, 49.
[2] *Men and Manners in America*, 20, note.

demand from the hour of dinner [1] till five in the morning, and long distances and heavy charges are all in their favor." [2]

As the visitor drove about the town he found nothing in the physical aspects of the country-town capital to indicate that L'Enfant ever had a vision or produced a plan for a city beautiful. Because real estate dealers had quarreled over the location of public buildings, the selection of the hill for the Capitol had led to the location of the White House a mile or more to the west, and for three decades the problem of building a compact city between the two had failed. The streets were all unpaved when Jackson was first inaugurated, and only Pennsylvania Avenue between the Capitol and the President's Mansion had been rescued from the mire when he left office. Hub-deep in mud in inclement weather, these country roads sent forth great clouds of dust on dry and sunny days. With the exception of the Avenue, not a single street approached compactness, the houses on all other streets being occasionally grouped, but generally widely separated, and in some instances so much so as to suggest country houses with their shade trees and vegetable gardens.[3] "It looks as if it had rained naked buildings upon an open plain, and every man had made a street in reference to his own door," wrote Nathaniel P. Willis, who knew his Washington.[4] Another writer of the day who was impressed with "the houses scattered in straggling groups, three in one quarter, and half a dozen in another," was moved to compassion for "some disconsolate dwelling, the first or last born of a square or crescent, yet in nebulous suffering like an ancient maiden in the mournful solitude of single blessedness." [5] Still another contemporary word painter tells us that even on the Avenue "the buildings were standing with wide spaces between, like the teeth of some superannuated crone." [6]

[1] Four o'clock.

[2] *Men and Manners*, 20.

[3] Frederick Seward's *Reminiscences*, 17–19.

[4] *American Scenery*, III, 49.

[5] *Men and Manners*, 17.

[6] *Public Men and Events*, I, 54.

At the foot of the Capitol, itself beautiful even then, were desolate waste lands being reserved for some ultimate Botanical Gardens, and a few miserable shack-like boarding-houses.[1] "Everybody knows that Washington has a capitol," wrote a satirical English observer, "but the misfortune is that the capitol wants a city. There it stands, reminding you of a general without an army, only surrounded and followed by a parcel of ragged little dirty boys; for such is the appearance of the dirty, straggling, ill-built houses which lie at the foot of it." [2] Where the Smithsonian Institution has long stood were innumerable quagmires reeking with miasma.[3] About the President's Mansion, a few pretentious houses, several still handsome homes after almost a century, had been built, and in this section, and in Georgetown, lived the people of fashion and the diplomats. "The Co't end," it was called. At the four corners of the Mansion of the Presidents stood the plain brick buildings occupied by the State, Treasury, War, and Navy Departments. On Capitol Hill a few good houses had been erected, especially on North A and New Jersey Avenue, South. Other than these, and those west of the White House, there was little but pastures and enclosed fields in the eastern, southeastern, and northeastern sections of the town.[4] East of Fourteenth Street, on the north side, but few houses had been built beyond F Street, and the "country home" of William H. Crawford, at the northeast corner of Fourteenth Street and Massachusetts Avenue, was still considered as remote from town as on that winter day after his defeat for the Presidency when no callers were expected because of the heavy snow.[5]

Looking down upon the little town from the skylight of the Capitol, Harriet Martineau could plainly discern the "seven theoretical avenues," but with the exception of Pennsyl-

[1] *American Scenery*, II, 55.
[2] Captain Marryat, *A Diary in America*, 163.
[3] *Public Men and Events*, I, 55.
[4] *Public Men and Events*, I, 54.
[5] *Life of Crawford*, 183.

vania, all were "bare and forlorn," and the city which has become one of the most beautiful and impressive in the world could then present to the naked eye only "a few mean houses dotted about, the sheds of the navy yard on one bank of the Potomac, and three or four villas on the other." [1] With the streets full of ruts, the sidewalks dotted with pools of muddy water, or in places overgrown with grass, with cows pasturing on many of the streets now lined with elegant homes, and challenging the right of way with Marshall or Clay or Jackson, it is not surprising that foreigners, even as late as the Thirties, were moved to imitate the sarcasm of Tom Moore. The difficulties of locomotion kept the pedestrian's eyes upon the ground, and the inconveniences, in making calls, of crossing ditches and stiles, and walking alternately upon grass and pavement, and striking across fields to reach a street, were more noticeable than the noble trees that lined the avenues.[2] Wretched enough in the daytime, the poorly lighted streets at night were utterly impossible. "As for lights," wrote a contemporary, "if the pedestrian did not provide and carry his own, he was in danger of discovering every mud-hole and sounding its depths." [3] More nearly possible to the fastidious were the narrower streets of Georgetown, with its more imposing and interesting houses, and more select society, where many of the statesmen lived, and not a few of the Government clerks, who rode horseback to the departments in the morning.

Even in the Thirties there were many beautiful drives and walks in the vicinity of Washington, and a few houses that were impressive to even the most critical English visitor. Visible for many miles, and easily seen from the town, loomed the pillared white mansion of Arlington, then the home of George Washington Custis, to which many of the aristocrats of the capital frequently found their way. There, during the

[1] *Retrospect of Western Travel*, I, 160. [2] *Ibid.*, I, 144.
[3] *Public Men and Events*, I, 54.

Jacksonian period, Robert E. Lee, standing in the room, whence, across the river, he could see the Capitol building, was united in marriage to the daughter of the house.[1] Within the city the most imposing mansions were those of John Tayloe, at Eighteenth Street and New York Avenue, designed by Thornton, and even then rich in political and social memories,[2] and the handsome residence of John Van Ness, the work of Latrobe, built at a cost of sixty thousand dollars to make a fit setting for the charm and beauty of Marcia Burns, at the foot of Seventeenth Street, on the banks of the Potomac. From the doorstep the master and his guests could watch the ships from across the sea mooring to the docks of Alexandria, and the merchantmen, bound for the port of Georgetown, laden with the riches of the West Indies.

The tourist in the Washington of the Thirties did not have the opportunity for sight-seeing that means so much to the capital visitor of to-day. Aside from the Capitol and the White House, there were no public buildings of architectural distinction. The churches had "nothing about them to attract attention," and while St. John's on Lafayette Square was then summoning to worship, it did not at that time have the virtue of quaintness or the mellowness of historical memories. A visit to the Patent Office was customarily made, and most tourists found something to interest them in the museum of the State Department, with its portraits of the Indian chiefs who had visited Washington.[3] Occasionally the venturesome would ascend to the skylight of the Capitol to survey the straggling and dreary town from the height.[4] But always there was the dignified and stately white building of the lawmakers and of the Supreme Court,

[1] Godfrey T. Vigne, in *Six Months in America*, thought that "in the distance" Arlington "has the appearance of a superior English country residence."

[2] The Octagon House still standing and being preserved by the Institute of American Architects.

[3] *Men and Manners*, 75.

[4] Miss Martineau tells of visits to the museum and the skylight, I, 159.

and thither tourists and citizens, men and women, daily found their way for the entertainment that never failed. Surrounded by its terraces, its well-kept lawns, its profusion of shrubbery, the visitor reached the entrance over its "beautifully gravelled walks," [1] and entered the rotunda with its four Trumbull paintings of Revolutionary scenes, to be more impressed with the vacant spaces for four more, and the explanation that "Congress cannot decide on what artist to confer the honor." [2] He would not fail to be delighted with the classic little Senate Chamber, redolent of the genius of Latrobe, and with the ease with which he might ignore the tiny gallery to find a hearty welcome on the floor. If a foreigner, he would be surprised to find a constant stream of fashionable ladies entering the chamber, crowding the Senators, accepting their seats, and attracting attention with their "waving plumes glittering with all the colors of the rainbow, and causing no little bustle." [3] There he would see Van Buren or Calhoun in the chair, and on the floor he would want to have Webster, Clay, Benton, Forsyth, Preston, and Ewing pointed out. And perhaps, like Miss Martineau, he would leave with the impression that he had "seen no assembly of chosen men and no company of the high born, invested with the antique dignities of an antique realm, half so imposing to the imagination as this collection of stout-souled, full-grown, original men brought together on the ground of their supposed sufficiency, to work out the will of their diverse constituencies." [4]

Having seen the Senate, he would seek the House of Representatives. Inquiring his way to the Strangers' Gallery from the rotunda, he would be directed to a narrow stairs, and, on ascending, would find himself in a large room of many columns, the work of the architect of the Senate, looking

[1] William H. Seward's *Autobiography*, I, 277. [2] *Ibid.*

[3] Miss Martineau comments severely upon the levity of the women, I, 180.

[4] *Retrospect of Western Travel*, I, 179.

down upon the seats of members arranged in concentric rows. Thence he would look down upon the bald head of the venerable Adams, the anæmic figure of Polk, the handsome form of Binney, and the ludicrous conglomeration of garbs representing the diverse tastes of the tailors of New York and the wilderness. If acquainted with one of the members, the visitor might be invited to the corridor behind the Speaker's desk, fitted with seats and sofas drawn about the fireplace at either end, where members and their guests were wont to lounge and smoke.[1] Having satisfied himself with the chambers of the lawmakers, the visitor would want to see the tribunal of interpretation, said by some to have more power in determining the law of the land than the members of Congress, and to observe the famous Marshall on the Supreme Bench. Descending to the basement of the Capitol, immediately under the Senate, he would be shown into a small plain room with low ceiling, and "a certain cellar-like aspect which is not pleasant," [2] and would probably be a little shocked at the figure of Justice, "a wooden figure with the eyes unfilleted, and grasping the scales like a groceress." [3] On cushioned sofas, on either side of the room, he might, if a favorite orator were making an argument, see gayly dressed ladies — for, like the Senate Chamber, the court was one of the fashionable resorts of the Thirties. But there, he would find dignity and quiet and decorum, in striking contrast with most of the American courts of that generation.[4] If fortunate, he might listen to the reading of a decision by Marshall, and observe Butler, the Attorney-General, "his fingers playing among his papers, his thick black eyes and thin, tremulous lips for once fixed, his small face pale with thought,"

[1] *Men and Manners*, 16. [2] *Ibid.*, 65.

[3] *Six Months in America*, 64.

[4] Both Hamilton (*Men and Manners*) and Vigne, the English barrister (*Six Months in America*), were shocked at the utter lack of respect for the dignity of American courts, but were impressed with the solemnity and decorum in the Supreme Court.

contrasting with the more composed countenances of Clay and Webster.[1]

In the days of Jackson, comparatively few families had a permanent residence in Washington, and to an English visitor the town had the appearance of a watering-place.[2] Many Senators and Representatives considered it so impossible that they left their families at home.[3] Attorney-General Butler at first refused to consider a position in the Cabinet because "Mrs. Butler did not like the idea of bringing her daughters up here."[4] When the wives and daughters did accompany the statesmen to the capital, it was the custom, with such as could afford to maintain an establishment, to take a house. These usually purchased, albeit many of the more desirable residences that could be leased were not for sale. An establishment could be maintained at a surprisingly low cost. Houses "suitable for the purposes of genteel people" could be had for from $50 to $300 a year, and even the large mansions, many of them standing and still occupied by fashionable families after almost a century, could be had for from $500 to $800 a year.[5] The servant problem did not exist, for domestics could be employed in abundance for $4 a month.[6] The Southerners, bringing their slaves with them, or buying them in the slave market at Alexandria, were able to entertain with a lavish display which set the pace socially, and made the Southern dominance easy. Foreigners were impressed, after hearing a senatorial orator rhapsodize in the Senate over the blessings of American liberty, to see him driven from the Capitol after his oration by one of his family slaves.[7] Others, not wishing to be burdened with a house,

[1] *Retrospect of Western Travel*, I, 165. [2] *Men and Manners*, 21.

[3] Senator Tazewell of Virginia was one of these.

[4] Van Buren to Butler, *Retrospect of Forty Years*, 39–43.

[5] *National Intelligencer*, Jan. 30, 1831, advertised a house in Georgetown on Gay Street, "convenient for the accommodation of a genteel family, having all necessary outhouses, stabling, etc.," for $300 a year payable quarterly.

[6] *Public Men and Events*, I, 55.

[7] Hamilton, in *Men and Manners*, comments severely upon this incongruity.

lived in the hotels, where other people's slaves waited upon them. In these, too, the cost of living was low, the leading hostelries taking guests at $1.75 a day, $10 a week, or $35 a month. Transients sat down to tables fairly groaning with food, and with decanters of brandy and whiskey at their elbows, free at these prices. The guest, in his room, could order real Madeira for $3 a bottle, sherry, brandy, and gin for $1.50, and Jamaica rum for $1. The statesman, leaving his hotel quarters for the Senate or the House, could, if he wished, pause at the bar of the hostelry for a toddy of unadulterated liquor and lump sugar for twelve and a half cents.[1] But the greater part of the public men lived in boarding-houses, and the "Intelligencer," the "Globe," and the "Telegraph" filled columns, at the beginning of congressional sessions, with the enticing advertisements of the landladies. Some few of these houses, such as Dawson's, associated with celebrities, live in history, but the majority were small, shabby, and uncomfortable. In these, however, romances sometimes blossomed, and the barmaid of one presided for a time over the establishment of a Cabinet member, and the landlady of another over the household of a Senator who aspired to the Presidency.[2]

Out of this life in hotels and boarding-houses, during the Jacksonian period, came the custom of statesmen forming themselves and families into "messes," each "mess" having a table to itself and contracting with the landlady or landlord for a caterer. In this way the lawgivers were socially grouped according to their intellectual and financial standing, and some of these "messes" were famous in their day. Friendships were formed that survived all the vicissitudes of time and political change. One of these, known as the "Woodbury mess," consisted of such a notable coterie of brilliancy and genius as Calhoun, John Randolph, Tazewell, Burges, and

[1] *Perley's Reminiscences*, I, 143.

[2] Peggy Eaton and Mrs. Hugh Lawson White.

Verplanck. About the table many celebrated measures were conceived and the strategy of many a fight was planned.[1] According to the law of the "mess" a member might invite a guest only with the consent of all the others, and it was understood that a failure to get unanimous consent should not be resented. Occasionally the guests were permitted to contribute something to the usual outlay. Daniel Webster was glad enough to pay his way on such occasions. The venerable Adams, who had a comfortable home on F Street[2] and was not considered a notably social animal, delighted to join his most interesting colleagues at the boarding-house or hotel table. "I dined with John C. Calhoun at Dawson's," he recorded. "Mr. Preston, the other Senator from South Carolina, and his wife were there, and Mangum, Southard, Sprague of Maine. Company sat late at table and the conversation was chiefly upon politics. The company was, at this time, adversaries of the present Administration — most of them were adversaries to the last."[3] Three days later: "Dined with Benj. Gorham and Edward Everett. Calhoun, Preston, Clay, and others were there."[4] The next evening: "Dined with Colonel Robert B. Campbell of S.C. at his lodgings at Gadsby's"; thirty people, including Calhoun and Preston, in attendance.[5]

It was inevitable that in a little city of twenty thousand, consisting in part of the cleverest men and women in the Republic, and devoted wholly to politics and society, celebrated sojourners should be fêted and lionized. Foreigners visiting America in the Thirties, and recording their impressions, have all paid tribute to the hospitality and brilliance of the capital, as compared with other and larger cities. The most famous of the visitors was Harriet Martineau, who arrived in the summer of 1834, in her thirty-second year, and

[1] *Retrospect of Forty Years*, 59.

[2] Near Fourteenth Street on the north side of the street.

[3] Adams's *Memoirs*, March 8, 1834.

[4] *Ibid.*, March 11, 1834.

[5] *Ibid.*, March 12, 1834.

in the full flush of her literary fame. Introduced to the President and the Senate leaders by the British Minister, it was the rumor at the time that six hundred people called upon her the day after her arrival.[1] "The drollest part of the whole," wrote a lady of fashion, "is that these crowds, at least in Washington, go to see the lion and nothing else. I have not met with an individual, except Mrs. Seaton and her mother,[2] who have read any of her works, or know for what she is celebrated. Our most fashionable exclusive,[3] Mrs. Tayloe, said she intended to call, and asked what were the novels she had written, and if they were pretty. The gentlemen laugh at a woman's writing on political economy. Not one of them has the least idea of her work."[4] But the fluency of the lioness captivated the men. Among her constant visitors were Webster, Clay, Calhoun, Preston, and Justice Story. When she entered the Senate Chamber or the Supreme Court room, the leading men of the Nation left their seats to pay her homage. Calhoun's "mess" gave her a dinner. Clay insisted that at Lexington she should occupy his house at Ashland, and that she should be the guest of his daughter in New Orleans. Calhoun assured her triumph in Charleston through letters to his friends. "No stranger except Lafayette ever received such universal and marked testimonies of regard," wrote a sympathetic observer of her reception.[5] When Thomas Hamilton, the English writer, author of "Men and Manners in America," reached Washington, a member of Congress escorted him, uninvited, to a ball on the evening of his arrival, with the assurance that the "in-

[1] Mrs. Margaret Bayard Smith, who recorded it in *First Forty Years of American Society*, Jan. 12, 1835, thought it exaggerated.

[2] Mrs. Seaton, wife of the editor of the *Intelligencer*.

[3] Mrs. Benjamin Ogle Tayloe lived in the house still standing on Lafayette Square, known in recent years as "The Little White House." She was a famous hostess. President W. H. Harrison contracted the cold that killed him while walking through the slush from the White House to the Tayloes' to offer a diplomatic post to the master of the house.

[4] *First Forty Years*, 356.

[5] *Ibid.*, 368.

trusion would be welcome." After passing "through a formidable array of introductions to distinguished persons, and after four hours of almost unbroken conversation, much of which could not be carried on without considerable expenditure of thought," the weary tourist, at three o'clock in the morning, rejoiced to find himself "stretched in a comfortable bed at Gadsby's." [1] The experiences of Hamilton and Miss Martineau were not exceptional.

Nor were American literary celebrities left in doubt as to the cordiality of their welcome in the best social circles of the capital. The winter of 1833 found Washington Irving in Washington, where he was not unfamiliar with the leading houses, living "in the neighborhood of the McLanes" and making "use of a quiet corner and a little interval of leisure to exercise a long neglected pen." [2] Despite the flood of invitations, he found time to report to Van Buren the attitude of McLane, and the hostilities, in select circles, to Kendall. "Washington Irving is here now," wrote John Tyler to his daughter. "He stands at the head of our literati. His productions are numerous and well spoken of in Europe." [3] Nor did society in those days lack their chronicler, for the first society letters from Washington were those of Nathaniel P. Willis written for the "New York Mirror." At that time he was "a foppish, slender young man, with a profusion of curly light hair, and was always dressed in the height of fashion." [4] The doors of the most exclusive homes were thrown open to this elegant youth, who, having traveled in Europe, affected a contempt for the masses. He became the faithful Pepys of the period, describing society people and events with liveliness and fancy, and imparting a strange interest to the most insignificant occurrences through the art of the telling. It was during this period, too, that the political

[1] *Men and Manners*, 17.

[2] Irving to Van Buren, Van Buren's *Autobiography*, 610.

[3] *Letters and Times*.

[4] *Perley's Reminiscences*, I, 107.

letters of Washington correspondents were introduced into American journalism. Matthew L. Davis, famous as the "Genevese Traveller" of the London "Times," and as the capital correspondent of the "New York Courier and Enquirer," was for years the confidant and companion of Senators, Justices, and Presidents. And James Gordon Bennett, young and clever, appeared upon the scene to give a new and spicy touch to reporting with his Walpolean letters of wit, sarcasm, and personalities, for the New York paper of James Watson Webb. Along with the democratization of politics in the Thirties went a popularization of the methods of the press.

The amusements of the Washington of this time were, for the most part, crude. The theater featured players scarcely celebrated in their own day, and most of the plays presented have happily been long since forgotten. Even these were interspersed with songs and farce acts. In 1820 the Washington Theater had been built, and hither, at long intervals, came celebrated artists, but they came "like angels, few and far between." From his rustic retreat in Maryland the elder Booth, half mad, all genius, occasionally emerged to curdle the blood of the statesmen and their families with his intense interpretations of the Shakesperian tragedies. From a Booth night Jackson was seldom absent. But of all the artists who played in the capital none created such a furor as Fanny Kemble. The elder statesmen were captivated by her art and charm. John Marshall and Justice Story were regular attendants, and the Chief Justice was lustily cheered as he entered the box. When she played Mrs. Haller in "The Stranger," and the audience was moved to tears, "the Chief Justice shed them in common with the younger eyes." [1] Inspiring audiences — those of the Thirties, with Marshall, Jackson, Webster, Clay, and Calhoun in the boxes or the pit. Great, not only in genius, but in their fresh capacity to enjoy,

[1] Story to Sarah Waldo Story, *Life and Letters of Story*, II, 117.

and when one of the most learned Justices of the Supreme Court could be moved to poesy in paying tribute to an actress's art.[1]

But even with a Kemble playing, the haughty little country capital refused to abandon its parties, and we have the record of a New Yorker finding "Fanny Kemble in the Washington Theater like a canary bird in a mouse trap," leaving the theater in the midst of a performance to attend "a delightful party at Mrs. Tayloe's," where he "met many distinguished people and all the Washington belles."[2] In those days the theater-goer purchased his tickets between ten and one o'clock, and the doors were thrown open at six, with the curtain rising promptly at seven. For the usual performances the boxes were seventy-five cents, the pit twenty-five. When the rain converted the streets into ribbons of sticky black mud, or the bitter cold made an invitation to the people from the "magnificent distances" unprofitable, the papers would announce a postponement, with an explanation.[3] The pleasure-seekers were not restricted, however, to the players of the Washington Theater, and occasionally a show would appear advertising "the Great

[1] Story wrote the following lines to Miss Kemble:

"Genius and taste and feeling all combine
To make each province of the drama thine.
She first to Fancy's bright creation gives
The very form and soul; it breathes — it lives.
She next with grace inimitable plays
In every gesture, action, tone and gaze.
The last to nature lends its subtlest art
And warms and wins and thrills and melts the heart.
Go, lovely woman, go. Enjoy thy fame.
A second Kemble with a deathless name."

(*Life and Letters of Story*, II, 117.)

[2] Hone's *Diary*, March 3, 1834.

[3] "The public is most respectfully informed that, in consequence of the weather, the performance advertised for Thursday is postponed until Saturday evening, September 17th, 1831." (*National Intelligencer*, Sept. 17, 1831.) "The Tyrolese Minstrels have to announce that, in consequence of the severity of the weather, their concert which was advertised for Saturday will be deferred until Monday evening." (*Ibid.*, Dec. 19, 1831.)

Anaconda of Java," and the "Boa Constrictor of Ceylon," both "so docile that the most timid lady or child may view them with safety and pleasure."[1] Such were the amusements offered for the entertainment of Jackson, Webster, Marshall, Calhoun, and Clay.

But for the men there were other forms of amusement, popular in their day. The racing on the National Course near the city made it difficult to maintain a quorum in Congress, and the statesmen mounted their horses to ride to the track to cheer their favorites and to bet their money. Even the President entered his horses and lost heavily on his wagers. There Jackson and a goodly portion of the Cabinet, and a formidable sprinkling of the leaders of the Opposition from Clay to Letcher, might be seen backing their judgment as to horseflesh with their purses. And when it was not horse-racing, it was cockfighting, with the President entering his own birds from the Hermitage, and riding with his friends to Bladensburg to witness the humiliation of his entries. It was a day of gambling, when statesmen, whose names children are now taught to reverence, played for heavy stakes for days and nights at a time, with Clay and Poindexter losing fortunes, and an occasional victim of the lure blowing out his brains. While most of the celebrities played in private houses, they could, if they preferred, find the notorious gambling-houses along the Avenue. Along with racing, cockfighting, and gambling went heavy drinking. "Since I have been here," wrote Horace Binney, after two years in Congress. "one man, an habitual drunkard, blew out his brains; two have died notorious drunkards, and one of them shamefully immoral. The honors are given to all, with equal eulogy and ceremonial."[2] The statesman of the Thirties who did not drink heavily was a rarity. Just as whiskey, brandy, gin, and wine were served in great decanters on the tables at hotels, "at the boarding-houses every guest had his bottle or interest

[1] Advertisement in the *Globe*.

[2] *Life of Binney*, 127.

in a bottle." [1] On the way to the Capitol, the statesman could quench his thirst at numerous bars — and often did. And in the basement of the Capitol building whiskey could be had. Never in American history have so many promising careers been wrecked by drunkenness as during the third decade. Frequently national celebrities would appear upon the floor of the House or Senate in a state of intoxication, and on at least one occasion the greater part of the house was hilariously drunk.[2] Thus, despite the miry streets, the drabness and rusticity, the Washington of the Jacksonian period was easily the gayest, the most brilliant and dissipated community in the country. A penetrating observer found, in its recklessness and extravagance, a striking similarity to the spirit of the eighteenth century in England, as portrayed in Thackeray's "Humorists," with "laxity of morals and the coolest disregard possible." [3] Its superior social charm was due to the fact that it was "the only place in the Union where people consider it necessary to be agreeable — where pleasing, as in the Old World, becomes a sort of business, and the enjoyments of social intercourse enter into the habitual calculations of every one." [4] A goodly portion of the women of good society, and other sojourners, were apt to contemplate a Washington season as "a sort of annual lark," which offered the most promising solution of the problem of a weary winter in the country. Willis explained the attractions of the country capital on the ground that "the great deficiency in all our cities, the company of highly cultivated and superior men, is here supplied." [5] Even the supercilious and scolding Captain Marryat of England found it "an agreeable city, full of pleasant, clever people, who come here to amuse and be amused," and he observed "much more *usage du monde* and Continental ease than in any other parts of the States." [6]

[1] Quincy's *Figures of the Past*.
[2] This charge was made on the floor by Henry A. Wise.
[3] *Perley's Reminiscences*, I, 120.
[4] *Men and Manners*, 20.
[5] *American Scenery*, II, 50.
[6] *Diary in America*, 163.

After spending several crowded weeks in the social and political heart of the town, Harriet Martineau concluded that, while life there would be "dreary" to women who loved domesticity, "persons who love dissipation, who love to watch the game of politics, and those who make a study of strong minds under strong excitement, like a season in Washington."[1] Ludicrous as it was in its incongruities, the little city bravely assumed the pose of a real capital, plumed itself on the superiority of its society, and made much of the fashions. At the crowded receptions the wondering visitor might very easily be jostled against Webster or Sam Houston, dandies like Willis or frontiersmen in boots and soiled linen, flirtatious belles and matrons, beauties and beasts. But there were many leaders of fashion who imitated the frivolities of European capitals, ordered their dresses from Paris or London, and regularly summoned coiffeurs to their homes to dress their hair for balls and receptions.[2] When Congress was in session fashionable women from every section flocked to the seat of government bringing their daughters for a Washington season. One of the resident society leaders, commenting on their coming, dolefully complained that they were "coming in such ton and expensive fashions, that the poor citizens cannot pretend to vie with them and absolutely shrink into insignificance."[3] The shops made much of their Paris finery. Mrs. Coursault announced "to the ladies of the metropolis that she has just returned from Paris with a most splendid assortment of millinery and goods, to be seen at the store of Mrs. Lamplier on the Avenue."[4] Mr. Palmieri advertised that he had "just received from Paris an elegant assortment of caps and pelerines direct from Mademoiselle

[1] *Retrospect of Western Travel*, I, 143.

[2] A. Lafore, a coiffeur from Paris, had his establishment at Mrs. Doynes's millinery store on the Avenue between Ninth and Tenth Streets, and advertised his skill in the local papers. *National Intelligencer*, Jan. 1, 1831.

[3] *First Forty Years*, Jan. 26, 1830.

[4] *National Intelligencer*, Jan. 2, 1831.

Minette's, the first Milliner of Paris, and a beautiful assortment of satin shoes."[1] Another announced "French dresses for balls," and still another, "the arrival from Paris of an elegant assortment of French jewelry."

The daily life of the fashionable ladies of the time began with breakfast at nine, when they amused themselves by comparing the conflicting descriptions of scenes they had witnessed the day before in the "Intelligencer" and the "Globe." By eleven they were apt to be on their way to the Capitol to enliven the solemnity of the Senate Chamber or the Supreme Court, unless a neglected call, an appointment with an artist, or an excursion interfered. Dinner was served from four to six, and soon afterwards milady retired to her boudoir to dress for some ball, rout, levee, or masquerade. Long drives through the mud — late hours with the breaking dawn greeting her return — and the weary lady would relax and warm awhile at the drawing-room fire before retiring for the night.[2] Contrary to the popular belief, there was much social brilliance during the Jackson Administrations. Nor is the prevailing impression that all the elegance, cleverness, and charm was confined to the drawing-rooms of the Whig aristocracy borne out by the facts. In truth, among the women of the Jacksonian circle there were two or three who were easily superior to the best the Whigs could offer, in intellect, culture, and beauty. Such was the bigotry of the times that there was a tendency for society to segregate into camps, but it was impossible to draw the party line on a number of the fascinating and brilliant women who presided over the households of Jacksonian Senators and Cabinet Ministers. While the Whigs generally remained severely aloof from the house of the President, they were unable to resist the invitations of the President's friends.

[1] *National Intelligencer*, Feb. 16, 1831.

[2] Miss Martineau thus describes the life of a lady of fashion, *Retrospect of Western Travel*, I, 145.

Among all the women of the period none approached Mrs. Edward Livingston in brilliance, charm, and elegance, nor did any of the ladies of the Whig circle, not even Mrs. Tayloe, who wondered if Miss Martineau's novels were "pretty," approach her in the lavishness and taste of her dinners and parties. "Mrs. Livingston takes the lead in the fashionable world," wrote Mrs. Smith, who found it hard to concede the virtues of the Jacksonians.[1] "I know that Mr. Livingston gives elegant dinners and his wines are the best in the city," recorded a press correspondent of the time.[2] "We dined by invitation with Mr. Secretary Livingston," wrote Justice Story, an enemy of the Jacksonians. "The dinner was superb and unequalled by anything I have seen in Washington except at some of the foreign ministers', and was served exclusively in the French style."[3] This captivating woman, of French descent, had known a childhood of romance in a marble palace by the sea in St. Domingo, had miraculously escaped the servile insurrection, and reached New Orleans to become the wife of Livingston. Wonderfully vivacious, eloquent in conversation, intelligently interested in politics, steeped in the literature of the ages, witty and spirited, her home in Lafayette Square more nearly resembled a salon than anything the capital has ever known. Even the most bigoted Whigs of the day were glad to lay aside their partisanship at her threshold, and leaders, still flushed with a verbal duel in the Senate, smiled amicably upon each other in her drawing-room. Here one might meet John Marshall, Joseph Story, and Bushrod Washington of the Supreme Court, Webster, Clay, Calhoun, Wirt, or Randolph. About her, too, she gathered a coterie of cultured women, and Mrs. John Quincy Adams and Mrs. Andrew Stevenson came and went in the house on the Square with as little ceremony as members of

[1] *First Forty Years*, Nov. 7, 1831.

[2] Quoted by Ellet in *Court Circles of the Republic*, 163 n.

[3] Letter to Mrs. Sarah Waldo Story, *Life and Letters of Story*, II, 117.

the household. The charm of the house was enhanced by the exquisite Cora, the daughter, who reigned as the belle and toast of the town until her marriage, captivating, among others, the impressionable young Josiah Quincy, who thought her "undoubtedly the greatest belle in the U.S.," and, if not "transcendently handsome," possessed of a "fine figure, a pretty face." Finding it "the height of the ton to be her admirer," the young Bostonian followed the fashion with all his heart.[1]

Intimately identified with Mrs. Livingston was Mrs. Stevenson, to whom the years had been kind since the days when, as Sally Coles, she was a protégée of Dolly Madison.[2] At this time she was the wife of the Jacksonian Speaker of the House, soon to become the hostess of the American Legation in London, and to witness, in that rôle, the coronation of Victoria. Strikingly handsome, tall and commanding, she resembled her friend in an ineffable graciousness of manner and an extraordinary conversational ability. Among the most famous hostesses of the Jacksonian circle were Mrs. Louis McLane, "a gay, frank, communicative woman" whose "self-complacence is united with so much good humor in others that it is not offensive," who gave popular weekly dinners and parties;[3] Mrs. Levi Woodbury, beautiful of form and feature, who resembled Dolly Madison in her suavity, ease of manner, and infinite tact, and presided over her many dinners and dances with dignity and grace, and made a practice of featuring the most dashing belles of Baltimore, Alexandria, and Georgetown;[4] and Mrs. John Forsyth, more conventional and retiring than the others, but yielding to none in culture and elegance, and having a certain advantage in her "group of graces."[5] Among the hostesses of the

[1] *Figures of the Past.* [2] Mrs. Wharton's *Social Life of the Republic,* 139, 179.
[3] *First Forty Years*, Aug. 29, 1831.
[4] Ellet's *Court Circles of the Republic*, 226.
[5] A poet describing one of the Adams parties referred to "Forsyth with her group of graces" — her beautiful daughters.

Opposition, Mrs. Benjamin Ogle Tayloe, a woman of grace and beauty, but lacking in the intellectual sparkle of Mrs. Livingston, maintained the most elegant establishment.

But these were only the most brilliant leaders, for the Jacksonian period was one of hectic social activity, with foreign ministers and Cabinet members entertaining constantly and lavishly, and the official underlings desperately bent on a ruinous and riotous imitation. It was a day of much pretense and pose, of ceremonious intercourse, and it was not easy to determine from the swallow-tails and the buff waistcoats whether the wearer were a Senator or a clerk.[1] It was a conversational period, and seldom has the American capital contained at one time so many excellent talkers. Nor was the talk mere chat and gossip. Even the women, especially from the South, were clever conversationalists, able keenly to discuss the politics of the day and the measures of the hour.[2] Even the busiest and greatest party leaders had the time and inclination for calls on bright women when they could enjoy the Johnsonian luxury of having their talk out. We have a picture of Clay "sitting upright on the sofa, with a snuff box ever in his hand," discoursing "for many hours in his even, soft, deliberative tone"; of Webster, "leaning back at his ease, telling stories, cracking jokes, shaking the sofa with burst after burst of laughter, or smoothly discoursing to the perfect felicity of the logical part of one's constitution"; of Calhoun, the "cast iron man," who "looked as if he had never been born," no longer capable of mental relaxation, meeting men and haranguing them by the fireside as in the Senate; of Justice Story, talking gushingly for hours, "his face all the while, notwithstanding his gray hair, showing all the nobility and ingenuousness of a child's."[3] The talk

[1] *Retrospect of Forty Years*, 60.

[2] Quincy, in *Figures of the Past*, was thus impressed, particularly with the daughter of Calhoun.

[3] These descriptions of Miss Martineau's are in harmony with those that sprinkle the pages of Mrs. Smith's work.

about the firesides and at the receptions, that were given over entirely to conversation, was by no means confined to art, eloquence, and poetry, for the Mother Grundys of gossip were numerous among the women seeking to amuse and be amused. There were personalities as well as personages in the years that Jackson directed a triumphant party and Clay led a brilliant and militant opposition.[1] The little town of twenty thousand was not so large that the ladies could not know, from observation or deduction, when Adams dined with Calhoun, when Webster called on Mrs. Livingston, and what Mrs. Tayloe served her guests at her last reception.

"Did you have candied oranges at Mrs. Woodbury's?" asked a lady who had dined with Mrs. Cass, of a friend who had dined with the wife of the Secretary of the Navy.

"No."

"Then they had candied oranges at the Attorney-General's," was the deduction.

"How do you know?"

"Oh, as we were on the way, I saw a dish carried; and as we had none at Cass's, I knew they were either for the Woodburys or the Attorney-General's." [2]

It was the golden age of gallantry as well as gossip, some flirtatious, some courtly. If the admirer of John Forsyth's daughter proposed in a Valentine Day verse [3] throbbing with adolescent passion, the more staid and sober-minded Francis Scott Key wrote, in a fine hand, religious hymns for the pleasure of her mother.[4]

The evening parties were the most popular form of entertainment, and the hostesses of the Cabinet circle set the pace. The invitations were sent out nine days in advance. Because

[1] Mrs. Smith's *First Forty Years*, Miss Martineau's *Retrospect of Western Travel*, and Adams's *Diary* all indicate a gossipy city.

[2] *Retrospect of Western Travel*, I, 152.

[3] The original from "Alphonse" in possession of Waddy Wood, Washington, D.C.

[4] This, too, in the possession of Waddy Wood.

of the exigencies of politics, and the exactions of an awakened "Democracy," these could be neither small nor exclusive in character, and from seven to nine hundred invitations were usually extended. Between nine and ten o'clock all the apartments would be thrown open. The muddy streets in front would be congested with carriages. The host and hostess, standing in the drawing-room, would receive their guests, and then the more serious would withdraw to quiet corners for conversation, the gay and frivolous would swing into the dance, and the devotees of chance would seek and find a remote corner for cards. Servants would gingerly thread their way through the throng with light refreshments until eleven o'clock when an elaborate supper would be served. By three o'clock the company would begin to retire, and usually, at daybreak, the lights would be extinguished.[1]

It was a day of social novelties. Ice-cream as a refreshment first made its appearance in the country capital at the home of the widow of Alexander Hamilton. Introduced at the White House immediately afterwards by Jackson, it took society by storm,[2] and Kinchy, the confectioner on the Avenue, who had a monopoly on ice-cream and ices, became as indispensable socially as the chef and the fiddler.[3] Of the dances, the most popular was the waltz, introduced two years before Jackson's inauguration, and, considered at first of questionable modesty, it soon won its way, and the matrons found it as alluring as the débutantes. Even then there were censorious people to see in the dreamy glide an example of the moral degeneracy of the age.[4] To accentuate their pessimism, the crowds were invariably so dense that the dancers could scarcely move, reminding an amused Kentuckian "of a Kentucky fight when the crowd draws the circle so close that the combatants have no room to use their

[1] *Court Circles of the Republic*, 180.
[2] *Perley's Reminiscences*, I, 168.
[3] *Retrospect of Forty Years*, 60.
[4] Mary C. Crawford, *Romantic Days of the Early Republic*, 207.

limbs." But despite the crowded quarters, the twenty-four fiddlers in a row bravely sought "by dint of loud music to put the amateurs in motion," until they jumped "up and down in a hole, and nobody sees more of them than their heads." [1] Queer, conglomerate crowds packed the balls and receptions of men in public life, forced to accept official society as they found it, and if members of Congress appeared at the dance in their morning habiliments and in unpolished boots, in worsted stockings and in garments fashioned by a backwoods tailor, they were not conspicuous.[2] All, or most, entered with zest into the social activities of the time. On the night of a big ball "the rolling of carriages sounded like continual peals of thunder, or roaring of the wind." In the dark, dismal streets, the lamps on the vehicles alone were visible, and these, moving rapidly in the blackness, "appeared like brilliant meteors in the air." [3] Sometimes, in the case of the more pretentious entertainers, like the foreign ministers, the streets in front of the houses were light as day from the line of flaming torches along the pavement. Fox, the British Minister, a relative of the great orator; Baron von Roenne, the Prussian, a brilliant jurist and publicist; and Baron Bodisco, the Russian, made great displays of equipages and appointments, and were noted for their wines and exotic entertainments. At the legations of Fox and Bodisco, great sums passed over the card table, the most famous statesmen of the time among the players, and the British Minister so seldom saw the sun that on the occasion of a funeral, while seated beside the wife of the Spanish Minister, he turned a puzzled look upon her with the comment, "How strange we all look by daylight!" Both ministers contributed not a little to the gayety of gossip, Bodisco, by his squat ugliness and courtli-

[1] Francis Blair's description, quoted in Rufus Rockwell Wilson's *Washington, the Capital City*.

[2] Hamilton, in *Men and Manners*, describes such garb at a ball given by the French Minister to the members of Congress.

[3] *First Forty Years*, Jan. 1, 1829.

ness, and Fox, by his whimsical refusal at dinners to go to the table until the dishes had cooled.[1] During the period the most celebrated functions were given at Carusi's Assembly rooms which could accommodate great numbers. Leaders of fashion and the socially ambitious of Baltimore and Alexandria, wishing to make an impression in introducing a débutante or to repay social obligations, found these rooms suited to their purpose. It was in these rooms that Washington society had its first presentation of the "Barber of Seville," and "John of Paris" in the winter of 1833.[2] The same year a Washington birthday party was given there, both rooms thrown open, "decorated and illuminated and with a band in each," and diplomats admitted without an entrance fee.[3] Hither all the ladies of the capital, unfamiliar with the dances, or wishing to learn new ones, found their way to learn from the popular Louis, only the inclemency of the weather and the impossible mire of the streets interfering with his profits.[4] Thus the fashionables of the Thirties managed to create the illusion of living in the great world, chattering in the Senate, bustling into the Supreme Court chamber, dining, dancing, flirting, gossiping, attending the theater to see a Booth or a Kemble, going to the circus to see the animals fed at eight o'clock, "in the presence of the audience,"[5] or riding to the National Course near town to witness the races, or attending an exhibit of the paintings of John G. Chapman

[1] Butler, in his *Retrospect of Forty Years,* refers to this peculiarity of Fox's (p. 61), and Bodisco, who gave the most brilliant dinners and dances, figured in the celebrated marriage to a girl of seventeen during Van Buren's Administration.

[2] *Washington Globe,* Feb. 1, 1833, announces these operas with Miss Hughes and Mrs. Anderson in leading rôles.

[3] Advertisement in *Washington Globe.*

[4] Announcing the opening of a spring school, and commenting on the general preference for the spring over the winter term, Carusi, in the *Globe* of Jan. 3, 1831, explained the disadvantages of the winter term to be "the disagreeable and long walks . . . the frequent inclemency of the weather, and the liability of sickness from exposure."

[5] Advertisement of Birchard & Company's Shows, *Washington Globe,* June 13, 1833.

on the Avenue.[1] Only on Sundays did the capital become quiet and sedate, for, after a pious morning pilgrimage to church, the ladies carrying a hymn or a prayer book and leaning on the arms of their escorts, they retired to the seclusion of their homes and the streets were deserted or given over to the promenades of the colored folks.[2]

In this Washington, where men were feverishly fighting for place and prestige, and women were engaged in a hectic struggle for social leadership, Death lurked always, for a less healthful spot could not easily have been found. Built originally in a swamp reeking with malaria, surrounded with morasses, and with not a few of these in the heart of the town, with sanitation poor and water wretched, the residents were constantly menaced by disease. With the gradual disappearance of the forests immediately surrounding it, the conditions became worse. The death-rate was as high as one in fifty-three, with August claiming the heaviest toll from fevers.[3] Between the fevers of the summers and the influenza of the winters, the residents had to be constantly on guard. Whiskey and quinine were taken with the regularity of bread and meat, and tourists were wont to sit late at their quarters "sipping gently a medicine which the doctors of the capital thought destructive of the influenza germs which were lying in wait for the unwary." [4] Fevers, pneumonia, influenza, and the cholera made the swampy capital of the Thirties as profitable to the doctors as to the coachmen.

Such, in brief, was the scene of the most dramatic and significant political battles that were staged in America between the foundation of the Republic and the Administration of Woodrow Wilson. Such was the day-by-day life of the men,

[1] Chapman had not then been given the contract for the historical paintings in the Capitol, rotunda, and exhibited fifty paintings on Pennsylvania Avenue, near Fourth Street, in the winter of 1833, charging twenty-five cents for admission and a catalogue. His advertisement in the *Globe*, Jan. 21.

[2] *Retrospect of Forty Years.*

[3] *Six Months in America*, 101.

[4] *Figures of the Past.*

now steel engravings, who played the leading rôles. And by bearing in mind the sordidness and pettiness of the environment, and of the men and women with whom they daily and nightly gossiped and dined and danced, it may be less of a shock to discover, in the unfolding of the story of these eight crowded years, that even the greatest were men of moral weaknesses and limitations.

CHAPTER II

THE RISING OF THE MASSES

I

WITH the election of 1828 a new era dawned in American politics. Up to this time the election of Presidents and the determination of policies had been a matter of manipulation among the congressional politicians. The possessors of property and the aristocrats of intellect had been the only classes with whom the politicians had concerned themselves. The Virginia Dynasty and the Secretarial Succession died on the day that the rising of the masses raised to the Presidency a man who had never served in the Cabinet, distinguished himself in the Congress, or appealed to the "aristocracy of intellect and culture." To the politicians, office-holders, and society leaders in Washington, the election of Andrew Jackson was something more than a shock — it was an affront. In the campaign he had been opposed by two thirds of the newspapers, four fifths of the preachers, practically all the manufacturers, and seven eighths of the banking capital. Respectability sternly set itself against the presumptuous ambitions of what it conceived to be a rough, illiterate representative of the "mob."

Four years before, the stage had been set for a bitter battle. The election of Adams, through the support of Clay, followed by the appointment of the latter to the first place in the Cabinet, had carried the suspicion of a bargain, and this suspicion had crystallized into a firm conviction with a large portion of the people. Throughout the Adams Administration, its enemies — and they were legion — harped constantly upon the "bargain," angering the crabbed Adams, and stinging Clay to furious denunciation, and this but served to intensify the bitterness of their foes.

The result was the most scurrilous campaign of vilification the country had known. A new school of politicians, forerunners of the astute and none too scrupulous managers of later days, sprang up to direct the fight for the grim old warrior of the Hermitage, and the fact that Clay took personal charge of the campaign for Adams was turned with telling force against his chief. Early in the campaign we find the satirical and caustic Isaac Hill, of the "New Hampshire Patriot," of whom we shall hear much, writing that "Clay is managing Adams's campaign, not like a statesman of the Cabinet, but like a shyster, pettifogging in a bastard suit before a country squire." And lest the motive for Clay's interest escape his readers, we find Hill writing again: "This is Mr. Clay's fight. The country has him on trial for bribery, and having no defense, he accuses the prosecutor."

This reference to the accusation of the prosecutor was inspired by the outrageous calumny that was heaped upon the head of Jackson. He was pictured as a usurper, an adulterer, a gambler, a cockfighter, a brawler, a drunkard, and a murderer. The good name of Mrs. Jackson, one of the purest of women, was wantonly maligned; and in the drawing-rooms of the intellectually elect she was not spared by the ladies who were shocked at the "vulgarity" of her husband. The Adams organs stooped to the attack, and while the "National Intelligencer," under the editorship of Joseph Gales, refused thus to pollute its columns, the "National Journal," under the editorial management of Peter Force, and specially favored by the Adams Administration, specialized on the slander of an excellent woman. A little later an attempt was made to justify the infamy of this proceeding by charging that Mrs. Adams had been assailed, but the extent of the assault was the charge that she was an English woman with little sympathy for American institutions.

While history has accepted Adams's indignant denial of the charge that he had personally sanctioned the attack on Mrs.

Jackson, the National Central Committee, in charge of his campaign, was busily engaged in the dissemination of the putrid literature. This has been thoroughly established by the testimony of Thurlow Weed, editor of the "Albany Journal," who refused to degrade himself by its circulation. When, early in August, before the election in November, he received "two large drygoods boxes" of the pamphlets, with a letter from the National Committee advising him that they contained "valuable campaign documents," with the request that he attend to their circulation "throughout the western counties of the State," he promptly "secured the boxes with additional nails and placed them under lock and key." And when the National Committee learned that they were not being distributed, and sent a representative to protest against his inactivity, he frankly informed the emissary that "not a copy had been seen or would be seen by an elector until the polls had closed." For this he was denounced in New York and Boston as "a traitor to the Administration," but the sagacious politician of Albany stoutly maintained that he "would not permit a lady whose life had been blameless to be dragged forth into the arena of politics." [1]

The charge of murder lodged against Jackson, by editor, hack-writer, and cartoonist, had reference to his execution of Arbuthnot, two Indian chiefs, and seven of his soldiers, and to his duel with Dickinson. Pictures of the coffins of the soldiers were printed on circulars and distributed from farmhouse to farmhouse in New England.[2] This gave Hill an opportunity to tickle Jackson with a rejoinder which was copied from the "New Hampshire Patriot" into all the Jackson papers of the country: "Pshaw! Why don't you tell the whole truth? On the 8th of January, 1815, he murdered in the coldest kind of cold blood 1500 British soldiers for merely

[1] Weed's *Autobiography*, 308–09.

[2] Bradley's *Life of Isaac Hill*. This circular may be seen in the Congressional Library.

trying to get into New Orleans in search of Booty and Beauty."

But all the scurrility of the campaign cannot be justly charged to the enemies of Jackson. His friends were almost as offensive. Adams had bribed Clay. He had bought the Presidency. While abroad he had pandered to the sensuality of the Russian Court. He was stingy, undemocratic, an enemy of American institutions, bent on the destruction of the people's liberties. He was an aristocrat, and had squandered the people's money in lavishly furnishing the East Room of the White House after the fashion of the homes of kings. He had even purchased a billiard table for the home of the President!

And so it went on for weeks and months — the ordinary slanders of a present-day municipal campaign. A foreigner traveling through the country during the summer and autumn of 1828 would have thought the election of Adams certain. In the marts, the counting-rooms, and the drawing-rooms, he would have found but one opinion; but the astute Adams sensed the coming disaster and recorded his misgivings in his diary. The temperamental Clay was depressed one day, to be exultant the next. But the new school of political leadership, managing the fight for Jackson, and devoting itself assiduously to the newly enfranchised "mob" in the highways and the byways, had no notion of defeat. The "hurrah for Jackson" which shocked the sedate, unaccustomed to such noisy acclaim of a presidential aspirant, and disgusted the "best people," was music to the ears of these modern politicians, who had carefully calculated upon the strength of the "mob." Their confidence was not misplaced. The result was an upheaval. Adams, Clay, Federalism, the Virginia Dynasty, the Secretarial Succession, were brushed aside by the rush of the cheering masses bearing their hero to the White House. History has decided that in this campaign "the people first assumed control of the governmental machinery which had been held in trust for them since 1789"; and that "the party and Administration which then came into power was the first in our history which represented the people without restriction, and with all the faults of the people." [1]

II

THE Administration circle in Washington was deeply depressed by the result, and society looked forward to the reign of the barbarians with mingled feelings of mirth and abhorrence. Although not unprepared for the defeat, the bitter Adams, meditating on his political blunders, recorded that "some think I have suffered for not turning my enemies out of office, particularly the Postmaster-General." [2] That John McLean, the official referred to, had been disloyal to his chief was common knowledge. The first reaction to defeat from the followers of the Adams Administration was toward laughter, levity, extravagant manifestation of cynical gayety, with an all too noticeable thawing of the frigidity of White House ceremonies. The dying régime put on its best bib and tucker in a hectic and hysterical demonstration of social hilarity. But this first reaction was short-lived. Very soon thereafter callers at Clay's home were "shocked at the alteration of his looks," and found him "much thinner, very pale, his eyes sunk in his head and his countenance sad and melancholy." [3] Mr. Rush (Secretary of the Treasury) was soon "alarmingly ill" — the "first symptoms of disease was altogether in the head." Mr. Southard (Secretary of the Navy) was confined to his room for three weeks. William Wirt (Attorney-General) suffered two attacks of vertigo, "followed by a loss of the sense of motion." General Porter (Secretary of War) "was almost blind from inflammation of the eyes and went to his office with two blisters, one behind

[1] Johnston and Woodburn's *American Political History*.

[2] Adams's *Memoirs*.

[3] Mrs. Smith's *First Forty Years*, Jan. 1, 1829.

each ear." Even the cold-blooded Adams, who appeared "in fine spirits," was soon "so feeble as to be obliged to relinquish his long walks and to substitute rides on horseback." [1] A social intimate of the leaders swept from power by the rising of the masses mournfully recorded that they would retire to private life "with blasted hopes, injured health, impaired or ruined fortunes, imbittered tempers, and probably a total inability to enjoy the remnant of their lives." [2]

On none did the blow fall with such crushing force as on the proud-spirited Clay. As the repudiated régime was approaching the end, the presiding genius of one of the favorite Administration drawing-rooms met him at a reception.

"What ails your heart?" he asked.

"Can it be otherwise than sad when I think what a good friend I am about to lose?"

For a moment he held her hand without speaking, his eyes "filled with tears."

"We must not think of this or talk of such things now," he said. And with that he relinquished her hand, "drew out his handkerchief, turned away his head and wiped his eyes, then pushed into the crowd and talked and smiled as if his heart were light and easy." [3]

On February 25th this lady made another poignant note: "Mr. Clay's furniture is to be sold this week."

Thus the old régime died hard, and in bitterness.

III

But "The King is dead — long live the King" — was the mood of the strange crowds in the streets of the capital — unusual creatures from the out-of-the-way places to whom the city was not accustomed. Never before had the inaugural ceremonies attracted the people of the farms and the villages, from every nook and corner. Long before the 4th of March

[1] Mrs. Smith's *First Forty Years.* Jan. 1, 1829.
[2] *Ibid.*, Jan. 12, 1829. [3] *Ibid.*

the city swarmed with all sorts and conditions, the rustic, the rural politician, the adventurer, along with politicians of influence and repute. They overflowed the city, filled all the hotels and rooming-houses, spread out to Georgetown, descended on Alexandria.[1] Webster, writing to his brother toward the close of February, said: "I have never seen such a crowd before. Persons have come five hundred miles to see General Jackson, and they really seem to think that the country has been rescued from some dreadful danger."[2] What they really thought was that they had come into their own. They hastened to "their capital," to witness the inauguration of "their President," and, in many instances, in the hope of entering into their reward.

Out of the maze of incomprehensible contradictions, we may gather that Jackson disappointed many of the faithful, who had planned a spectacular entrance to the capital, by entering quietly and unannounced in the early morning. Elaborate preparations had been made, a pompous reception committee of the socially elect and politically pure had been organized, headed by John P. Van Ness, the dean of society and husband of the exquisite Marcia Burns, and plans had been perfected for leading a great throng into the country to meet and escort him to the accompaniment of gun fire into the city. Reaching the capital four hours before he was expected,[3] he went directly to Gadsby's where he took lodging.[4]

But the committee was not to be wholly deprived of its prerogatives. The moment the news reached it and the crowds, the celebration began. "I hear cannon firing, drums beating, and hurrahing. I really cannot write, so adieu for

[1] Mrs. Smith's *First Forty Years.*

[2] Webster's *Correspondence.*

[3] Mrs. Smith's *First Forty Years.*

[4] Buell, in his *Life of Jackson,* says he went to the Indian Queen, "where he was temporarily domiciled." Mrs. Smith and President Adams, who were on the ground, agree that he stopped at Gadsby's. It is possible that he went first to the Indian Queen and then removed to Gadsby's.

the present," wrote Mrs. Smith. The mob surged down the Avenue to the hostelry famous for its whiskey, brandy, game, and the imposing ceremony of the host, packed the streets and fought for the privilege of entering and shaking the hand of the man of the hour. From the moment of his arrival until he took the oath of office he was accessible to the most humble and obscure. Importuned and petitioned by ambitious politicians, the old man courteously heard them all, to the last man, and, according to all contemporaries, kept his own counsel as to prospective appointments. Even as late as March 2d, the observant Webster wrote his brother that the President-to-be was close-mouthed, and predicted that there would be few removals.[1] The crafty Isaac Hill, of the "New Hampshire Patriot," had arrived early upon the scene, and we are indebted to him for a side-light on Jackson's methods and mood, and the scenes about the hotel. Almost daily this persistent aspirant for place wormed his way into the presence of the source of all patronage. Jackson was cordial, remembered, quoted, laughed about witticisms in Hill's paper during the campaign, but said "little about the future except in a general way." There was cruel hilarity in that crowded room at Gadsby's over the maneuvers of the office-holders to retain their places. A "funny story" was told of Wirt writing to Monroe "soliciting his influence with the General to keep him on the pay roll."[2] An old translator of twenty years' experience in the State Department had, in conversation, expressed a curiosity to know where a Democrat could be found to translate diplomatic French, and this was jokingly related to Jackson. "Oh, just tell him," said the General, "that if necessary I can bring Planche's whole Creole Battalion up here. Those French fellows, you know, who helped to defend New Orleans against the Red Coats

[1] Webster's *Correspondence.*

[2] Wirt wrote Monroe asking his advice about resigning, and Monroe advised this course, but expressed the opinion that Jackson would not want to dispense with his services.

that had just made all the translators here take to the woods for their lives." This flare of spirit gratified and encouraged the spoilsmen. "Good, was n't it?" Hill wrote to his assistant in Concord. "Besides his courage and truth, Old Hickory has a fund of humor in his make-up, but most of his sallies, like the above, are likely to be a little bit cruel."

About the time that Hill was writing to his assistant editor, he was meeting daily, at the home of Obadiah B. Brown, a preacher-politician, where Amos Kendall, a Kentucky editor, then obscure, but destined to become the master mind of the Administration, was holding forth, and organizing a number of fellow journalists who had been useful in the campaign, to compel recognition. There, in the home of the jovial preacher, Kendall and Hill were making common cause with the smiling Major M. M. Noah of New York, Nathaniel Green of Massachusetts, and the quiet but sagacious Gideon Welles of Connecticut. More political history was being made in the humble abode of Brown than in the crowded, smoke-laden room at Gadsby's.[1] The Kentucky editor does not seem to have encountered the same reticence in Jackson that Hill had found. After his first call at Gadsby's, we find him writing his wife: "He expressed his regards for me and his disposition to serve me, in strong terms." And a few days later, after his second call, he writes: 'The other day I had a long conversation with General Jackson. At the close of it, after saying many flattering things of my capacity, character, etc., he observed, 'I told one of my friends that you were fit for the head of a department, and I shall put you as near the head as possible.' "[2]

It is significant of the change of the times that, while the practical politicians of the new school were encouraged and jubilant, the seasoned veterans of political battle-fields were discouraged and not a little disgruntled. Amusing tales of the discomfiture of these were gayly carried to the politicians

[1] *Perley's Reminiscences*, I, 96.

[2] Amos Kendall's *Autobiography*.

of the Opposition in the salon of Mrs. Smith, who recorded, toward the close of February, that "every one thinks there is great confusion and difficulty, mortification and disappointment at the Wigwam, as they call the General's lodgings. Mr. Woodbury[1] looks glum, as well as several other disappointed expectants."[2]

The battle royal occurred in the selection of the Cabinet. The one principle on which Jackson was determined was the exclusion from his Cabinet table of any aspirant for the succession. He had been profoundly impressed by the demoralizing effect of the intrigues of the presidential candidates in the Cabinet of Monroe.[3] This, however, did not deter the two powerful men of the party, Calhoun and Van Buren, from exerting themselves to pack the Cabinet with men favorable to their respective aspirations for the chief magistracy. Of the latter's plans the President-elect knew nothing. He had probably decided to ask the clever New York politician to accept the portfolio of State before leaving the Hermitage. He had been intimate with Van Buren in the Senate; had been impressed with his tact, diplomacy, and ability, and especially with his genius in the creation, consolidation, and drilling of a party, and in formulating its policies. He was not unmindful of the part the "Red Fox"[4] had played in his nomination and election. In view of all the conditions the selection of Van Buren was logical and inevitable.[5] It was just as inevitable that Calhoun, the Vice-President, should be hostile to the choice. Primarily, we may be sure, the South Carolinian recognized in the suave and subtle New Yorker a dangerous rival for the succession. Whether he was even that early interested in strengthening the South at the expense of the North is not so certain. However that may be, he appeared in the throng of wire-pulling politicians at

[1] Later in the Cabinet.

[2] Mrs. Smith's *First Forty Years*, 283.

[3] Adams, Crawford, and Calhoun.

[4] Van Buren was thus known in his day.

[5] Van Buren in his *Autobiography* ascribes his selection to the party managers.

Gadsby's, earnestly urging that Senator Tazewell of Virginia should be placed at the head of the Cabinet. This able statesman but a little time before had maintained close political relations with Van Buren,[1] but he was an extreme State-Rights advocate, entirely satisfactory to Calhoun. During the half-concealed struggle over the Cabinet, Van Buren, who had been elected Governor of New York and was staying in Albany, was well served in Washington by James A. Hamilton, whose mission was to keep in intimate touch with events and inform the New Yorker of all developments. Thus it happened that Hamilton was with Jackson when, at ten o'clock one morning, Calhoun called for a conference with the President-elect. "I know what it is about," said Jackson to Van Buren's agent. "He cannot succeed. I wish you to remain until he leaves." It was during this conference, the last he ever had with the President on patronage matters, that Calhoun made his final stand for Tazewell, or against Van Buren. With great solemnity he urged the appointment of the Virginian, largely because of "his great knowledge and wisdom," but partly on the ground that it would assure the support of Virginia for the Administration. It is doubtful whether, up to this time, Calhoun had appreciated the political sagacity of the man with whom he dealt. Jackson listened to his importunity with courteous attention, but did not commit himself. One suggestion he made, however, which must have warned the great Carolinian that his motives were divined. When Calhoun stressed the importance of cultivating Virginia, Jackson blandly inquired whether it would not be useful to have the support of New York. Calhoun's reply disclosed his animus against the "Little Magician." The appointment of Clinton, had he lived, might have guaranteed the support of the Empire State, but the selection of no other citizen of that State would. He left, no doubt,

[1] See letter of Tazewell to Ritchie regarding the establishment of a party organ in Washington in Ambler's *Life of Thomas Ritchie.*

with the feeling that he had failed in his mission, and never again approached Jackson on the subject of appointments. And the moment he left, a detailed story of the conference was given to Hamilton, who promptly sent it to his chief in Albany.[1]

When Jackson reached the capital he had made no decision as to the Treasury, and there he was to be buffeted about by many cross-currents. Van Buren, who was socially and politically intimate with Louis McLane of Delaware, was anxious that he should be named for the post, and the gentleman himself was on the ground ready to respond to the summons that failed to come. The political tacticians at Gadsby's reached the decision early that the place should be awarded to Pennsylvania, and Samuel D. Ingham, who had rushed to Washington as a representative of one of the factions, with an application for a subordinate position in the Treasury, became an active candidate for the more important honor. This was displeasing to Jackson, who favored Henry Baldwin, but in this preference he was unable to secure any important support among his advisers.[2] Strangely enough, powerful influences almost immediately rushed to the support of the man who would have been delighted with a comparatively obscure position. The Pennsylvania congressional delegation, on which he had served for years, unanimously endorsed him. Stranger still, Calhoun, with whom Jackson at this juncture had no desire to break, became an ardent supporter of his candidacy. He had served in the House of Representatives many years before with the mediocre Pennsylvanian, and had found in him one of his most faithful idolaters. That his influence, and the desire to recognize him in the making of the Cabinet, was the determining factor, was the consensus of opinion at the time.

But here again appeared cross-currents difficult to under-

[1] See Hamilton's *Reminiscences*, 101.
[2] See *ibid.*, p. 97, on Ingham's original ambition.

stand. South Carolina, usually so subservient to the wishes of her great statesman, but now cool toward him, was uncompromisingly hostile to his favorite for the Treasury. The other leading members of the South Carolina delegation, known to be opposed to Ingham and to prefer McLane to him, had hesitated from motives of delicacy to make their views known to Jackson; and Van Buren's favorite for the position authorized Hamilton, Van Buren's emissary, to notify the General of their willingness to call if their opinion was wanted.[1] On February 17th, the Carolinians, including Senator Hayne, McDuffie, Hamilton, Archer, and Drayton, filed into the throne room at Gadsby's, and Hamilton, who acted as spokesman, began by tactfully commending the selection of Van Buren, and then turned to the Treasury. Before he could announce his candidate, Jackson interrupted with the announcement that Ingham had been chosen. Nothing daunted, Hamilton suggested as a better choice the brilliant Langdon Cheves of South Carolina. "Impossible," snapped the grim old man. Then why not McLane? That, too, was instantly dismissed, and the Carolinians left Gadsby's in a rage. "I assure you I am cool — damn cool — never half so cool in my life," Hamilton exclaimed immediately afterwards.[2]

For the War Department there was no such competition, and after an unsuccessful attempt had been made to conciliate Tazewell with the post, Jackson, who was anxious to have among his advisers one of his old friends and managers, satisfied himself with the selection of Senator John H. Eaton of Tennessee.

The processes of reasoning leading to the appointment of

[1] Hamilton, in his *Reminiscences*, p. 99, makes this unqualified statement. Professor Bassett, in his admirable *Life of Jackson*, p. 416, says that Jackson told Calhoun to notify the delegation of his willingness to see them. Knowing the delegation to be opposed to the man he favored, and to prefer Van Buren's candidate, it seems more probable that Hamilton was the emissary and not the Carolinian.

[2] The Carolinian's opposition to Ingham was due to his tariff views.

Senator John Branch of North Carolina as Secretary of the Navy have been lost to history and there is no clue. We know that Van Buren and his friends strongly urged the selection of Woodbury of New Hampshire; and McLane expressed the contemporary state of mind in a letter to his friend: "By what interest that miserable old woman, Branch, was ever dreamed of, no one can tell." This much we know — that Branch himself did not have the most remote idea of entering the Cabinet when the invitation reached him from Gadsby's, and he withheld his acceptance until he could consult with a number of his friends.[1] Two reasons have been advanced as probable. The one, popular at the time, was that Jackson's advisers thought that something should be done to promote the social prestige of the Administration; and the other, generally accepted by historians, that the appointment was made as another concession to Calhoun. While the Carolinian made no request for his inclusion in the Cabinet, Branch was one of his most loyal followers.

There is no real justification for astonishment over the decision of the conferees at the Wigwam to ask Senator John McPherson Berrien of Georgia to accept the position of Attorney-General. Not only was he a brilliant member of the Senate, noted as an orator, but his professional reputation in his section was almost as great as that of Webster in New England. His votes in the Senate on the party measures of the Adams Administration had been pleasing to Jackson, and, whether he was named as another gesture of good-will toward Calhoun, as generally assumed, or not, his appointment could not have been displeasing to the Vice-President.

While the Postmaster-General had not hitherto been a member of the Cabinet, the Jackson board of strategy, wishing to manifest its appreciation of John McLean, who had held the post under Adams while exerting himself on behalf

[1] From speech of Branch, quoted in Haywood's brochure on Branch, pp. 14–15.

of Jackson, determined to raise the position to the Cabinet and retain him.[1]

Thus the Cabinet was completed, and after a fashion indicative of no desire on the part of Jackson to quarrel with his Vice-President. Van Buren, who did not enter into the President's calculations as to the succession, had been given the most desirable post, but his friends, McLane and Woodbury, had been set aside for Ingham and Branch, both devoted to the political fortunes of Calhoun. The latter was represented by half the Cabinet, Ingham, Branch, and Berrien, and no stretch of the imagination could make the other two members, Eaton and McLean, other than absolutely independent of the wily politician of Kinderhook. The processes through which all this was speedily changed enter into one of the most fascinating dramas of political intrigue in the history of the Republic.

IV

WHILE the President-elect was holding his conferences, with the mysterious Major Lewis going in and out at Gadsby's and playing with the destinies of men, and the streets were seething with an incongruous crowd shouting their "Hurrah for Jackson," Jackson was remaining coldly aloof from the occupant of the White House. He had carried to Washington a bitter resentment against Adams and his personal lieutenants, because of the dastardly attacks upon the woman then buried at the Hermitage. He made no call of courtesy, and Adams was stung to the quick. Especially painful to the old Puritan was the thought that he had been considered capable of a vulgar assault upon the good name of a woman. After much struggling with his pride, he made the first advance by sending a messenger to Jackson to inform him that the White House would be ready for his occupancy on the 4th of March.

[1] Adams knew of McLean's treachery, and in his *Memoirs* denounces him bitterly.

"He brought me the answer," Adams records, "that the General cordially thanked him, and hoped that I would put myself to no inconvenience to quit the house, but to remain in it as long as I pleased, even for a month." [1] A few days later, Adams sent his messenger to say that his packing might require two or three days beyond the 3d, and Jackson replied that he did not wish to put him to the slightest inconvenience, "but that Mr. Calhoun had suggested that there might be danger of the excessive crowds breaking down the rooms at Gadsby's, and the General had concluded, if it would be perfectly convenient to us, to receive his company at the President's house after the inauguration on Wednesday next." Whereupon Adams "concluded at all events to leave the house on Tuesday." [2] Thus the closing days of his Administration must have been bitter, indeed, to the proud old Puritan of the White House. Deliberately ignored by his successor, tortured by the thought of the treachery of McLean and others, the co-workers of his régime, depressed, embittered, or in hiding, he appears to have been utterly forgotten by the society of the capital as well as by the general public. Justice Story observing his isolation was moved to write in bitterness to a friend that he had never "felt so forcibly the emptiness of public honors and public favor." Certainly no generous sympathy was felt for him by his triumphant foes. When, on the last Sunday before the inauguration, the pastor of the President's church unhappily selected for his text, "What will ye do on the solemn day?" one of Jackson's courtiers, who had attended the services, hurried back to Gadsby's, and the company assembled there went into gales of laughter, and agreed that it would be, for some, a "solemn day."

That day was heralded by the thunder of cannon — a day of warmth and sunshine. All roads led to the Capitol, and from an early hour the thoroughfares were thronged

[1] Adams's *Memoirs*, Feb. 24, 1829. [2] *Ibid.*, Feb. 28, 1829.

with the eager, enthusiastic, motley crowd, rejoicing audibly in the event. Down the Avenue the good-natured mob fought its way, the splendid Barronet and the stately coaches splashed by the wagons and the carts, women and children in exquisite finery crowded by women and children in homespun and rags, statesmen jostled by uncouth frontiersmen, the laborer brushing inconsiderately, and perhaps a little arrogantly, against the banker — for it was the People's Day. When, at eleven o'clock, the aristocratic Mrs. Smith set forth with her company, she found the Avenue one living mass, flowing sluggishly eastward, with every terrace and portico and balcony packed, and with all the windows of the Capitol crowded, some to observe the approach on the west, and others to witness the ceremony on the east. When the mob caught sight of Jackson and his party walking from Gadsby's in democratic fashion, it pressed in upon him, impeding his approach, but seeming in nowise to challenge his displeasure, for he alone of his party walked with bared head. The spectators on the south terrace thrilled to the scene — an American king going to his coronation, acclaimed and accompanied by the plain people. The ceremonies over, he fought his way to his waiting horse — and down the Avenue he rode, followed by the most picturesque cortège that ever trailed a conqueror — gentlemen of society and backwoodsmen, scholars and the illiterate, white and black, the old hobbling on crutches and canes and children clinging to their mothers' gowns, walking and riding in carriages and wagons and carts — following to the People's House.

There the unwieldy mob, in carnival mood, hundreds only accustomed to the rough life of the frontier, stormed the mansion, fighting, scrambling, elbowing, scratching. Waiters appearing with refreshments were rushed by the uncouth guests, resulting in the crash of glass and china. Men in heavy boots, covered with the mud of the unpaved streets, sprang upon the chairs and sofas to get a better view of the hero of the hour.[1] Women fainted, some were seen with bloody noses, and Jackson was saved from being crushed only by the action of some gentlemen in making a barrier of their bodies. After this the old soldier beat a hasty retreat through the back way to the south, and sought relief at Gadsby's.[2] "I never saw such a mixture," wrote Justice Story. "The reign of King Mob seemed triumphant." And Mrs. Smith writing of her experience said: "The noisy and disorderly rabble . . . brought to my mind descriptions I have read of the mobs in the Tuileries and at Versailles."

And on the day that Jackson was enjoying, or trembling at, the popularity of his triumph, where was Adams? The day before the inauguration he had removed to the home of Commodore Porter on the outskirts of the city; and at the time the surging multitude was all but drowning the roar of the cannon with its cries for Jackson, the dethroned President, finding the day "warm and springlike," had ordered his horse, and, accompanied by a single companion, had ridden into the city "through F Street to the Rockville turnpike," and over that until he reached a road leading to the Porters' — reminded of the passing of his power by the neglect of the people.[3]

Henry Clay shut himself in his house and did not leave it during the day — tormented by bitter regrets.

V

Almost immediately Jackson began to get the reaction on his Cabinet and his policies. The disaffections in the house of his friends, which were to cause him so much embarrassment during the first two years of his Administration, began to appear before the shouts of the crowd on the White House lawn had died away. We have it on the authority of the

[1] Wilson's *Washington, the Capital City*, I, 251.
[2] Mrs. Smith's *First Forty Years*, 295.
[3] Adams's *Memoirs*, March 4, 1829.

capital gossips of the day that when McLean, the Postmaster-General, who had betrayed Adams, heard of his new chief's plans for wholesale dismissals of postmasters, he warned Jackson that in his proceedings against those officials who had participated in politics he would be forced to include in the proscription the supporters of Jackson as well as those who had been faithful to Adams; that Jackson, for a moment nonplussed, sat puffing at his pipe, then arose, and, after walking up and down the room several times, stopped abruptly before his obstreperous minister, with the question: "Mr. McLean, will you accept a seat on the bench of the Supreme Court?" — and that McLean instantly accepted.[1] This is vouched for by Nathan Sargent, who says that on the evening of the interview Lewis Cass told him, at a reception at the home of General Porter, that McLean, with whom he was intimate, had just described the interview to him.[2] The civic virtue of Mr. McLean has been explained on the theory that he entertained presidential aspirations and did not care to incur the displeasure of the many postmasters who were friendly to his ambition. However that may be, he secured a position of which he was not unworthy, and Jackson probably saved himself some trouble by meeting a sudden crisis in a truly Jacksonian way.

It is reasonable to assume that during the brief moments he walked the floor puffing his pipe, he determined upon McLean's successor. One week before his inauguration, he had given James A. Hamilton a list of applicants for office with the request for an opinion and report, and among these was the application of William T. Barry of Kentucky for a place on the Supreme Bench. The applications had been returned to him with the recommendation that the Kentuckian be appointed. He was known to Jackson as an "organization man." It was probably the matter of a mo-

[1] *Perley's Reminiscences*, I, 98.
[2] Sargent's *Public Men and Events*, I, 165–66.

ment, for one of the President's quick decision, to make the exchange — McLean for the Bench, Barry for the Cabinet.[1] His efforts to soothe the injured feelings of Senator Tazewell, whose heart had been set on the portfolio of State, were not so successful. After the disappointed statesman had refused the War Department, some of the Jackson tacticians conceived the idea of offering him the mission to London, and for a few days the Virginian seemed tempted. But one week after the inauguration, he wrote the President that domestic reasons precluded an acceptance. Keenly disappointed and concerned, Jackson, after a consultation with one of his advisers,[2] wrote a personal note to Tazewell requesting him to call at the White House. It is not incomprehensible that in his angry mood the proud Southerner should have resented the earnest importunity of the direct Jackson, and he left the President with the statement to McLean that he had not liked the General's manner in looking him through and through and telling him he must go. He had looked upon it as a military order, and considered the matter at rest. This opened the way, however, for the recognition of Van Buren's friend, Louis McLane, whose ruffled feelings were smoothed by the appointment to the English Court. But within a week two of Jackson's party friends and supporters, McLean and Tazewell, had been alienated and were ripe for the seduction of the Opposition.

Meanwhile, as soon as Clay could recover from the shock of defeat, he began the organization and solidification of a bitter and stubborn opposition to the Administration. As early as the first of January it was evident that "the aim of the defeated party is to get a majority in the Senate and thereby to control the President." [3] During the first few weeks

[1] Hamilton, in his *Reminiscences,* p. 100, tells of his report to Jackson on Barry's application.

[2] Hamilton. See Hamilton's *Reminiscences,* 90–91.

[3] Mrs. Smith thus writes in the *First Forty Years,* and her salon was the center of Whig gossip.

of the new Administration the iron sank deep into the souls of the dispossessed office-holders and their friends. It was manifest that there was something more than a new master in the White House — that a régime had passed, a dynasty had fallen. Previous Presidents had entered office with the good wishes of most of their political opponents, but it was clear from the beginning that the dispossessed had steeled themselves against conciliation, were planning to find fault on general principles, and to exert themselves to the utmost to wreck the Administration. The Cabinet was greeted with derision and the Whig drawing-rooms made merry over the "millennium of the minnows." All the members of the new official family were ridiculed with the exception of Van Buren and even he, while conceded to be a "profound politician," was "not supposed to be an able statesman."[1] The vitriolic and vindictive Adams, nursing his wrath to keep it warm, poured forth on the pages of his diary vituperative denunciations of the Cabinet, together with the gossip of the malicious. Ten days of the new régime, and he had rendered the verdict that "the only principles yet discernible in the conduct of the President" were "to feed the cormorant appetite for place, and to reward the prostitution of canvassing defamers."[2]

While Adams indulged in these unfriendly reflections merely to feed his personal vanity, and to record his superiority, Clay, equally bitter, was not content to shut his reflection up between the covers of a book. To him defeat had been especially bitter. He hated Jackson with vindictive malice because the latter really credited the "bargain" story, and had sanctioned its circulation. His overpowering passion was to reach the Presidency. He had entered the official household of Adams as the head of the Cabinet when the "Secretarial Succession" seemed definitely established, and had looked forward to succeeding his chief at the end of

[1] Mrs. Smith's *First Forty Years*. [2] Adams's *Memoirs*, March 14, 1829.

his second Administration. The fact that there had been no second Administration had been due, in part, to the prevalent opinion that Clay had entered into a bargain for power, and he faced retirement from public life feeling that his great opportunity had failed him and that his reputation had been stained. He was the type of man whose bitterness must find relief in action. From the moment he recovered from the shock of the election, he dedicated himself to the pursuit of Jackson.

In judging of the sincerity of his unrelenting opposition during the next eight years, it is well to bear in mind that before Jackson had perfected a policy, or proclaimed a principle, Mr. Clay attended a banquet given in his honor within a stone's throw of the White House, at which he assailed the President with an intemperance of denunciation never exceeded in later years. This was evidently personal. One week after the inauguration he said to Mrs. Bayard Smith: "There is not in Cairo or in Constantinople a greater moral despotism than is at this moment exercised over public opinion here. Why, a man dare not avow what he thinks or feels, or shake hands with a personal friend, if he happens to differ from the powers that be."[1] On the very day this remarkable statement was recorded by the chronicler of the Whig drawing-rooms, Adams wrote in his diary: "Mr. Clay told me some time since that he had received invitations at several places on his way to Lexington to public dinners, and should attend them, and that he intended freely to express his opinions."[2] A little later Adams notes that while riding he passed Mr. Clay in a carriage driving toward Baltimore on his way to Kentucky — pale, stern, and sour. On that journey, and without having at that time any particular actions of the new Administration on which to base an attack, he spoke wherever the opportunity was afforded, and always with a vehement denunciation of President Jackson.

[1] *First Forty Years*, March 12, 1829. [2] Adams's *Memoirs*, March 12, 1829.

The inauguration was over; the people from afar, having seen "their" President and visited "their" White House, had returned to their homes; and Henry Clay, the most consummate of politicians, one of the most eloquent of men, was already meditating upon the organized assault that was to be made upon the new régime. Now let us acquaint ourselves with the advisers with whom the President had surrounded himself officially.

VI

By common consent the Whig aristocracy conceded that Martin Van Buren was the strong man of the Cabinet because of an uncanny cleverness as a politician, while denying him the qualities of statesmanship or intellectual leadership. Even as a politician tradition would have him of the superficial, manipulating, intriguing sort. History had generally accepted this tradition until Mr. Shepard's masterful biography [1] focused attention upon his career, and the publication of his fascinating "Autobiography" disclosed his intellectuality. He stood out among the politicians of his time, to whom history has been kinder, because of his refusal to indulge in the popular personal attacks or to stoop to disreputable intrigues. A man of even temper, blessed with a sense of humor, he found it not only possible but profitable and pleasurable to maintain social relations with political opponents, and all that the embittered Adams could see in this was that "he thought it might one day be to his interest to seek friendship." In senatorial debates he had discussed principles and policies calmly, instead of indulging in flamboyant discourses flaming with personalities — and this was accepted in his day as evidence that he held his principles lightly. Adams wrote that "his principles are always subordinate to his ambition." [2]

This "superficial politician" was the greatest lawyer

[1] American Statesmen Series.

[2] Adams's *Memoirs*, April 4, 1829.

elected to the Presidency before the Civil War, and, with the possible exception of the second Harrison, the greatest lawyer-President we have had. Living in a community overwhelmingly Federalistic, this "trimmer without principles" became a bitter opponent of Federalism. With all the rich and powerful of the locality allied with Federalism, this "courtier" entered the other camp. When Burr was a candidate for Governor, with the support of Van Buren's preceptor in the law, this young man, who "was under the influence of his evil genius," ardently supported the Clinton-Livingston candidate, who was elected. When he entered politics, he found the spoils system thoroughly established in New York, and political proscription practiced by both parties, but that was not to prevent his enemies from charging him with its initiation. He did not quarrel with the system. He used, but never abused it. And in the days of his limitation to State politics, he displayed qualities of statesmanship, patriotism, and courage. New York Federalism did not dismiss him as a mere schemer and intriguer when he led his party in the State Senate. He met the Federalist attack upon the War of 1812 upon the floor of the Senate, and not in party caucus. When Federalism fought every needful measure, he became as much the spokesman of the war party in Albany as Clay, Calhoun, and Grundy in Washington. In reaching an estimate of Van Buren, it is important to bear in mind that this alleged man of indecision, without initiative or constructive capacity, was the author of "the most energetic war measure" adopted in the country.[1] As a member of the Constitutional Convention of New York, dealing with the extension of suffrage, when Chancellor Kent, giving free rein to his aristocratic tendencies, was opposing the extension, and mere demagogues were advocating the immediate letting down of the bars to all, it is significant, both of his Americanism and

[1] Benton's characterization of Van Buren's Classification Bill; *Thirty Years' View*

his wisdom, that Van Buren scorned both the rôle of reactionary and demagogue, and proposed the plan for the gradual extension of suffrage in a speech couched in the language of seasoned statesmanship. Thus, at the time he entered National life, there was nothing in his career to justify the conventional estimate of his public character.

With the inauguration of Adams, soon after he had entered the United States Senate, Van Buren became the recognized leader of the Opposition, and he set himself the task of organizing and militantizing a party to fight the Federalistic trend of the President. There were various elements on which he could draw. With his genius for organization and direction, he made it his work to seek a common ground upon which all could stand together in harmony. He fought the principles and policies of the Administration in dignified fashion, without recourse to scurrility; but he capitalized every mistake and gave it fullest publicity through the circulation of carefully prepared speeches, after the fashion of the present day. Careful to discriminate, even in his attacks, between personal and political wrongdoing, he treated Adams with the utmost courtesy. With a party formed, he drilled it as carefully as was ever done by the Albany Regency. He instilled into it the party spirit. He mobilized an army. With this he fought the Administration on the floor.

But he was one of the first, if not the first, to take the people outside the halls of Congress into consideration. To create a party without as well as within the Congress, he arranged for the circulation of carefully prepared senatorial speeches for the moulding of public opinion in the highways and the byways. Thus he was probably responsible for the delivery of the first congressional speeches intended solely for campaign use.

In person he was slight, erect, and scarcely of middle height. His intellectuality was indicated by his high, broad forehead, and his bright, quick eye. His smile, which was habitual, was genial and seemed sincere. His features, generally, were pleasing. His manner was always courtly, and he made a study of deportment. No professional diplomat of the Old World, living in the atmosphere of courts, could have been more polished. Contemporaries have described him as "extraordinarily bright and attractive, but without anything supercilious."[1] In social life he was a favorite. Few men of his period were better fitted for the drawing-room. An entertaining talker, he could converse intelligently upon a multitude of subjects and could pass from a political conference with the Kitchen Cabinet to a social call on Adams, or a chat with Clay, without effort or embarrassment. Fond of feminine society, he could be as charming to a débutante as to a grande dame, and we find him delighting the brilliant Mrs. Livingston with his intellectual charm, while captivating her daughter, Cora, with his juvenile levity. Fastidious to a degree, he could enjoy the unconventional moments of Jackson in his shirt-sleeves and with his pipe, and make the pleasure mutual. This premier of an Administration that contemporaries of the Opposition loved to describe as plebeian and vulgar "was perhaps as polished and captivating a person as the social circles of the Republic have ever known."[2] As we shall see, nothing ruffled him. He never forgot his dignity nor lost his temper. He was all suavity. He was all art.

He lives in history as a politician and President and is never thought of as an orator. He belonged rather to the type of parliamentary speaker which followed the scintillating period when Pitt declaimed in stately sentences and Fox thundered with emotional eloquence — the conversational type which is still prevalent at Westminster. He made no pretense to an artful literary style, but his speeches were in good taste. We have the tradition that he not only prepared

[1] Ellet's *Court Circles of the Republic*, 149.

[2] Senator Foote's *Casket of Reminiscences*, 59.

his speeches with infinite care, which is probable, but that he rehearsed them before a mirror, which is debatable. It is said that on his retirement from the Senate, and at the sale of his household goods at auction, "it was noticed that the carpet before the large looking-glass was worn threadbare," and that "it was there that he rehearsed his speeches." [1] That he was something of an artist and an actor we shall see in the course of the recital of the events of the Jackson Administration.

Secretary of the Treasury Ingham was a Pennsylvania paper manufacturer who possessed little learning and stood in no awe of genius. His career had been that of a petty but persistent plodder who knew the ways of cunning. His mind was prosily practical, and he thought solely in terms of money. His fourteen years in Congress had been barren of achievement, but his business training had given him a certain advantage over more brilliant men in the work of the committees. He was the forerunner of the machine politician of a later day, skillful in intrigue, unscrupulous in methods, and resourceful in the work of organization. His general character is not easily deduced from the conflicting opinions of his contemporaries. One of these, unfriendly to the Jackson régime, wrote that he "is a good man of unimpeachable and unbending integrity"; [2] while Adams, after relating an incident tending to an opposite conclusion, tells us that "there is a portrait of Ingham in Caracci's picture of the Lord's Supper" — which is the nearest approach to a description of his appearance that can be found. There is a general agreement, however, as to the inferiority of his talents, and in our political history he is scarcely the shadow of a silhouette.

Quite a different character was Secretary of War Eaton, a gentleman of education, polish, amiability, capacity, and wealth. The possession of a fortune deprived him of an in-

[1] *Perley's Reminiscences*, I, 65. [2] Mrs. Smith's *First Forty Years*.

centive to the full exertion of his talents, and he frankly preferred leisure to labor, discouraged the approach of clients, and liked nothing better than a quiet corner of his library at his country home near Nashville. There was nothing in his appearance, his manner, or conversation remotely to suggest the frontiersman, and, on the contrary, observers were impressed by his dignity and poise, his courtliness and courtesy. Even in the bitter days when society was in league against his wife, we find one of her harshest critics writing that "every one that knows esteems, and many love him for his benevolence and amiability."[1] He possessed many advantages for a political career. Having the time and money to devote to politics, he early developed a genius for organization, and an uncanny capacity for intrigue. The campaign of 1828 found him entrusted with much of the important work — the delicate missions. Wherever Jackson lacked or needed an organization, or one in existence required stiffening, there went Eaton, doing his work furtively, and on the surface nothing but its achievement indicated that it had been undertaken.[2] It was his fine Italian hand which wrought such havoc with Clay's forces in Kentucky. When that State began to waver as to Clay, Jackson determined to force the fighting in a territory at first thought hopelessly lost to the Democracy. Even Benton found his way to the "dark and bloody ground," but tradition has it that it was the suave and furtive Eaton, who appeared in different parts of Kentucky, making no speeches, and half concealing himself in a mantle of mystery, who divorced from Clay so many of his supporters. There is a sinister aspect to the general description of his activities; and his enemies, and Jackson's, always insisted that he had parceled out jobs with a lavish hand. A man of culture, a soldier of acknowledged gallantry, a lawyer of ability, he was destined to an unhappy notoriety, but he deserved a better fate.

[1] *First Forty Years*, Feb. 25, 1829.

[2] Buell's *Life of Jackson*.

The patrician of the Administration was Secretary of the Navy Branch, who, like Eaton, had inherited an ample fortune, and had divided his time between politics, the practice of the law, and the management of a large plantation. At the time he entered the Cabinet, he had distinguished himself in the politics of North Carolina, had served three terms as Governor, and was a member of the United States Senate — scarcely the record of an obscure man. As chief executive of his State, his record had been far from that of a colorless time-serving politician without constructive qualities or vision. If his messages were couched in the lofty, pompous phrases of the period, they were not without substance. He was a pioneer in the field of popular education, the leader of a crusade against capital punishment for many crimes, an advocate of the substitution of imprisonment for the death penalty, and he urged the establishment of a penitentiary based on the idea of reformation. A man of great wealth, and an aristocrat by temperament, he led a fight against imprisonment for debt.[1] His, too, is the distinction of having in that early day proposed the strict regulation of the medical profession as a protection of the public against impostors. A planter, and the owner of many slaves, he insisted, while Governor, on the protection of the legal rights of the blacks; and the petition of the entire population of Raleigh, the importunities of a hundred and twenty young women, the plea of State officials, were not sufficient to persuade him to save from the gallows a young white man who had murdered a slave.[2] In the Senate, while not distinguished as an orator, he was considered a strong debater and was respected as a man of courage and deep convictions.

The portrait of Branch, which hangs in the Navy Department in Washington, suggests, in the slender profile and luminous eyes, the poet, rather than the politician. He is described by one who saw him often in his Washington days as "tall, well-proportioned, graceful in gestures, and affable and kindly in manner." [1] He had the graciousness of the Southern aristocrat of the old school, and was devoted to the social standards and customs of his section. Strongly attached to his home and family, having the poet's love of the artistic, he surrounded himself with beauty, and his home at Enfield was a comfortable and stately mansion surrounded by a smooth lawn, in the midst of gardens, orchards, and shade trees. His political career and the course of the Jackson Administration were to be greatly influenced by his devotion to his wife and daughters, and to his social ideals.

In John McPherson Berrien, the Attorney-General, we have a character with whom history has played strange pranks. When he entered the Cabinet, he was conceded to be one of the most polished orators of his time and one of the famous lawyers of the South. His Washington début in the Supreme Court, in a case involving the seizure of an African slave ship, had been a spectacular triumph.[2] All contemporaries agree as to his extraordinary gifts of eloquence. Perley Poore describes him as "a polished and effective orator." [3] Another contemporary found him "a model for chaste, free, beautiful elocution." [4] Still another has it that "he spoke the court language of the Augustan age." [5] Even the blasé John Marshall, who listened to Webster and Choate, was so impressed that he dubbed him "the honey-tongued Georgian youth." [6] He had been in the Senate three years when a speech upon the tariff impelled the press of the period to describe him as "the American Cicero" — a designation that clung to him

[1] Ellet's *Court Circles of the Republic*, 155.
[2] Senator Foote describes it, in his *Casket of Reminiscences*, p. 14.
[3] *Perley's Reminiscences*.
[4] *Sketches of Public Characters*. New York, 1830.
[5] Lucian Lamar Knight, *Reminiscences of Famous Georgians*.
[6] Northern's *Men of Mark in Georgia*.

through life. The greatest speech made by any of the leaders of the Opposition on the Panama Mission was the constitutional argument of Berrien.[1] As a man he was cold and reserved, an aristocrat in manner, as in feeling. He made a virtue of not cultivating the multitude, scorned all compromise with his convictions, firmly believed in himself, and was not at all impressed with opposition. Utterly without tact or diplomacy, caustic and sarcastic, he incurred bitter enmities, but his admirers, who liked to compare him with Cicero, took pride in this weakness.[2] As a political leader, he was dictatorial and demanded obedience without question. The slightest hesitation on the part of his tried and truest friends was usually followed by coldness on his part. Selfish to a degree, he was always keen for his personal advancement.[3] Few more brilliant men have ever been Attorney-General of the United States.

If Postmaster-General Barry was unknown to Washington, it was a matter of indifference to him. In politics he was an exotic. Entering Congress as a young man, he could have remained indefinitely, but congressional life did not allure him. For twenty years he had been an influential State politician, serving in the legislature until sent to the United States Senate to fill an unexpired term. It is an interesting commentary on his preference for State office that he resigned from the Senate, where he might have remained, to become Chief Justice of the State Supreme Court. Living in Lexington as a neighbor of Henry Clay, he had been for many years one of the great leader's most ardent supporters, and it is significant of the character of the man that, while he supported Clay against Jackson in 1824, the "bargain" story transformed him into a bitter foe.

In view of their relations to the Jackson Administration

[1] This speech was incorporated in the 4th volume of *Elliot's Debates* as an exposition of the Constitution.

[2] Knight's *Reminiscences*.

[3] Miller's *Bench and Bar of Georgia*.

years later, the estimate of Barry reached by Amos Kendall in 1814, and recorded in his "Autobiography," is interesting, and serves to account for the feeling, scarcely concealed, with which the journalist-politician afterwards undertook the unraveling of the difficulties into which Barry had plunged the Post-Office Department. It was when Kendall was on his way to Kentucky that he first met the Lexington politician and went down the Ohio River with him and Mrs. Barry with "servants, horses, and carriages," in a boat thirty feet long, with three apartments. At the end of the journey Kendall wrote: "He appears to be a very good man but not a great man. For our passage he charged nothing, and in every way treated me like a gentleman. His lady seems to be a woman of good disposition, but uneducated." In contradiction to this estimate, we have another in which he is described as possessing extraordinary abilities, active business habits, an exact knowledge of men and things, and as being "a great orator."[1] And this same authority describes Mrs. Barry as "frank, lady-like, free from affectations, possessing a fine person and agreeable manners." Parton tells us that he was "agreeable and amiable, but not a business man" — which is the final verdict of history. In person he was above the medium height, but slender and thin in face. He was modest in demeanor, and energetic — even though he did not always properly direct his energy — and fond of society. He became Postmaster-General because, according to the Jackson standard, he had richly earned the reward.

Such was the Jackson Cabinet which accompanied him into office. There have been greater Cabinets, but many inferior to it, and few with men possessing greater ability than Van Buren or Berrien, or more social distinction than Branch. There was not a single member who did not possess at least good ability, and Jackson had, or thought he had, what he said he proposed to have, a Cabinet without a pres-

[1] Ellet's *Court Circles of the Republic*, 148.

idential aspirant. It is strange that the one man who developed into a candidate almost immediately was the one to whom he became most ardently attached.

We shall now note the first troubles of the official family.

CHAPTER III

THE RED TERROR AND THE WHITE

I

THIRTEEN days after the inauguration, the Senate, having confirmed the Cabinet, adjourned, and the Administration could look forward to almost nine months of non-interference from the Congress. The pre-inaugural prediction that the President would adopt a policy of proscription of his political foes was almost immediately justified by events. The "spoils system," as an important cog in the machinery of political parties, thus frankly recognized, dates from this time. Through all the intervening years the civil service reformers have indulged in the most bitter denunciation of Jackson on the untenable theory that but for him public offices would never have been used as the spoils of party. Some of the most conscientious of historians have created the impression that the adoption of a proscriptive policy was due to something inherently wrong in the President. As a matter of fact, Jackson was the victim of conditions and circumstances, and the new political weapon grew out of the exigencies of a new political era.

For many years political parties had been chaotic, vapory, and indefinite; and if the politics of the young Republic had not been drifting toward personal government, it had been partaking of the nature of government by cliques and classes. The first Message of John Quincy Adams had made the definite division of the people into political parties inevitable — these parties standing for well-defined, antagonistic policies. Van Buren had early caught the drift and had cleverly organized a party standing for principles and policies, rather than for personalities. John M. Clayton, soon to become one of the outstanding figures of the Opposition to the Jackson Administration, who had seldom voted even in presidential elections because of his indifference to the mere ambitions of individuals, understood that in 1828 something more was involved, and threw himself into the contest in support of Adams. And Clay was even then looking forward to the organization of a party pledged to internal improvements and a protective tariff.

The Jackson Administration marks the beginning of political parties as we have known them for almost a century.

It was in this compaign, too, that the masses awakened to the fact that they had interests involved, and possessed power. Previous to this the aristocracy, the business and financial interests, and the intellectuals, alone, determined the governmental personnel. Men went into training for the Presidency, and, as in a lodge, passed, as a matter of course, from the Cabinet to the Vice-Presidency, and thence to the chief magistracy. An office-holding class, feeling itself secure in a life tenure, had grown up.

As we have seen, the election of Jackson was due to the rising of the masses. Thousands who had never before participated in politics played influential parts in the campaign. The victory, they considered theirs. Thus they had flocked to Washington as never before to an inauguration, rejoicing in the induction of "their" President into office, and all too many pressing claims to recognition and entertaining hopes of entering upon their reward. Before the inauguration, the grim old warrior, awaiting the opportunity, at Gadsby's, to take the oath of office, had been fairly mobbed by ardent partisans of his cause, demanding the expulsion of the enemy and the appointment of his supporters to office. The Jackson press had been particularly insistent upon this point. Duff Green, of the "National Telegraph," had early announced that he naturally assumed that the office-holders who had actively campaigned for Adams would make way for the victors. This same feeling had spread into every community in the country. Isaac Hill, writing in the "New Hampshire Patriot" immediately after the election, had sounded the onslaught for the Democracy of New England.[1] And soon after reaching Washington, and sensing the atmosphere at Gadsby's, the New England editor had written joyously to a friend: "You may say to all our anxious Adamsites that THE BARNACLES WILL BE SCRAPED CLEAN OFF THE SHIP OF STATE. Most of them have grown so large and stick so tight that the scraping process will doubtless be fatal to them."

Before Jackson's entry into the White House, the scenes in and about Gadsby's were scarcely less than scandalous. A great perspiring mob swarmed in the streets in front, crowded the tap-room, jostled its way in the halls, and, notwithstanding the efforts of Major Lewis, it demanded and secured admission to the President's private apartment. All admitted themselves responsible for Jackson's election. Amos Kendall, encountering a pompous stranger on the Avenue, was invited to look upon the man who had "delivered Pennsylvania." [2] James A. Hamilton, who was close to Jackson in the early days of the Administration, was importuned by an Indianian, who had taken the electoral vote of the State to the Capitol, to intercede on his behalf for the Register's office at Crawfordsville, or the Marshalship. This typical office-seeker had "calculated to remain a few weeks . . . hoping that some of these violent Adams men may receive their walking papers." He carried letters of recommendation from all the Democratic members of the

[1] "Every State in New England is now ruled by the same aristocracy that ruled in 1798 — that ruled during the late war. . . . A band of New England Democrats have encountered the dominant party at vast odds — they have suffered every species of persecution and contumely. Shall these men not be protected by the Administration of the people under General Jackson? If that Administration fail to extend this protection, then indeed it will fail of one of the principal objects for which the people placed them in power by at least two to one of the votes of the Union."

[2] Kendall's *Autobiography*, 307.

State Legislature "for any office I can ask." But, in view of the brisk competition, would not Hamilton kindly recall that he had received letters from the Hoosier bearing on the campaign, and personally testify to the important part he had played? [1] Others depended upon the length of their petitions, and two applicants from Pennsylvania, for the same office, had signers so numerous that the number had to be estimated by the length of the sheets.[2]

Meanwhile there is no question but that Jackson was eager to serve his friends, if not to punish his enemies. From the moment of his election, he had entertained no illusions as to the character of the opposition his Administration would encounter. It was an open secret that his enemies, long before the inauguration, had begun to organize for the discrediting of his Administration. He was familiar with the bitterness of Clay. And, with the determination to make his Administration a success, from his point of view, he turned his attention to preparations for the fight. His military training told him that it was fatal to enter a campaign with traitors in the camp. The disloyalty from which Adams had suffered had not been lost upon him.[3] And he had fixed convictions as to political organization. "To give effect to any principles," he said, "you must avail yourself of the physical force of an organized body of men. This is true alike in war, politics, or religion. You cannot organize men in effective bodies without giving them a reason for it. And when the organization is once made, you cannot keep it together unless you hold constantly before its members why they are organized." [4] Thus party politics, in the modern sense, began with Jackson, and the spoils system grew out of the exigencies of party politics. Vicious though it may be, it is significant of its appeal to the rank and file of party workers, upon

[1] Hamilton's *Reminiscences*, 98.

[2] *Ibid.*

[3] Adams turned out but five.

[4] Quoted by Francis P. Blair to Buell, author of the *Life of Jackson*.

whom party success depends, that politicians of all parties, including Lincoln, have adopted it without shame.

It does not appear that Jackson was greatly influenced in his course by his advisers, of either his constitutional or Kitchen Cabinet. Van Buren, who has been wrongfully accused of so many things, and among others, of having been the dominating influence as to the spoils system, heard of the plan for sweeping changes with grave misgivings. "If the General makes one removal at this time," he said in a letter to Hamilton written from Albany, "he must go on. So far as depends on me, my course would be to restore by a single order every one who has been turned out by Mr. Clay for political reasons, unless circumstances of a personal character have since arisen to make the appointment in any case improper. To ascertain that will take a little time. There I would pause." This, from the head of his official family.

And the most intimate of his advisers, of the Kitchen Cabinet, Major Lewis, is reported to have written to the President: "In relation to the principle of rotation in office, I embrace this occasion to enter my solemn protest against it; not on account of my office, but because I hold it to be fraught with the greatest mischief to the country. If ever it should be carried out *in extenso*, the days of this Republic will, in my opinion, be numbered; for whenever the impression shall become general that the Government is only valuable on account of its offices, the great and paramount interests of the country will be lost sight of, and the Government itself ultimately destroyed." With the possible exception of Eaton, who was a practical politician in the modern sense, and Van Buren, to the extent just indicated, none of the members of the Cabinet were spoilsmen at heart; and Amos Kendall, the genius of the Kitchen Cabinet, would unquestionably have preferred to be spared the pain of turning men out of office. To be sure, the jovial but vindictive Duff Green, who spent much time at the elbow of Jackson in the early months of the Administration, was insistent upon the punishment of enemies, but the responsibility for the adoption of the policy rests upon the President himself.

And the result was that the spring and summer months of 1829 were filled with the clamor of importunate pleas, not unmixed with threats and curses, from the office-seekers. In many instances the wives and daughters of the applicants fluttered down upon Washington to reënforce the husband and the father.[1] One of the General's most ardent supporters left the capital two days after the inauguration bitterly denouncing him for his failure to appoint the irate one to a position not then vacant.[2] Cabinet officers were harassed, bombarded, followed from their offices to their homes and back again, until several of them confessed that life had become a burden, and they were forced to close their doors to applicants until a late hour in the afternoon to find time for the transaction of public business.[3] Such aspirants as were not upon the ground in person were either represented by friends who were, or they peppered the members of the Cabinet with letters. One peculiarly offensive candidate for the collectorship of customs in New York wrote to an equally disreputable friend: "No damn rascal who made use of an office or its profits for the purpose of keeping Mr. Adams in and General Jackson out of power is entitled to the least leniency save that of hanging. Whether or not I shall get anything in the general scramble for plunder remains to be seen, but I rather guess I shall. I know Mr. Ingham slightly, and would recommend that you push like the devil if you expect anything from that quarter." [4] And in the letter from Ingham to the seeker of "plunder" we have abundant evidence that the advice was accepted: "These [his duties] cannot be postponed; and I do assure you that I am com-

[1] Hamilton's *Reminiscences*, 98.

[2] McMaster's *History of the People of the United States.*

[3] Hamilton's *Reminiscences*, 98.

[4] Samuel Swartwout to Jesse Hoyt, in Mackenzie's *Life of Van Buren.*

pelled daily to file away long lists of recommendations, etc., without reading them, although I work eighteen hours out of the twenty-four with all diligence. The appointments can be postponed; other matters cannot; and it was one of the prominent errors of the late Administration that they suffered many important public interests to be neglected, while they were cruising about to secure or buy up partisans. This we must not do."[1] The same man, having written an insolent letter to Van Buren, was sharply rebuked by him. "Here I am," wrote the Secretary of State, "engaged in the most intricate and important affairs, which are new to me, and upon the successful conduct of which my reputation as well as the interests of the country depend, and which keep me occupied from early in the morning until late at night. And can you think it kind or just to harass me under such circumstances with letters which no man of common sensibility can read without pain? . . . I must be plain with you. . . . The terms upon which you have seen fit to place our intercourse are inadmissible."[2]

Nor was this clamor for office confined to the more important positions — it reached down to the most menial places, to those of the gardener, the janitor, and messenger. Worse still — men in position to serve were even appealed to for place by members of their immediate families. Thus we find Amos Kendall writing to his wife: "I had thought before of trying to get some place for your father, but I cannot do anything until I am myself appointed. I hope in a year or two, and perhaps sooner, to find some situation that will enable him to live near us, and comfortably."[3]

Meanwhile the clerks in Washington lived in a state of terror. Men who had long worked in harmony, and on terms of intimacy, were afraid to talk to one another. Every one

[1] Ingham to Jesse Hoyt, Shepard's *Life of Van Buren*, 210–11.
[2] Shepard's *Life of Van Buren*, 210.
[3] Amos Kendall's *Autobiography*, 286.

suddenly assumed the aspect of a spy and an informer. "All the subordinate officers of the Government, and even the clerks are full of tremblings and anxiety," wrote one woman to a correspondent. "To add to this general gloom, we have horrible weather, snowstorm after snowstorm, the river frozen up and the poor suffering." [1] The majority of the subordinates and clerks, many the ne'er-do-wells of distinguished families, assuming that they were assured of a life position, had lived up to, and beyond, their meager incomes, and suddenly found themselves unfit for other employment and confronted with dismissal.[2] And slowly, but surely, the dismissals came, leaving many in desperate straits, without sufficient funds to reach their homes, and unfit to earn a livelihood if they did. Some were driven to desperation. One dismissed employee of the Custom House in Boston went "in a transport of grief" to Ingham with a plea to be informed of the cause of his dismissal, only to be told that offices were not hereditary.[3] One clerk in the War Department cut his throat from ear to ear; another in the State Department went stark mad. But all appeals for sympathy were met by the proscriptionists with the stern reminder: "The exclusive party who were never known to tolerate any political opponent raise and reiterate the cry of persecution and proscription at every removal that takes place. They have provoked retaliation by the most profligate and abandoned course of electioneering; the most unheard-of calumny and abuse was heaped upon the candidate of the people; he was called by every epithet that could designate crime, and the amiable partner of his bosom was dragged before the people as worse than a convicted felon. What sympathy do men of such a party deserve when complaining that the places which they have abused are given to others?" [4]

[1] *First Forty Years*, 283.

[2] Amos Kendall in a letter to his wife describes the extravagant lives of these clerks. *Autobiography*, 278.

[3] Schouler's *History of the United States*, 457.

[4] Isaac Hill, quoted in Cyrus Bradley's *Life of Hill*.

A dark picture — and yet only darker than similar pictures in years to follow because, in 1829, the policy was new and caught the office-holders unprepared. So gloomy has the picture been painted that the student of the times is prepared to learn of a general massacre of the placemen. There was no such massacre — no such massacre as followed the election of Lincoln. One is prepared to hear that all the enemies of Jackson were driven from office, but, as a matter of fact, the majority of the Federal office-holders during his régime were unmolested. This could not be said of Roosevelt's Administration, nor of Cleveland's. The exact number of removals during the first year of Jackson's Administration cannot be determined with precision. Schouler,[1] while making no attempt definitely to fix the number, says that "some have placed the number as high as two thousand." In view of the evidence of contemporaries available, it does seem that a fairly accurate idea should be obtained. It is interesting to observe in this connection that while Jackson's enemies were dealing in sweeping generalities, his defenders were furnishing figures.

And among the defenders none is more reliable than Thomas H. Benton, whose veracity or personal honesty has never been impeached or questioned, and he tells us [2] that there were whole classes of office-holders that were not molested; that those whose functions were of a judicial nature were not disturbed, and that in the departments at Washington a majority remained opposed to Jackson through his two Administrations. More important still — he tells us that Jackson not only left a majority of his enemies in office, but that in some instances he actually reappointed personal and political enemies where they were "especially efficient officers." And he lays stress upon the point that where men, who had bitterly fought Jackson in the election, were not reappointed, a hue and cry was raised that they had been de-

[1] *History of the United States.*

[2] *Thirty Years' View*, I, 160.

nied a right. Corroborating this, we have the evidence of Amos Kendall,[1] who wrote, after the Administration had been in power a year and a half: "He [Jackson] is charged with having turned out of office all who were opposed to him, when a majority of the office-holders in Washington are known to be in favor of his rivals. In that city the removals have been but one seventh of those in office, and most of them for bad conduct and character. In the Post-Office Department, toward which have been directed the heaviest complaints, the removals have been only about one sixteenth; in the whole Government, one eleventh." And to the evidence of both Benton and Kendall, either one of whom would have been incapable of deliberate falsehood, we may add the less reliable, because more prejudiced, evidence of Isaac Hill, given in a public speech at Concord in the late summer of 1829. "It is worthy of observation," he said, "that at least two thirds of the offices of profit at the seat of the National Government, after the removals thus far made, are still held by persons who were opposed to the election of General Jackson." [2] A more detailed study of the removals actually made show that, while there were 8600 post-offices in 1829, less than 800 postmasters were removed, and these, largely, in the more important centers, leaving 7800 undisturbed.

One of the most serious charges against Jackson in connection with these removals is that he practiced duplicity, reassuring a trembling office-holder one day only to remove him, without warning, on the next; and this story is based upon what the officer in charge of Indian affairs under Adams declares to have been his personal experience. According to his story, Eaton, his superior officer, suggested that he should see the President to meet some charges that had been made against him; that on visiting Jackson he had made a solemn denial, satisfied the President, and been presented by him to the members of his household; that on the

[1] Kendall's *Autobiography*. [2] Bradley's *Life of Hill*.

next day a gentleman entered the Indian Office, and, after looking around, explained that the place had been offered him by the President that morning, but that he did not intend to accept; that the position was afterwards offered to others, and that the dismissal finally reached him in Philadelphia while there on official business. This places Jackson in a sinister light; but our commissioner adds, that one close to the Administration said: "Why, sir, everybody knows your qualifications for the place, but General Jackson has been long satisfied that you are not in harmony with his views in regard to the Indians." [1] This raises the question whether a President chosen by the people is entitled to his own governmental policies or should be forced to accept such as may be handed to him by subordinates who received their appointments by preference, and not from the hands of the people. That this removal was the President's own idea may be gathered from the fact that Eaton, Secretary of War, under whom Indian affairs came, was not in favor of the dismissal.

It is worth recording that Van Buren kept his department comparatively free from the spoils idea. But even the most intense partisan of Jackson will be hard pressed to find any proper reason for the spiteful recall of William Henry Harrison from Bogota, where he had just presented his credentials as United States Minister to Colombia. This recall was opposed very earnestly by Postmaster-General Barry, who frankly said to the President:

"If you had seen him as I did on the Thames, you would, I think, let him alone."

"You may be right, Barry," Jackson replied. "I reckon you are. But thank God I did n't see him there." [2]

Dark though the picture is from the viewpoint of the civil service reformer, there is another possible point of view. All

[1] McKinney, *The Office-Holder's Sword of Damocles.*

[2] Story related by William Allen to Buell.

the officials dismissed from places were not high-minded, conscientious public servants, for among them were numerous criminals. The dismissal of Tobias Watkins an Adams appointee and a personal friend of the former President, to make place for Amos Kendall, was the occasion for a great outburst of indignation from the Opposition. Within a month the product of the spoils system had discovered frauds on the part of the "martyr" to the amount of more than $7000, and an arrest followed. He was convicted and served his time in prison. Nor was that of Watkins an isolated case. Thus the collector at Buffalo [1] had procured false receipts for money never paid and was given credit at the Treasury; the collector at Key West [2] had permitted an unlawful trade between Cuba and Florida; the collector at Bath, Maine,[3] was dismissed for personally using $56,315 of the public funds; the collector at Portsmouth [4] was shown to have engaged in smuggling; the collector at St. Marks [5] was shown to have been plundering live-oak from the public lands; the collector at Petersburg [6] had used $24,857 of the public money; the collector at Perth Amboy [7] had made false returns, appropriated to his own use $88,000 of the public money, and fled to Canada; the collector at Elizabeth City, North Carolina,[8] had converted $32,791 to his personal use and joined the other "martyr" to the spoils system on Canadian soil.[9] In brief, the introduction of the spoils system had resulted, in eighteen months, in the uncovering of peculations in the Treasury Department alone of more than $280,000 by men whose dismissal from office had called forth the unmeasured denunciation of Jackson's enemies, and it is manifestly unfair to withhold these facts while placing emphasis upon the "dismissal of collector to make way for Jackson's henchmen."

[1] M. M. Cox. [2] William Pinckney. [3] John B. Swanton. [4] Timothy Upham. [5] D. L. White. [6] J. Robertson. [7] R. Arnold. [8] Asa Rogerson.

[9] These facts are taken from Ritchie's *Richmond Enquirer*, and are quoted in Professor Tyler's *Letters and Times of the Tylers*.

Thus, throughout the spring and summer of 1829, the President and his Cabinet were bored, harassed, and tortured with importunities for place, denounced as ingrates because they left any of the enemies in office, and damned by the enemy for every dismissal that was made.

II

THE spring and summer was the time of the Red Terror.

The White Terror of retaliation began with the meeting of the hostile Senate in December.

The enemies of Jackson sought the earliest possible opportunity to denounce the wholesale dismissals, and the brilliant orators of the Opposition in the House made intemperate attacks, while in the Senate Webster spoke against the policy of proscription, without, however, adopting the absurd position that the President did not possess the constitutional power.[1] The early part of the session was given over to denunciations of the removals, and to a frankly hostile scrutiny, on the part of the Senate, of all nominations requiring onfirmation. It foreshadowed the bitter party battles of the next eight years by rejecting the nominations of some of Jackson's most ardent supporters in the campaign, and by taking the ridiculous position that journalists should be excluded from appointive office. This proscription, or massacre of the editors, was aimed at men, comparatively new to public life, who were speedily to develop into the most brilliant and sagacious of the Jacksonian leaders. Long and acrimonious executive sessions became the rule of the Senate. In some instances, action upon nominations was postponed for months under provocative circumstances that were not lost upon the fighting figure at the other end of the Avenue. The charge was made that a number of the President's nominees were "vicious characters." It was in the early days of this session that a comparatively new Senator, elected upon

[1] Lodge's *Life of Webster*, 167.

the supposition that he would support the President and his policies, and destined to be the only member of the Senate to realize personally upon that body's venomous hostility to the Administration, stepped forth to organize and direct the fight against the confirmation of nominees in whom the President was deeply interested. John Tyler led the first onslaught on the Administration.

It is important to pause to contemplate Tyler's character and career, because he typifies those Democrats who were so soon to enter into coöperation with the Whigs in opposition, and because history has been unjust in underestimating both his capacity and courage. We shall find him pursuing Jackson throughout the greater part of his Presidency, and paying the penalty to the people with a manliness which found little emulation among men to whom history has been more gracious.

John Tyler was the scion of a family distinguished in law and in politics. His father was a fine Revolutionary figure, and one of the first lawyers in Virginia. He inherited his father's ability, predilections, and prejudices. Within three months after his admission to the bar, he was employed in every important case in the county, and when, at the age of twenty-seven, he abandoned his practice to enter Congress, his income was $2000 a year, which was $1300 more than Webster's at the same age.[1] On reaching Washington, he was cordially welcomed by the Madisons into the White House circle. He was fond of the society of the President's house, disliked the French cooking, but found consolation in the excellent champagne of which he was very fond.[2] He found Clay, with whom he was to be associated in the fights against Jackson, in the Speaker's chair, and fell under the spell of his fascination. It was then, too, that he formed his intense admiration for Calhoun.

[1] Professor Tyler's *Letters and Times of the Tylers*, I, 236.

[2] Letter to his wife, in *Letters and Times of the Tylers*, I, 288.

His hostility to Jackson and Jacksonian methods was first manifested in his support of the resolutions censuring the General for his course in Florida. There is no doubt that at this time he had formed a deep-seated prejudice against the military hero. "We are engaged with Jackson and the President," he wrote home at the time. "I do not hesitate to say that the constitutional powers of the House of Representatives have been violated in the capture and detention of Pensacola and the Barancas; that Jackson overstepped his orders; and that the President has improperly approved his proceedings, and that the whole are culpable." [1] But there was a more powerful and less personal reason for his enmity to the Jackson Administration, which developed during this period. He had already become a sectionalist. Like Calhoun in later life, and Webster in 1820, he began to sense a struggle between the sections over the balance of power. Thus early he commenced to question the permanency of the Union. In the Missouri fight, in a strong speech against the restriction of slavery, he alone, among all participating on his side, advanced the proposition that the Congress possessed no constitutional power to pass a law prohibiting slavery in the Territories.[2] We find him writing [3] that "men talk of the dissolution of the Union with perfect nonchalance and indifference." When, in his thirty-first year, he voluntarily retired to private life to retrieve his fortunes, he had made an impression so profound that it was predicted that he would rise to high station.[4]

When in 1827 he became a candidate for the Senate against the brilliant and vitriolic John Randolph of Roanoke, we find the elements working that were to ripen him for the break with the Jackson Administration, and for association with Clay's party of incongruities and nondescripts. After

[1] Letter to Dr. Curtis, in *Letters and Times of the Tylers*, I, 305.

[2] *National Intelligencer*, Sept. 15, 1859.

[3] To Dr. Curtis.

[4] The prediction of Justice Baldwin of the Supreme Court.

the inauguration of Adams, he had written Clay commending his action in throwing his support to the Puritan, assuring him of his contempt for the "bargain" story, and unnecessarily adding a fling at Jackson: "I do not believe that the sober and reflecting people of Virginia would have been so far dazzled by military renown as to have conferred their suffrage upon a mere soldier — one acknowledged on every hand to be of little value as a civilian." [1] When Randolph so viciously attacked Adams and Clay on the "bargain" story, Tyler became his most uncompromising foe. In some manner his letter to Clay found its way into the newspapers, resulting in much feeling, letter-writing, charges and counter-charges and journalizing, and the supporters of Tyler interpreted the use of the letter as an attempt to coerce him into support of Jackson in 1828. If such was the purpose, it failed. He was elected without having pledged himself, and at a complimentary dinner after his election, he referred to Jackson in a sneering fashion.

And now we begin to understand the underlying causes that took Tyler and other Southern Democrats out of the party and into the Whig ranks during the Jackson period. On reaching Washington in December, 1827, we find him writing to a correspondent: "My hopes are increased from the following fact . . . that in the nature of things, General Jackson must surround himself by a Cabinet composed of men advocating, to a great extent, the doctrines so dear to us. Pass them in review before you — Clinton, Van Buren, Tazewell, Cheves, Macon, P. P. Barbour, men who, in the main, concur with us in sentiment. Furthermore, General Jackson will have to encounter a strong opposition. He will require an active support at our hands. Should he abuse Virginia by setting at nought her political sentiments, he will find her at the head of the opposition, and he will probably experience the fate of J. Q. A." [2] The Cabinet, when an-

[1] *Letters and Times of the Tylers*, I, 360.

[2] Letter to John Rutherford, in *Letters and Times of the Tylers*, I, 378.

nounced, does not seem to have satisfied him, albeit Van Buren, of whose views on slavery extension he appears to have been misinformed, was a member. The presence of Berrien and Branch ought, perhaps, to have reassured him, but they were a minority, and they did not satisfy Calhoun, of whom they were devoted disciples.

Thus, from the very beginning of the Jackson régime, Tyler was suspicious, and ripe for the Opposition. In the spoils system he found a pretext for dissatisfaction, and he proceeded to develop this into a rather petty persecution. It would be a mistake to underrate the effect of his opposition. He was highly respected by his colleagues. His dignity, courtliness, urbanity, and ease gave him a certain social prestige. He was an interesting and likable companion, and his polished conversation had impelled an English novelist [1] to describe it as superior to that of any one he had met in America. His appearance was not against him. Tall and slender, of patrician mould, his Roman nose, firm mouth, broad and lofty brow, and honest blue eyes combined to give him a distinction that marked him in an assembly. He was not a mere professional politician of a type to be developed later in the Republic. His letters to his daughter [2] concerning her studies, on poetry, fiction, and history, denote a discriminating student and lover of literature. It was this occasional detachment from the political world which made it possible for him, during the famous debate on the Foot Resolution, to entertain himself in the Senate Chamber in the reading of Moore's "Life of Byron." We shall now observe him launch the White Terror against the Red.

III

Among the nominations, mostly for comparatively minor positions, sent to the Senate by Jackson were those of a "batch of editors." [3] Strangely enough, this seems to have rather

[1] G. P. R. James. [2] *Letters and Times of the Tylers.*

[3] Tyler's term, in *Letters and Times of the Tylers*, I, 408.

affronted the somewhat ponderous dignity of that body. So strongly did it then impress the Senate that it has made an ugly impression upon a number of historians. Even Schouler[1] is distressed to find so many mere "press writers" on the list. Whether the fact that they were mere editors was enough to make them "infamous characters," we are left to conjecture. The secret of the strange antipathy to a class long conceded to be among the most influential of any nation is probably to be found in the fact that until this time the lawyers were conceded a monopoly in public station. There was a reason for Jackson's change of policy, and it grew out of the organization of party and the democratization of government. Unlike his predecessors, he had not depended for support, nor did he expect to look exclusively for support to the professional politicians and the wealthy. As a candidate his appeal had been — for the first time in American history — to the people. As a President he proposed to look to the same quarter. With the people actually established as the ultimate power in the State, according to the theory of American institutions, he was not unmindful of the necessity of reaching the people with his case. He was the first President fully to appreciate the power of the press. He could see no reason why men capable of presenting and popularizing a policy or principle should be excluded from the privilege of helping put it in operation.

In the campaign of 1828 he had been opposed by the greater portion of the press, but he had found champions — men of capacity and talent, who had fought the good fight for him, and not without effect. The assumption that all these men were bribed by the promise of place would be a violent one indeed. And the "batch of editors" whose names he sent to the Senate were men who had long been attached to the cause that Jackson personified. Some had more recently allied themselves with the cause, but in every

[1] *History of the United States.*

instance there was a sound reason for the change of front, and in these cases it does not appear that they had met the President in the campaign or had any expectations.

And these men, having received recess appointments, were at their posts or on their way. Those already at their posts had given ample proof of their capacity. One, against whom considerable bitterness was felt, had speedily uncovered the peculations of a highly respectable predecessor who was not a "press writer," and that gentleman was languishing in the penitentiary. The Senate, apparently, did not consider this a service to the State worthy of reward. While there can be no doubt that the partisan enemies of Jackson were delighted at the opportunity personally to affront him, and while it is certain that Clay's friends were anxious to punish one, and Adams's friends to humiliate another, the actual conspiracy to defeat the confirmation of the editors originated with John Tyler, in close coöperation with Senator Tazewell of Virginia — who was still smarting under his defeat in the contest with Van Buren for the secretaryship of State.

The editors who thus fell under the haughty displeasure of the Senate were Major Henry Lee, James B. Gardner, Moses Dawson, Mordecai M. Noah, Amos Kendall, and Isaac Hill.

Charges of a personal nature were made against Lee, who had been appointed consul-general to Algiers. He was a half-brother of Robert E. Lee and a man of brilliant parts. During the campaign he had lived with Jackson at the Hermitage "writing for his election some of the finest campaign papers ever penned in this country."[1] One who saw him there at the time has recorded his impressions. "He was not handsome, as his half-brother, Robert E. Lee, but rather ugly in face — a mouth without a line of the bow of Diana about it, and nose, not clean-cut and classic, but rather meaty, and, if we may use the word, 'blood meaty';

[1] Henry S. Wise, *Seven Decades of the Union*, 99.

but he was one of the most attractive men in conversation we ever listened to."[1] He had served in the Virginia House of Delegates with Tyler, and had been a college mate. "Moreover," writes Tyler, "I regarded him as a man of considerable intellectual attainments and of a high order of talent."[2] But this did not operate in his favor. He had assisted in the writing of Jackson's inaugural address, and is said to have been mostly responsible for its literary form. The fact that his morals were not considered impeccable was sufficient as a pretext, and the news of his rejection reached him in Paris, where he died. Tyler afterwards protested that he had found it painful to vote against his confirmation, and had expressed his opinion of Lee's "innocence of certain more aggravated additions to the charge under which he labored."

Isaac Hill, of the "New Hampshire Patriot," was easily slaughtered on the ground that during the campaign he had "slandered Mrs. Adams." In addition to the publication of his paper, the most vigorous and clever Jacksonian organ in New England, he conducted a publishing house, and his offense lay in having published a book in which Mrs. Adams was described as an "English woman" with little sympathy for American institutions. The hollowness of this excuse is evident in the fact that several Senators who had been shocked at this offense had regaled drawing-rooms with jokes of Mrs. Jackson's pipe, and on Mrs. Eaton's being a proper "lady in waiting" for the President's wife since "birds of a feather flock together."[3] The real reason for his rejection was that he had incurred the bitter enmity of the Opposition by his telling paragraphs during the campaign. Immediately after his rejection, two Senators hastened to the home of John Quincy Adams with the news, and the old

[1] Henry S. Wise, *Seven Decades of the Union*, 99.

[2] Letter to Richard T. Brown, in *Letters and Times of the Tylers*, I, 409.

[3] Mrs. Smith, in *First Forty Years*, p. 253, refers to such conversations.

man made the comment in his diary that night that Hill "was the editor of the 'New Hampshire Patriot,' one of the most slanderous newspapers against the late Administration, and particularly against me, in the country."

Mordecai M. Noah, editor of the "National Advocate" of New York City, appointed surveyor and inspector of the port of New York, appears to have tickled the risibles of the Senators of the Opposition, though his distinguished career entitles him to the respect of posterity. One important and memorable service to the Nation should have made him immune from the common hate. Sixteen years before he had been sent as consul to Tunis with a special mission to Algiers. We had been paying an annual tribute to Algiers for the privilege of navigating the Mediterranean, and Noah, the journalist, had denounced the practice and declared that the money could be better spent in the building of warships. He succeeded on his Algerian mission in ransoming American prisoners who were being held in slavery, but such was the bigotry of the time that, after his work was done, he was recalled on the flimsy pretense that his Jewish religion was impossible in Tunis. At the time he was honored by Jackson, he was not only distinguished by his public service, but because of his journalistic genius, and he had written his "Travels in England, France, Spain, and the Barbary States." He deserves his place in Morais's "Eminent Israelites of the 19th Century." But he had rendered valuable service to Jackson in the campaign, and the bigoted members of the Senate rejected him with much hilarity.

The first setback the Opposition received came in the consideration of the nomination of Amos Kendall, of the "Kentucky Argus." He had, at the time, served for months with marked ability as auditor of the Treasury, rooting out old and vicious practices, uncovering the crimes of his predecessor, but he had left the camp of Clay to do yeoman service for Jackson, and that was quite enough. Adams himself was deeply interested in his humiliation. In the midst of the campaign he had been consulted by Clay touching upon "testimony given by Amos Kendall before the Senate of Kentucky intended to support charges against Mr. Clay of corrupt bargaining with me"; and, on Clay's representation, no doubt, describes the editor as "one of those authors to let, whose profligacy is the child of his poverty." But the vote on Kendall was a tie, and Calhoun cast the deciding vote in his favor.

Tyler was delighted with his work. "On Monday we took the printers in hand," he wrote. "Kendall was saved by the casting vote of the Vice President . . . Hendricks [Indiana], who was supported by the last Administration, was induced to vote for him and in that way he was saved. Out of those presented to the Senate, but two squeezed through, and that with the whole power of the Government here thrown in the scale."[1] Kendall tells an interesting story which shows that the friends of Calhoun were quietly at work to convince the rejected editors that their humiliation had been brought about through the secret influence of Van Buren. Even then the Little Magician, as Van Buren was called, was considered the greatest obstacle in the way of the South Carolinian's progress toward the White House, and it was the evident purpose to send the editors, miserable "press writers" though they were, back to their papers to fight the aspirations of Van Buren. Before the vote was taken on Kendall, he was approached by Duff Green, of the "National Telegraph," Calhoun's organ, and assured that the Van Buren influence was responsible for the fight against him. This aroused the curiosity of the clever Kendall, who "had never heard of such influence," and he instantly surmised the meaning of the message. Thus, when Green, predicting his rejection, suggested that the Kentuckian could return to the "Argus," the latter replied that he would remain in Washington in that event.

[1] Letter to R. W. Christian, in *Letters and Times of the Tylers*, I, 408.

The effect of these rejections on Jackson was like a slap in the face. It aroused all the lion in his nature. He had grown fond of the editors who had so vigorously fought his battles, and his heart was set on their reward. It was the Senate's first challenge, and it was instantly accepted. It was clear that nothing could be done for Lee, where the vote was unanimous, but Jackson decided to renominate Noah, and we find Tyler writing to Tazewell: "The President this morning renominated Noah. This is a prelude to Hill's renomination. Your presence, I apprehend, would be immaterial, as the result of any vote upon these subjects would not be varied. Monday is fixed for the consideration of Noah's case."[1] On the second attempt, Noah was confirmed, like Kendall, with the casting vote of Calhoun.

But the President had other plans for his favorite, Hill, over whose sharp retorts the General had so heartily chuckled during the campaign. Webb, the editor of the "Courier and Enquirer" of New York, denounced in his paper the Senate's rejection of Hill. "Isaac Hill," he wrote, "is a printer and was the editor of the 'New Hampshire Patriot.' He was always the friend of his country and its republican institutions, and when that country, during the late war, was about to be sold by traitors to the enemy; when the war was declared wicked and unjustifiable, and the Hartford Convention meditated the formation of a separate treaty with England, his voice was heard in the Granite State and in the mountains of Vermont, animating the people and arousing them to a just sense of their danger, and the blessings of freedom. He was a thorn in the side of the Tories, and though living in the hotbed of the Opposition, he pursued his course fearlessly, independently, and successfully." Writing from Jefferson Barracks, General Henry Leavenworth entered his protest, a non-partisan one: "Isaac Hill with his 'New Hampshire Patriot' did more than any one man known to me to put

[1] *Letters and Times of the Tylers*, I, 408.

down the 'peace societies' during the war," he wrote, and he described enlistments under him following Hill's patriotic exhortations.

It is more than probable that these protests were not uninspired, and that the fine Italian hand of Amos Kendall, who had already become the managerial genius of the Administration, was in them. Certain it is that the most effective move was that of Kendall in writing to the Democracy of New Hampshire that the President "has entire confidence in Mr. Hill and looks upon his rejection as a blow aimed at himself," and putting it up to the legislature to "wipe away the stigma cast upon this just and true man, by the unjust and cruel vote of the Senate." The New Hampshire Democrats understood, and a little later Isaac Hill walked down the aisle of the Senate that had humiliated and rejected him to take the oath as a Senator of the United States.

Thus the Senate's fight against Jackson began at the earliest possible moment. Clay had begun his denunciations of the Administration before it was three weeks old; and the Senate sought an opportunity personally to affront the President before he had announced a policy or a programme.

CHAPTER IV

JACKSON BREAKS WITH CALHOUN

I

THE definite break between Calhoun and Jackson was one of the most dramatic and far-reaching in its political effects of any similar quarrel in American history. It furnished Clay with new material for the building of his party. It decisively committed the party of Jackson to the defense of the Union. It eliminated Calhoun from the list of presidential possibilities, dropped the curtain on the South Carolinian that the Nation had known for two decades, and raised it on another with whom the world is well acquainted. It divided his life into two distinct parts. It made Martin Van Buren President.

The Calhoun who was to become one of Clay's most vituperative and intemperate lieutenants in the fight against the Administration differs as radically from the ambitious politician who had intrigued for the election of Jackson as the Webster of the Great Debate differed from the Webster of the Rockingham Resolutions.

The greatest biographer of the Carolinian [1] fixes the time that he became the personification of the slavery cause as 1830 — the date of the quarrel — and says that "up to that time he is, in spite of his uncommonly brilliant career, only an able politician of the higher and nobler order, having many peers and even a considerable number of superiors." Of the three great figures, Clay, Webster, and Calhoun, he was admittedly the strongest intellectually, and the one most unmistakably touched with genius. Nature made him a statesman. Swept into Congress on the wave of patriotic enthu-

[1] Von Holst.

siasm following the attack on the Chesapeake, his audacity, independent thinking, militancy, and genius combined to place him in the very lead of the party of Young America that clamored for the War of 1812. He sounded the first clear official war note in his report on that part of Madison's Message dealing with our relations with England; and after the delivery of his first war speech one of the leading editors of the day hailed "this young Carolinian as one of the master spirits who stamp their names upon the age in which they live." [1] In his haughty assumption of equality with the oldest and most experienced members of the Congress, he suggests the younger Pitt. His war speeches were classics of argumentation, sober, and yet pulsating with patriotic passion. If any sectional thought crossed his mind then, it never touched his tongue. He was a superb Nationalist — one of the most splendid figures of his time. Summoned into Monroe's Cabinet as Secretary of War, he disclosed a high order of executive as well as legislative ability. Finding the department in confusion, he brought order out of chaos, and established system. A former officer of the great Napoleon was impressed with the resemblance between Calhoun's plan of army organization and that of the Corsican.[2] Even his friends were agreeably astonished at his aptitude for organzation and general executive duties. And this furthered his presidential plans, and a strong party in the Congress perfected plans to advance him to the White House on the expiration of Monroe's term.

It is not now fashionable to think of him as a designing and ambitious politician, but one of his biographers has commented on his tendency to stoop "to cover with an approving and admiring smile a resentment which is lurking in the corner of his heart, and on the other side to break off all social intercourse with old and highly respected associates, merely

[1] Ritchie, in the *Richmond Enquirer*.

[2] General Bernard, chief of staff of the engineers.

because others whose services he wished to secure might not like these connections." [1] And yet, despite his efforts, his candidacy appears to have made no impression upon the country. Among the publicists he was strong; but the people were not impressed. He was the original "young man's candidate," but this weakened him among the older and more important leaders. "His age, or rather his youth," wrote one,[2] "at the present moment is a formidable objection to his elevation to the chair." Nevertheless, placing his reliance on the younger element, he pushed on. Even in Massachusetts he was charged with having "newspapers set up" to support him.[3] Certain it is that Webster favored his election as long as it seemed possible of achievement, and when failure there seemed certain, the greatest of his future rivals earnestly urged his election to the Vice-Presidency.[4] To the latter position he was elected through a combination of the friends of Adams and Jackson.

And now we find the presidential fever consuming him. He becomes the practical, scheming, not overly scrupulous politician — a rôle he is not popularly supposed to have ever filled. From the very beginning he set to work to undermine the Administration of his chief. His apologists explain that when the "bargain" story was advanced, he was forced to choose between the two factions that had combined to elect him, and preferred to go with the Jackson forces.[5] Whatever his motive, he entered into no half-hearted opposition. This notable activity against Adams and in favor of Jackson has been ascribed to a presumptive premonition that the latter was certain to reach the Presidency, and, in view of Jackson's assurance that he would be satisfied with one term, Calhoun calculated that the defeat of Adams would shorten his period

[1] Von Holst, 58. [2] Joseph Story.

[3] Adams's *Memoirs*.

[4] Webster wrote to his brother: "I hope all of New England will support Mr. Calhoun for the Vice-Presidency." (Webster's *Correspondence*.)

[5] Von Holst, 62–63.

of waiting by four years.[1] So ardently was he panting for the Presidency at this time that he summoned his friends to assist in the establishment of a paper, impatiently brushed aside the objections as to cost, and calling Duff Green to the editorship of the "National Telegraph," created the most powerful party organ that had existed in this country up to that time.[2] Less than a year after Adams's inauguration, Calhoun was actively organizing for his defeat. We find him inviting a Philadelphian to his chamber in the Capitol to urge him to coöperate with the Opposition party on the ground that "because of the manner in which it came into power it must be defeated at all hazards, regardless of its measures." [3] This insistence on the defeat of the Administration, "regardless of its measures," was the reasoning of an ambitious politician, none too scrupulous, in a pinch, in his methods. The rest is known — how Calhoun threw his influence to Jackson in 1828, and was reëlected to the Vice-Presidency with the hero of the Hermitage. Close students of the period are now convinced that preliminary to this alliance an agreement had been made that Calhoun was to succeed to the Presidency after four years.

At this time he was in the full maturity of his wonderful power, and the future must have seemed secure. Quincy, who saw him about this time, found him "a striking looking man, with thick black hair brushed back defiantly," and he comments on Calhoun's policy of cultivating and fascinating all young men visiting the National capital.[4] The world is too familiar with the tragic features of the great Carolinian to require a description. The rugged carving, the low broad brow, the spare frame almost amounting to attenuation, the penetrating gaze of the "glorious pair of yellow-brown shining eyes," the bushy brows and the sunken sockets —

[1] Sargent's *Public Men and Events*, I, 108. [2] *Ibid.*, 109.

[3] Sargent tells of his interview with Joseph McIlvaine, Recorder of Philadelphia, I, 108.

[4] Quincy's *Figures of the Past.*

Calhoun looked unlike any other man in history.[1] He was a commanding figure at the time of the quarrel which was to change the entire course of his life, and to alter his political character.

II

WE have seen that Calhoun was annoyed with Jackson over matters of patronage, but the development of the quarrel to the breaking point is to be traced in the story of a debate and two dinners.

While it has not been customary to attach any party significance to the Webster-Hayne debate, it was conducted along party lines and was a party battle. To such a seasoned observer of parliamentary fights as Thomas H. Benton, it was little more than a party skirmish.[2] Even Webster, at the time, evidently looked upon Hayne's assault upon him as political in its character. Some time before he had sent Senator White of Florida to Calhoun to warn him that by permitting his friends to attack New England, he was playing into the hands of Van Buren, who would capture New England States that would otherwise go to the South Carolinian. And Calhoun, no less alive to the political significance of the promised fight, had, according to White's story to Adams, been impressed. "He said Calhoun seemed to be considerably at a loss what to do," wrote Adams at the time; "that he did not know what things were coming to; that he had no feeling of unfriendliness to me, and would by now have visited me but for fear of being misrepresented; that if I had consulted him four years ago, and not have appointed Clay Secretary of State, I should now have been President of the United States." [3] This purported warning of Webster to Calhoun is

[1] Jefferson Davis in his *Memoirs* describes Calhoun's eyes as "yellow-brown," while his contemporary biographer, Jenkins, tells us they were dark blue. It seems unlikely that Davis, who knew him well, could have been mistaken.

[2] Benton's *Thirty Years' View*, I, 13–40.

[3] Adams's *Memoirs*, Feb. 28, 1830.

given color by the former's action during his great speech, in turning his fine black eyes upon the latter, in the chair, while quoting:

> "A barren sceptre in their gripe
> Thence to be wrenched by an unlineal hand,
> No son of their's succeeding"

— a prophecy said to have caused Calhoun to "change expression and show some agitation."[1]

Whether the attack on Webster and New England was conceived for the purpose of serving a party or sectional end, the records show that the Administration leaders who participated in the debate, Grundy, White, and Livingston, followed the Webster-Hayne exchange with elaborate indictments of New England Federalism, and John Forsyth, the real floor leader of the Administration, while contributing little to the discussion, was notably busy upon the floor. That the party phase was uppermost in the minds of the politicians and the press immediately following the verbal duel of the giants may be deduced from the nature of the press comments. One paper, having a correspondent at the capital, summed up the result: "The opposition party generally contend that Mr. Webster overthrew Mr. Hayne; while, on the other hand, the result is triumphantly hailed by the friends of the Administration as a decisive victory over the eastern giant."[2] And in keeping with the theory that the mass attack on New England Federalism was to capture that section for the Administration,[3] we find the speech of Hayne being extensively circulated over the New England States. There can be no doubt that Webster literally dragged in the really great issue of the Union, that Hayne was forced to accept that diversion, and by so doing gave to the debate its immortal character. Jackson was delighted with Hayne's first

[1] March's *Reminiscences of Congress.*

[2] *Philadelphia Gazette.*

[3] March's idea.

speech, and interested in the second, but on a more mature consideration Webster's glowing defense of the Union went home to the old patriot at the White House. It is because of the effect of the debate upon Jackson's Administration, and not merely because it occurred during his Presidency, that we cannot dismiss it as remote from the party politics of the time.

It should be borne in mind that the Daniel Webster who emerged from the debate was not the same public character who had entered it. By that epochal utterance he obliterated the one vulnerable point in his career — for the Daniel Webster of 1829 was vulnerable. He entered politics in New Hampshire as a Federalist — "liberal Federalist," to use the phrase of his biographer.[1] Notwithstanding this "liberality," he was to become considerably smirched by party loyalty during the war with England. This war was the occasion for his first public utterance, when, on July 4, 1812, he bitterly denounced the war with true Federalistic fervor at Portsmouth. This speech, printed and circulated for propaganda purposes against the war, ran into two editions, and led to his selection as a delegate to the notorious Rockingham County mass meeting. Here it fell to him to prepare the address known to history as the "Rockingham Memorial" to which the advocates of the sinister doctrine of Nullification pointed approvingly up to the Civil War. The notoriety of this document resulted in his election to Congress, where his record was everything it should not have been.

His first move was to heckle the President by calling upon him for information as to the time and manner of the repeal of the French decrees — which was in line with his previous denunciation of France. The enemies of the War of 1812 were bitter against the French, just as the enemies of the World War, over a century later, were bitter against the English. And while his country was at war with a powerful

[1] Henry Cabot Lodge.

foe, he voted against taxes necessary for the waging of it; fought the compulsory draft of men for the miserable little army on the ground that the States alone had the right to resort to conscription; and even threatened the dissolution of the Union with the suggestion that "it would be the solemn duty of the State Governments to protect their authority over their own State militia, and to interpose between their citizens and arbitrary power." He stubbornly resisted the attempt to extend martial law to all citizens suspected of treason; actually declaimed against the bill to encourage enlistments; opposed the war policy of the war Administration and urged a defensive warfare. And, of course, he intemperately denounced the embargo.

This course made him by long odds the most conspicuous Federalist in the House, and while he opposed the Hartford Convention, he does not appear to have looked upon it as seditious or treasonable, and as late as 1820, in his Boston speech, utterly ignored by his biographers, he practically proclaimed the right of secession. In brief, throughout the second war against England he was found just on the safe side of the line of sedition. His position at the time was notorious, and Isaac Hill, in the "New Hampshire Patriot," was openly accusing him of trying to dissolve the Union and to array the North against the South.

Thus, the Webster that Hayne assailed had skeletons in his closet. His reputation as an orator was greater than that of any living American. Behind him was his Plymouth Oration which had rivaled Washington Irving as a best seller;[1] his Dartmouth College plea, which had moved John Marshall to tears; his Bunker Hill Address, which had been read with avidity in England and translated into French; and his plea for Greek independence, which had been read all over the world. Such was the Daniel Webster who was challenged by Hayne — or the Democrats — or the Administration.

[1] Lodge's *Life of Webster*, 118.

Robert Y. Hayne was a knight of Southern chivalry, who in youth, like the ancient Greeks and Romans, had studied oratory as an art, from his first boyhood triumph moving with dash and audacity to his destiny, and at thirty-two entered the Senate of the United States.[1] His reputation as an orator previous to the great debate promised that the contest would not be one-sided. His character as man and publicist commanded universal respect and even the affection of political friend and foe alike.[2] And he entered the contest with one distinct advantage over his adversary: there were skeletons in Webster's closet; there were none in Hayne's.

III

THERE is no doubt but that on the day Hayne opened his attack, he was in fine fettle. Never had the Senate Chamber presented a more inspiring scene. Before him, with folded arms, sat the most coveted prey in the covey of the Opposition. From the Vice-President's chair, Calhoun, the god of his idolatry, encouraged him with the compliment of a happy expression. About him were grouped the prominent "Jackson Senators" ready to encourage him with their approving smiles.[3] There was a gallant and confident air in the orator as he "dashed into the debate like a Mameluke cavalry upon a charge." [4] In a moment he was in the full swing of his eloquence, and, as he poured forth his sarcasm, and marshaled his facts against the Federalism of New England, and threw wide the door revealing the Webster skeletons in the closet, the realization was borne to all that they were listening to one of the most effective speeches ever heard in the Senate.

[1] Senator Foote, in *A Casket of Reminiscences*, 34–36, describes his early struggles to overcome defects in enunciation, and Ludwig Lewisohn, in his *History of Literature in South Carolina*, refers to his first oratorical triumph.

[2] March, an idolater of Webster, in his *Reminiscences of Congress*, is almost extravagant in his praise, and Benton, in his *Thirty Years' View*, is even more complimentary.

[3] Sargent's *Public Men and Events*, I, 172.

[4] March's *Reminiscences of Congress*.

The Democrats were jubilant — the enemy concerned — Webster was a mask, as unresponsive as the sphinx. The blows at Federalism — at New England — at Webster, fell like the hammer on an anvil. The speaker's deadly parallel on Webster and his tariff record was a superb piece of clever oratory. His analysis of New England Federalism in the War of 1812 was a stinging indictment — it was a conviction and a sentence.

The Democrats and Jackson Senators were naturally delighted. This was a political speech that Hayne was making, and he was crucifying Federalism and parading the closet skeletons of its greatest living champion, and shaming the section that refused to be converted to the new faith. And when the orator fell into the trap cleverly prepared for him by Webster, and, ostentatiously encouraged by Calhoun with numerous notes of suggestions sent by the pages from the chair, entered upon his exposition of the theory of Nullification, it is improbable that the delighted Jackson Senators caught the full significance of the departure. Duff Green, in the "National Telegraph," the Calhoun organ, then supporting the Administration, was in a frenzy of delight. Andrew Jackson, who had kept in close touch with the debate, sending Major Lewis daily to the Senate Chamber, and was immensely pleased with the political or party features of the speech, wrote the orator a cordial letter of congratulation.

The depression of the Federalists, the New Englanders, and the Opposition generally, was correspondingly great. A professional observer,[1] writing of the event in later years, tells us that "the immediate impression from the speech was most assuredly disheartening to the cause Mr. Webster upheld." And Henry Cabot Lodge accepts the statement that "men of the North and of New England could be known in Washington in those days by their indignant and dejected looks and downcast eyes."[2]

[1] March's *Reminiscences of Congress.* [2] Lodge's *Life of Webster*, 177.

The day Webster began his reply was the coldest of the winter, a biting wind filling the streets with clouds of dust, and Margaret Bayard Smith, sitting before a blazing fire, and free from the interruption of callers because "almost every one is thronging to the Capitol to hear Mr. Webster reply to Colonel Hayne's attack on him and his party," wrote regretfully of the growing tendency of women to monopolize the seats both in the gallery and upon the floor.[1] The reader is too familiar with that splendid oration to justify, for our purposes, any analysis or extended reference to the substance. His replies to Hayne's attacks on the war policy of the Federalists, and upon his own inconsistencies, while clever, were not, in truth, convincing answers, and it was upon these points that the Jackson Senators were centering their attention. Thus it is not remarkable that the full import of his speech was momentarily lost upon the heated partisans. Even Benton, refusing to believe that the Union was in danger, or in any way involved in the debate, did not care for Webster's peroration, finding the sentiment nobly and oratorically expressed, "but too elaborately and too artistically composed for real grief in the presence of a great calamity — of which calamity I saw no sign." [2] To Benton, the debate was a party combat and nothing more. Nor is there anything in the notes recorded by Adams to indicate that he was impressed with the Webster speech except as a defense of Federalism.[3] The party issue had, for the moment, obscured all else. If in Charleston, the home of Hayne, Webster became the idol of the old Federalists, and of the Democratic mechanics, Hayne won the affectionate admiration of the merchants of Boston, who had his speech

[1] *First Forty Years*, 310.

[2] *Thirty Years' View*, I, 142.

[3] Adams, in his *Memoirs*, refers to the speech as "a remarkable instance of readiness in debate — a reply of at least four hours to a speech of equal length. It demolishes the whole fabric of Hayne's speech, so that it leaves scarcely a wreck to be seen."

printed on satin for presentation to him.[1] The Democratic members of the Legislature of Maine, thinking only of the denunciation of Federalism, ordered two thousand copies published and distributed as "a fearless unanswerable defense of the Democracy of New England" — showing that the Nullification feature was overlooked in the party contest involved. Some contemporaries thought the battle a draw.

And Jackson? Parton tells us that Major Lewis, who had been stationed in the Senate during the debate, on returning from the Capitol after hearing Webster, found Jackson up and eager for news. On being told that the New England orator had made a powerful speech and demolished "our friend Hayne," the old man replied that he "expected it."[2] A few days later the full import of Hayne's speech must have dawned upon Jackson and his political intimates, and there is significance in the powerful speech delivered a little later in the debate by Edward Livingston, Senator from Louisiana, intimate friend of the President, who was destined to enter the Cabinet and to frame Jackson's immortal challenge to Nullification. After the speeches of Webster and Hayne, that of Livingston stands out as the greatest made during the prolonged discussion. He attempted again to center the fire on Federalism, and in so doing brilliantly defended the Union against Nullification, and vigorously defended the Jacksonian policies against the attacks to which they had been subjected during the remarkable debate. If the personal views of Jackson and the Administration are to be sought in any of the senatorial speeches, they will be found, not in the speech of Hayne, but in that of Livingston, which, for that reason, is entitled to more consideration from historians than it has received. We shall now see that within two months Jackson was to find a way to say the last word in the Great Debate of 1830.

[1] Letter from Washington Alston Hayne, grandson, to Jervey, Hayne's biographer.

[2] Parton's *Life of Jackson*.

IV

For some reason the Nullifiers miscalculated the stern old patriot of the White House. Perhaps it was his opposition to the tariff; possibly his South Carolina nativity — whatever the cause, the extreme State Rights party claimed him as its own. It is scarcely probable that, previous to the Webster-Hayne debate, Jackson had ever given any serious consideration to the danger of disunion, and most probable that the views advanced by Hayne in the Nullification part of his speech first impressed him with the fact that a sinister doctrine, brilliantly advanced and powerfully supported, was preparing to challenge the authority of the Nation. But he had kept his own counsels. He may have discussed the danger with Livingston or Van Buren, but no public announcement of his position had escaped him up to the time of the Jefferson dinner in the April following the Great Debate. This dinner, it is now reasonable to conclude, had been arranged with a definite object in view — to create the impression that, in a contest, the President would be friendly to the doctrine of Calhoun and Hayne. The significance of the selection of Jefferson's birthday as the occasion was not lost upon the President or his Secretary of State. It was the first formal observance of the great Virginian's natal day, and among the leaders in the preparations were some "with whom the Virginia principles of '98 had, until quite recently, been in very bad odor."[1] It was clear to the Red Fox that the intent was "to use the Virginia model as a mask or stalking horse, rather than as an armor of defense." The plan, as it developed, was to undertake, through various toasts and their responses, to associate this doctrine with Jeffersonian Democracy. Of the twenty-four toasts, practically every one bore upon this subject. The President, Vice-President Calhoun, the Cabinet were to be guests.

[1] Van Buren's *Autobiography*.

It was a subscription dinner, and outside the conspirators in charge the purchasers of tickets had no other thought than that it was intended solely as a tribute to the memory of the sage of Monticello.

Talking it over with Van Buren, Jackson soon convinced himself as to the motive of the conspirators. By prearrangement, Van Buren met Jackson at the White House, in the presence only of Major Donelson, the President's secretary, to determine upon the attitude to be taken and the toasts to be proposed. While the Nullifiers were jubilating over the promised participation of the President, he was locked in with his Secretary of State deliberating on the wisdom of showing by his toast his familiarity with the purpose of the conspirators, and his determination to preserve the Union at all hazards. The conferees decided upon that aggressive course, and the toasts were framed accordingly.

"Thus armed," wrote Van Buren years later, "we repaired to the dinner with feelings on the part of the Chief akin to those which would have animated his breast if the scene of this preliminary skirmish in defense of the Union had been the field of battle instead of the festive board." [1] When Benton arrived that night, he found a full assemblage, with the guests scattered about in groups excitedly examining the list of toasts, and discussing their significance. The congressional delegation from Pennsylvania, on scenting the conspiracy, left the hall before the dinner began. Many others, not caring to associate themselves with such a movement, retired, thus depriving themselves of a triumph. But many remained, among them four members of the Cabinet, Van Buren, Eaton, Branch, and Barry. During the toasts, which were so numerous and lengthy that they required eleven columns in the "National Telegraph," Jackson sat stern and impassive, betraying nothing of his intention. At length, the regular toasts given, the volunteer toasts were called for,

[1] Van Buren's *Autobiography*, 414.

and Jackson rose. As he did so, Van Buren, who was short in stature, stood on his chair to observe the effect better.[1] Straightening himself to his full height, and fixing Calhoun with his penetrating eye, he paused a moment, and then, following the hush, proposed the most dramatic and historical toast in American history:

"Our Federal Union: It must and shall be preserved." [2]

There was no possible misunderstanding of the meaning. From the time of the delivery of the Webster speech the value of the Union had been discussed with a disconcerting freedom of expression. The rumor was afloat in the capital that Calhoun had sinister designs, and proposed to place himself at the head of a disloyal movement of the extreme State Rights men. The toasts of the evening had told their tale of the dinner conspiracy. And Jackson's brief, meaningful sentence cut like a knife. It was something more than a toast — it was a presidential proclamation.

Without a word more, Jackson lifted his glass as a sign that the toast was to be drunk standing. Calhoun rose with the rest. "His glass trembled in his hand and a little of the amber fluid trickled down the side." [3] There was no response. Jackson stood there, silent and impassive — clearly the master of the situation. All hilarity had gone. Jackson left his place, and, going to the far end of the room, engaged Benton in conversation, but not upon the subject of the dinner.

[1] Van Buren's *Autobiography*, 415.

[2] Van Buren is authority for the statement that the President, who had prepared the toast as given in the text, really gave it — "Our Union — it must be preserved," and that Hayne left his seat and hastened to him to beg him to insert the word "Federal." "This," says Van Buren, "was an ingenuous suggestion, as it seemed to make the rebuke less pungent, although it really had no such effect. The President cheerfully assented because, in point of fact, the addition only made the toast what he originally designed it to be — he having rewritten it in the bustle and excitement of the occasion, on the back of the list of regular toasts which had been laid before him, instead of using the copy in his pocket, and having omitted that word inadvertently." (Van Buren's *Autobiography*, 415).

[3] Isaac Hill's description.

When all were seated, Calhoun, who had remained standing, slowly and hesitatingly proposed:

"The Union: next to our liberty, the most dear."

Then, after a pause of half a minute, he proceeded in such a fashion as to leave doubt as to whether the concluding sentence was a part of the toast, or a brief speech:

"May we all remember that it can only be preserved by respecting the rights of the States, and by distributing equally the benefits and burdens of the Union."

Within five minutes after Calhoun had resumed his seat, the company of more than a hundred had dwindled to thirty — men fled from the room as from the scene of a battle.

The story of that Jacksonian toast spread over the country, justifying, as Benton admits he then realized, the peroration of Webster's speech, and proclaiming to the people the existence of a conspiracy against the Union, and the determination of Jackson to preserve it at all cost. That toast made history. It marked the definite beginning of the history-making quarrel of Jackson and Calhoun, and the beginning of the exodus from the Democratic or Jacksonian party of the Nullifiers and Disunionists, who were to be warmly welcomed by Clay into the party he was about to create to wage war on the Jackson Administration.

V

ANOTHER dinner was to complete the break of Calhoun and Jackson.

In the spring of 1830, President Jackson gave a dinner at the White House in honor of former President Monroe. During the evening, while the President and his predecessor were engaged in animated conversation concerning the days when the latter was in the White House and the former in the field in Florida, Finch Ringgold, marshal of the District, turned to Major Lewis with the observation that Calhoun had been an enemy of the President in relation to his Florida campaign. It was not, however, a revelation to Lewis at the time.

During Jackson's first successful fight for the Presidency, the anniversary of the battle of New Orleans was celebrated, with Jackson as the guest of honor. James A. Hamilton had participated in the celebration as the representative of the Tammany Society of New York; and, joining the Jackson party at the Hermitage, had accompanied it to New Orleans. During the conversation *en route*, there was some discussion of the charges that had been made against Jackson in the presidential contest of four years before relative to his conduct in the Seminole War, and the assertion had been made that Crawford, a member of Monroe's Cabinet, had urged his arrest. It was expected that a similar attack would be made in the campaign then beginning. Learning that Hamilton expected to return by way of Georgia, Major Lewis requested him to visit Crawford, then living in retirement there, and ascertain just what had occurred in the Cabinet meeting. The motive of Lewis was to arm himself, if possible, to repel the attack, and to effect a reconciliation between Jackson and the Georgian. Finding on his arrival in Georgia that to reach the home of Crawford he would be forced to go seventy miles out of his way, Hamilton requested John Forsyth to ascertain from Crawford "whether the propriety or necessity for arresting or trying General Jackson was ever presented as a question for the deliberation of Mr. Monroe's Cabinet." [1] Passing through Washington on his way home, Hamilton spent two days in the same house with Calhoun, and frankly made inquiry of him also. The latter answered with an emphatic negative. The impression Hamilton received from the conversation was that Calhoun had been favorable to Jackson and Crawford hostile. On reaching New York he wrote Major Lewis of his inability to see Craw-

[1] Hamilton to Forsyth, Van Buren's *Autobiography*, 369.

ford and of his conversation with Calhoun. The reply of the Major shows conclusively that, up to this time, there was not the slightest suspicion that Calhoun had been unfriendly to Jackson, and the sole impression made upon Lewis by Hamilton's letter was that, since the subject of arresting or reprimanding Jackson had not been broached in the Cabinet, a grave injustice had been done the Georgian which ought to be righted. Soon afterwards, Hamilton heard from Forsyth to the effect that Crawford informed him that in a meeting of the Cabinet Calhoun had urged the propriety of arresting and trying Jackson.[1] Very soon after the receipt of Forsyth's amazing letter, Hamilton received a note from Calhoun, suggesting the impropriety of disclosures as to Cabinet proceedings and asking that no use be made of his name. Realizing now the serious possibilities of a complete airing of the old controversy, Hamilton filed Forsyth's letter away and mentioned it to no one. For eighteen months this letter was undisturbed. Then, in the autumn of 1829, when Major Lewis was his guest in his New York home, some evil spirit impelled Hamilton to show the letter to Jackson's intimate who dwelt with him in the White House. Lewis made no disclosure until after the Monroe dinner. In the meanwhile, as we have seen, the relations between Jackson and Calhoun had become strained, and the Major convinced himself that, since the fight was inevitable, his idol should be furnished with all available ammunition. In telling him of Ringgold's statement at the dinner, Lewis added that it was supported by the revelations of the Forsyth letter, and Jackson demanded the fatal note.

On learning of Jackson's demand, Forsyth took the precaution first to send a copy of his letter to Hamilton to Crawford for verification in writing, or for such corrections as the facts might necessitate. The reply, with a minor correction,

[1] This he afterwards amended to the extent of saying that Calhoun had urged a reprimand of some sort.

together with the Forsyth letter to Hamilton, were thereupon turned over to Jackson.

The effect on the President was to infuriate him. Setting his jaws, he wrote a sharp note to Calhoun demanding an explanation. This was the beginning of one of the most acrimonious controversies in American politics.

VI

WITH Crawford as the witness against Calhoun, it is essential to turn for a moment to the career of this remarkable and singularly unfortunate statesman. No student of the period, not poisoned by the prejudices and jealousies of Adams, who filled the pages of his diary with grotesque caricatures of his rivals, can escape the conclusion that William H. Crawford was one of the purest and ablest statesmen of his day. At the time he entered the Senate, in his thirty-fifth year, he was a splendid figure — handsome, virile, magnetic, independent in thought, and audacious in action. He was the great war leader in the Senate, as was Calhoun in the House. He had made the most profound impression on the business men of the Nation of any publicist since Hamilton by his fight for strict governmental economy, for the scrutinizing of all expenditures, and by his championship of the National Bank in a brilliant and exhaustive speech in reply to Clay. After two years as Minister to France, Madison called him into his Cabinet to unravel the hopeless tangle in the War Department. He served as adviser to Madison during the remainder of his Administration, continued as the official adviser of Monroe through the eight years of his Presidency, and was urged by Adams to continue in a similar capacity under him. He was soon transferred from the War Department to the Treasury, where he served for nine years to the complete satisfaction of the business men of the Republic.

Even as early as the close of the Madison Administration, a powerful element, opposed to the precedent which pointed to Monroe for the succession, centered on Crawford. Numerous newspapers strongly urged his election, offers of support poured in upon him, and had he at that time entered actively into the plans of his friends, there is every reason to believe he would have been chosen. When the Congress convened, the majority favored his candidacy. The caucus was postponed. The Administration put forth its utmost exertions for Monroe. Crawford remained inactive. And when he definitely put his claims aside, a number of his friends refused to participate in the caucus, in which, notwithstanding his own lack of interest and the prestige of the Administration, Monroe was barely nominated by a vote of 65 to 54 for Crawford.

The Cabinet of Monroe was so constituted as to make it a house divided three ways against itself. Adams, Calhoun, and Crawford were all members, all were presidential candidates, and none had a clearer right to aspire to the succession than the one who had lacked only twelve votes of the nomination in 1816. The three-cornered fight began in earnest as early as 1821. With Adams, Crawford's relations were far from friendly, as we may judge from the numerous vindictive comments in the former's diary. Between Crawford and Jackson no love was lost, and we find the Georgian writing to a correspondent of Jackson's "depravity and vindictiveness."[1] But Calhoun was to prove the most unscrupulous and hostile of his foes.

It was not unknown to Crawford that Calhoun had earnestly sought the alienation of his supporters at the time of Monroe's election. And, as the election of 1824 approached, Calhoun's personal organ at the capital became intemperate in its attacks upon him. But the climax, involving Calhoun, was reached in the spring of 1824, when the "A. B." papers appeared in Calhoun journals, followed by a formal charge in the House of Representatives, filed by Ninian Edwards

[1] Letter to Judge Tait, Shipp's *Life of William H. Crawford*, 152.

of Illinois, alleging irregularities and misconduct in office against the Secretary of the Treasury. Here we have the issue direct between Calhoun, seldom accused of being an unscrupulous intriguer, and Crawford, against whom history has lodged the charge. The connection between Calhoun and the attack appears clear enough. Edwards was Calhoun's friend. The paper that published the "A. B." papers was Calhoun's paper and was edited by a clerk in Calhoun's office.

Immediately after making the charges, Edwards was appointed Minister to Mexico — on the recommendation of Adams, Secretary of State. During the two weeks previous to Edwards's departure for his post, Calhoun made almost daily visits to his room in a lodging-house, spending from one to two hours with him on each occasion.[1] Nor does Adams, judger of men and motives, appear entirely free from complicity in view of his efforts to dissuade Monroe from summoning Edwards back to Washington to testify in the investigation ordered by the House on the demand of Crawford. The investigation disclosed that Edwards was a liar, and the committee, including Webster, Livingston, and Randolph, unanimously reported that "nothing has been proved to impeach the integrity of the Secretary of the Treasury or to bring into doubt the general correctness and ability of his administration of the public finances."

There is ample justification for the conclusion that Calhoun was directly implicated in an unscrupulous attempt to blacken the reputation of a rival, and that Adams shared with him in the earnest desire that the investigation should be postponed until after the presidential election.

In the early stages of the contest everything indicated Crawford's triumph. Then Tragedy intervened. As a result of the administering of lobelia by an unskilled physician, Crawford suffered a stroke. For a time he lost both sight and

[1] Crawford in his letter to Calhoun quotes Senator Noble of Indiana, who lived in the same lodging-house with Edwards, to this effect. Shipp's *Life of Crawford*, 247.

the power of speech. His nervous system was shattered. He lost the use of his lower limbs. But such is the pull of an overshadowing ambition that even in this plight he refused to withdraw from the race. The Opposition press was not above exaggerating his condition. And at such a time the caucus was held. The galleries were packed, but the attendance on the floor was slight. Out of the 261 members, only 68 were present, the friends of Calhoun, Adams, Clay, and Jackson having reached an agreement not to enter the caucus. Thus the contest was thrown into the House, where Clay went over to Adams and elected him.

There are few more poignant pictures associated with the failure of lofty political ambitions than that in the country home of the Georgian where he sat with his family about the blazing fire, awaiting the news from the Capitol.[1] His reputation had been dishonestly assailed, his health was broken, his fortune was gone, and, after having almost touched the Presidency, he calmly awaited the final word of failure. The daughters, who adored him, in their efforts to soften the expected blow, told him of their joyous dreams of a return to "Woodlawn," the Georgia country home, where all could be much happier. When the expected messenger arrived and announced the election of Adams, the defeated statesman, without a change of tone or countenance, merely remarked that he thought it would be Jackson. The next day a letter from the new President urged him to continue in the Cabinet, Jackson called, "frank, courteous, and almost cordial," and a little later Thomas Jefferson wrote his frank regrets.[2] And thus, having declined the Adams invitation, after a remarkable career in the service of his country, William H. Crawford, poorer than the day he entered public life, and physically a wreck, returned to "Woodlawn" in its magnificent

[1] Crawford's Washington country home was situated near Thomas Circle, five blocks from the Willard Hotel, and all beyond was farmlands.

[2] The scene at the Crawford home is elaborately described by an eye-witness in Shipp's biography of Crawford.

oak forest, with its charming, winding driveways, with its peach and apple blossoms, and its gardens and its shrubbery. And here under an ancient oak he was to sit for many evenings with his children and his friends. That he sometimes thought over the lost hope, we may be sure; that he often associated it with Calhoun, there can be no doubt.

VII

THE first act of Jackson's, on being told of Calhoun's hostility in the Monroe Cabinet, was to call for a copy of Crawford's letter to Forsyth, and to enclose it in a letter to the Vice-President, expressing his surprise and asking for his version. The next development in the controversy came in the form of a long letter from Calhoun, practically admitting the charge, and elaborately condemning and damning Crawford for the betrayal of a Cabinet secret. This reply was delivered to Jackson on a Sunday on his way to church, and he wrote a brief and significant answer on his return to the White House on the same day. The closing words sealed the doom of Calhoun as far as the Presidency was concerned. "In your and Mr. Crawford's dispute I have no interest whatever," he wrote. "But it may become necessary for me hereafter, when I shall have more leisure and the documents at hand, to notice the historical facts and references in your communication — which will give a very different view to the subject. Understanding you now, no further communication with you on this subject is necessary."

About this time he sent Calhoun's letter to Van Buren, who refused to read it, explaining that he would be accused of fomenting the trouble and preferred to know nothing about it. When the messenger returned to Jackson with the comment of his Secretary of State, he replied, "I reckon Van is right. I dare say they will try to throw the blame on him." [1]

[1] Van Buren, in his *Autobiography*, p. 376, convincingly exonerates himself from all complicity.

And of course Van Buren was right. After many conferences on the subject with Calhoun, Adams recorded in his diary that "Calhoun is under the firm persuasion that the author of this combustion is Martin Van Buren, who has used the agency of James A. Hamilton in producing it, and that Hamilton, as well as Forsyth, had been a go-between to and from Nashville." [1] The denial of Van Buren at the time was discounted by the anxiety of Hamilton, after talking with Forsyth in Georgia, to have Crawford's statement in writing. Nothing, however, could have been more effective in eliminating Calhoun from the presidential race.

That he appreciated his predicament and fought desperately to extricate himself is shown in various ways. Wirt declared, at the time, that "he has blasted his prospects of future advancement," and Adams described him as a "drowning man." But the most conclusive evidence of Calhoun's desperate efforts is to be found in the numerous notations in Adams's journal. The first entry is to the effect that he had "received a letter from John C. Calhoun . . . relating to his personal controversy with President Jackson and William H. Crawford. He questions me concerning the letter of Gen. Jackson to Mr. Monroe which Crawford alleges to have been produced at the Cabinet meetings on the Seminole War, and asks for copies, if I think proper to give them, of Crawford's letter to me, which I received last summer, and of my answer." It is characteristic that the only comment of Adams is an impartial damnation of the trio, Jackson, Calhoun, and Crawford, and especially of the Carolinian for his "icy-hearted dereliction of all the decencies of social intercourse with me, solely from terror of Jackson." But the day following, we find Adams delving into his diary of 1818. "I thought it advisable," he writes, "to have extracts from it made of all those parts relating to the Seminole War and the Cabinet meetings concerning it. As the copy must be made by an

[1] Adams's *Memoirs*, Jan. 30, 1831.

entirely confidential hand, my wife undertakes the task."[1] A little later[2] we find a Mr. Crowninshield applying to him on behalf of Mr. Crawford for a written verification of the Cabinet incident. And four days after that we have Calhoun writing again "requesting statements of the conduct of Mr. Crawford in the deliberations of the Cabinet upon the Seminole War."[3] The same day Wirt[4] informs Adams that he has received a similar note from the Georgian, and asks for a conference.

That night Adams went to Wirt's lodgings on Capitol Hill and found him in bed and asleep. He was awakened, however, by a fellow lodger, and a four-hour conference followed, with Adams reading the former Attorney-General the letter from Crawford and the answer sent, and also from the Adams diary of May to August, 1818.

It seems that Adams was not prompt in complying with Calhoun's request, and a third letter reached him pressing him for a statement of Crawford's conduct and opinions expressed at the Cabinet consultation on the Seminole War, causing the former President to comment sourly in his diary that he would give no letter until he had seen all the correspondence, and knew precisely the points in dispute.[5] There appears to have been little disposition on the part of Calhoun to meet this requirement, for Adams notes that he had received from Calhoun "an extract" from Crawford's letter to Forsyth, but not all the correspondence.[6] On the next day, the Carolinian, who was evidently devoting himself feverishly and exclusively to the hopeless attempt to save himself, sent "a further extract from the Crawford letter."[7] The unpleasant old Puritan, thoroughly enjoying the torture of the fighting politicians, calmly awaited all the correspond-

[1] *Memoirs,* Jan. 15, 1831.
[2] *Ibid.,* Jan. 26, 1831.
[3] *Ibid.,* Jan. 30, 1831.
[4] Attorney-General in Monroe's and Adams's Cabinets.
[5] *Memoirs,* Feb. 4, 1831.
[6] *Ibid.,* Feb. 4, 1831.
[7] *Ibid.,* Feb. 5, 1831.

ence, and thus a week later we learn from the diary that "Mr. Martin took me aside and delivered to me a letter from Vice-President Calhoun with a bundle of papers, being the correspondence . . . ," and that the messenger "said that Mr. Calhoun wished to have the papers returned to him to-morrow morning."[1]

On the following day Wirt, having moved to Gadsby's, was there informed by Adams that he had received the correspondence, but "that Mr. Calhoun had withheld two important papers; one, the letter from General Jackson to Mr. Monroe of Jan. 6, 1818, and the other, Crawford's last letter to Calhoun, which, he sent me word, he had returned to Crawford."[2] A few days later a Dr. Hunt called upon Adams, "more full of politics and personalities than of physic," with the announcement that "Mr. Calhoun's pamphlet is to be published to-morrow morning."[3]

To Adams the issue was clear — a battle between Calhoun and Van Buren for the Presidency. The next day this pamphlet, bearing the elaborate title, "Correspondence between General Andrew Jackson and John C. Calhoun, President and Vice-President of the United States, on the Subject of the Course of the latter in the deliberations of the Cabinet of Mr. Monroe on the Occurrences in the Seminole War," was published at midnight by Duff Green in the "National Telegraph." "In my walk about the Capitol Square," writes Adams, "I met E. Everett, R. G. Amory, E. Wyer, and Matthew L. Davis, all of whom, with the exception of Wyer, spoke of the pamphlet. I received a copy of it under cover from Mr. Calhoun himself."[4]

Then the war opened in earnest. The "Telegraph" favorably commented upon the pamphlet, and the "Globe" un-

[1] *Memoirs*, Feb. 12, 1831.

[2] This letter of Crawford's was returned to the writer, according to Shipp's *Life of Crawford*, p. 210, which contains the letter — a vicious philippic — and Calhoun's brief note on returning it.

[3] *Memoirs*, Feb. 16, 1831.

[4] *Ibid.*, Feb. 17, 1831.

favorably. Adams found that "the effect of Mr. Calhoun's pamphlet is yet scarcely perceptible in Congress, still less upon public opinion," and that, while the Administration was at war with itself, "the stream of popularity runs almost as strongly in its favor as ever." [1] Not content with the pamphlet alone, the "National Telegraph" followed it with Crawford's letter to Calhoun, and another of Forsyth's, and Adams observed with interest that "in all this correspondence Van Buren is not seen; but James A. Hamilton, intimately connected with him, is a busy intermeddler throughout." [2] This notation was in line with the gossip of the capital at the time of the controversy.

A little more than a week after the appearance of the pamphlet, Calhoun published his correspondence with Hamilton in the "Telegraph," and Duff Green, in the same issue, editorially charged Van Buren with responsibility for the rumpus. And this was met on the following day by the latter in a letter to the paper positively denying any interest in the controversy, or any knowledge of Hamilton's correspondence with Forsyth or Calhoun. Green responded by writing Van Buren down as a liar.[3] Thus the controversy raged, drawing politicians, one after another, into the fight. But in this fearsome medley of charges and counter-charges one fact stood out — that Calhoun had misrepresented his conduct in the Monroe Cabinet to Jackson, and, on being betrayed by Crawford, had incurred the deadly enmity of the President. As far as Jackson was concerned in the public controversy, the matter rested with Calhoun's initial letter of admission that he had opposed Jackson's course in the war. He prepared an elaborate statement of the facts for the purposes of history, turned it over to the editor of the "Globe," who became his literary executor, and he, in turn, permitted Kendall to study it when

[1] *Memoirs*, Feb. 21, 1831. [2] *Ibid.*, Feb. 22, 1831.

[3] It was not until Jackson had asked Hamilton for Forsyth's letter that the latter told Van Buren of its contents. Van Buren's *Autobiography*, 373.

he was planning a biography of the President.[1] But of all this the public knew nothing.

The inevitable storm had broken. Van Buren, suavely in the background, was clearly the beneficiary, Calhoun just as clearly the victim. After this the great Carolinian lost interest in the Presidency, all concern with party, and henceforth, with occasional attacks on Jackson, concentrated on sectionalism and slavery. His disaffection was to carry with it that of his more ardent supporters, and thus in scarcely more than a year Calhoun, Tyler, Tazewell, and the men who looked to them for guidance, passed from the Administration camp to join the Opposition. And the incident had one immediate effect — inseparable from it — the disruption of the Cabinet with the eradication of the last vestige of Calhoun influence from all the executive branches of the Government.

[1] Benton's *Thirty Years' View*, I, 168.

CHAPTER V

MRS. EATON DEMOLISHES THE CABINET

I

At the time the politicians were discussing the open rupture with Calhoun, two horsemen might have been seen riding slowly through Georgetown, and out on the Tenallytown road, engaged in earnest conversation. It was not a novelty, however, to the people of the ancient river town, for this had long been a favorite route of Jackson and Van Buren on their daily rides. On this occasion Jackson had been discussing the painful lack of harmony in his Cabinet and had expressed the hope that his troubles were about over.

"No, General," said Van Buren, a little nervously, "there is but one thing that will give you peace."

"What is that, sir?" snapped the grim one.

"My resignation."

"Never, sir; even you know little of Andrew Jackson if you suppose him capable of consenting to such a humiliation of his friends by his enemies."

To understand the conditions leading to such a suggestion from Van Buren, it is necessary to refer to the serious petticoat entanglement in which Jackson found himself within a few weeks after his inauguration, because of the presence of Senator Eaton in his Cabinet. It is an amusing fact that the first real democratic administration in American history should have been all but wrecked on a social issue. Aside from the agreeable work of "turning the rascals out," little had occurred to disturb the serenity of the new Administration between the inauguration and the meeting of the Congress in the following December but this social war. The call to battle had been sounded even before Jackson had taken the oath of office; the battle raged with unprecedented fury for many months, finally wrecking the Cabinet and advancing Van Buren to within sight of the White House. It has not been uncommon for women to change the course of political and dynastic history in other countries, but to this day the case of the captivating Margaret O'Neal is unique in the United States.

The pretty daughter of a popular tavern-keeper, whose old-fashioned house was a favorite with statesmen and their wives, she had developed into womanhood under the eyes of men famous in the State. Here Jackson lived during his senatorial service, and grew fond of the vivacious child he often held on his knee. With the education a doting father lavished upon her, and with her intimate contact with men of ability and women of refinement, she found herself, on the threshold of life, the intellectual peer of the best of her sex. It is not unnatural that this clever and beautiful girl should have incurred the jealous displeasure of the less attractive spouses of the elder statesmen. Her rare beauty alone would have done that had she been as virtuous as Cæsar's wife should have been. Perley Poore [1] describes her as of medium height, straight and delicate and of perfect proportions; with a skin of delicate white, tinged with red, and with an abundance of dark hair clustered above her broad, expressive forehead; with a nose of perfect Greek proportions, a finely curved mouth, a firm, round chin — the Aspasia of Washington. When, in addition to her physical and intellectual charms, it must be recorded that she occasionally played the rôle of barmaid, permitting such liberties as men in the early stages of their cups would take, it is easy to understand why the more sedate matrons of the little capital were prone to look upon her as beyond the pale. She had married a purser in the navy, and even her enemies at the time conceded that the match was a *mésalliance* because of her intellectual superi-

[1] *Perley's Reminiscences*, I, 122.

ority. In time the husband sailed across the sea, leaving his comely young wife in the rather free-and-easy atmosphere of her father's tavern. The moral conditions of the capital were not such as to spare the most virtuous, thus situated, from the tongue of gossip. A contemporary has said that the Washington of those days "resembled in recklessness and extravagance the spirit of the England of the Seventeenth Century, so graphically portrayed in Thackeray's 'Humorists.' . . . Laxity of morals and the coolest disregard possible, characterized that period of our existence." [1]

Living at the O'Neal tavern at the time was the wealthy Senator Eaton, who had manifested more than a passing interest in "Peggy," as she was called, before her marriage. Gossip had it that he became more than ever attentive when the sailor went to sea. When, after a drunken debauch, which the gossips, without the slightest justification, ascribed to the worthless seaman's knowledge of his wife's friendship for the Senator, the husband shot himself, and Eaton was found in her company with increasing frequency, the case was complete as far as the drawing-rooms were concerned. All that evidence could not furnish, the imagination did, and pretty Peggy stood pilloried in the community.

It was at this juncture that Eaton asked the advice of Jackson as to a marriage. With characteristic impulsiveness the old warrior replied that if he loved her he should marry her and save her good name by the act. Thus, on January 1, 1829, the future Secretary of War was married to the tavern-keeper's daughter, and instantly the drawing-rooms began to buzz. One of the patrician ladies of the time of the wedding poured forth the chatter of the social set. Here we find that Mrs. Eaton "had never been admitted into good society"; that while "very handsome" she was "not of an inspiring character" and had a "violent temper"; that notwithstanding this she was "irresistible" and "carries

[1] *Perley's Reminiscences.*

whatever point she sets her mind on." The enemies of Jackson were laughing in the drawing-rooms and diverting themselves "with the idea of what a suitable lady in waiting Mrs. Eaton will make for Mrs. Jackson," and were repeating "the old adage, 'Birds of a feather flock together.'" [1] In arriving at an understanding of Jackson's vigorous defense of the lady of his Cabinet, it is well to bear in mind that the same scandal-mongers were rolling the name of Mrs. Jackson on their tongues. The same letter relates how one of Mrs. Smith's gentlemen callers "laughed and joked about Mrs. Jackson and her pipe."

The marriage might have remained merely one of the innumerable morsels with which ladies sometimes regale the drawing-rooms but for the announcement that Eaton had been invited into the Cabinet — and that spread the controversy to the politicians. Among these Senator John Branch had the courage or the insolence personally to press the point upon Jackson that, because of social complications, the appointment of Eaton would be "unpopular and unfortunate." [2] Jackson heard his future Secretary of the Navy in stern silence, and appointed Eaton Secretary of War. The inauguration was scarcely over when the petticoat battle began. The most fashionable minister at the capital at the time, at whose church Mrs. Smith, the Branches, the Berriens, and the Inghams worshiped,[3] importuned, no doubt, by the society women of the city, and quite probably encouraged by the Cabinet ladies of his congregation, persuaded a Philadelphia minister to write the President of the alleged irregularities of Mrs. Eaton. Some of these ministerial charges are unfit for print. Jackson sent a stinging reply, and at the same time employed detectives to investigate the charges. The search of the sleuths was unavailing, and the situation became so embarrassing to the Philadelphia clergyman that

[1] *First Forty Years*, 253.
[2] Haywood's *Branch*.
[3] Rev. J. N. Campbell.

he demanded that the Washington minister should reveal himself.

Thus, on the evening of September 1, 1829, a unique conference was held at the White House, when Jackson confronted the two clergymen, in the presence of witnesses, and forced them to admit that they had no evidence. One of the worst charges had been that a certain physician, conveniently dead, had said that Mrs. Eaton had undergone a premature *accouchement* when her husband had been more than a year at sea — the date fixed as 1821. When confronted by the fact that the first husband had not gone to sea until 1824, the clergyman lightly changed the date to conform. This disgusted and enraged Jackson. Because he cross-examined the gentlemen of the cloth regarding a matter affecting the reputation of a woman, some historians have been resentful of his severity.[1] The purpose was to convince the members of the Cabinet, who were present, that their ladies were working a grave injustice upon the wife of a colleague in refusing her social intercourse. But far from satisfying the women, the discomfiture of the minister and the utter collapse of the case only embittered them the more against her. The minister was placed in a painful position, dubbed by the irrepressible "Ike" Hill as "the chaplain of the conspiracy," and described by Mrs. Smith[2] as having been "rendered incapable of attending to his ministerial duties to such a degree as to produce great dissatisfaction in his congregation."

Meanwhile months had gone by and Mrs. Eaton was still snubbed. Mrs. Calhoun, a thorough aristocrat, had positively refused to call. Mrs. Ingham, whose own reputation was not unquestioned, took her cue from Mrs. Calhoun. Branch tells us that when, in May, his wife and daughters joined him in Washington, they found Mrs. Eaton "excluded from society," and that he "did not deem it their duty to endeavor

[1] Schouler, III, 492. [2] *First Forty Years*, 311.

to control or counteract the decision of the ladies of Washington."[1] Miss Berrien had accepted the verdict of the women, and her father was openly expressing his admiration for "the heroic virtues of John Branch for hazarding his place rather than permit his wife and daughters to associate with the wife of John H. Eaton."[2] Parties were given and Mrs. Eaton was not invited; at public receptions she was snubbed.

This was all meat and drink to Adams, who recorded in his diary, after some scandal gossip with Mrs. Rush: "I told Mrs. Rush that this struggle was likely to terminate in a party division of Caps and Hats." It is this suggestion as to party divisions which imposes upon the historian the necessity of dwelling upon this strange petticoat squabble. It is scarcely an exaggeration to say that, when Martin Van Buren appeared at social functions with the pretty Peggy on his arm, he made himself President of the United States.

When the Red Fox arrived in Washington and noted the passionate determination of the iron man at the White House to force a social recognition of Mrs. Eaton, he could not have been unmindful of his advantage. He was a widower. No wife or daughters were with him to be compromised. His biographer[3] makes the point that he called upon the accused woman in response to common instincts of decency, and that his failure to have done so would have amounted to a striking public condemnation. But he did something more than merely call upon her — he became an active and aggressive partisan of her cause, and by so doing endeared himself to Jackson. Common decency did not demand that he feature her at his dinners and receptions, or enter into an agreement with two unmarried members of the diplomatic corps to do likewise.[4] It is impossible to account for this extraordinary partisanship on any other grounds

[1] Haywood's *Branch*.
[2] Adams's *Memoirs*, March 18, 1830.
[3] Shepard.
[4] Vaughan of Great Britain and the Russian Minister.

than his desire to curry special favor with the President. His conduct and activities became the subject of jests and quips. "It is asserted that if Mr. Van Buren persists in visiting her [Mrs. Eaton], our ladies will not go to his house," wrote one of the stubborn dames.[1] With the ladies of the Cabinet giving large parties, the wife of Eaton was omitted from the invitation lists, and Van Buren countered with dinners and dances at the British and Russian Legations at which Mrs. Eaton was treated with marked distinction. But even here "cotillion after cotillion dissolved into its original elements when she was placed at its head." [2] At the Russian Legation, Madame Huygens, wife of the Dutch Minister, on finding that her seat was beside Mrs. Eaton at the table, haughtily took her husband's arm and stalked impressively from the room. Because of this affront, Jackson was prone to make it an international incident by demanding the recall of the Minister, but Van Buren's sense of humor intervened. In sheer delight Adams wrote: "Mr. Vaughan . . . gave a ball last night which was opened by Mr. Bankhead, the Secretary of the British Legation, and Mrs. Eaton; and Mr. Van Buren has issued cards also for a ball which is to be given in honor of the same lady. I confine myself to the Russian and Turkish war." [3] In the late summer of 1829 the effect of the struggle upon both Jackson and Van Buren was apparent. The President, disgusted, worn, and sick at heart, was confiding to his correspondents his partiality for the calm of the Hermitage. And Adams, riding about the environs, and encountering Van Buren, similarly taking the air, spitefully wrote: "His pale and haggard looks show it is already a reward of mortification. If it should prove, as there is every probability that it will, a reward of treachery, it will be but his desert." [4]

[1] Mrs. Smith.

[2] Mary C. Crawford, *Romantic Days of the Early Republic,* 219.

[3] *Memoirs,* March 3, 1830. [4] *Ibid.,* July 8, 1829.

When the winter came and the social season opened, the contest naturally intensified. Ingham, Branch, and Berrien gave large parties from which Mrs. Eaton was excluded, while "on the other hand the President made her doubly conspicuous by an over display of notice." [1] At one of the President's drawing-rooms she was surrounded by a crowd eager to please the host, but Mrs. Donelson, mistress of the White House, held aloof. This rebellion under his own roof caused the aged President the deepest pain. Adams records a melodramatic appeal by Van Buren to Mrs. Donelson, which was highly colored by the ardent Pepys, but such an appeal was made.[2] The effect of the fight was disastrous to the Administration. The members of the Cabinet were speedily involved by their wives, and for a time Eaton and Branch did not speak. It was at this juncture that Jackson determined to intervene, and "to bring them to speaking terms." [3] His intermediary for the purpose, Colonel Richard M. Johnson,[4] was not a Talleyrand, and his lack of tact in his talks with Branch, Berrien, and Ingham made matters all the worse. When the relations of the Cabinet members became threatening, Jackson demanded that they meet and reach a basis for official intercourse at least. The meeting was held at the home of Berrien, attended by Branch, Eaton, and Barry. The negotiations were conducted with dignity and decorum, Branch satisfactorily explained invitations to the ministers who had accused Eaton's wife, and the two shook hands as a token of reconciliation.[5] Meanwhile Congress was in session. All attempts to hold Cabinet meetings had long been abandoned. The lines were drawn tightly. The slights and indignities to Mrs. Eaton had become all but intolerable. And much was being heard of the alleged frailty and indis-

[1] Adams's *Memoirs*, Feb. 6, 1830.

[2] Van Buren probably gives the true story in his *Autobiography*, 343–44.

[3] Adams's *Memoirs*.

[4] Later Vice-President and noted as slayer of Tecumseh.

[5] Letter from Branch, in Haywood's *Branch*.

cretions of Mrs. Ingham — stories that seem to have been well known at the time, but to have been given renewed currency by Eaton.[1]

It was at this juncture that Van Buren, riding with Jackson, proposed the acceptance of his resignation. Meditating the step for some time he had been unable to muster the courage to broach the subject. For four days the President and his Secretary of State rode the Tenallytown road earnestly debating the propriety of the plan, and on the fourth day, just as they reached their turning-point at the Tenallytown Gate, Jackson gave a reluctant consent and suggested the British Mission. But the grim old warrior was loath to part with his one strong friend in the Cabinet, and early the next morning he summoned Van Buren to the White House, and in great agitation, and with significance, explained anew that it was his custom to release from association with him any man who felt that he ought to go. Thoroughly alarmed, Van Buren, with emotion, withdrew all he had said, and announced a willingness to retain his post until dismissed. Deeply touched, Jackson proposed another discussion on their afternoon ride. It was that afternoon that it was agreed to call others into the conference; and the next night Van Buren had as dinner guests Jackson, Barry, Eaton, and Major Lewis. Finally Eaton agreed to follow with his resignation. Would Peggy consent, asked the tactful Fox. Her husband thought she would. The next night the five met at dinner again, with Eaton reporting his wife's acquiescence in the plans. But when, a few days later, Jackson and Van Buren, out for a stroll, stopped at the Eaton house, their reception from the mistress was so cold and formal that the Secretary commented upon it, and Jackson shrugged his shoulders in silence. But the die was cast. The plan was made. Van Buren and Eaton would resign, thus paving the way for the resignation of the Calhoun followers, and a

[1] *First Forty Years*, 311.

reorganization of the Cabinet — with the Calhoun influence entirely eliminated.[1]

II

THE decision made, the old President must have felt a sense of ineffable relief. His Cabinet had been a failure and he realized it. His dissatisfaction with a majority of its members was not due entirely to their hostility to Mrs. Eaton. The fight against the National Bank was in its incipiency and he looked upon Ingham as a tool of the Bank; the Nullification doctrine was being promulgated and he considered Berrien a Nullifier — and in both surmises he was right. He thought Branch pompous, incompetent, and subservient to petticoat rule. And we may be sure that whether or not the Cabinet was to be reorganized in the interest of Van Buren, the relations of all three toward the Carolinian entered into his decision to rid himself of them. There is evidence that he quite early determined to displace Berrien, but nothing of record to indicate the cause. In the man selected for his place, however, we have ample justification for the suspicion that the Red Fox had poisoned his mind against his Attorney-General. It was on the suggestion of Van Buren, very soon after the formation of the Cabinet in 1829, that the Attorney-Generalship was offered to Louis McLane, who, in disgust, had retired to Wilmington for the practice of his profession, with the inducement that he would later be transferred to the Supreme Bench on the death of the rapidly failing Justice Duval. Before breakfast one morning, after a hard ride over the wretched mud roads, Hamilton, the lieutenant of Van Buren, arrived at the McLane home with the proposal, which was accepted. Nothing, however, was done — another mystery that died with Jackson and his Secretary of State.[2]

But the coast was now clear. A strong workable Cabinet

[1] The story of the resignation is told in detail in Van Buren's *Autobiography*.
[2] Hamilton, in his *Reminiscences*, p. 130, tells of the ride to Wilmington.

after Jackson's own heart could be created. The manner in which he went about ridding himself of the undesirable members of the old Cabinet is graphically illustrated in the account left by Branch.[1] It is easy to visualize the scene in the President's room, whither he has summoned Branch to inform him of the resignations of Van Buren and Eaton. There is a "solemn pause." The Secretary, sensing the intent, smiles, and suggests that the grim one is not "acting in a character nature intended him for"; that he is not a diplomatist, and should speak frankly. Whereupon Jackson, "with great apparent kindness," explains his purpose, points to a commission as Governor of Florida upon the table, and announces that it will be a pleasure to fill in the name of the visitor. Branch haughtily declares that he had "not supported him for the sake of office," and soon retires. Returning to his office, Branch prepares and sends in his resignation courteously, but not omitting to mention that the action was taken in response to the President's wish. Whereupon Jackson, splitting hairs, writes a protest against the statement that his correspondent's resignation had been asked. "I did not," he writes, "as to yourself, express a wish that you would retire." But since the Cabinet had come in "harmoniously and as a unit," and two were voluntarily retiring, it had become "indispensable" to reorganize completely the official household "to guard against misrepresentation." More correspondence follows, ending with a gracious acceptance of the resignation, coupled with an expression of appreciation of the "integrity and zeal" with which the Secretary of the Navy had discharged his duties.[2]

Ingham made the President's task easy with a brief note of resignation, and passed permanently from public life.[3] But

[1] Published in Haywood's *Branch*.

[2] Letters published in Haywood's *Branch*.

[3] During the Bank controversy Ingham attacked Jackson and defended the Bank. He died in Trenton, New Jersey, in 1860, never having held office after leaving the Jackson Cabinet.

Berrien was loath to go. In discussing the situation with friends, he made no secret of his desire to retain his post, but on learning that Jackson had no such notion, he withdrew in a friendly and dignified letter.[1]

The period between the announcement of Van Buren's resignation and the appointment of the new Cabinet was rich in food for the gossips. What would become of the Red Fox? Would Mrs. Eaton have her triumph in the elevation of her husband to some other post of distinction? And what would be the factional complexion of the new Cabinet? John Tyler, sending his budget of gossip home, rather questioned the rumor that Van Buren would be groomed for Vice-President and thought he would prefer to go abroad. It had also reached Tyler that Hugh L. White might become Secretary of War, and that "Livingston is to rule the roost," and he lamented that in the latter event "the Constitution may be construed to mean anything and everything." He had likewise heard that McLane would be Secretary of the Treasury, "but how," he asked, "can he ever be acceptable to the South with his notions on the tariff and internal improvement?"[2] Meanwhile there appears to have been a rather definite plan on the part of Jackson and Van Buren for the building of the new Cabinet.

III

EITHER the President or Van Buren could very plausibly have been responsible for the decision as to Livingston and the State portfolio, but the fact remains that the proffer of the post was made through the latter. The Louisiana statesman was spending his summer vacation at his country place on the Hudson when a mysterious letter reached him from the New York politician, summoning him instantly to Wash-

[1] Berrien's position is clearly disclosed in conversations with Francis Scott Key, who wrote Roger Taney. See Tyler's *Life of Taney*.

[2] *Letters and Times of the Tylers*, I, 423.

ington, and warning him, on leaving, to conceal his destination. Observing both the summons and the injunction, he proceeded at once to the capital, and with some misgivings accepted the post of Secretary of State.[1] That this was Van Buren's appointment seems more than probable.

For the Treasury, Louis McLane, Minister to England, a subordinate, as such, to Van Buren, with whom he had worked in perfect accord politically, and whose wife was ambitious for Cabinet honors,[2] was summoned home from London. As Van Buren had, at this time, selected the London post for himself, this appointment was unquestionably his own.

The one embarrassing hitch came in the selection of a Secretary of War. It was the plan to have Senator Hugh L. White of Tennessee relinquish his seat for the War Office, thus opening the way for the election of Eaton to his old position in the Senate. But White was cold to the proposition. The mutual friends of the President and the Tennessee Senator importuned him to no effect. James K. Polk strongly urged him. Felix Grundy added his appeal. Another wrote him: "The old man says that all his plans will be defeated unless you agree to come."[3] Jackson himself did not hesitate to go with White's brother-in-law to Virginia to request Senator Tazewell, an intimate of White's, to exert his influence — but to no avail. The reason for this refusal, furnished by a kinswoman, throws light on the general understanding as to the purpose of the Cabinet reorganization — he did not intend to "thereby aid in the elevation of Mr. Van Buren to the Presidency."[4] Thus did Jackson's earnest wish to serve his friends, the Eatons, fail at a critical juncture. After the

[1] At Philadelphia, where he met Dallas, an intimate, Livingston appears to have discussed nothing more important than his rosebuds at Montgomery Place. Hunt's *Life of Livingston.*

[2] *First Forty Years,* 252, 319.

[3] Letter from F. W. Armstrong, quoted in Nancy Scott's *Memoir of Hugh Lawson White.*

[4] Nancy Scott's *Memoir of Hugh Lawson White.*

place was also refused by Representative Drayton of South Carolina, an enemy of Nullification, Jackson turned to his old co-worker in the War of 1812, and Lewis Cass, then Governor of Michigan, entered the new Cabinet. This was probably Jackson's personal appointment, albeit years before, while acting as judge advocate in the court-martial of General Hull, Van Buren had learned to his discomfiture that Cass was no ordinary man.[1] More successful in caring for his friend Isaac Hill than for the Eatons, a proffer of the Navy portfolio to Senator Levi Woodbury of New Hampshire created a senatorial vacancy that fell to the fighting journalist. Incidentally the relations between Van Buren and Woodbury were close.

In finding a successor for Berrien the President was handicapped by the general opinion of his friends, including Van Buren, that his retention would serve a good purpose. During the period of uncertainty numerous names were canvassed, the favorite of the politicians being James Buchanan.[2] The first suggestion of Roger Taney was made to Jackson by a Washington physician who had ventured to say that he knew "a man who will suit for Attorney-General." The disinterestedness and high character of this truly great and much-maligned man shines forth in his conduct during this period of negotiations. He not only did not press his claims, but urged the retention of Berrien, and, under his instructions, his brother-in-law (Key) did likewise. Thus we find Key calling upon Livingston, Barry, and Woodbury, urging the keeping of Berrien on the ground that "it would have a good effect upon the affairs of the party, both as to its bearing on the Indian and the Eaton questions."[3] All three agreed, but confessed a delicacy about broaching the subject unless consulted. In the midst of these negotiations, Key

[1] Van Buren commenced the cross-examination of Cass in a flippant manner, but was almost instantly sobered by the demeanor and dignity of the witness. Young's *Life of Lewis Cass*.

[2] Key's letter to Taney, Tyler's *Life of Taney*.

[3] Tyler's *Life of Taney*.

was summoned to the White House and informed of the intention to invite Taney into the Cabinet. Again Key urged the wisdom of retaining Berrien; the President firmly rejected the idea, and thus, on his personal judgment, Jackson secured the services of one of the strongest figures to be associated with him in his most bitter battle.

Livingston, McLane, Cass, Woodbury, and Taney — this at any rate was not the "millennial of the minnows." But the new Cabinet was not to be received with universal acclaim. The Calhoun followers grumbled that it was a Van Buren Cabinet; and Tyler, thinking in terms of State Rights, complained bitterly that State-Rights men had been left "entirely out in the cold." [1]

Nor did the Eaton trouble dissipate instantly on the passing of the first Cabinet. The retired members stoutly insisted on every occasion that they had been forced out because of their refusal to coerce their wives to associate with naughty Peggy. After his return to his North Carolina home, Branch, in a voluminous letter, charged all the responsibility for the disruption of the Cabinet to the social issue. Berrien, albeit not only willing but anxious to remain, on his return to Georgia eulogized Jackson at a complimentary dinner in his honor, but added that when he attempted to prescribe rules for the association of the families of his Ministers he scorned the dictation.[2] And Duff Green was so active and persistent in ascribing the upheaval to the Eaton affair that Key was convinced "that that matter had not occasioned the change in the Cabinet." [3] The gossips of the drawing-rooms, distressed at being deprived of a choice morsel, set their teeth into it with a grim determination to hold on. Mrs. Bayard Smith, as though personally affronted, wrote to a friend: "The papers do not exaggerate, nay do not retail one half his [Jackson's]

[1] *Letters and Times of the Tylers*, I, 423.
[2] Miller's *Bench and Bar of Georgia*.
[3] Letter to Taney, Tyler's *Life of Taney*.

imbecilities. He is completely under the domination of Mrs. Eaton, one of the most ambitious, violent, malignant, yet silly women you ever heard of." And a few days later she returns to the attack: "Mrs. Eaton cannot be forced or persuaded to leave Washington. . . . She . . . believes that next winter the present Cabinet Ministers will open their doors to her. Mrs. McLane has already committed herself on that point. Previous to her going to England, while on a visit here, in direct violation of her most violent asseverations previously made, she visited this lady, and instantly became a great favorite with the President."[1]

However, if Mrs. Eaton lingered, others departed with undignified celerity. As soon as the robes of office fell from his shoulders, Eaton began a search for Ingham to administer a personal chastisement. The latter, who had been peculiarly offensive, and whose own wife was a victim of the gossips, would not fight a duel. He did not care to fight at all. Thus began an amusing chase. Eaton lay in wait for him in the streets, while the dignified ex-Minister of Finance carefully picked his way home through the muddy alleys and back yards into the back door of his house. At length the chase became uncomfortable. A stage-coach was chartered. The Inghams' baggage was packed. Two hours before daybreak, the coach driver might have been seen lashing his horses through the mud and water of the capital, bearing on their way to Philadelphia the erstwhile Cabinet Minister and his family.

The first Cabinet, which almost immediately put on a drawing-room comedy, went out with a rip-roaring farce, with seconds bearing ominous messages, and with Cabinet officers lying in wait in the shadows, creeping through alleys, brandishing pistols, and in the darkest hours before the dawn lumbering in stage-coaches out of the capital city to escape a shot.

[1] *First Forty Years*, 320.

The thoroughly frightened Ingham openly charged that Eaton intended to murder him, and the letters of the former secretaries concerning the "murder conspiracy" added mightily to the amusement of the enemies of the Administration and to the chagrin and disgust of its friends. "Before you receive this," wrote a Washingtonian to Senator John Forsyth, "you will have seen the disgraceful publications of Eaton and Ingham, which, of course, are the sole topics of conversation here. The rumor was that the President was engaged the day before yesterday in investigating the matter, and I know that he had a magistrate with him taking depositions."[1] The hilarity of Jackson's enemies was vividly expressed in a cartoon, entitled "The Rats Leaving a Falling House," published in Philadelphia, and, with childish delight, Adams records in his diary that "two thousand copies of this print have been sold in Philadelphia this day," and that the ten thousand copies struck off "will be disposed of within a fortnight."[2]

Van Buren was sent to the English Court. Eaton was made Governor of Florida and later Minister to Spain, where Mrs. Eaton, in the most dignified Court in Europe, became a brilliant success. Ingham passed from public life. Branch affiliated with the Whigs in 1832 and in 1836, and was made Governor of Florida by Tyler. Berrien became one of the orators and leaders of the Whigs, and one of the founders of the Know-Nothing Party. Thus, after two years of disorganization and domestic turmoil, the Jackson Administration, with a powerful Cabinet, and, for the first time, a definite policy, began to strike its stride. At least two of the new Ministers were to play leading and spectacular parts in the great party battles that were to follow.

It must have been with a sense of ineffable relief that Jack-

[1] MS. letter of Arthur Schaaf to Senator John Forsyth, written from Georgetown June 25, 1831, furnished the author by Mr. Waddy Wood, Washington, D.C.

[2] *Memoirs*, April 25, 1831.

son, seated at the head of the Cabinet table, surveyed the new men with whom he had surrounded himself — a feeling in which the public shared. But as his glance moved about the table it no doubt lingered with greatest confidence and satisfaction upon the three whose very appearance bespoke character, intellectuality, and power. At his right hand the tall figure, with the student's stoop, the meditative manner, the benevolent expression, which had stood beside him in the stirring days of New Orleans — the scholarly Livingston. Near by he recognized in the imposing figure with the robust, well-knit frame, the huge head, the bushy brows, the penetrating, fighting blue eyes of Cass, a man of the solidity and strength that he admired and trusted. The one strange figure about the table, destined to prove more nearly a man after his own heart than any other who was to serve him in the Cabinet, was Taney — thin and delicate like Jackson himself, with the student's stoop of Livingston, but without his calm. Between these three and the others, there was a decided descent, although they were men of ability and reputation.

IV

Edward Livingston was one of the strongest characters of his time, a Nationalist as intense as Webster, who was to pen a document as virile and militant as Webster's speech for the Union — one of the most brilliant, talented, and polished publicists the Republic has known. This premier of the greatest of democrats, was a thorough aristocrat, tracing his lineage back to the English peerage. Compared with him, the Opposition leaders and even their ladies of the drawing-rooms lamenting the social crudities of the Jacksonians were of mongrel breed. And yet this highest type of aristocrat was, by preference, one of the most ardent of democrats. When, in his thirtieth year, he entered the National House of Representatives from his native city of New York, he had behind him every advantage and before him every opportunity.

Distinguishing himself by brilliancy in debate, vigor in attack, when he left Congress his militant leadership of the Jeffersonian party had convinced Hamilton that he had to be destroyed.[1] Jefferson made him district attorney; the people elected him to the mayoralty of New York, and the attempt to serve in both capacities wrought his financial ruin. While personally directing the fight against the yellow fever plague, he was himself stricken, and he recovered only to find that his assistant in the district attorney's office had squandered $100,000 of the public money on wine and women. Without a moment's hesitation he conveyed all his property to a trustee for sale, beggared himself completely, and resigned both his offices. The public protested against his abandonment of the mayoralty, and for two months the Governor refused to accept his resignation, but he knew that the path of duty led to the replenishment of his purse. Thus, at thirty-nine, leaving behind him the prestige of his family connections and his own career, he turned toward Louisiana, then the Promised Land, and set forth for New Orleans. There he immediately took high rank in his profession, established a lucrative practice, and soon acquired valuable real estate abutting the river which promised a fortune. The story of how he was deprived of this through the incomprehensible spite of President Jefferson constitutes one of the most fascinating chapters in the history of American litigation.[2] But Livingston was sustained by infinite patience, a happy philosophy, and natural buoyancy of temperament, and he soon found other matters to enlist his interest. When Jackson reached New Orleans to defend the town, it was Livingston who aroused the militant spirit of the people with his martial eloquence, and served as the soldier's aid, translator, and adviser. It was in these days amidst the barking of the English guns that Jackson discov-

[1] Hamilton took the stump in a vain attempt to defeat his reëlection.

[2] Senator Beveridge, in his monumental work on John Marshall, gives in detail the legal phases of the controversy, IV, 100–16.

ered in Livingston the man he could trust as a patriot and fighter in two of the bitterest battles of his Presidency.[1] It was soon after this that Livingston began the greatest undertaking of his life — one so far-reaching in its effect on humanity as to carry his name to the thinkers, philosophers, and philanthropists of every land. The "Livingston Code" alone entitles him to a place high on the scroll of humanitarians who have served mankind. Victor Hugo declared that he would be "numbered among the men of this age who have deserved most and best of mankind." Jeremy Bentham was tremendously impressed. Dr. H. S. Maine, author of the "Ancient Laws," pronounced him "the first legal genius of modern times." Villemain, of the Paris Sorbonne, described his work as "a work without example from the hand of any one man." From the Emperor of Russia and the King of Sweden came autograph letters, from the King of the Netherlands a gold medal and a eulogy, and statesmen and philosophers of Europe vied with kings and emperors in paying homage. The Government of Guatemala, not content with translating his "Code on Reform and Prison Discipline," and adopting it without the change of a word, bestowed upon a new city and district the name of Livingston. Jefferson wrote: "It will certainly array your name with the sages of antiquity"; Kent and Story, Madison and Marshall joined in the common praise, and he was elected a member of the Institute of France. Such was the prestige he took to Washington, when, in his fifty-ninth year, he again entered the House as a Representative from New Orleans.

He was now an old man, but of unusual vigor, and able to wear out younger men with his long pedestrian jaunts. He loved society and mingled with it freely, unable to escape it if he would because of the social and intellectual brilliance of his wife and the charm and beauty of his daughter. His fame

[1] Hunt's *Life of Livingston* describes in detail Livingston's activities in connection with the battle of New Orleans.

was seemingly secure. His reputation was world-wide. His conversational gifts were of an uncommon order. His friends and social intimates were confined to no party, and embraced the best of both. After a brief period in the House he had entered the Senate where he stood among the foremost. Such was the man Jackson called to the head of his Cabinet — one whose character and career suffer nothing by comparison with those of his most distinguished predecessors, Jefferson, John Quincy Adams, and Henry Clay.

V

We are not concerned with the Roger B. Taney who wrote the Dred Scott decision, but with that portion of his career, little known and appreciated, which convinced Jackson that he was worthy of wearing the mantle of John Marshall. And that is by far the most dramatic phase of his life — his battling years. Born and reared on a Maryland plantation, among horses and slaves, he grew up to be an independent, self-reliant youth. At Dickinson College he refused to take down a portion of a lecture which assailed our republican governmental system. As valedictorian of his class he suffered torments from a morbid fear of public speaking. Thus even as a student he was independent in thought, courageously devoted to his convictions, brave in battle, but miserably self-conscious on parade.

On graduating, he returned to the woods and fields of the plantation, abandoned his books, and gave himself up to the joys of fox-hunting, leading the life of the old-fashioned English country gentleman. When he took up the study of law in Annapolis, however, he abandoned this outdoor life in turn, and, declining all social invitations, devoted himself to his studies, and to fighting his native timidity, in a debating society. Here also he studied the methods of two of the Nation's greatest advocates, Luther Martin and William Pinkney.

And, strangely enough, this great lawyer in the making, began the practice of the law as a side issue to politics. In the quiet rural community of his nativity, where there was little litigation and no opportunity for professional distinction, he settled, for the sole purpose of entering the House of Delegates. This, however, in compliance with the wishes of his aggressively Federalistic father. Thus, at the age of twenty-two, we find young Taney responding to the roll-call as a pronounced Federalist of the school of Hamilton. It is noteworthy that he was defeated in the next election because of the Jeffersonian revolution of 1800.

This setback changed the course of his career. An uncompromising Federalist with Federalism apparently dead, politics no longer promised a future, and he turned now to the serious consideration of the law, and located at Frederick where the Democrats were overwhelmingly predominant. In this community, rich, intellectual, cultured, and hospitable, he instantly took his place among the leaders of the bar and entered upon a lucrative practice. A Federalist from principle, he did not hesitate, when called to lead the forlorn hope. As a Federalist, he opposed the War of 1812. Up to this point his political career was similar to that of Webster.

And it is in the divergence of the two careers at this point that the future of Taney turned. He fought the war until the die was cast, and then threw himself with intense fervor into the support of his country against the foreign foe. Contemptuous of the disloyalists of his political family, he summoned the Federalists to the unqualified support of the American arms, and such was his prestige that a large portion of the party in Maryland followed his lead.[1] By subordinating party to country, he all but obliterated party lines, and when he was nominated for Congress as a war Federalist he all but wiped out the normal Democratic majority. Had he gone to

[1] These came to be known as the "Coodies," and Taney was known as "King Coodie" to indicate his unquestioned leadership. Tyler's *Life of Taney*.

Washington at that time as a lone Federalist supporting the war, to face Webster, fighting the organization of the army and the appropriations, his national reputation would have come eighteen years before it did. For his was no half-hearted hate of the disloyalty of his party co-workers. This is the first decisive action upon which an interpretation of his political character may be predicated.

Meanwhile, restricting himself more and more to his profession, frequently associated with Luther Martin in the most important litigation, his reputation spread throughout the State, and the politician was merged with the lawyer. It was in connection with one of his most sensational cases that he took a position on slavery and the right of abolitionists to be heard that throws a high light on his character and courage.

An abolitionist minister from Pennsylvania had gone to Maryland and made a ferocious attack on slavery in a public meeting attended by some slaves. The excitement and feeling against him were intense. To the sensitive slave-owners the speech seemed a deliberate incitation of the slaves to insurrection. The minister's life was in danger. It required supreme courage for a Maryland lawyer in that slave-holding community to stand between the abolitionist and the popular clamor against him, and Taney stepped from the professional ranks to plead his cause, not perfunctorily, but with a passionate defiance worthy of the highest traditions of his profession. He made his defense on no less grounds than "the rights of conscience and the freedom of speech." And he spoke on slavery even as Garrison or Lincoln might have spoken. In a courtroom crowded with slave-owners who were his neighbors, he touched boldly on the pathos and the tragedy of the institution. After this daring defense before a slave-holding jury, the hated abolitionist was acquitted — and the records of the American courts record no nobler triumph.

The death of Pinkney and the disqualification of Martin

soon advanced Taney to the head of the Maryland bar. It was one year after he had established himself in Baltimore that he first allied himself with the supporters of Andrew Jackson. During the campaign of 1824 was published a letter written by Jackson to Madison seven years before, urging the recognition of those Federalists who had broken with their party to support the War of 1812, and suggesting the name of Colonel Drayton of South Carolina.[1] Discriminating between the anti-war Federalists and the pro-war Federalists, Jackson here declared that had he been commander of the military department in which the Hartford Convention was held, he would have court-martialed the three leaders of the Convention. This announcement of his views had attracted to his standard many pro-war Federalists of Maryland, and the most notable acquisition was Roger B. Taney. He was impelled to his course with no thought of political reward. His whole mind and heart were in his profession. Jackson knew nothing of Taney's partiality at the time, and only learned of it about the time he was seeking a successor for Berrien. At no time in his life had the Maryland lawyer been so thoroughly satisfied with his lot. He had been made Attorney-General of the State on the unanimous recommendation of the bar, and this was the only office to which he ever aspired. It was in line with his work and left him at home with his family and his books. Such was his situation, when, through a non-political suggestion, he was offered the position in the Cabinet of Jackson.

At this time he was in his fifty-fourth year, with no taste for the trickery and intrigues of politics, and he asked nothing better for his leisure hours than meditative tramps through the woods, a canter on his horse, a volume of poetry or history, or the delights of his home, presided over by the sister of the author of "The Star-Spangled Banner." An ar-

[1] Drayton was Congressman from Charleston during the Nullification fight and strongly supported Jackson.

dent Catholic, he was strict in the observance of his religious duties. Always vehement in his views, and uncompromising in his convictions, he was almost unpleasantly decisive in the expression of his political opinions. Such was his lofty conception of official propriety that while in office he was to refuse to accept the slightest token of appreciation from people with whom he had official relations.[1] He had all the courtesy and courtliness of his culture, all the caution of the painstaking lawyer, and all the circumspection of the man jealous of his honor. He was to become the most virile assistant of Jackson in the bitterest fight of his Presidency, the most trusted of his Cabinet, because the most like Jackson in the vigor of his blows.

VI

To describe Lewis Cass as an American politician would be damning with faint praise, for he was something infinitely more and greater — he was an empire-builder of the company of Clive and Rhodes, one of the most robust figures in American history. His first remembered view of the world was that of being held in his mother's arms, and looking out the windows of his New Hampshire home upon the bonfires blazing in celebration of the ratification of the Constitution. Crossing the Alleghanies on foot, with a knapsack on his back, sleeping beneath the stars, his Americanism had expanded in the contemplation of the magnitude of the Republic. Riding the circuit, as Western lawyers did in those days, he was a witness of the stubborn battles against the wilderness, and he had enough imagination to see, in the rough men wielding axes, Homeric figures. And it was while pursuing his lonely way through the virgin forests of

[1] Tyler relates the incident of a personal friend of Taney's, temporarily connected with the custom house in New York, sending him a box of cigars without his card, while he was Attorney-General. Not knowing who sent them, Taney put them aside. After leaving office, and learning the donor's identity, he wrote an appreciative note enclosing the price of the cigars.

Ohio that he found time for the assimilation of his reading and learned to be the independent and courageous thinker he became.

He had established a sound reputation at the bar, when the War of 1812 added that of a gallant and brilliant soldier. To him especially are we indebted for the shameful story of Hull's cowardly surrender of Detroit — an act so maddening that Cass broke his sword in protest. But his reputation as lawyer and soldier pales by comparison with the reputation he was to make as an empire-builder.

Never was a ruler confronted by more disheartening difficulties than Cass, when, in 1813, he became the civil Governor of Michigan. For two years he was forced to battle against anarchy and famine. Organized society was demoralized. The country was disorganized. The savages had driven away the cattle of the settlers, and the French especially were in desperate straits. The war-whoops of the red men had so terrorized the people that they were afraid to settle down to the cultivation of the land. The morale of the Territory was pathetically low. And Cass, with the empire-builder's decision and genius, instantly formed his plan to combat the threatened disintegration. The people had to be fed — he fed them from the public stores, drew upon the Government for further assistance, personally directed the battle against famine — and won. The confidence of the people had to be restored as a preliminary to progress — he determined to restore it by demonstrating his mastery of the savages. Organizing the young men, he personally led them against the Indians in a bloody skirmish — and won. He repeated it — and won. Again — and won. And thus the terror of the people passed, and they returned to their homes.

He then turned to the organization of civil government. Courts were created, civil officers selected, territorial divisions established, new counties were carved, and he began an elaborate policy of road-building and internal improvements.

One of his first acts was to establish a school system, and to encourage the building of churches with the assurance of religious liberty.

This accomplished, he turned with his usual zeal to the Americanizing of the people, many of whom were French, and to encouraging the migration of colonists. Knowing the industry and energy of his native New England, he planned to draw immigrants from that section hoping that the French would learn by their success to emulate their example. But here he had another battle to overcome the general notion of the Eastern States that the land of Michigan was valueless. In time he succeeded.

And then he found time to challenge the right of the British across the border to interfere in the affairs of the Territory. In those days Michigan was only a Territory on the outskirts, and it was easier for the National Government to ignore insults than to challenge a mighty empire by protesting against them. As late as 1816 vessels were stopped on their way to Detroit and searched by British agents. Cass, with lawyer-like care, collected his evidence, transmitted it to Washington, vigorously protested to the British authorities — and won.[1]

Nowhere, perhaps, does his vision as an empire-builder, shine more luminously than in his letter to Calhoun, Secretary of War, proposing a scientific expedition in 1819, under the sanction and with the coöperation of the Federal Government.[2] This was the programme of a statesman. And he asked for experts for the expedition — engineers, zoölogists, botanists, mineralogists. Determining to accompany the expedition, it is interesting to note the sagacity of the reason he assigns: "I think it very important to carry the flag of the United States into those remote sections where it has never been borne by

[1] See McLaughlin's *Life of Cass*, 99, 100, for details of his fight against British insults and interference.

[2] See Smith's *Life of Cass* for letter.

any one in public station." This was the most important expedition ever undertaken by the American Government up to that time, and was so regarded by the press of the period.

If we add to this, his successful negotiations of treaties with the Indians under dramatic circumstances, we have the work and record of "The Father of the West" — empire-builder from 1813 until he entered the Cabinet of Jackson in 1831.

And this man of action, fighting life-and-death battles on the fringe of civilization, found time for the gratification of literary tastes. Here he suggests the Roosevelt of a much later day. When starting forth on an expedition into the wilderness, it was his custom to supply himself with a small library for his entertainment while floating in canoes on the rivers or the lakes. His articles in later years disclose the scholar.[1] Just before entering the Cabinet he had delivered a scholarly address at Hamilton College which has been preserved in a number of the popular collections of orations.[2]

Livingston the Nationalist.

Cass, the Empire-Builder.

Taney, the Crusader.

Out of the career of any one of these might be woven a romance. All were of heroic mould, veritable Plutarchian figures. And we shall see that the time had arrived when Jackson would need the wisest and most courageous of counselors — for Henry Clay was returning in shining armor to lead the bitterest of partisan battles against the Administration.

[1] "France: Its King, Court and Government"; "Three Hours at St. Cloud's"; and "The Modern French Judicature." He also, on the request of Jackson, wrote the best account of the battle of New Orleans.

[2] See McLaughlin's *Life of Cass;* Young's biography, written during Cass's lifetime, in Smith's *Life of Cass.*

CHAPTER VI

KITCHEN CABINET PORTRAITS

I

FROM the beginning the virile, militant, driving factors behind Jackson's policies were found outside his official family. The "Kitchen Cabinet," so called in derision, was more influential in the moulding of events than the old-fashioned, conventional statesmen who advised their chief in the seclusion of the Cabinet room. Had Jackson depended wholly on his Cabinet for the support of his policies, he would have been constantly confused by divided counsels. On scarcely any of the vital issues of his Presidency did he have the hearty coöperation of his constitutional advisers. But never before, nor since, has any President been served by such tireless organizers of the people, such masters of mass psychology, such geniuses in the art of publicity and propaganda. These men, the small but loyal and sleepless group of the Kitchen Cabinet, were the first of America's great practical politicians.

Of this group the master mind was Amos Kendall, born in a New England farmhouse in the latter days of the eighteenth century. In youth, he preferred study to play, and because of a premature solemnity he was familiarly known as "The Deacon." His timidity was as painful as that which tortured Charlotte Brontë. The stupid act of a teacher in ridiculing his reading of an oration came near putting a period to his education, and at Dartmouth he was almost moved to tears by professorial praise of one of his essays. His college days were so serious and laborious that his health suffered, and his constitution was impaired. He played no pranks and had no dissipations. Taking his politics seriously, the overwhelming preponderance of Federalists did not restrain him from belligerently espousing the cause of the minority. It is significant of his instinctive bent that when he turned to politics he shed his timidity and stood forth a passionate militant. Graduating from the college that Webster loved, he declined his diploma, partly because of indifference, but largely because of his personal dislike of the president. Thus early he entertained no illusions, and had the courage of both his convictions and his prejudices.

Meanwhile the second war with England was on, and he was beginning to detest the New England Federalists for their disloyalty and illiberality. The pulpits rang with bitter denunciations of Madison, and ministers proclaimed from the pulpits that Democrats were "irreligious profligates." [1] In Boston, Kendall heard the eloquent Harrison Gray Otis ferociously denounce the war, and he hastened home to enlist, to be rejected for physical disabilities.

In his twenty-fifth year he set forth from his bleak New Hampshire home to seek his fortune, and we are able to sense the spirit and temper of the youth from the jottings of his journal. At Boston he heard Edward Everett whom he thought a "youth of great promise." At Washington he attended a White House levee, finding Dolly Madison "a noble and dignified person," the President's "personal appearance very inferior," and meeting Felix Grundy and Lewis Cass. Thence he passed down the Ohio, a guest of Major Barry, and became a citizen of Kentucky.

At Lexington he entered the home of Henry Clay, engaged by Mrs. Clay as a tutor for the children. In later years, when he was the mysterious power in the Jackson Administration, and Clay the leader of the Opposition, the drawing-rooms of Washington buzzed with a fantastic tale, intended to prove his depravity and ingratitude. Harriet Martineau,[2] while in the capital, heard it and incorporated it in her book. According to this story "tidings reached Mr.

[1] Kendall's *Autobiography*, 73.

[2] *Retrospect of Western Travel*, I, 156.

and Mrs. Clay one evening that a young man, solitary and poor, lay ill of a fever in a noisy hotel in the town. Mrs. Clay went down in the carriage without delay, and brought the sufferer home to her house, where she nursed him with her own hands till he recovered. Mr. Clay was struck with the talents of the young man and retained him as a tutor of his sons, heaping benefits upon him with characteristic bounty." Unhappily for the tale, Kendall was not ill, Mr. Clay was at Geneva at the time of his employment and during the entire period of his stay in Ashland, and the "benefits heaped upon him" consisted of $300 a year with board and lodging, and the privilege of using Mr. Clay's library. Soon after leaving the service of the Clays, we find him recording in his diary: "Rode to Lexington and visited H. Clay. I found him a very agreeable man, and was familiarly acquainted with him in half an hour."

However, his sojourn at Ashland was pleasurable and profitable. Mrs. Clay, deeply interested in him, chaffed him on his timidity, criticized the stiffness of his bows, and drove him to his room to practice before the mirror, admitted him to her social gatherings, called upon him to read his poetry to her friends, and rallied him about his love affairs. Thus the "mediocre" and vulgar "writer for pay" of the Jackson régime was once considered fit for the social circle in the home of Henry Clay.

Scarcely had he been admitted to the bar when he was enticed by Colonel Richard M. Johnson into the editorship of the "Georgetown Patriot"; and it is illuminative of his character to find him, when the slayer of Tecumseh, a little later, upbraided him for refusing personally to abuse the Opposition, writing in his diary: "I shall give Richard my vote, but I shall not be his tool."[1] His editorials constructive, his specialty banking and currency, he soon found himself in the editorial chair of the "Frankfort Argus," where he was

[1] Kendall's *Autobiography*, 175.

instantly engaged in bitter political controversies. Whether in argument, where he excelled, in invective, or in wit, he invariably scored heavily on the Opposition. For his generation and community, his editorial code was lofty. He promised himself never knowingly to misrepresent; if, through mistake, he did, to rectify the mistake without being asked; never to retract a statement he thought true; to resent an insult in kind; to defend himself, if assaulted, by any means necessary, even to killing, and never to run. So great was his professional self-respect that on one occasion, when vulgarly assailed in an Opposition paper, he had his answer printed in bill form and circulated by hand, rather than befoul his own journal with a suitable reply.

In seeming contradiction, however, we have his merciless bombardment of the unfortunate Shadrach Penn, editor of a Louisville paper, who had a genius for attracting the ridicule of his intellectual superiors; for while Kendall was peppering him from Frankfort, George D. Prentice was bombarding him from Louisville, and between the two, he was driven whimpering from the State.[1]

The physical courage of Kendall may be read in his encounters with irate victims. In one controversy he was spared the necessity of killing an assailant with a dirk by the timely interference of friends. In another he put an opponent to flight by cracking a whip and displaying the sparkling silver handle in the sun. He never ran.

Under his editorship the "Argus" became a powerful political factor in Kentucky. He inaugurated the plan of printing legislative speeches, specialized on political news, intelligently discussed international affairs, launched a campaign in favor of public schools, reviewed contemporary books, dipped into religious subjects with his "Sunday Reflections," and significantly began a fight against the National Bank in a series of articles combating the Supreme

[1] Henry Watterson's oration on Prentice, "Compromises of Life."

Court decision as to its constitutionality. If, thirteen years later, he was not to flinch under the lashings of the Bank press, it may have been because he had become seasoned to the punishment more than a decade before when he was described as a "political incendiary."

His friendly relations with Clay were maintained at least until the autumn of 1827, when, on a trip to New Hampshire, he wrote his wife of dining with the orator in Washington. But the campaign of 1828 found Kendall and the "Argus" valiant in the cause of Jackson, with Clay and his friends "casting aspersions upon his motives and character." [1] In revenge for these attacks he sought the privilege of taking the electoral vote of Kentucky to Washington. Meanwhile, after the election, and before his departure, he had been informed by an emissary from the Hermitage that Jackson intended to offer him an appointment.

The Kendall lingering at the capital awaiting an appointment presents an interesting study. It is disappointing to note a certain humility and manner usually associated with the lower order of place-hunters. He was evidently ardent in his pursuit of a position. His inexperience is disclosed in his disgust on finding so many obscure politicians pretending to the distinction of having elected Jackson. And yet, so anxious was he for place, that he was willing to accept one paying an inadequate salary, and he wrote his wife that in that event he might persuade Duff Green to pay him $1000 a year for writing for the "Telegraph." [2] During the weeks of waiting before the inauguration, he was not a little embarrassed for funds, and yet, under these drab conditions, he did not lack for invitations of a social nature. Meeting General Macomb and finding him "a Jackson man," he expressed the hope that he might "find him a valuable acquaintance." [3] Meanwhile he was investigating houses and

[1] Kendall's *Autobiography*, 303.

[2] *Ibid.*, 278. [3] *Ibid.*, 279.

rents, and concluded to economize by taking a house in Georgetown. "The house I contemplate taking," he wrote, "is in a charming neighborhood on First Street, near Cox's Row."

Receiving his appointment as Fourth Auditor, he dropped from public view. Dinners and parties saw him no more. He immediately assumed the rôle of a recluse. Taking his duties seriously, he uncovered the crimes of his predecessor and sent him to jail. His rules for the conduct of subordinates were such as to merit the approval of business men — rules that the office-holder of those days scarcely understood. After a week in office he wrote his wife: "The labor is very light, and when I am master of the laws under which I act, will consist of little more than looking at accounts and signing my name." Thus we find him systematizing his work to dedicate the greater portion of his time to the political work of the Administration. "Hamilton," said Martin Van Buren, a month later, "Kendall is to be an influential man. I wish the President would invite him to dinner, and if you have no objection, as you are so intimate with the General, I wish you would propose to him to invite Kendall to meet us at dinner to-morrow."[1] The invitation was extended and accepted, and the Red Fox, who had a genius for picking men, was notably attentive to the timid subordinate.

During the five years he held his inferior post, Kendall became more powerful than any Cabinet Minister in the determination of Jacksonian policies. A little later, a contemporary observer of men at the capital described him as "secretive, yet audacious in his political methods, a powerful and ready writer, and the author of many of Jackson's ablest State papers."[2] There in his office we may picture him, alone, with pad and pencil, preparing elaborate political war maps, and literature for propaganda, or in earnest

[1] Hamilton's *Reminiscences*, 130.

[2] Rufus Rockwell Wilson, *Washington the Capital City*, I, 263.

conversation with Lewis and other members of the Kitchen Cabinet, forging thunderbolts with which to smite the foe. And it was very soon after he had left this subordinate post that Harriet Martineau was impressed with the uncanny mystery of the "invincible Amos Kendall."

"I was fortunate enough," she wrote, "to catch a glimpse of the invincible Amos Kendall, one of the most remarkable men in America. He is supposed to be the moving spring of the Administration; the thinker, the planner, the doer; but it is all in the dark. Documents are issued, the excellence of which prevents them from being attributed to the persons that take the responsibility for them; a correspondence is kept up all over the country, for which no one seems answerable; work is done of goblin extent and with goblin speed, which makes men look about them with superstitious wonder; and the invincible Amos Kendall has the credit for it all. President Jackson's letters to his Cabinet are said to be Kendall's; the report on Sunday mails is attributed to Kendall; the letters sent from Washington to remote country newspapers, whence they are collected and published in the 'Globe' as demonstrations of public opinion, are pronounced to be written by Kendall; and it is some relief that he now, having the office of Postmaster-General, affords opportunity for open attack upon this twilight personage. He is undoubtedly a great genius. He unites with all his 'great talents for silence' a splendid audacity.

"It is clear he could not do the work he does if he went into society like other men. He did, however, one evening. . . . The moment I went in, intimations reached me from all quarters, amid nods and winks, 'Kendall is here,' 'There he is.' I saw at once that his plea for seclusion (bad health) is no false one. The extreme sallowness of his complexion, the hair of such perfect whiteness as is rarely seen in a man of middle age, testified to his disease.[1] His countenance does not

[1] Kendall is thus described at forty-five.

help the superstitious to throw off their dread of him. He probably does not desire this superstition to melt away, for there is no calculating how much influence is given the Jackson Administration by the universal belief that there is a concealed eye and hand behind the machinery of Government, by which everything could be foreseen, and the hardest deeds done. A member of Congress told me this night that he had watched through five sessions for a sight of Kendall, and had never obtained one until now. Kendall was leaning on a chair, his head bent down, and eyes glancing up at a member of Congress with whom he was in earnest conversation, and in a moment he was gone." [1]

Such was the cleverest most audacious, and powerful member of the Kitchen Cabinet — a man who made history that historians have written and ascribed to others who merely uttered the words or registered the will of this indomitable journalist and politician.

II

When Jackson left the Hermitage, he was accompanied by Major William B. Lewis, who had been intimately identified with his campaign for the Presidency. This unobtrusive man found lodgment with his chief at Gadsby's, where he interested himself in analyzing the characters of office-seekers for the guidance of his friend. After walking with Jackson from the hotel to the Capitol, and seeing him inducted into office, he announced his plan to return to the quiet life of Tennessee.

"Why, Major," exclaimed the astonished Jackson, "you are not going to leave me here alone, after doing more than any other man to bring me here!"

Moved by the sincerity of the appeal, Lewis remained on in Washington through the eight years of the reign, living at the White House, and enjoying a greater personal intimacy with the President than any other politician of the time. Accepting

[1] *Retrospect of Western Travel*, I, 155–57.

an insignificant auditorship at the Treasury as an excuse for staying on, he interpreted his real function as that of a political bodyguard. He came and went in the President's private apartments at will. No formalities were interposed between these two strangely different men. No secrets formed a veil. In the midst of the bitter fights against his idol, Lewis moved quietly and uncannily about, gauging sentiment, determining the drift, analyzing men and motives, guarding Jackson against the surprise attack. When the ferocious onslaughts were at their worst in the Senate, Lewis could be found somewhere in the shadows of the chamber watching every movement of the enemy, and critically, if not always wisely, passing judgment upon the strategy of the Administration forces; and when the fight was over, he hastened to the White House, sure to find Jackson sitting up in his room with the picture of Rachel and her Bible on the table before him, awaiting the report.

There was this difference between Lewis and the other members of the Kitchen Cabinet — they all loved Jackson; but where the others thought of him as the personification of a party, Lewis could only think of him as the friend of the Hermitage. He had fought and wrought for his election, not to score a party victory, but to vindicate the man. Of Jackson's comfort, happiness, and prestige he was supremely jealous, but there were times when he rebelled against the audacious proposals of others, more given to thinking of party, to stake the General's reputation and success upon a party issue.

He has been called the "great father of wire-pullers," [1] a closet man's definition of a great manipulator of men. At the time the public began to speculate on the presidential possibilities of Jackson, the Major was his neighbor. He was not a penniless adventurer or soldier of fortune. There was nothing in politics for himself for which he cared a

[1] Sumner's *Life of Jackson.*

bauble. He was living comfortably on his large productive plantation, with slaves in the fields, and books in the library. Jackson had learned to love and trust him years before when he was chief quartermaster on the General's staff in the campaign of 1812–15, and in the final settlement the Government was found to be indebted to him to the amount of three cents — which was never paid. When the Jackson movement became serious, the Major, knowing the General's strength and weaknesses, took charge of all confidential matters. To just what extent he contributed to Jackson's election no one ever knew — but all knew that he had played an important part. He conducted all the correspondence, and carefully scrutinized, and often revised, the General's letters; and another of his functions was to serve as a sort of valet for all State occasions when Jackson should be carefully groomed.

He possessed the qualities that Jackson lacked. Where Jackson was impulsive, he was deliberative; where Jackson was prejudiced, he was tolerant; where Jackson was rash, he was prudent, if not timid; where Jackson was a man of action, he was a man of thought; and while Jackson had ideas, he furnished the vehicle to bear them in parade. During the many months preceding the election of 1828, this practical, polished politician was studying the political war map, and quietly planning successful battles in this State and that. He knew the politics of each State, the personalities and prejudices entering in, the dominating motives of all politicians, even to those never known outside their own little communities, and he knew how to play one force against the other without appearing in the game. Knowing as he did all the cross-currents of local politics, nothing ever arose that he could not deal with intelligently.

During the eight years in the White House, Lewis was a whole regiment of Swiss guards — always on duty and alert. "Keep William B. Lewis to ferret out and make known to you all the plots and intrigues hatching against your Administration, and you are safe," was Jackson's advice to Polk when the latter was entering the White House. We shall find him implicated in some of the most important events of his time, making history, and yet escaping the historian. His great advantage was his perfect understanding of Jackson's character. He often became a buffer, protecting the President against unpleasant revelations. If he thought a disclosure necessary as a protection to the grim old warrior, he told his secret; if he thought it would merely arouse to useless wrath, he buried it; and sometimes, as in the case of the Crawford letter, he bided his time for months before revealing it. All the politicians of his day passed in review before him, Democrats and Whigs, Nullifiers and Nationalists, friends and enemies, and he silently catalogued them through a Bertillon system of his own. His advice to Jackson was that of a friend to a friend, seated about the blazing White House hearth, discussing politics and men in the midst of the tobacco smoke, as they might have done in the private life of the Hermitage.

He did not possess Kendall's genius for programmes, nor Blair's for propaganda, but he was invaluable in the field of personalities. He alone of the three sometimes doubted and drew back in fear. When Jackson vetoed the Maysville Bill, Van Buren found Lewis's countenance "to the last degree despondent." [1] He dreaded and doubted the effect of the veto of the measure rechartering the Bank, and later, the withdrawal of the deposits. Having been Federalistic himself, in other days, he had a fellow feeling for Louis McLane when that politician found himself in trouble. But doubting and trembling though he sometimes was, Van Buren has testified that "no considerations or temptations, through many of which he was obliged to pass, could weaken his fidelity to the General or his desire for the success of his Administration." [2]

[1] Van Buren's *Autobiography*, 325. [2] *Ibid.*, 579.

In the early stages of the Bank controversy, he alone of the members of the Kitchen Cabinet maintained friendly relations with Biddle.[1]

Concerning his status among the Jacksonian leaders, biographers and historians have radically disagreed. Even among the later writers this disagreement persists, and where one dismisses the theory that he was a politician, far-sighted and astute, as without sufficient evidence,[2] another concludes that "in a day of astute politicians, Major Lewis was one of the cleverest." [3] The truth appears to be that while he was not a moulder of policies and creator of programmes, he was one of the most clever manipulators of men and masters of personal intrigue who ever served a President. In the Kitchen Cabinet he was the personal manager — the political secretary.

III

THE most militant of the Kitchen Cabinet was Isaac Hill, whose name was anathema to the Federalists of New England. A poor boy educated in a printshop, slight and lame, hurling picturesque phrases and bitter reproaches at the powerful enemy, excoriating it with his satire and sarcasm, and slashing it with the keen blade of his wit, it is not surprising that the impression handed down by the Intellectuals of the Opposition is unfavorable. Where they have not dismissed him with a shrug, they have damned him as a dunce — and largely because he gave virility to a minority and made it militant, and, despite overwhelming odds, established in the hotbed of proscriptive Federalism a vigorous Democratic paper which was quoted from New Orleans to

[1] In the *Correspondence of Nicholas Biddle* (Houghton Mifflin Company, 1919) are numerous letters between the banker and Lewis, indicative of a desire on the part of the latter to conciliate the former and save his chief from the hazards of a bitter fight.

[2] Professor J. S. Bassett's *Life of Jackson*, II, 399.

[3] Professor Frederic Austin Ogg's *Reign of Andrew Jackson*.

Detroit, and from Boston to St. Louis. If he lacked the depth and the constructive faculty of Kendall, and the literary finish of Blair, he possessed a genius as a phrase-monger which spread his fame and served his party, and in the heat of a campaign, one of his stinging paragraphs was as effective as one of Kendall's leaders. There was no finesse in his fighting — he fought out in the open, in full range of his foe, and with any weapon on which he could lay his hands. If the intensity of his partisanship amounted to unfairness, it had been made so by the intolerance and bigotry of the Opposition of his section. Since no member of the Kitchen Cabinet more insistently demanded of Jackson the adoption of the spoils system, it is not unprofitable to inquire into the origin of his state of mind.

His life was a tragedy. Born in abject poverty, a cripple from childhood, he had seen his father and grandfather become mental wrecks. Under this cloud, in this state of penury, he looked out upon the world. Shut off by his infirmity from physical labor, he had no money for an education, and he lived on an unpromising New Hampshire farm, where there were no schools, libraries, or books, and few papers. But before he was eight he had read the Bible through. Two years before he had read the story of the Revolution from books borrowed, and had supplemented his reading by having a relative, who had fought with Washington, describe the burning of Charlestown and the Concord fight. There was infinite pathos in his passion for the printed page. But college was out of the question, the printing-office the only possible substitute, and thus, after a long apprenticeship, he took over a wobbling paper at Concord and became an editor.

Throwing discretion to the winds and with a sublime audacity, he took up the challenge of the powerful majority; and it required courage to pursue that course in the New Hampshire of 1809. To be a Democrat (Republican) there in those days was to offend God; boldly to preach hostility to Federalism was to proclaim blasphemy and invite destruction. The Federalistic press opened their batteries of abuse upon the obscure youth. One paper solemnly announced the discovery that he was a direct descendant of the witches who had suffered at Salem. Hill returned a spirited fire, and rejoiced in the combat. "I have hit them, for they flutter," he said.[1] In the campaign of 1810 he fairly galvanized the prostrate friends of the National Administration into life and incurred an unbelievable hatred of the Opposition. When this crippled boy was brutally assaulted on the streets of Concord, the Federalist press of New Hampshire gloated over the attack. Nor was it above sneering at his infirmity.

Throughout the War of 1812 he was a pillar of strength to the Republic in New Hampshire. During the darkest days it was said that he was worth a thousand soldiers in heartening the patriots.[2] With the approach of the campaign of 1828, Hill's paper, the "Patriot," began to bombard the Adams Administration, and Clay, who was to shudder later at the wickedness of the spoils system, promptly deprived him of the public printing.

Thus the campaign of 1828 began. The stinging paragraphs of Hill made the rounds of the Democratic press of the country, and in his own State he was shamelessly assailed. Not satisfied with maligning his personal character, his enemies stooped to references to the insanity of his father in disseminating the story that he was crazy.[3] In view of this cruel personal persecution, it was but human that, on the election of Jackson, his voice should have been for war on all the Federalist office-holders. Thus his psychology is easily

[1] Bradley's *Life of Hill.*

[2] General Leavenworth's letter, quoted in Bradley's *Life of Hill.*

[3] Hill took notice of this brutality: "There is an Almighty Power Who tempers the wind to the shorn lambs, Who will preserve us from such a calamity, and Who will not suffer our intellectual vision to be dimmed until our work shall be accomplished."

understood. Because of his political convictions, he had been proscribed. A cripple, he had been personally attacked in the streets. In suffering he had been ridiculed. The insanity of his father had been made the subject of vulgar jests. His personal character had been assailed. And in the hour of victory, all the pent-up hatred of the years was let loose upon the vanquished foe.

Hill was the Marat of the Kitchen Cabinet, the fanatic, calling for heads — more heads — and unseemly in his mirth as they fell.

In appearance he was not prepossessing. Below the medium height, he was spare as well as crippled. In his high forehead and the expression of his eyes his intellect was indicated, and he carried himself with that haughty air of superiority which men, forced to fight for their existence, are apt to assume. This was described by his enemies as "demoniacal." He always dressed plainly as a workingman. Without imagination or dreams, severely practical and to the point, conscious of his limitations, and passionately devoted to both his convictions and prejudices, there was nothing about him to appeal to the fashionable or the intellectually elect. In no sense dazzling in his gifts, hesitating instead of eloquent, shocking the Senate of his time by reading his speeches, and proud of his profession, he was not pointed out to travelers who wrote books, nor lionized in the drawing-rooms, nor dignified by the complimentary notices of the women letter-writers or diarists of his day. He has come down largely as his enemies have painted him, and their very hate of him discloses his effectiveness as a politician.

He was one of the Republic's first uncompromising partisans — "My party, right or wrong."

IV

An Administration and party paper had been considered important in the political circles of the Republic from the beginning, but it was left to the editors of the Kitchen Cabinet to develop it to the highest degree of efficiency. The "National Journal," Court paper of the Adams Administration, had awakened the Opposition to an appreciation of the practical value of a powerful party paper. Duff Green and the "Telegraph," in a sense, met the requirements, but even then there were Democrats of influence and aspirations who found something lacking. To Van Buren, the editor, devoted to Calhoun, was unsatisfactory. It is inconceivable that he felt the need for a more aggressive pen for the Opposition. Nevertheless, in the summer of 1826, while planning a more vigorous attack on the Adams Administration, he had an "animated conversation" concerning the need of a strictly party paper with Calhoun, at the latter's house in Georgetown. The Carolinian urged the adoption of the "Telegraph" as the party organ, with Van Buren pressing the advantage of prevailing upon Thomas Ritchie of the "Richmond Enquirer" to accept the editorship of a new party paper at the capital.[1] Failing to persuade Calhoun, the Red Fox cleverly approached Senator Tazewell of Virginia, an ardent friend of the Carolinian, and persuaded him to join in an invitation to the Richmond journalist.[2] Ritchie declined, however, on the ground of his attachment to Virginia and his reluctance to leave old friends and associates.[3] Thus, at the beginning of the Administration, it seemed that Duff Green and the "Telegraph" were destined to become the pen and organ of the Jacksonian Democracy.

At a White House levee in the winter of 1830–31, under the very nose of Jackson, and under his roof, the intriguing Green drew the proprietor of a Washington printing-house aside to tell him confidentially of the hastening rupture of Jackson and Calhoun, and of the plans in incubation for the advancement of the presidential aspirations of the latter. Calhoun

[1] Van Buren's *Autobiography,* 541.

[2] Ambler's *Thomas Ritchie,* 109.

[3] *Ibid.,* 247.

organs were to be acquired or established in all the strategic political points in the country, and when the rupture came these were to follow the lead of the "Telegraph" in a nationwide denunciation of Jackson. The printer was offered the editorship of one of these papers, and a liberal amount for his Washington plant. Thoroughly devoted to the political fortunes of the President, and not relishing the idea of being the depositary of a secret which threatened the President's position, the printer consulted freely with his friends, and, on their advice, carried the story to the White House.

Benton tells us that the story did not surprise Jackson, who was "preparing for it."[1] Thus we are told that in the summer of 1830 he had been impressed with a powerful editorial attack on Nullification in the "Frankfort Argus," had made inquiries as to the identity of the author, and had authorized the extension of an invitation to assume the editorship of an Administration paper in the capital. The version of Benton differs in material points from the version of Amos Kendall,[2] who was far more intimately identified with the launching of the new paper than either Benton or Van Buren. Here we have it that the idea was not Jackson's, and that when plans for a Jacksonian organ were presented to him "he entirely disapproved." At that time Jackson was unable to bring himself to believe in the treachery of Green. When ultimately, however, he saw the drift, he gave his "tacit consent."

Here Kendall's story clashes with the theory, put forth by Green, that Van Buren was the directing genius behind the whole project. When the President finally gave his "tacit consent," the practical politicians of the Kitchen Cabinet took charge. The various governmental offices were visited for an understanding as to what portion of the Government printing could be expected. When Van Buren, then at the

[1] Benton's *Thirty Years' View*, I, 128, gives the version of the establishment of the *Globe* which Van Buren in his *Autobiography* quotes.

[2] Kendall's *Autobiography*, 370–74.

head of the State Department, was approached, he announced that he would not give a dollar of the printing of his department, on the ground that "were such a paper established its origin would be attributed to him, and he was resolved to be able to say that he had nothing to do with it." This is typical of Van Buren, and is no doubt true. But the responses from all the other departments were satisfactory and the plans were pushed.

Having positively settled upon the paper, the next step was to find a managerial genius. In a conference between Kendall and Barry, the Postmaster-General, the latter suggested the availability of Frank P. Blair, then writing occasionally for the "Frankfort Argus," though not attached to the paper in a regular capacity. The correspondence with Blair was conducted by Kendall. The Kentuckian, surprised, momentarily hesitated, and it was not until Kendall had agreed to bear an equal part of the responsibility that he consented.

While Blair was getting his affairs in order in Kentucky, Kendall proceeded with the arrangements in Washington, and when the editor reached the capital nothing remained unsettled but the name and a motto. The two agreed to call the paper the "Globe," and the motto, suggested by Blair, "The World is Governed Too Much."

Thus there appears no reason to doubt that Kendall's version is the correct one, that Jackson was no more a leader in the movement than Van Buren, and that the idea was conceived by the little group of new and practical politicians, then coming to the fore, and who, while friends of Jackson, were interested in "measures more than men."

V

THE arrival of Frank Blair in Washington was an historical event, not appreciated at the time, and scarcely properly appraised to this day. But the ugly, illy dressed stranger, who presented himself at the White House immediately after reaching the capital, gave little promise, in his appearance, of the power within him. Instead of a large, raw-boned, husky Kentuckian expected, Major Lewis, who met him, was confronted by a short, slender man, poorly garbed, and rather timid and retiring than otherwise. The Major was frankly disappointed and probably disgusted. But when the editor was presented to Jackson, that genius took note neither of his dress nor appearance. Although expecting foreign diplomats and distinguished statesmen to dinner, he could see no reason why the unimposing little man, with the ill-fitting clothes and the ugly visage, should not remain as his guest. Assuming that he would be alone, Blair accepted, and, to his horror, he found himself in the presence of ministers in all the splendor of their official regalia. Unaccustomed to such show, and feeling the conspicuousness of his garb, he fled to a corner, hoping to escape notice. But Jackson, who never judged men by their appearance, least of all by their clothes, sought him out with the kindest intentions, and placed him beside him at the table. This act of courtesy, painful to Blair at the time, was understood and appreciated, and not only won his ardent support, but his deepest affection.

Although unknown to Jackson, who would have been uninterested if he had known, Frank Blair was qualified by blood to sit at the table of the first gentleman of the land. His grandfather had been acting president of Princeton when Witherspoon, signer of the Declaration, was summoned to New Jersey to accept the presidency. Born forty years before becoming editor of the "Globe," he had displayed, in college, the remarkable intellectual qualities that were to make him the adviser of Presidents, and one of the most influential moulders of public opinion of his time. He distinguished himself as the best rhetorician and linguist of his class.[1] The

[1] George Baber's *Blairs of Kentucky, Register of Kentucky Historical Society,* vol. XIV.

weakness of his voice discouraged his ambition for forensic distinction. In the Governor's Mansion at Frankfort he was married, early in life, to a charming woman noted for "her extraordinary mental force and her sagacity." [1]

Like Kendall and Barry, Blair had begun his political career as an ardent supporter of Clay, and like them, had broken with him on the "bargain" story. According to Blair's contention through life, Clay had confided to him in advance that, if such a contingency as did develop should arise in the congressional caucus, he would throw his support to Adams, and that he had protested against the plan. Whether true or not, that event marked the end of Blair's interest in the political ambitions of the man from Ashland. From 1823 to 1827 he played a conspicuous part as one of the principals in the famous fight between the New and the Old Courts which all but reduced the State to a condition bordering on anarchy. This part of his career is difficult to understand. The New Court Party, with which he was affiliated, was a revolutionary organization mustering its strength from the indebtedness and poverty of the people. It proposed to relieve the condition of the poor through methods frankly revolutionary and worse. During the period of the court fight, and while acting as the clerk of the revolutionary court, two events completely changed the course of his career. He broke with Clay and allied himself with the Democratic Party; and he became a regular contributor to the columns of the "Frankfort Argus," and a journalist by profession. On abandoning the court clerkship he immediately identified himself with Kendall in the publication of the paper, and the combined genius of these two extraordinary men converted the little Western journal into one of the most powerful and popular of the Jacksonian organs. All the credit appears to have gone to Kendall and none to his associate, for after the

[1] George Baber's *Blairs of Kentucky*, *Register of Kentucky Historical Society*, vol. XIV.

election it was Kendall and not Blair who was assured of recognition from the incoming Administration. After Kendall went to Washington, Blair, without the slightest notion of ever following, remained in Frankfort, writing special articles in support of Jacksonian policies for the "Argus." Thus he plied his trenchant pen against the Bank, excoriated Nullification, attacked Clay, and damned Calhoun. He had suffered financial reverses, been forced to sacrifice much property, and was in distressed circumstances. Later, when he was assailed by Senator Poindexter as having gone to Washington as a "beggar," he was indignantly to repel the charge. "The editor of the 'Globe' resigned, on leaving Frankfort to take charge of the press here," he wrote, "the clerkship of the circuit court, the fees of which alone averaged $2000 annually, and the presidency of the Bank of the Commonwealth, and other employments which made his annual income upward of $3000 — a sum twice as great as the salaries of the judges of the Supreme Court, and a third greater than that of the Governor of the State."[1] Nevertheless, it was the state of his finances which had necessitated the temporary suppression of the fact that he had accepted the editorship of the "Globe."

Once in the editorial chair, he assumed a militant attitude, and frankly announced that the paper would be devoted "to the discussion and maintenance of the principles which brought General Jackson into office"; and as early as April, 1831, four months after the first appearance of the paper, he began vigorously to advocate the reëlection of his idol in the White House.

The first issue appeared on December 7, 1830, published twice a week. In its initial days the inevitable quarrel between Blair and Green simmered, and while the "Globe" and the "Telegraph" were nervously toying with their pistols, the actual fight did not commence until Green published the Calhoun letters. Thereafter the contest was acrimonious and

[1] *Globe*, Feb. 17, 1834.

continuous. The immediate result of this battle was to impress Blair with the necessity of a daily publication, requiring a much larger outlay in money than either Blair or Kendall or both were able to advance. This, however, did not discourage the plucky little Kentuckian in the least. He called upon the friends and supporters of Jackson in the capital and throughout the country to subscribe for six hundred copies and pay for them in advance at the rate of ten dollars per annum. This money was easily collected, and thus, without the advance, by Blair, of a dollar of capital, the "Globe" was placed upon a firm and sure foundation.[1]

The journalistic genius of the little editor almost immediately gave the paper first rank in importance among all the papers then published in the country. Some of his admirers have said that "he became the master of a style of composition that compared favorably with that of Junius." [2] However that may be, he unquestionably was forceful, entertaining, and at times, eloquent. He could be dignified and argumentative without being dull. He knew how to appeal at once to the lover of pure English and the uneducated artisan of the city or the frontiersman in the wilderness. He was a pioneer among the journalists who have known how to produce a paper that would be as welcome on the library table of the student as in the hut of the farmer on the outskirts of civilization. The secret of his strength was his direct method. There was nothing of equivocation or compromise in his character. He did not qualify away all force for the sake of conservatism. He liked to cross the Rubicon, burn the bridges, and devastate the country. Any one could understand precisely what he meant. He was intense in his convictions, and he had the audacity, inseparable from political genius, to

[1] This is Kendall's story in his *Autobiography*. He gives no hint that Jackson contributed a penny. George Henry Payne, in his *History of Journalism in the United States*, says that the establishment of the *Globe* cost Jackson $50,000 a year, but as this version is Green's, it is not at all convincing or probable.

[2] Baber's *Blairs of Kentucky*.

move in a straight line, prepared to meet the enemy even on ground of the latter's choosing. His gift of satire and sarcasm was a joy to his fellow partisans who delighted in him. At first intended as their spokesman, he became their leader. Politicians soon learned that it was not necessary to carry suggestions to the editor of the "Globe" — they went to his sanctum to get them. Capable of a skillful use of the rapier, he preferred the meat-axe. Nothing pleased him so much as the crushing of the skulls of the enemies of Jackson, and if these should happen to be Democrats, all the greater was the joy of the operation.

This slashing, brilliant style delighted Jackson, who, strangely enough, had a profound admiration for the fluent writer. The old warrior took him to his bosom. That the editor of the "Court journal" should be mistaken was unthinkable to the President; and when any one asked him for information on any subject with which he was unfamiliar, he would invariably reply: "Go to Frank Blair — he knows everything." And Jackson believed it. Firmly convinced that the people were entitled to all public information, when any such came to his attention he would instantly say, "Give it to Blair." [1] He consulted the little ugly Kentuckian constantly on all matters of domestic policy, on party matters and patronage, and even on delicate points concerned with international programmes. The intimacy of this relationship soon trickled down from the capital to the party workers in the most remote sections, and, in time, the paper took its place with the Bible in all well-regulated Democratic households. Jackson himself is said to have read nothing during his Presidency but the Bible, his correspondence, and the "Globe." [2] The Democratic press throughout the country got its cue from Blair's editorials, and he, astute politician and advertiser, took pains to cultivate intimate relations with all papers supporting the Administration. Many arti-

[1] Van Buren's *Autobiography*, 323.

[2] *Perley's Reminiscences*, I, 191.

cles, written by Kendall in the office of the "Globe," and sent to country papers for publication as their own, were afterwards collected and reproduced in the Administration organ to indicate the trend of public opinion.

Naturally the enemies of the Administration in Congress looked upon Blair and his paper with venomous hatred, and not without cause. No head was too distinguished for his bludgeon, and it descended with resounding whacks upon the craniums of the greatest as well as the least of these, leading to many furious protests and denunciations on the floor of the House and Senate. The "Congressional Globe" is thickly sprinkled with references to the paper. There was nothing of novelty in a statesman rising to a question of personal privilege to explain that the editor had done him an injustice in describing him as a liar, an anarchist, or a traitor. Occasionally Clay, or some lesser light, would rise to protest against the action of the President in conveying information, to which the Congress was entitled, through the columns of his organ. Henry A. Wise would complain that "the Secretary of the Treasury has already informed Congress and the country, through the columns of the 'Globe' of Saturday last," that a certain policy would be pursued.[1] Or perhaps he would merely desire to explain that a certain editorial was a "total perversion of the facts." [2] Or maybe it was John Quincy Adams who took the floor to describe the editor of the "Globe" as "the ambassador of the Executive," an ambassador being "a distinguished person sent abroad to lie for the benefit of his country." [3] One member would secure recognition to "indignantly repel the charge made against him by the 'Globe' of being an anarchist and a revolutionist." [4] Even Webster was not impervious to the darts of the journalist, and did not think it beneath his dignity formally to

[1] *Cong. Globe*, April 14, 1836. [2] *Ibid.*, April 20, 1836.
[3] *Ibid.*, May 13, 1836.
[4] Mr. Williams of Kentucky, *ibid.*, May 30, 1836.

protest against an editorial paragraph, "flagitiously false," which had reflected upon him as chairman of the Finance Committee.[1]

With the politicians, the country press, and the party leaders in the Congress treating the "Globe" as the editorial reflection of the President, it is not surprising that the diplomatic corps should have accepted the general assumption, and that the foreign offices of Europe should have attached no little significance to any of its observations on international affairs. Of the truth of this we have one very striking illustration.

While Livingston was Secretary of State, James Buchanan was the American Minister at St. Petersburg, charged with the negotiation of a highly important commercial treaty. All went well until the terms of the treaty had been practically agreed upon, when he had an interview with the brilliant Count Nesselrode, Minister of Foreign Affairs, who protested against what he termed the unfriendly attitude of the American press toward the Emperor and Russia, apropos of Poland. Not only, he complained, had the "Globe," which he characterized as "the Government paper," failed to correct the false impressions of the press generally, but it "had itself been distinguished by falsehoods." He hoped, therefore, that the President "would adopt measures to remove this cause of complaint in the future, at least against the official paper in Washington." [2] Recovering as quickly as possible from his astonishment, Buchanan explained that the press in the United States was not subject to governmental supervision, but the practical-minded Nesselrode was not at all impressed. He baldly charged that the "Globe" "formed an exception to the rule and was a paper over which the Government exercised a direct control." Such being the Russian understanding, the Count was disappointed at the failure of

[1] *Cong. Globe*, June 3, 1836.

[2] Buchanan to Livingston, Buchanan's *Works*, II, 299.

Livingston, when he had met the Russian Minister to the United States in New York City, to offer assurances that no more offensive articles would appear in that journal, and even more chagrined to learn, after that interview, that the "Globe" had been "more violent than before." Buchanan was forced to concede that the "Globe" was commonly called the "official paper," but earnestly protested that it was free from governmental control. He was "persuaded that even the influence of Mr. Livingston over the editor" was not much greater than his own, and he had no influence at all. Here Buchanan was on safe ground, but Nesselrode was not so easily convinced. With a disconcerting smile of incredulity, he suggested that "General Jackson himself must certainly have some influence over the editor." Finding himself in a blind alley, Buchanan was lamely admitting that the President might have such influence, when Nesselrode, taking instant advantage of the admission, and without waiting for the conclusion of the sentence, requested him to ask Jackson to "exercise it for the purpose of inducing the 'Globe' to pursue a more cautious course hereafter." Buchanan, glad of the opportunity to drop the subject, hastened to assure the Count that it would afford him great pleasure "to make his wishes known to the President." [1]

Thus, such was the genius of Blair and Kendall in impressing themselves upon the affairs of the Nation that, within three years after the establishment of the "Globe," they had become political powers in the Republic, and so much international figures that their editorials were carefully read in the foreign offices of Europe.

Of the members of the Kitchen Cabinet, Lewis's influence in determining the political fate of men, and Hill's in establishing the system of spoils, were of no small importance, but the publicity work of Blair and Kendall, more than any other one thing, contributed to the solidarity of the party, and the

[1] Buchanan's *Works*, II, 300–01.

general popularity of Jackson and his measures. Benton, Van Buren, Forsyth, were masterful managers of Jackson's congressional battles, where he frequently lost to Clay, but the practical politicians of the Kitchen Cabinet, through the free use of patronage and the press, aroused and organized the masses with the ballots for the succession of successful battles at the polls.

CHAPTER VII

CLAY LEADS THE PARTY ONSLAUGHT

I

HENRY CLAY sat in the little library at Ashland reading a letter from Webster. "You must be aware of the strong desire manifested in many parts of the country that you should come into the Senate," the letter ran. "The wish is entertained here as earnestly as elsewhere. We are to have an interesting and arduous session. Everything is to be attacked. An array is preparing much more formidable than has ever yet assaulted what we think the leading and important public interests. Not only the tariff, but the Constitution itself, in its elemental and fundamental provisions, will be assailed with talent, vigor, and union. Everything is to be debated as if nothing had ever been settled. It would be an infinite gratification to me to have your aid, or rather, your lead. I know nothing so likely to be useful. Everything valuable in the government is to be fought for and we need your arm in the fight."

The meaning was perfectly clear to Clay. The man in the White House, contrary to Whig expectations, was disclosing masterful qualities of leadership. The veto of the Maysville and Lexington Turnpike Bills had left no room for doubt as to his attitude toward internal improvements. No Executive had ever before so freely exercised the power of presidential rejection.[1] On the tariff he was known to favor such reasonable reductions as would conciliate the Southern States, and his brief reference to the National Bank in his first Message, disconcerting in itself, had been followed by ominously hos-

[1] The public improvement feature of internal improvement was of less importance with the politician than the pork-barrel phase. See Schouler's *History*.

tile action on the part of several State Legislatures.[1] Meanwhile Jackson's candidacy for reëlection was practically announced. Major Lewis, in his subterranean manner, had been busy and with the usual results. The "New York Courier and Enquirer," organ of Van Buren, was advocating his reëlection, and the President's followers, quietly encouraged by Kendall and Lewis, had placed him in nomination in the legislatures of five States.

Under these conditions the old party of Adams grew restive and impatient for a strong leader, and instinctively turned to the magnetic figure of Ashland. Already his nomination for the Presidency in 1832 was a foregone conclusion. The enthusiastic acclaim which had greeted him on his political tours during his retirement had impressed his sanguine temperament as a sure omen of success. He would have preferred to have remained in retirement pending the election, but the party demand for his leadership in Washington was insistent. The Opposition needed a figure around which it could rally, and as a party leader Webster was a failure. With much reluctance Clay decided to respond to the call. The election in Kentucky had been a keen disappointment, and the enemies of the Administration had a bare majority in the legislature, but it was enough, and he was elected.

Early in November he reached the capital, "borne up by the undying spirit of ambition," looking "well and animated," to be received with "the most marked deference and respect." [2] From this time on, throughout Jackson's Presidency, he was to remain the brilliant, resourceful, bitter, and unscrupulous leader of the Opposition — as brilliant and remarkable an Opposition as has ever confronted a Government in this or any other country.

And such a politician! There have been few remotely like him, none his superior in personal popularity. His unpre-

[1] Benton's *Thirty Years' View*, I, 187.
[2] *First Forty Years*, Nov. 7, 1831.

cedented sway over a party was due, in large measure, to his remarkably fascinating personality, his audacity and dash, his amazing powers of ingratiation, and his superb eloquence which acted upon the spirit of the party workers like the sound of a bugle to a battle charger. No American orator, perhaps, has ever approached his effect upon a partisan audience. Fluent, and at times capable of passages of inspired eloquence, a consummate master of the implements of sarcasm and ridicule, his was the oratory that moves men to action. He could lash his followers to fury or move them to tears. His speeches often lacked literary finish, and, at times, in their colloquialisms descended beneath the dignity of the man's position, but even these occasional descents to buffoonery contributed to his popularity. He often spoke the language of the people — Webster and Calhoun, never. The contribution of new ideas to a discussion was not his forte. But he could gather up the material at hand, and weave it into a speech of fervent declamation which created the momentary impression that he was breaking virgin soil. His oratory was in his personality and his delivery. His voice was an exquisite musical instrument, with a clarion note that carried his words to the outskirts of the greatest throng. When he spoke, his expressive countenance glowed with his genius, his eyes flashed or caressed, his commanding figure seemed to grow, and in his combined dignity and grace he looked the part of the splendid commander of men, and the inspiring crusader of a cause. No man of his time, among all the great orators of that golden age, could so hold an audience literally spell-bound, Prentiss alone approaching him.

In personal intercourse, no politician ever possessed more of the seductive graces. There his magnetism was compelling. When he cared to put forth all his powers of attraction, no one could withstand his charm. Webster was godlike and compelled admiration; Clay was human and commanded love. Calhoun once said of him: "I don't like Clay. He is a bad man, an impostor, a creature of wicked schemes. I won't speak to him, but, by God, I love him!" His effect on both men and women has been ascribed to the fact that, masculine and virile though he was, he possessed feminine qualities that led to a sentimental feeling toward him. Men would follow him, knowing him to be wrong; stake their political fortunes on him, though they knew it would mean their own undoing; and women wept over his defeats and idolized him as a god.

As a political leader he was an opportunist. He often changed his tack to meet the passing breeze, but with the exception of his Bank reversal nothing could force him to admit it. As we proceed with the story of the party battles of the Jackson Administrations, we shall be impressed at times with his capability for trickery, demagogy, misrepresentation, deliberate misinterpretation, and dogmatic arrogance with his own friends and supporters. He brooked no equals. He accepted no rebuke and few suggestions, and led his party with a high-handedness that would have wrecked a lesser man.

His personal habits were not the best, and yet they were not of a nature that greatly shocked his generation. Adams thought him "only half educated" and was disgusted by the looseness of his public and his private morals.[1] But Adams was not in harmony with his times. Clay was an inveterate gambler — but so were a large portion of the public men in the Washington of the Thirties. And while a heavy drinker, he does not appear to have often been noticeably under the influence, as was Webster. But these vices never interfered with his work or diverted him for a moment from the pursuit of his ambition.

It was a militant figure that strode down the Avenue to the Capitol to lead the fight, with the stride of an Indian, his well-shaped feet encased in shoes instead of the boots

[1] Adams's *Memoirs*.

generally worn at the time, and fastidiously attired as was his wont — a Henry Clay, in shining armor, his sword shimmering.

II

FIVE days after Congress convened, the Baltimore Convention nominated Clay for the high office he long had sought. It had been inevitable from the hour he rode out of Washington after the inauguration on his way to Baltimore. During his retirement, his letters of 1829 and 1830 furnish proof of his candidacy, albeit he carefully conveyed the impression that he was a little indifferent to the nomination, and more than doubtful of the result of the election.[1] In a letter to a political follower he early predicted that if Jackson could unite New York, Virginia, and Pennsylvania upon his candidacy, opposition would be futile.[2] Two months later, Webster assured him of the support of Massachusetts, but feared that a first nomination from that State would "only raise the cry of coalition revived."[3] And three days after his nomination at Baltimore, Clay had written of his skepticism of success, with the encouraging comment: "Something, however, may turn up (and that must be our encouraging hope) to give a brighter aspect to our affairs."[4] Thus, when he entered the Senate we may be sure that it was with the fixed determination that something should "turn up." It was his belief, as we have seen, that Jackson's election depended upon his ability to carry Virginia, Pennsylvania, and New York. At the time he entertained no hope of diverting Virginia from Jackson, but he hoped to carry Pennsylvania or New York, or both. Upon the former he pinned his faith — and there the tariff was strong, and the National Bank had its headquarters there, with its ramifications into every

[1] Colton's *Life and Correspondence of Clay.*
[2] Clay to Senator Johnson, Clay's *Works*, IV, 265.
[3] Clay's *Works*, IV, 275.
[4] *Ibid.*, IV, 321.

section of the country. His platform had been carefully thought out and thoroughly discussed in the correspondence of 1829 and 1830. It embraced internal improvements, a protective tariff, and the rechartering of the Bank. Thus, when Congress met, the Opposition candidate and his platform were before the people, and the congressional battles of the session were but heavy skirmishes preliminary to the battle for the Presidency.

As he looked over the personnel of Congress, Clay must have rejoiced over his advantage. There, by his side, sat Webster, with all the prestige of his great name and in all the splendor of his genius. Presiding still over the deliberations of the Senate was the stern-visaged political philosopher and sage who had definitely broken with Jackson — Calhoun. It could not have taken him long to discover, in the young Hercules with the harshly carven features, the brilliant possibilities of John M. Clayton. And there, harboring a secret grudge, and suffering acutely from the wounds inflicted on his mentor in the chair, sat the eloquent Hayne, meditating revenge. In Thomas Ewing of Ohio, a robust partisan and able debater, he found a fighter after his own heart. And while they were of the State Rights persuasion, and hostile to the tariff and internal improvements, he could scarcely have failed to catch in the eyes of the erudite Tazewell and Tyler of Virginia something of a promise that was to be fulfilled.

And against him, he saw John Forsyth and Benton, men of character and power, supported by Felix Grundy and Hugh White, "Ike" Hill and Mahlon Dickerson of New Jersey.

His was manifestly the advantage in the Senate.

But in the House his advantage was much greater, for among the members of the Opposition was the most brilliant array of great orators ever assembled in a single Congress. John Quincy Adams had reëntered public life as a Representative from Quincy — as full of fire and pepper as ever in his youth; Edward Everett, the most scholarly and polished orator of his generation; Rufus Choate, the greatest forensic orator the Republic has produced; Richard Henry Wilde, who combined the qualities of a graceful poet, a vigorous debater and eloquent orator, and a sound scholar; Tom Corwin, the wit and the slashing master of polemics; and greater perhaps than all, as a congressional orator, the fiery and indomitable George McDuffie of South Carolina.

And against this combination the best the Administration could do was to put forth the commonplace plodder James K. Polk, assisted by Churchill C. Cambreleng of New York.

If Jackson had the advantage of position, Clay had all the prestige of genius on his side. Thus the two parties faced each other for the battle.

III

A LESS provocative Message than that with which Jackson opened the Congress could hardly have been penned. It was conciliatory and in good taste. But Clay's voice was for war. It was his determination that something should "turn up," if he had to turn it up, for the purposes of the election, and he had instilled his spirit into his followers. Instantly the gage of battle was thrown down in the consideration of the nomination of Van Buren as Minister to England. A pettier piece of party politics is scarcely found in the history of the Senate. Among all the Opposition Senators, there were probably none who doubted his capacity or questioned his integrity. With the Calhoun faction it was personal spite; with Clay, Webster, and Clayton it was partisan spleen. Six months before, Van Buren had ridden out of Washington with Jackson by his side, and had sailed for England. In London he was at once received into the most brilliant society. He became an intimate of the Duke of Wellington, and Talleyrand, Ambassador from France, cultivated him, while Rogers, the poet, entertained him frequently at his famous breakfasts. He had been charged with an important mission — nothing less than the negotiation of an agreement that would prevent the recurrence of the causes of estrangement between the two peoples growing out of the occurrences incidental to England's participation in European wars.[1] Welcomed to the most exclusive drawing-rooms, cultivated by the most powerful of English statesmen, with the prestige in London of having adjusted, while in the State Department, the long-standing differences relative to the West Indian trade, he was in position to achieve triumphs for his country when his nomination was sent to the Senate.

And there, Clay, Webster, and Calhoun eagerly awaited its coming. They had been busily engaged for weeks in preparing the attack. Each drew all his particular friends into the conspiracy, many of them entering reluctantly rather than incur their displeasure. The charges against Van Buren were transparently political. The Calhoun faction were prepared to contend that he had engineered the quarrel of the President and the Vice-President and had disrupted the Cabinet. Clay's special point was to be that he had introduced the policy of proscription, destined to destroy American institutions, and he was to join with Webster in viciously assailing him for his instructions to our Minister to England in the negotiations on the West Indian trade.

The latter reason for refusing to confirm the nomination of Van Buren was the only one that rose to the dignity of a pretense. For some time the United States had been negotiating with London for the opening of trade in American vessels between this country and the British possessions, but without success. During the preceding Administration, while Clay was Secretary of State, extravagant claims were advanced by the American Government, and, by angering England, had only served to make a settlement more remote. When Van Buren became Secretary of State, and McLane

[1] Jackson refers to his instructions in his Message of December, 1831.

was sent to London, he was charged with the duty of reopening negotiations, and was given certain instructions for his guidance. Among these was the abandonment of the untenable claims of Clay, and the concession of the British point of view upon them. This was denounced as a weakness and a surrender, and as an intentional reflection upon the previous Administration for party purposes. As a matter of record, the instructions furnished McLane by Van Buren were predicated upon the report submitted to Clay, after the failure of the preceding negotiations, by Albert Gallatin, the Minister to England under Adams.[1] It consequently follows that when Clay, thoroughly familiar with his own Minister's report to him, and with the fact that Van Buren had merely followed it in his preparation of the instructions, vehemently denounced the latter for deliberately and maliciously reflecting upon the previous Administration, he was tricking the Senate and the country. He, at least, knew better. And the mere fact that McLane was further instructed to stress the fact that the preceding Administration had been repudiated by the people at the polls, and the new régime should not be held accountable for the mistakes of the old, while in doubtful taste, was scarcely an offense so heinous as to justify the proposed humiliation of Van Buren.[2] The other charges had less substance. It has never been convincingly shown that Van Buren had any part in engineering the quarrel between Jackson and Calhoun, and years after retiring from the Presidency, Jackson solemnly exonerated him from any complicity.[3] Equally unproved, and unprovable, was the claim that he had precipitated the Cabinet crisis, and the charge that he had introduced the policy of proscription might well have emanated from some one other than Clay.

[1] Benton, by quoting the instructions and Gallatin's report, shows the dishonesty of the simulated indignation. (*Thirty Years' View*, I, 216–17.)

[2] Rufus King had furnished a precedent when he described the John Adams Administration to the British. (King's *Works*.)

[3] Benton's *Thirty Years' View*, I, 217.

The clear intent of the conspiracy was to destroy Van Buren and his prospects for the Presidency.

When the nomination reached the Senate, nothing was done for five weeks. Meanwhile the leaders of the conspiracy were carefully preparing their speeches for publication and wide distribution. On the submission of the report, the venom behind the remarkable procrastination was revealed in a resolution, entrusted to one of the lesser lights,[1] to recommit the nomination with instructions to investigate the disruption of the Cabinet and whether Van Buren had "participated in any practices disreputable to the national character." This, offered as a weak contribution to the attempt to blacken Van Buren's reputation, having served its purpose, was withdrawn without action. Then the orators began. One after another, with a cheap simulation of sorrowful regret over the necessity of injuring an amiable man, poured forth his protest against the nomination. Clay, of course, made a slashing onslaught. Webster confined himself to attacking the victim because of his instructions to McLane. Clayton and Ewing, Hayne and seven others recited their elaborately prepared partisan harangues under the approving eye of Calhoun in the chair.

The principal reply, and only four were made, was that of Senator John Forsyth, the accomplished floor leader of the Administration, and one of the most eloquent and resourceful of men. He vigorously protested against a partisan crucifixion, and sarcastically commended the fine public spirit of Senators who could voluntarily bring such distress upon themselves to serve the public good. This fling went home to many. Hayne, in later years, admitted that he had spoken and voted against his judgment at the behest of party,[2] and John Tyler, who was incapable of a pose, voted for the confirmation, "not that I liked the man overmuch," but because he could find no principle to justify his rejection, and

[1] Senator Holmes of Maine. [2] Jervey's *Robert Y. Hayne.*

did not care to join "the notoriously factious opposition . . . who oppose everything favored by the Administration." [1] Indeed, the cooler and wiser heads among the enemies of the Administration considered the attack a serious political blunder. Adams, on learning of the plan, warned that "to reject the nomination would bring him [Van Buren] back with increased power to do mischief here." [2] And Thurlow Weed, of the "Albany Journal," uncannily wise and prophetic, sounded a solemn warning through his editorial columns that such persecution of Van Buren "would change the complexion of his prospects from despair to hope." The plan persisted in, and "he would return home as a persecuted man, and throw himself upon the sympathy of the party, be nominated for Vice-President, and huzzahed into office at the heels of General Jackson." [3]

This was the view of Kendall and Blair, and of Benton, who refused to participate in the Senate debate. The latter felt that, though "rejection was a bitter medicine, there was health at the bottom of the draught." He alone among the senatorial friends of the rejected Minister appears to have had the prescience to appreciate the ultimate advantage. To one Senator, rejoicing over the rejection, he turned with triumphant mien: "You have broken a Minister and made a Vice-President." But the enemies of the Administration and of the victim were jubilant. "It will kill him, sir, kill him dead; he will never kick, sir, never kick," exclaimed Calhoun in the presence of "Old Bullion." [4] And there was an immediate reaction. Instead of killing, it made Van Buren. He instantly became a party martyr, and idol.

On the evening of the day the news of his rejection reached London, Van Buren appeared at a party at Talleyrand's, smiling, suave, undisturbed, as though he had scored a tri-

[1] *Letters and Times of the Tylers*, I, 427.
[2] Adams's *Memoirs*, Dec. 22, 1831.
[3] Weed's *Autobiography*, 375.
[4] Benton's *Thirty Years' View*, I, 219.

umph. It was probably on that day that he heard from Benton, urging that he hold himself free for the Vice-Presi dency.

The speeches of Clay, Webster, Hayne, and Clayton were published, the veil of secrecy having been lifted from the executive session for this party purpose, and the effect was wholly different from that expected. It had been the part of Kendall and Blair to see to that. While the Senators were talking, they had been busy with their pens, and when the action was taken the Democratic press furiously denounced the rejection, the rank and file of the party rose *en masse* to proclaim the victim a martyr, mass meetings were called in New York, Philadelphia, and Albany to arraign the Senate, and the Democratic members of the New York Legislature sent the President a letter of condolence. The Legislature of New Jersey declared that after its favorite son, Senator Dickerson, its choice for Vice-President would be the martyr. And Isaac Hill took the stump in New Hampshire to denounce Webster as disloyal to friendship and as a sniveling hypocrite.[1]

But the success of the conspiracy acted upon Clay like the taste of blood on a tiger, and with an insinuative reference to Livingston's indebtedness to the Government, which he knew had been discharged to the penny, he would have applied the political proscription of the Whigs to the philosopher in the State Department but for the indignant protest of Dallas. Thus the character of the fight to be waged against the Administration was clearly revealed within a month after Clay's return to public life.

IV

THE first month, too, witnessed an assault on the most vulnerable point of the Administration lines, and an open invitation to Calhoun and the Nullifiers to join their political

[1] Bradley's *Life of Hill.*

fortunes with the party of Clay. Both the attack and the invitation came from John M. Clayton, who was almost to rival Clay in the leadership of the Whigs, and to surpass him in some of the qualities of leadership. When he entered the Senate practically unknown, he was the youngest member of that body, but there was enough in his physical appearance and bearing to set him out in any group as one destined to command. Over six feet in height, his figure well filled out; of clear complexion, with large gray eyes of intellectual power, and an enormous, superbly shaped head, he looked both the physical and mental giant. It only required the personal contact to attract men to him as steel shavings are attracted to the magnet. His manner was easy and graceful, his disposition kindly and benevolent, his wit keen, his conversational powers far beyond the average. With a remarkable memory and an unusual gift for analysis, he entered the Senate well equipped in a thorough knowledge of literature and history. He had great talents and just fell short of genius. As an orator, he was logical, forceful, at times dramatic and eloquent. Hating the Jacksonians, he surveyed the field for an opportunity to attack, and he found it in the Post-Office Department.

One of Jackson's most unfortunate appointments had been that of Barry as Postmaster-General. A genial and likable politician, a loyal friend, an ardent champion of the President, and, personally, a man of undoubted integrity, he was pitifully lacking in business ability, in a capacity for organization, and was all too credulous of his subordinates. Within two years after Jackson's inauguration, the politicians knew that his department offered a rich field for investigation. Knowing this, Clayton introduced his celebrated resolution inquiring into its abuses. That the Administration circles were not at all satisfied that nothing could be uncovered is evident in the excitement the resolution caused, and every effort was made by Administration Senators to block it.

In his initial speech in support of his resolution, Clayton sounded the keynote of the Whig campaign against the proscriptive policies of Jackson, but more significant still was his appeal, the first openly made, to Calhoun, to join with the followers of Clay in a concerted assault upon the Administration.

While the young Senator from Delaware was speaking, Calhoun sat in the chair of the presiding officer. Turning in his direction, Clayton made the first bold bid for his support of the party Opposition.

"But it will be seen," he said, "whether there be not one man in this nation to breast its [Administration's] terrors whenever the President hurls his thunders. There are hawks abroad, sir. Rumor alleges that that plundering falcon has recently swooped upon a full-fledged eagle that never yet flinched from a contest, and, as might be naturally expected, all await the result with intense interest. It is given out that the intended victim of proscription now is one distinguished far above all in office for the vigor and splendor of his intellect. . . . But if that integrity and fairness which have heretofore characterized him through life do not desert him in this hour of greatest peril, we may yet live to see one, who has been marked out as a victim, escape unscathed even by that power which has thus far prostrated alike the barriers of public law and the sanctity of private reputation."

The appeal was entirely unnecessary, if not intended merely as a public tribute to a newly acquired ally, for Calhoun and his friends were already hostile to the Administration. It is historically interesting only in that it shows the cleverness of the National Republicans, soon to adopt the name of Whigs, in undertaking to coalesce with all elements of the Opposition, no matter how divergent, or even inconsistent, the causes leading to the disaffection.

Thus, within a few weeks after the assumption of the leadership by Clay, we find Jackson's favorite humiliated by the rejection of his nomination; another wantonly insulted by the questioning of his personal integrity; a movement launched to blacken the Administration through an investigation of its most vulnerable department; and a plan conceived for the consummation of an unholy alliance of incongruous elements.

V

MEANWHILE Clay, devoted to the protective tariff policy, anxious to save it from crucifixion by consent, and with a political eye on the political effect of his championship in Pennsylvania, without which he thought Jackson's reëlection impossible, had been busy formulating a new tariff which was to create more party clashes.

Within a month after Congress met, he called a meeting of the friends of the protective tariff to determine plans for party action. The then existing "tariff of abominations" [1] was doomed by public opinion. Two months before he wrote a friend acknowledging a revision inevitable, and announcing plans for one not compromising to the protective principle.[2] The conference called by Clay met at the home of Edward Everett, Representative from Boston, with the presidential nominee himself presiding. He summoned his friends, not to consult, but to take orders. He disclosed his plan — a repeal of all duties on tea, coffee, spices, indigo, and similar articles, and thereby reduce the revenue as much as seven millions that year without interfering with the prevailing duties that had been imposed for protective purposes. Jackson intended to destroy the protective system through the accumulation of revenue. It was the duty of its friends to save it through the reductions proposed.

If we may accept Adams as a faithful reporter, Clay's manner was "exceedingly peremptory and dogmatical."

[1] So described by Senator Smith of Maryland.
[2] Clay to Brooke, Clay's *Works*, IV, 314.

Various questions, indicative of doubt, were asked. Everett, mindful of the ominous protest of the South, thought the plan might be interpreted as "setting the South at defiance" Adams, who had a mind of his own, reported that the Committee on Manufactures in the House, of which he was chairman, was "already committed upon the principle that the reduction of the duties should be prospective, and not to commence until after the extinguishment of the public debt"; and he suggested that the Clay plan would be, not only "a defiance of the South, but of the President and the Administration." The spirit of Clay is well disclosed in his none too gracious reply that "to preserve, maintain, and strengthen the American System, he would defy the South, the President, and the Devil; that if the Committee on Manufactures had committed themselves . . . they had given a very foolish and improvident pledge; and that there was no necessity for the payment of the debt by the 4th of March, 1833."

This led to some debate between the former President and his premier, with Adams insisting that Jackson's desire to extinguish the debt should be "indulged and not opposed," and that the President's idea "would take greatly with the people." This view piqued and mortified Clay, who had found all the party leaders in the conference becomingly obsequious with the exception of Adams. That Adams was equally disgusted we may gather from his description of Clay's manner as "super-presidential," and from the following entry in his journal: "Clay's motives are obvious. He sees, that next November, at the choice of presidential electors, the great and irresistible electioneering cry will be the extinguishment of the public debt. By instant repeal of the duties he wants to withdraw seven or eight millions from the Treasury and make it impossible to extinguish it by the 3rd of March, 1833. It is an electioneering movement, and this was the secret of these movements, as well as of the desperate efforts to take the whole business of the reduction of the tariff into his own hands." [1] The Democratic opinion that Clay was partly actuated by a petty partisan desire to deprive the Administration of the credit for wiping out the national debt, corroborated as it is by Adams, is plausible enough. At the same time, it was manifestly Clay's purpose to rally the protected industries to his standard in the presidential campaign.

Meanwhile the lobbyists of the protected interests, flocking to the capital, crowded the rotunda every morning, mixing with the statesmen. Here, at the time, was the Republic in miniature — lobbyists, statesmen, correspondents, and plebeians mingling in a common arena, with the visiting tourists ranged about to view the celebrities in their moments of conversational unbending.[2] Clay made the presentation of his plan the opportunity for his first political speech of his campaign. The Senate was crowded to hear him. It was not enough that he should acknowledge the approach of the extinguishment of the public debt, and base his argument for the reduction of duties upon that fact. The possibility of the passing of the debt during the Administration of Jackson was clearly annoying, and he attempted, laboriously, and at considerable length, to deprive it of any credit. The plan of the Administration to reduce no duties on unprotected articles previous to March, 1833, and to make a gradual and prospective reduction on protected articles, he denounced as a scheme to "destroy the protecting system by a slow but certain poison." There was nothing remarkable in his first speech except its affectation of modesty, and his reference to old age and declining power.

But he was soon to find the incentive for his greatest speech upon the tariff. Hayne attacked the protective system with all the vigor and venom of a Nullificationist in the making; and Clay replied in the brilliant fighting protec-

[1] Adams's *Memoirs*, Dec. 22, 1831. [2] *Perley's Reminiscences*, I, 46.

tionist speech which ranks as one of the masterful efforts of his life, and was to be used as a textbook for the advocates of the system for fifty years. Read even to-day, after the lapse of almost a century, it has a familiar sound, and transmits its pulsations from the printed page as though the reader felt the heartbeat of the orator.

Among the Southerners in the Senate, this speech created the greatest excitement and the gravest forebodings, with John Tyler assailing both the principle of protection and the method of framing bills under the principle. But the most significant note struck by Tyler was the warning that the continuance of the protective policy would inevitably lead to the disruption of the Union. The speeches of both Clay and Tyler were sent broadcast over the country. That of the former delighted protectionists and impressed all. Harrison Gray Otis wrote enthusiastically from Boston, but both James Madison and James Barbour gently questioned the taste of the partisan attack on Albert Gallatin as a "foreigner."[1] Highly complimentary letters were received by Tyler from John Marshall and James Madison, both of whom favored the reduction of the tariff.[2]

And throughout it all, Clay found himself unable to maneuver Jackson or his friends into a position of opposition to the system. Amos Kendall and Blair had their hopes tied to another issue. They had no thought of sacrificing the electoral vote of the Keystone State. The leaders of the Senate opposition to the tariff were Hayne and Tyler, neither of whom was longer considered as in the confidence of the President. Clay's speech, widely distributed in Pennsylvania, Ohio, and New York, proved him a champion of the system, but nothing occurred in the Senate to prove Jackson an enemy. This was the situation when the real battle was transferred to the House of Representatives.

[1] Clay's *Works*, IV, 328–29.

[2] *Letters and Times of the Tylers*, I, 438.

VI

THROUGH some trickery or blunder, that portion of the Presidential Message relating to "relieving the people from unnecessary taxation after the extinguishment of the public debt," was referred to the Committee on Ways and Means a majority of whose members were hostile to the protective system; and to the Committee on Manufactures was referred that part concerning "manufactures and the modification of the tariff" — a dual reference of the same subject to rival committees. At the head of the Committee on Manufactures was John Quincy Adams — certainly not a spokesman of the Administration; and the chairman of the Committee on Ways and Means was George McDuffie of South Carolina, a protégé of Calhoun, and now an implacable foe of Jackson.

In feverish haste McDuffie, representing the extreme free-trade school, began the preparation of his report and the formulation of his bill to get in before the more deliberate Adams. He proceeded independently of the forthcoming report and tentative Administration measure from Secretary McLane, such was his precipitation. Adams, more considerate, awaited the report, in the meanwhile making many morning calls upon the Secretary.[1] Strangely enough, the former President had favorably impressed many Southerners by his admission that existing rates were unfair to the South. His position, as on a more notable occasion later, was unique. Even Jackson was actively making overtures to him. The ever-convenient Colonel Johnson of Tecumseh fame, approaching the old Puritan with a suggestion of a reconciliation, tactfully hinted that he thought the President should make the first move. The cautious Adams, not at all averse, reminded the emissary that Jackson had broken, not he; to which Johnson replied that the General had been poisoned by "scoundrel office-seekers" when he first reached the capi-

[1] Adams in his *Memoirs* makes numerous references to these calls.

tal. Would Adams dine at the White House, if invited? The wily old man parried with the reminder that such would only be the courtesy customarily accorded all members. But would Adams dine at the White House with a small and select company? He would not — and on similar grounds. At the end of his rope, the anxious Johnson asked Adams for a suggestion, only to receive the reply that it was a matter for Jackson to decide.[1] The next day Adams received a note from Johnson to the effect that Jackson had "expressed great satisfaction" over the conversation and sent his "personal regards and friendship," together with the assurance that he was "anxious to have social and friendly intercourse restored." Thinking it over, the suspicious Adams could not but meditate upon the attacks from Clay's friends if he should cross the threshold of the White House — and there the matter appears to have rested finally.[2]

There has never been another character in American history quite like Adams. His real portrait, self-painted, peers at the world from between the covers of his monumental diary, in which he communed with himself unreservedly, and expressed his opinion of men and their motives with brutal frankness. He was a professional statesman of a high order. Entering upon diplomatic duties in his youth, he knew the cross-currents of world politics at an age when most Americans are laboriously projecting themselves into the politics of their immediate neighborhood. From his earliest years he had been in contact with great minds, and with men of power and broad vision. A thorough scholar, he was, at the same time, a man of the world. Conscious of his ability and his advantages, cold and reserved, and dignified to the point of frigidity, it is not difficult to understand his supercilious attitude toward men less favored, and yet placed in lofty station. Inspired by the highest ideals of public service, holding himself under such rigid discipline as to have

[1] Adams's *Memoirs*, March 2, 1832. [2] *Ibid.*, March 3, 1832.

made himself immune to the small vices, placing duty above friendship, scarcely ever yielding his dignity to mirth, and on those rare occasions smiling sardonically, he stood upon an isolated peak — of humanity, and yet separated from it.[1] No one living the monastic life could have lived more by rule, or have scourged himself more faithfully to his tasks.

Of friendships, he knew little from experience. Naturally of a suspicious disposition, he suspected treachery where it was not. Holding to no ordinary standard of perfection, he could not forgive the imperfections of his fellows. Even the transcendent genius of Clay could not hide from him the great man's lack of education. One searches the pages of his diary in eager quest of some complimentary references — there are scarcely any. That he bitterly realized his isolation is clearly disclosed. "I am a man of reserve," he wrote, "cold, austere and forbidding manners. My political adversaries say a gloomy misanthrope; my personal enemies, an unsocial savage. With a knowledge of the actual defects of my character, I have not had the pliability to reform it." That such a man, entertaining such an opinion of his own merits and the failings of his contemporaries, should have consented to serve in the lower House of Congress, after having served in the Presidency, can only mean that he loved his country and sought the opportunity for service. That it was not to punish his enemies, we shall find on more than one occasion when he took his stand with the Administration of the man who displaced him. Not least among the merits of Adams was his capacity to work in serious coöperation with McLane in the moulding of the tariff of 1832.

Quite a different type, and in some respects a greater genius, was George McDuffie. His career was a mingling of romance and tragedy. A child of poverty, the protégé of a Calhoun,[2]

[1] March, in his *Reminiscences of Congress*, describes him as "cold, passionless and inscrutable as the Egyptian sphinx, whose fate, too, his own resembled."

[2] Brother of John C.

he had while yet in college been regarded "as a young man of extraordinary talents," albeit at that time "he had not that passionate and eloquent declamation which he was afterwards to display in Congress."[1] After hearing his great speech on the tariff in 1827, Josiah Quincy, who heard him, described him as "the most sensational orator of the time."[2] In the fight against the Panama Mission, Sargent thought him "decidedly the most violent and aggressive speaker arrayed against the Administration."[3] His passionate and impulsive nature frequently led to personal encounters; and in reaching an understanding of his irritable and sour disposition, it is profitable to know that just before entering Congress he had been wounded in the spine in a duel, and never afterwards knew a day free from personal discomfort. This wound, which ultimately killed him, changed a good-tempered and jovial man into the irritable, morose, and nervous creature known to history.[4] The indifference of the protectionists to the interests of the South, and the intemperate attacks of the abolitionists upon the Southern people, acted upon the diseased genius as an irritant and drove him to extremes. Even so, he rejected Nullification as a remedy, and insisted that the sole recourse of the Southerners was revolution.[5] Intellectually honest, morally clean, physically ailing, he put such of himself as he cared for the world to see into his public acts. He withdrew into himself — taciturn, lonely. "A spare, grim looking man, who was an admirer of Milton, and who was never known to smile or jest," as Perley Poore describes him.[6] His health gone, his life uncertain, an idolized wife taken from him within a year, his leader's

[1] O'Neall's *Bench and Bar of South Carolina.*

[2] *Figures of the Past.*

[3] *Public Men and Events*, I, 117.

[4] O'Neall's *Bench and Bar of South Carolina.*

[5] "I know that he had no faith in Nullification." (O'Neall.) "It would seem that he was willing to rest the case of the State upon the bare right of revolution." (David F. Houston's *Study of Nullification in South Carolina.*)

[6] *Perley's Reminiscences*, I, 81.

aspirations wrecked, his section threatened, it is not strange that he poured forth on Andrew Jackson such torrents of eloquent vituperation.

VII

Standing not on ceremony, McDuffie hastened to report a bill, accompanied by an elaborate report in the nature of an indictment of the protective system, which "ought to be abandoned with all convenient and practical despatch, upon every principle of justice, patriotism and sound policy." The bill provided an immediate reduction of duties on all articles except iron, steel, salt, cotton-bagging, hemp and flax, and on everything made of cotton, wool, and iron, to a basis of twenty-five per cent ad valorem. On the excepted articles the reduction was to be gradual, tumbling to twenty-five per cent at once, to eighteen and three quarters per cent on June 30, 1833, and to twelve and a half per cent one year later.

With Adams still laboring on his bill, McDuffie called his up with a slashing speech. This prodigiously long philippic was historical in that it tended to force the issue of Nullification a little earlier than its sponsors had planned.

In the meanwhile the Administration measure, with McLane's report, had been submitted, providing for the repeal of the existing tariff after March 3, 1833, and the reduction of the revenue to the financial requirements of the Government. This contemplated the reduction of the revenue to $12,000,000 a year, and the arrangement of the rates so as sufficiently to protect the great interests involved.

Using the Administration measure as a basis, Adams thereupon prepared his bill and report. In his statement the patriotic statesman, indifferent to the clamor of party, or class, or section, shines forth luminously. It may have been unnecessary to expose the protectionist's fallacy that raising the duties lowers the price of the domestic product; equally unnecessary to warn the Southerners that a persistence in their course would lead to appalling consequences, but he made these points. In presenting his bill, Adams frankly explained that it was based on the Administration measure, with some changes as to details.

With the Adams bill before it, the House made short shrift of the McDuffie measure. The protectionists were in despair. The Legislatures of Pennsylvania and Connecticut passed condemnatory resolutions, and mass meetings were held protesting against reductions. An unsuccessful attempt was made to substitute the Clay Senate plan. And yet Clay himself was fairly well satisfied, and on its passage in the House wrote that "with some alterations it will be a very good measure of protection."[1] At the time he wrote, however, he was convinced that the alterations would be made in the Senate and accepted by the House, and upon the failure of these plans to materialize hangs another story of politics.

The Senate lost no time making amendments, and as it was now July, with all anxious to adjourn, no time was wasted on unnecessary speeches, and the amendments, which were numerous, were hurried through. In a few instances, not many, the protectionists lost, but on the whole theirs was the victory when the bill went back to the House. There a few of the Senate amendments were accepted, but the majority were rejected and the bill was thrown into conference.

And here enters one of the comedy-tragedies of politics. Calhoun was absent, Tazewell in the chair, when the measure was returned to the Senate. The motion for a conference carried. And then it was, in the naming of the Senate conferees, that Tazewell either made a blunder or turned a trick. Hayne, named as the minority member, was expected to act badly, but the protectionists pinned implicit faith in Wilkins of Pennsylvania and Dickerson of New Jersey, the

[1] Clay to Brooke, Clay's *Works*, IV, 340.

former a business man, manufacturer, banker from a protectionist State, the latter with a powerful protectionist constituency. Unhappily the friends of the Senate bill did not attach sufficient importance to the candidacy of both men for the Vice-Presidential nomination with Jackson — to the pull of personal ambition. Whatever their special motives in surrendering to the conferees of the House, they gave only a perfunctory support to the Senate amendments and capitulated.

The amazement and indignation of Clay and his followers were unbounded. Clay sharply cross-examined Wilkins and Dickerson upon the proceedings in the conference, and then had to content himself by joining Webster in a warm denunciation of the surrender. There was nothing to be done, however, but for the Senate to recede, and the bill was passed and promptly signed by Jackson.

Thus the tariff battle on which Clay relied to strengthen him in the pre-presidential contest was practically barren of party significance. By no sophistry or reasoning could the protectionist States of Pennsylvania and New York be turned against Jackson, who had promptly signed the bill that Adams had sponsored, and which had been supported by such Administration Democrats as Isaac Hill, Dickerson, Marcy, Wilkins, Grundy, White, and Benton.

The tariff issue was dead before the campaign was fairly begun.

VIII

If Clay had failed to embarrass the Administration on the tariff, the keen Jacksonian politicians were to be more successful in embarrassing Clay on the land question. This was a peculiarly delicate subject for Clay to touch in the midst of the campaign. In the Southern and Western States more than 1,090,000,000 acres remained the property of the National Government — a vast empire. The proceeds from the sale of these lands had been originally dedicated to the payment of the national debt; and now with the extinguishment of the debt in sight, all manner of schemes were advanced as to the future disposition of the lands and the proceeds. For a number of years Benton, with characteristic tenacity, had been urging his plan of graduated prices, with free grants to actual settlers, and he had won Jackson over to his theory with Edmund Burke's proposition, advanced in his speech on the disposition of the crown lands in England, that the principal revenue to be had from uncultivated tracts "springs from the improvement of the population of the kingdom." The sturdy Missourian looked with repugnance upon the idea of considering these uncultivated acres as sources of revenue, rather than as an opportunity for settlers, and he gradually converted the Democratic Party to his point of view.

To make matters all the more embarrassing to Clay, his party had been placed in the position of deliberately withholding this vast domain from the axe of the pioneer and the spade of the cultivator, in the interest of the manufacturers of the East. This had resulted from the unfortunate wording of an official report of Richard Rush, a colleague of Clay's in the Cabinet of Adams, in which he had lamented the preference of the American people for agricultural over manufacturing pursuits. The report had been referred to Clay whose practiced political eye instantly saw the possibilities in the perversion or exaggeration of the meaning of these paragraphs, and he had fruitlessly urged their elimination. The Democrats were quick to grasp their opportunity. The protectionists, Clay and his friends, planned that the National Government should, by holding on to the lands, retard their settlement by maintaining prices prohibitive to the settler; they proposed to maintain a large labor market in the industrial labor centers of the East where competition would be keen enough to keep down wages. For the sake of the protected interests, they were ready to sacrifice the opportunities of the poor of the Eastern cities and make them the galley slaves of the factories; retard the development of the West, and immolate the national interest on the altar of greed. And there was just enough truth in these charges, rather luridly put forth, to make them exceedingly dangerous in a presidential year.

The issue had been accentuated by the suggestion of McLane, Secretary of the Treasury, that the public lands should be sold to the States in which they were located, and the proceeds apportioned among all the States in the Union. This, naturally enough, made an instant appeal to the States most intimately concerned, and six of the new Commonwealths hastened to petition Congress for the cession. This brought the subject before the Senate, and in the spring of 1832 two motions were submitted, one to inquire into the wisdom of reducing the price of the public lands, the other into the expediency of the McLane proposition.

And it was at this juncture that the Jacksonians turned the trick on Clay and forced him into the open as an aggressive enemy of the wishes of the new States. With a regular Senate Committee on Public Lands, composed of men intimately acquainted with the subject, the amazing motion was made and carried that the matter be referred to the Committee on Manufactures of which Clay was chairman. The friends of the candidate bitterly protested against the reference; and Clay himself "protested," "entreated," and "implored" that the reference be changed to the Committee on Public Lands. "I felt," he said later, "that the design was to place in my hands a many-edged instrument which I could not touch without being wounded."[1]

Unable to extricate himself from the embarrassment, Clay set to work, and in a short time submitted a report, accompanied by a bill, providing against the reduction of the price of

[1] Clay's *Works*, IV, 331.

the land, but for granting to Ohio, Indiana, Illinois, Alabama, Missouri, and Mississippi twelve and a half per cent of the proceeds from the sale of lands within their borders, to be applied to the purposes of education and internal improvements. This, of course, was a frank attempt to prevent the resentment of the people of these States from asserting itself at the polls. The remainder of the proceeds was then to be apportioned to the remaining States, according to their population, to be used for the schools, internal improvements, and negro colonization. The act was to remain in force for five years, provided no war intervened, in which event all the proceeds were to be used in defraying the expenses of the conflict. In this way Clay attempted to maintain the existing economic conditions while satisfying the new States whose electoral votes he sought.

If the political intent of the reference to Clay's committee had been in the least open to doubt, all such was removed by the action of the Senate in thereupon ordering the matter referred to the Committee on Public Lands. Again Clay vehemently protested. He had not wanted to report upon the subject. He had protested against the reference. But the reference having been made, and the report submitted, he protested anew against the reflection upon his committee implied by the new reference.

At the head of the Committee on Public Lands was Senator King of Alabama, but Clay was right in ascribing the authorship of the report, soon to be submitted, to Thomas H. Benton.[1] This report vigorously assailed the reasoning and conclusions of Clay; attacked the disposition to look upon the public lands as useful primarily for revenue and secondarily for settlement, and reversed the order; and deprecated the suggestion of the use of the money to be distributed

[1] "He [King] has availed himself of another's aid, and the hand of the Senator from Missouri is as visible in the composition, as if his name had been subscribed to the instrument." (Clay's speech of June 20, 1832.)

among the States for the colonization of the negroes as calculated to "light up the fires of the extinguished conflagration which lately blazed on the Missouri question." It favored the reduction of the price of land to one dollar per acre during the next five years; then to fifty cents, with fifteen per cent of the proceeds to be apportioned among the States. Whatever may have been the objections to the Democratic plan, it gave promise of an earlier redemption of the wilderness by the cultivation of man, and the more speedy enhancement of the land of the pioneers already in possession.

Keenly appreciative of the purpose of his enemies, Clay delivered a long and powerful speech, his second campaign speech in the Senate, plausibly defending his position, explaining Rush's meaning, and attempting to divert the greed of the new States into a different channel. That he made a profound impression may be properly assumed from the fact that the bill passed the Senate, although it was checked by a hostile House.

Thus his friends flattered themselves that he had scored a triumph and outwitted his foes. The old school politicians still gauged public opinion by the roll-calls of the Congress. The new school, which came in with Jackson, were least of all concerned with the views of the politicians at the capital. They were interesting themselves with the plain voters, and were devising means for reaching these in the campaign to follow. They had sensed the feelings and the prejudices and suspicions of the pioneers of the new States. They were an agricultural people and easily inflamed by the suggestion that their interests were to be subordinated or sacrificed to the interests of the Eastern industrial centers. They wanted the speedy felling of the forests, the cultivation of the fields, the building of homes and schools and churches, and the Benton plan of reduced prices and preëmption for actual settlers appealed to them as in harmony with their desires.

And thus, while the friends of Clay were rejoicing in what

they conceived to be the unanswerable logic of the Clay report, the politicians of the Kitchen Cabinet, Kendall and Blair, were rejoicing in having, in documentary form, the proof that Clay and the protectionists were hostile to the wishes of the new States. Amos Kendall knew that "free trade and free lands" was a shibboleth that these pioneers could understand. And while Clay, Webster, and Clayton were rejoicing over the passage of the bill in the Senate, Kendall and Blair were joyously arranging to spread the story of that triumph to the voters of the new States. After all, they had succeeded in their purpose. They had a Clay and a Jackson report to hold side by side, and the event disclosed that the politicians of the Kitchen Cabinet were wiser than the politicians of the Senate house.

CHAPTER VIII

CLAY FINDS HIS ISSUE

I

DURING the early days of the Jackson régime, a remarkable and little remembered figure passed furtively in and out of the closet of the President, playing a quiet, but none the less effective, part in the moulding of policies. This was none other than James A. Hamilton, son of the creator of the National Bank. Then a trusted brave of the tribe of Tammany, the reflector of Van Buren, the supporter of Jackson, he had fought the Federalist machine of New York, been made acting Secretary of State by the President pending the arrival of Van Buren, and later been appointed District Attorney of New York. For several years on the eve of portentous events he glided into the capital. That the son of Alexander Hamilton should have had such intimate relations with the President who denounced what he thought to be the persecution of Aaron Burr, is one of the mysteries of history.

When the first Jackson Message was under consideration, Hamilton, in response to the requests of Van Buren, Lewis, and others, reached Washington to confer with Jackson. He hastened to Van Buren, who was no doubt prolific of suggestions; thence to the White House to be cordially received. The following morning he breakfasted with the President, who urged him to remain at the White House while revising the Message. In going over the draft, which he found the "work of different hands," he was surprised to find that "the Bank of the United States was attacked at great length in a loose, newspaper slashing style." He found much to do. It was four o'clock in the morning when Jackson, hearing some one tinkering with the fire in the grate, entered Hamilton's room in his nightgown.

"My dear Colonel, why are you up so late?" he asked.

"I am at my work which I intend to finish before I sleep," Hamilton replied.

At which the mulatto who slept on a rug in Jackson's room was sent in to keep Hamilton's fire going. At eight in the morning the latter appeared in the President's room to report the completion of his task.

"What did you say about the Bank?" Jackson asked instantly.

"Very little."

And the son of Alexander Hamilton read the brief paragraph challenging the constitutionality and the expediency of the Bank his father had created, and declaring that it had "failed in the great end of establishing a uniform and sound currency."

"Do you think that is all I ought to say?" asked Jackson.

"I think you ought to say nothing about the Bank at present," was the response.

"Oh, but, my friend, I am pledged against the Bank, but if you think that is enough, so let it be." [1]

Some students of the period are prone to ascribe Jackson's hostility to the Bank to a personal grievance of Isaac Hill. The flimsy assumption that the President's Bank policy was born of the quarrel of the Concord editor with Biddle, because of the retention in the presidency of the Portsmouth branch of Jeremiah Mason, is unimpressive. Equally absurd to deny that the Mason incident played no part. According to some, Hill, in his attempt to force the removal of Mason, was wholly actuated by a desire to get political control of the institution; to others, to the inability of the editor-politician to get a loan. The truth is that the hostility to Mason was not confined to politicians, but was shared by many of the

[1] Hamilton's *Reminiscences*, 150.

merchants of New Hampshire. This hostility was due to Mason's austere action, on discovering that some bad loans had been made on speculative ventures, in exacting hard terms of the local merchants. The petition sent to Biddle by Hill contained the names of sixty members of the legislature, and most of the business men of Portsmouth, of both parties.[1] The president of the Portsmouth branch was a great lawyer, a statesman of reputation, an orator of power, and a partisan as bitter and intolerant as ever breathed the proscriptive air of New Hampshire. In the correspondence which followed between Secretary Ingham, who is said to have had a personal grievance,[2] and Nicholas Biddle, the president of the Bank, who has been variously described according to the bias of the writer, was unquestionably flippant and intolerant of suggestions from the Administration. While his position in the Mason incident can be justified, he was unnecessarily arrogant and tactless; but quickly realizing his mistake, he thereafter changed his tone, and throughout the summer and autumn of 1829 made every effort to conciliate the President. His letters of this period to the heads of the various branches insisting that the Bank be kept out of politics smack of sincerity.[3] But the harm had been done, and there is every reason to conclude that Amos Kendall was deeply concerned in the President's decision to attack the Bank in his first Message. Certain it is that a letter from Kendall to Noah in November led the "New York Courier and Enquirer" to launch its editorial campaign against the institution. This letter, announcing the presidential decision to attack in his first Message, and presenting an argument in support of the position he was to assume, was sent by Noah to the newspaper,

[1] Hill's explanatory speech in the Senate, March 3, 1834, differs radically from the generally accepted story, and has the ring of truth.

[2] Schouler, IV, 44.

[3] In Reginald C. McGrane's *Correspondence of Nicholas Biddle*, see Biddle to John Harper, 67; to John Nichol, 72; to Robert Lenox, 72; to A. Dickens, 77; to Major Lewis, 80; to Samuel Jaudon, 82.

and "a portion of Amos Kendall's letter, with a head and tail put to it . . . was published as an editorial the next morning"; and this "was the first savage attack on the United States Bank" in the columns of that paper.[1] And almost immediately afterwards James Gordon Bennett, writing for the "Courier and Enquirer," began a series of powerful articles in support of the policy of that journal.[2]

Indeed, if an explanation for Jackson's position must be sought in the Kitchen Cabinet, it would be more profitable to seek it in the principles of Amos Kendall, who had written against the Bank long before he had met the President, and while still on friendly terms with Clay. Others of Jackson's intimates were equally hostile. The views of Benton had been urged for years; and Hugh L. White, Senator from Tennessee, one of his confidential advisers in the early days of his Administration, had long distrusted the institution as tending to extravagant speculation, and as threatening the liberties of the people through its increasing influence in elections.[3] But Jackson himself needed no propagandists at his elbow. He had been prejudiced against the Bank for twenty years by Clay's slashing speech against it when the first Bank applied for a recharter.[4]

In his Message of December, 1830, Jackson dismissed the Bank in a paragraph, clearly indicative of unfriendliness; and in December, 1831, he scarcely mentioned it at all, except to call attention to his previous statements. But from the moment the first Message was read, Biddle's complacency was disturbed. His correspondence during the next two years shows him active and alert in attempts to conciliate his foe in the White House. Less than a week after one son of Alexander Hamilton had penned the first warning of war, Biddle was reading a letter from Alexander Hamilton, Jr., a brother, assuring him that the die was cast, the war inevitable, and

[1] Pray, *Memoirs of James Gordon Bennett*, I, 148.
[2] *Ibid.*
[3] *Memoir of Hugh Lawson White*, 80.
[4] Parton, II, 654.

warning him against the presidential aspirations of Van Buren, to whose political fortunes his brother was then attached.[1] Biddle replied that the Bank views of the Message were Jackson's, honestly held, and that for the time the Bank's policy would be one of "abstinence and self-defense." [2] "The expressions of the Message were the President's own," he wrote the head of the Washington branch immediately afterward, ". . . and inserted in opposition to the wishes, if not the advice of all his habitual counsellors. It is not, therefore, a cabinet measure, nor a party measure, but a personal measure." [3] And had he not ample encouragement in the letters of Major Lewis, a household guest of Jackson's, recommending the appointment of certain men to the directorship of the branch in Nashville? [4] Nevertheless, he was not at all positive that the recharter might not be made a party measure. Especially concerned with Van Buren's attitude, he was being constantly warned against him, but his advices were contradictory. Within a month he was reassured by one correspondent [5] and alarmed by Clay, who wrote him from Ashland that, while in Richmond, Van Buren had entered into a conspiracy with politicians to destroy the Bank.[6] And to add to the mystic maze of contradictions, Major Lewis wrote, in a "confidential" note, that the report that Jackson would veto a bill rechartering the Bank "must be some mistake because the report was at variance with what I had heard him say upon the subject." [7] Still another correspondent [8] informed him that Van Buren had told him that "he disapproved of that part of the message and was not hostile to the Bank."

About this time Jackson journeyed to the Hermitage, and

[1] *Correspondence of Nicholas Biddle*, 88.
[2] *Ibid.*, 91.
[3] Biddle to Samuel Smith, *ibid.*, 94.
[4] *Ibid.*, 97.
[5] Charles Augustus Davis, *ibid.*, 101.
[6] Clay to Biddle, *ibid.*, 105.
[7] Lewis to Biddle, *ibid.*, 103.
[8] Roswell L. Colt, *ibid.*, 104.

Biddle asked a leading citizen of Nashville to "feel him out." The banker's correspondent entertained the President at his home, and after a confidential chat felt justified in advising Biddle that he was "well convinced that he will not interfere with Congress on the subject of the renewing of the charter." [1] By this time, however, Biddle had convinced himself that political expediency would determine the President's attitude, and in a letter to one of Jackson's personal friends he pointed out the disastrous political results to the Administration if the impression gained ground that it was "unfriendly to sound currency." He even graciously indicated the line the next Message might take to save the Administration from that embarrassment.[2] But before that suggestion reached its destination, Clay solemnly wrote him that only a devoted friend of the Bank in the Presidency would make a recharter possible, and warned him against Van Buren. He was convinced that the Jacksonian politicians had determined to make the Bank question the issue in the next campaign. "I have seen many evidences of it," he wrote. "The editors of certain papers have received their orders to that effect, and embrace every occasion to act in conformity with them." [3] But when Congress met in December, and Jackson reiterated his views on the Bank, Biddle was earnestly urged from Washington to meet the issue at once by applying for a new charter. This advice was finally rejected. Congress, he wrote, was favorable, "and moreover the President would not reject the bill," but many members favorable to the recharter would prefer not to vote that session. Then, too, time was working the removal of prejudices.[4]

At the beginning of the session, December, 1831, with the charter five years to run, we are confronted with the mys-

[1] Josiah Nichol to Biddle, *Correspondence of Nicholas Biddle*, 106.
[2] Biddle to Nichol, *ibid.*, 107.
[3] Clay to Biddle, *ibid.*, 110.
[4] Biddle to Clay, *ibid.*, 115.

tery of the injection of the issue at that time. We know, however, that the strain of uncertainty had been telling on Biddle's temper. The vultures that play on the political necessities of corporations were beginning to swoop down upon him. Duff Green, of the "National Telegraph," had applied for a $20,000 loan.[1] And mindful of the importance of propaganda, he had already decided to cultivate the press by paying it well for the publication of Bank literature.[2] But just before the opening of the congressional session, his negotiations with McLane and Livingston of the Cabinet, both friendly to the Bank, had again diverted him from his disposition to fight. In October the Secretary of the Treasury had sat in the marble-front building in Philadelphia and told him of confidential communications with the President. Anxious to keep the Bank question out of the campaign, Jackson had reluctantly consented, on the importunities of Livingston and McLane, to omit all references to the Bank in his Message. Biddle feared it would be a mistake. Would it not be better merely to remind Congress of his previous comments, and leave the decision "with the representatives of the people?" The fact that this course was followed is one of the ironies of history.[3] Hardly had this decision been reached when Clay wrote from Ashland urging an immediate application for a new charter. This was a sensational reversal of views. Not only had he previously advised Biddle differently, but in August, 1830, he had taken strong grounds against such application so long before the expiration of the existing charter. "I am not prepared," he said then, "to say whether the charter ought, or ought not to be renewed on the expiration of its present term. The question is premature. I may not be alive to form any opinion on it. It belongs to posterity. It ought to be indefinitely postponed." [4] This

[1] *Correspondence of Nicholas Biddle*, 124. [2] *Ibid.*, 126.
[3] See Biddle's memorandum on conference, *ibid.*, 128.
[4] Speech at Cincinnati, Clay's *Works*, VII, 396.

speech was to be used with deadly effect by Blair in the "Globe" a little later.[1] Even then, before reaching Washington, Clay had determined to "turn up" the Bank charter as an issue.

II

WHEN Congress met, Jackson had concluded to postpone his fight on the Bank. Three reasons entered into the decision — the friendliness of his Secretary of the Treasury to the institution, the realization that a majority in Congress favored the recharter, and the fear that a contest during the session would throw the tremendous weight of the Bank's influence against him in the election. Most of his advisers, including Benton, were anxious to postpone the contest. Just as Biddle had thought that time would operate to the advantage of the institution, Benton was confident that it would work to its detriment, and he wished to strengthen the anti-Bank lines in the Senate and to have Van Buren in the chair when the contest came. McLane's pronouncedly pro-Bank report had deeply embarrassed the President's supporters. Creating indignation in some quarters, consternation in others, Jackson hastened to explain it away in a letter to Hamilton; but just how he persuaded himself that the views of the report did "not express any opposition to those entertained by myself," is not clear.[2]

The Bank supporters had eagerly seized upon the McLane report, and Webb, of the "New York Courier and Enquirer," now deserting the Administration on the Bank question, commented glowingly upon its author and his views. That this was gall and wormwood to Jackson and his intimates is evident in the correspondence which passed beween them. "The

[1] Commenting on it in the *Globe*, Jan. 14, 1832, Blair concludes: "The object of the Bank and politicians who build their hopes upon its power is at once to procure a new charter from a Congress which has not been elected by the people to pass upon that question."

[2] Hamilton's *Reminiscences*, 234.

article . . . was calculated if Blair had replied, to do McLane irreparable injury in a political point of view, because it might have brought him and the President into seeming collision," wrote Major Lewis to Hamilton.[1] And all this time, McLane, who was one of Hamilton's correspondents, was frankly admitting to the latter that he had "most earnestly urged Mr. Clay not to attempt to pass a Bank bill at this session, insisting that, if deferred to the next session, he was satisfied that he could, by that time, induce Jackson to approve it"; but that Clay had "persisted in the hope, that if the President approved the bill, he would lose the support of those of his party who had approved his opposition to the Bank, and a vast many others who approved of the State Bank system." Or, on the other hand, "if the President vetoed the bill, he would lose Pennsylvania and his election." [2] Thus it is clear enough that if Jackson could have determined, the Bank would not have been an issue in 1832.

But Clay was pressing Biddle, and the latter devoted the whole of December to feeling his way. "I think they [the Jackson leaders] are desirous to have the Bank question settled by a renewal before the next presidential canvass, with any modifications to free the President from the charge of an entire abandonment of his original opposition," wrote one who had "seen a letter from the Private Secretary of the President to a gentleman" in Louisville.[3] "Last night I had a long conversation with McLane," wrote the president of the Washington branch, "and I am authorized by him to say that it is his deliberate opinion and advice that a renewal of the charter ought not to be pressed during the present session, in which I concur most sincerely. The message is as much as you could expect. It shows that the Chief is wavering. If pressed into a corner immediately, neither McLane nor myself will answer for the consequences." [4] From another cor-

[1] Hamilton's *Reminiscences*, 235–36. [2] *Ibid.*, 234–35.
[3] Edward Shippen to Biddle, *Correspondence of Nicholas Biddle*, 136. [4] *Ibid.*, 138.

respondent Biddle learned that Barry, Woodbury, and Taney were hostile, being "under the influence of Blair, Lewis, Kendall & Co. who rule our Chief Magistrate"; that Blair had written a slashing attack upon the McLane report, which was only moderated after the Secretary of the Treasury had threatened to resign if the original were published. "I fear you will yet have trouble with our wise governors," he added.[1] A Virginia Congressman urged reasons for an immediate application. Jackson's popularity was on the wane, especially in Congress, and his reëlection notwithstanding being certain, he would have more prestige in the next Congress. Calhoun, still Vice-President, would be serviceable among the Bank's enemies in the South, and McDuffie, a follower of Calhoun, would be chairman of the House Committee to pass upon the application.[2]

"My own belief," wrote the wily Clay, "is that, if now called upon, he [Jackson] would not negative the bill, but that if he should be reëlected, the event might and probably would be different." At any rate, all the friends of the Bank with whom Clay had conversed "expect the application to be made." [3] In corroboration of Clay's views, Webster wrote that, as a result of conversations, he had been strongly confirmed in his opinion "that it is expedient for the Bank to apply for a renewal of the Charter without delay." [4]

Confused by such a medley of counsel, Biddle decided to have the situation studied on the ground. Thomas Cadwalader, a trusted Bank agent, could be depended upon to leave party considerations out of his survey, and on Tuesday, the 20th of December, this servitor took up his quarters at Barnard's Hotel.[5] The next day found him closeted, first with McLane, who warned him of a certain veto, and advised

[1] Robert Gibbs to Biddle, *Correspondence of Nicholas Biddle,* 139.

[2] C. F. Mercer to Biddle, *ibid.*, 140.

[3] Clay to Biddle, *ibid.*, 142.

[4] Webster to Biddle, *ibid.*, 145.

[5] Site of the Willard, 14th Street and the Avenue.

him to canvass Congress to ascertain whether the Bank could muster the two thirds necessary to override it. A preliminary survey that day was discouraging, and the evening found the agent again with McLane, who reiterated his plea for a postponement until after the election. On Thursday the agent met McDuffie, who urged an immediate application until "staggered" by what Cadwalader had learned of the probable vote to override the veto. He then advised the Bank to feel its way cautiously. Friday found him dining with Senator Smith, a Democrat, who opposed the agitation of the question that session, since it would mean a Jackson and anti-Jackson vote, and lose the Bank ten votes it could depend upon the next year.[1] It did not take the sagacious agent long to sense the selfish political motives of the Clay leaders. "It is evident," he wrote Biddle, "that W.'s [Webster's] opinions are guided, in some degree, by party feelings — as seems to be the case with most of the Clay men." In John Quincy Adams he found a cooler head, and one in whose judgment he had more confidence. Where Webster had urged that the application be made if "a bare majority in Congress could be mustered," Adams favored postponement "unless a strong vote can be ascertained." But, thinking the situation over on Christmas Day, and after another and more favorable canvass of the available votes, he began to lean toward the Clay opinion. In the case of a postponement some of the Bank's friends would be "luke-warm," Webster would be "cold or perhaps hostile," if the Bank bent to the Government influence. After another conference with McLane, he thought he would advise the Bank to start the memorial. In this disposition he was confirmed by a visit on Christmas night from the brother of the Secretary of State, a Whig and a follower of Clay, who brought the solemn assur-

[1] These ten, Dickerson of New Jersey, Dallas and Wilkins of Pennsylvania, Smith of Maryland, Mangum of North Carolina, Forsyth of Georgia, Poindexter of Mississippi, Kane and Robinson of Illinois, and Hendricks of Indiana.

ance that Livingston, McLane, and Cass would prevent the veto. The outcome of it all was that Cadwalader was won over to the Whig plan.[1] The moment the agent returned to Philadelphia, McLane, assuming the chilly dignity of resentment, wrote Biddle, restating his position and curtly declaring that he could not, "as one of the constitutional advisers of the President," object to the exercise of his veto power.[2] But three days later, Webster, in a reassuring note, wrote that the decision to present the memorial was "exactly right." [3]

The Whig politicians were determined that the Bank should be dragged into politics, and they had their way. The desire of Biddle to accept compromises proposed by McLane were ruthlessly brushed aside by his political friends. The story of the meeting at which Clay forced the issue is significant and dramatic. McLane had summoned Biddle to Washington and submitted a proposition for a recharter which, he contended, would meet with the approval of the President. After returning to Philadelphia and consulting with his directors, an agreement was reached to accept the compromise. Hurrying back to the capital, Biddle conceived the unhappy notion of first consulting with the political friends of the institution in the Congress, before calling upon McLane. Fatal error!

An historical political conference was called. There, of course, was Nicholas Biddle, financial American autocrat of his time, elegant, suave, polished to scintillation, a lover of literature, a brilliant conversationalist, with a graceful epistolary style, which was as dangerous to him as loquacity to a diplomat. He had been schooled in tact while serving as the Secretary of the American Legation at Paris under Monroe. Clever, unscrupulous, practicing diplomacy where

[1] For Cadwalader's reports see *Correspondence of Nicholas Biddle,* 146–61.
[2] McLane to Biddle, *ibid,* 165.
[3] Webster to Biddle, *ibid.,* 169.

straightforward methods would have served better, he had assiduously cultivated public men until he had created a bi-partisan Bank party in both branches of the Congress. In his Philadelphia home the great men of his day partook of his hospitality. Before Jackson reached the Presidency, the president of the Bank of the United States was in better position to foresee the proceedings of Congress than the responsible Chief Executive of the people. Instead of concealing his power, he loved to flaunt it in the face of authority. "Emperor Nicholas" smiled and bowed blandly to his title.

And there, of course, was Clay, leader of his party, the greatest genius in the Senate, seemingly destined to the presidential dignity, and for years one of Biddle's most trusted friends and advisers. He had been on the pay-roll of the Bank as its counsel in Kentucky and Ohio.

There, too, was John Sergeant, there by right as chief counsel of the Bank, but there, too, by right, as Clay's running mate in the election, for he had been nominated for Vice-President.

And there sat Webster, upon whose eloquence and wisdom the Bank had learned to lean. But he sat there that day, less as the champion of the Bank than as a partisan supporter of Clay and Sergeant.

The compromise proposition was submitted by Biddle, and, after some pretense at discussion, it was vetoed by Clay and Webster, on the ground that "the question of a recharter had progressed too far to render any compromise or change of front expedient." [1]

A little nonplussed, Biddle and Sergeant retired for further consideration, and returned to the conference with the politicians in the evening still convinced that the McLane compromise should be accepted. And it was then that Clay and Webster, by assuming an injured air, literally blackmailed their Philadelphia friends into the acceptance of their plan,

[1] Weed's *Autobiography*, I, 373.

asserting their ability at the time to carry the charter through in the face of a veto, but significantly adding that they would no longer be responsible for anything that might occur "if in the heat of the contest the Bank, abandoning its reliable friends, should strike hands with its foe." [1] Thus it was neither Jackson nor Biddle that forced the Bank into the campaign of 1832, but Henry Clay, thinking solely in terms of politics and self-interest, as he saw them.

III

THE winter roads between Philadelphia and Washington were ribbons of mud, cut across by frozen streams. A stage-coach, bumping and splattering through the mire, struck an obstruction, turned over, and General Cadwalader, with the Bank's memorial in his pocket, arose from the wreck with an injured shoulder that was to delay its presentation to the Congress. But three weeks after the conference in Washington it was delivered into the hands of its friends.

In the Senate it was presented by a Democrat, George M. Dallas of Pennsylvania, acting under strict instructions from the Legislature of his State, but very much against his personal judgment. In the House it was entrusted to one who could act with greater spirit, because of venomous hostility to Jackson — the vehement and picturesque McDuffie.

On the motion of Dallas, a select committee was chosen in the Senate to consider the memorial, composed of four friends of the Bank and one enemy. In the House, the fighting began at once. Instead of requesting a select committee, McDuffie asked a reference to his own Committee on Ways and Means — packed with friends of the Bank. This was good tactics. Andrew Stevenson, Speaker of the House, and a Jacksonian Democrat, could clearly not be entrusted with the selection of a special committee. An animated debate followed, and the McDuffie motion prevailed by a narrow

[1] Weed's *Autobiography*, I, 373.

margin of ten votes. But that was not to be the end of the matter — not so long as there was a Jackson in the White House, a Benton in the Senate, and a Kendall on the side lines. The plan of parliamentary warfare was devised by the master parliamentarian from Missouri. It contemplated numerous amendments and elaborate discussion in the Senate; and in the House, an investigation into the condition and methods of the Bank. Benton immediately furnished a new member of the House, Clayton, with an indictment in many counts, some justifiable, and others having nothing more substantial than gossip behind them. But even these served. The debate was brisk. James K. Polk led for the Administration in the strongest speech of his congressional career; and McDuffie, sincerely believing in the purity of the Bank, and fearing the effect of opposition to an investigation, making only a perfunctory objection. At the time it was presented, Biddle was relying for information on Charles Jared Ingersoll, who had been sent to Washington in an attempt to conciliate Jackson, and was in constant communication with Livingston and McLane. It is significant of Jackson's methods that his Secretary of State authorized Ingersoll to inform Biddle that the President had nothing to do with the resolution, wished to end the matter that session, and would sign a rechartering measure if satisfactorily framed.[1] But the easy capitulation of McDuffie in permitting the passage of the resolution caused poignant distress in Bank circles. Ingersoll concluded that the Carolinian preferred to have the tariff debate precede that on the Bank.[2]

Thus the investigation was ordered. The apologists for the Bank among historians persist in the fallacy that its enemies had no expectation of finding anything wrong. This is a remarkable conclusion. Benton thoroughly expected it. The son of Alexander Hamilton had no doubt of it.[3] Jackson

[1] Ingersoll to Biddle, *Correspondence of Nicholas Biddle*, 187. [2] *Ibid.*, 188.
[3] Hamilton's *Reminiscences*, 243.

was serious about it. "The affairs of the Bank I anticipated to be precisely such as you have intimated," he wrote to Hamilton. "When fully disclosed, and the branches looked into it will be seen that its corrupting influence has been extended everywhere that could add to its strength and secure its recharter. I wish it may not have extended its influence over too many members of Congress." [1]

The committee of investigation submitted three reports. The majority report charged usury, the issuance of branch bank notes as currency, the selling of coin, loans to editors, brokers, and members of Congress, donations to roads and canals, the construction of houses to rent and sell, and the sale of stock obtained from the Government through special acts of Congress. The minority report, and that of Adams, who reported separately, were laudatory of the institution. Nothing was proved. Campaign material was furnished, and nothing more.

In the midst of the fighting, on May 30th, Nicholas Biddle moved upon the capital and took personal charge of his forces. He entertained at dinners at Barnard's. He daily repaired to the Capitol to meet emergencies. He conferred freely with Livingston and McLane, hoping through them to conciliate the President. So positive was he that the investigation, by proving nothing, had disarmed hostility, that he wrote expansively, on his arrival, of his willingness to consider with Jackson such modifications as would satisfy the President.[2] In less than a week he was disillusioned of the idea of an easy triumph. "It has been a week of hard work, anxiety and alternating hopes and fears," he wrote Cadwalader, "but I think that we may now rely with confidence in a favorable result." [3] All through June the battle raged in the Senate, and it was not until July 3d that the "Emperor Nicholas"

[1] Hamilton's *Reminiscences*, 244.

[2] Biddle to Cadwalader, *Correspondence of Nicholas Biddle*, 191.

[3] *Ibid.*, 192.

was able to write of the passage of the bill by that body, and to "congratulate our friends most cordially upon their most satisfactory results." The victory was achieved by a vote of 28 to 20, with Dallas, Wilkins, and Poindexter, among the Democrats, voting for the bill. In the House, the Bank won by a vote of 106 to 84.

"Now for the President," wrote Biddle. "My belief is that the President will veto the bill, though that is not generally known or believed." [1] And Clay at the same time wrote: "The Bank bill will, I believe, pass the House, and if Jackson is to be believed, he will veto it." [2] Thus, at this stage, it is evident that Biddle had reconciled himself to Clay's plan of making the fate of the Bank the issue in the campaign. Among Jackson's friends there was no doubt as to his intentions. Both McLane and Livingston had warned the banker. Three months before, Hamilton had written a friend that, in the event of its passage, Jackson would promptly veto the measure. "He is open and determined upon this point. I conferred with him yesterday upon the subject. I told him what the Opposition avowed as their motive for pushing the bill at this session. He replied: 'I will prove to them that I never flinch; that they were mistaken when they expected to act upon me with such considerations.'" [3]

IV

When the bill reached Jackson, he knew that he could not count on the unanimous support of his Cabinet on the veto. Livingston, McLane, and Cass were frankly antagonistic to his purpose, Woodbury was uncertain, while Barry, always acquiescing in his chief's policies, scarcely counted. Among all the men who sat about the table in the Cabinet room, the only one who heartily sympathized with his intent was Roger

[1] *Correspondence of Nicholas Biddle*, 192. [2] Clay's *Works*, IV, 340.
[3] Hamilton's *Reminiscences*, 243.

Taney. In February, Ingersoll had found him against the Bank, but Livingston then "hoped to convert him"; and while the Bank representative had "found him just now closeted with Kendall," this was so far from discouraging him that he had not even despaired of Kendall and Lewis, and felt that he had established "a good understanding" with Blair of the "Globe." [1] On the day the bill reached the White House, Taney was absent from Washington, but he had gone over the ground thoroughly with the President, and had written him a letter setting forth reasons why, in the event of the bill's passage, it should be vetoed.

On the day of its passage, Martin Van Buren landed in New York, and the following morning he started for the capital. It was midnight when he reached Washington, but, in compliance with a letter from Jackson, which awaited him on landing, he proceeded through the dark streets to the White House where he was instantly ushered into the President's room. The grim old fighter was sitting up in bed, supported by pillows, his wretched health clearly denoted in his countenance.[2] But there was the passion of battle in his blood, and it flashed in his eye as he eagerly grasped the hand of his favorite, and, retaining it, poured forth the story of the Bank Bill, and expressed his satisfaction on the arrival of a faithful friend at such a critical juncture. When Van Buren expressed the hope that he would not hesitate to veto the bill, Jackson's face beamed. "It is the only way," said the Red Fox, "you can discharge the great duty you owe to the country and yourself." [3] By Van Buren, the old man's gratification was easily understood, for he knew of the desertion of the greater part of the Cabinet.

There is some confusion among those who should have known as to the authorship of the Veto Message. In this instance Hamilton was not called in, albeit sympathizing

[1] Ingersoll to Biddle, *Correspondence of Nicholas Biddle,* 183.

[2] Van Buren's *Political Parties in the United States,* 314. [3] *Ibid.*

heartily with Jackson's purpose. According to one of his biographers [1] the ideas were contributed by Livingston, Benton, Taney, and Jackson, and the phrasing was by Amos Kendall, Blair, and Lewis. In view of Livingston's negotiations with Biddle, we may safely accept his denial of having had any part in the Message. It was inevitable that Benton should have been consulted. And it is known that Taney was summoned back to Washington to assist in the framing. During the entire time it was being written, Van Buren, who remained at the capital, with the document open to his inspection, did not have any "direct agency in its construction." [2] His enemies at the time, however, insisted that he was a party to the phrasing. "Mr. Van Buren arrived at the President's on Sunday," a correspondent in Washington wrote Biddle, "and to-day the President sent to the Senate his veto on the Bank Bill." [3] That Major Lewis and Blair were called in to assist in the actual wording is quite probable, but it may be set down as positive that the greater part of the document as it reached the Senate was the product of the pen of the mysterious recluse, Amos Kendall.

That such a Message from such a pen at such a time should be strikingly strong and couched in such language as to appeal to the electorate of the Nation was inevitable. It has been fashionable to describe it as demagogic because of its appeal to the masses and its protest against the conversion by the rich of governmental agencies to their personal ends, and because of its objections to the foreign stockholders in the Bank of the United States. It was, of course, a campaign document — intended as such. Jackson understood perfectly that the presentation of the memorial for a recharter four years before the expiration of the existing charter, and in the year of the presidential election, was a campaign move on the part of Clay. He knew that Clay was appealing to

[1] Buell. [2] Van Buren's *Political Parties in the United States*, 218.
[3] *Correspondence of Nicholas Biddle*, 193.

wealth and power — he appealed to the people. And his appeal was to the people of the United States.

In this stirring appeal to the prejudices of the people, as well as to their interests, as the Jacksonians saw it, there was but one real blunder, and that in phrasing. In discussing the constitutionality of the Bank, Jackson said: "Each officer who takes an oath to support the Constitution, swears that he will support it as he understands it, and not as it is understood by others." Upon this was to be predicated the assertion that Jackson had announced a philosophy of chaos, with each petty officer passing upon the constitutionality of laws, and irrespective and in contempt of the Supreme Court. The more conservative friends of the President interpreted the words employed as meaning "that in giving or withholding his assent to the bill for the recharter of the Bank, it was his right and duty to decide the question of its constitutionality for himself, uninfluenced by any opinion or judgment which the Supreme Court had pronounced upon that point, farther than his judgment was satisfied by the reasons it had given for its decision." [1] But there were other expressions in the Message that must have appeared as little short of appeals to anarchy to the more conservative element. "It is to be regretted that the rich and powerful too often bend the acts of Government to their selfish purposes." "Every man is equally entitled to protection by law; but when the laws undertake to add to these natural and just advantages artificial distinctions, to grant titles, gratuities, and exclusive privileges, to make the rich richer and the powerful more potent, the humble members of society — the farmers, mechanics and laborers — who have neither the time nor the means of securing like favors to themselves, have a right to complain of the injustice of their government." "There are no necessary evils in government. Its evils exist only in its abuses." "Many of our rich have

[1] *Political Parties in the United States*, 313–14, and 317.

not been content with equal protection and equal benefits, but have besought us to make them richer by act of Congress."

Here was a Message striking an entirely new note in American politics, and not without justification. So completely had the country been under the domination of the powerful, politically, financially, and socially, previous to the Jackson régime, that the Message was actually hailed with delight by the followers of Clay.

"As to the veto message," wrote Biddle, "I am delighted with it. It has all the fury of the unchained panther, biting the bars of his cage. It is really a manifesto of anarchy, such as Marat and Robespierre might have issued to the mob of the Faubourg St. Antoine; and my hope is that it will contribute to relieve the country from the domination of these miserable people." [1] The personal organ of Clay, the "Lexington Observer," commented thus: "It is a mixture of the Demagogue and the Despot, of depravity, desperation and feelings of malice and vengeance partially smothered. It is the type of the detested hypocrite, who, cornered at all points, still cannot abandon entirely his habitual artifice, but at length, finding himself stripped naked, in a tone of defiance says: 'I am a villain; now do your worst and so will I.'" [2] So little did the Bank and its supporters understand the psychology of the "mob" that it published and circulated thirty thousand copies of the Message at its own expense!

But if the Whigs were pleased with its tone, the Democrats were delighted. Either Blair or Kendall in a fulsome editorial in the "Globe" found it "difficult to describe in adequate language the sublimity of the moral spectacle now presented to the American people in the person of Andrew Jackson," and that "in this act the glories of the battle-field are eclipsed — it is the crowning chaplet of an immortal fame." [3]

[1] *Correspondence of Nicholas Biddle*, 196.

[2] Balir reproduced this in the *Globe* of July 26th in the nidst of the campaign.

[3] *Washington Globe*, July 14, 1832.

And Hugh Lawson White, himself a banker, a statesman, a man of property, and a patriot of impeccable purity, declared that it would give to Jackson a more enduring fame and deeper gratitude than the greatest of his victories in the field.

Both parties were satisfied with the Message.

V

NEVER in the history of the Republic had feeling been aroused to a more dangerous pitch than during the period of the Bank fight. Senator White, a calm, well-poised man of years, was not at all certain that even he could escape a personal encounter. "Everything here is in a bustle," he wrote. "Nothing out of which mischief can be made is suffered to slumber. Ill blood is produced by almost every event; and a great disposition is manifested by some to appeal to the trial of battle. . . . No man can tell when or with whom he is to be involved. I will do all that a prudent man ought to do to avoid difficulties, but should it be my lot to have them forced upon me, my reliance is that Providence will guide me through them safely." [1]

The debate in the Senate following the Veto Message was significant. The great Field Marshals of the Bank, who had maintained silence until now, appeared upon the scene with impassioned speeches of denunciation and solemn warning. The import of the speeches of Clay and Webster could not have been clearer. They were designed to intimidate the electorate into voting against Jackson by the most gloomy predictions of panic and distress. Webster, who spoke first and made by long odds the most powerful presentation against the Veto, dwelt with funereal melancholy upon the President's determination to overturn American institutions, basing this absurd theory on the unhappy sentence referred to above.

[1] *Memoir of Hugh Lawson White*, 80.

But the one note he struck in the beginning and pounded to the end was that of intimidation. The country was prosperous and yet there was "an unaccountable disposition to destroy the most useful and most approved institutions of the Government." Unless Jackson should be defeated at the polls the Bank would fall, and in its fall pull down the pillars of prosperity and involve all in a common ruin. The Bank would have to call in its debts at once. The distress would be especially acute in the States on the Mississippi and its waters — where votes were needed for Clay. There thirty millions of the Bank's money was out on loans and discounts, and how could this be immediately collected without untold suffering and misery? The great orator, however, evidently afraid that his hints at the election had been too subtle, soon threw off the mask boldly.

"An important election is at hand," he said, "and the renewal of the Bank Charter is a pending object of great interest, and some excitement. Should not the opinions of men high in office and candidates for reëlection be known on this as on other important questions?" And thence he argued that the life of the Republic, the preservation of the Constitution, the salvation of society from anarchy, and the prosperity of the people, were all inseparably interwoven with the National Bank and the candidacy of Clay. "No old school Federalist," says Van Buren, "who had grown to man's estate with views and opinions in regard to the character of the people which that faith seldom failed to inspire, could doubt the efficacy of such an exposition in turning the minds of all classes of the community in the desired direction." [1]

If the Veto was satisfactory to the Whigs — to the surprise of the Democrats — Webster's avowed purpose to make it the issue in the campaign was satisfactory to the Democrats — to the equal astonishment of the Whigs. When

[1] *Political Parties in the United States*, 321.

the great New England orator sat down, Hugh Lawson White of Tennessee, a banker, fluent, logical, and forceful, lost no time in accepting Webster's "issue."

"I thank the Senator," he said, "for the candid avowal, that unless the President will sign such a charter as will suit the directors, they intend to interfere in the election, and endeavor to displace him. With the same candor I state, that after this declaration, this charter shall never be renewed with my consent. . . . Sir, if under these circumstances the charter is renewed, the elective franchise is destroyed, and the liberties and prosperity of the people are delivered over to this moneyed institution, to be disposed of at their discretion. Against this I enter my solemn protest."

Even the most ardent supporters of Clay will hardly point to his speech on the Veto as evidence of his power. Compared with Webster's or White's, it was mere froth, lacking in both substance and style, and only notable in its insistence that the failure of the recharter would be fatal to the West, as the continuance of Jackson in office would be subversive of all government.

The reply of Benton was characteristic in its slashing style, its exhaustive appeal to facts and figures, and chiefly important as a campaign argument in its elaborate discussion of the relations of the Bank with the Western States. Not to be outdone in dire predictions, he insisted that the triumph of the Bank would mean the end of free institutions; that "no individual could stand in the States against the power of the Bank, and the Bank flushed with the victory over the conqueror of the conquerors of Bonaparte"; that "an oligarchy would be immediately established, and that oligarchy, in a few generations, would ripen into a monarchy." He realized that all nations must ultimately perish. "Rome had her Pharsalia and Greece her Chæronea, and this Republic, more illustrious in her birth, was entitled to a death as glorious as theirs." He would not have her "die by poison" or "perish in corruption," but "a field of arms and glory should be her end."

And he, too, eagerly accepted the challenge of Webster: "Why debate the Bank question now, and not before?" he asked. "With what object do they speak? Sir, this *post facto* debate is not for the Senate, nor the President, nor to alter the fate of the Bank Bill. It is to arouse the officers of the Bank — to direct the efforts of its mercenaries in their designs upon the people — to bring out its streams of corrupting influence, by inspiring hope, and to embody all its recruits at the polls to vote against Jackson. Without an avowal we would all know this; but we have not been left without an avowal. The Senator from Massachusetts commenced his speech by showing that Jackson must be put down; that he stood as an impassable barrier between the Bank and a new charter; and that the road to success was through the ballot boxes at the presidential election. The object of this debate is then known, confessed, declared, avowed; the Bank is in the field; enlisted for the war; a battering ram — the catapulta, not of the Romans but of the National Republicans [Whigs]; not to beat down the walls of hostile cities, but to beat down the citadel of American liberty; to batter down the rights of the people; to destroy a patriot and a hero; to command the elections and to elect a Bank President."

Thus the politicians sounded the keynotes of the two parties in the approaching campaign in the country.

The debate was not to end without its serio-comedy. Benton had criticized Clay for lack of decent courtesy to the President, and when he resumed his seat, Clay arose to question the Missourian's qualification to pass on decent courtesy, and to revive the story that Benton had once said that should Jackson ever reach the Presidency, Senators "would have to legislate with pistols and dirks." Benton excitedly denied it. The lie was passed. The angry statesmen were called to order and forced to apologize to the Senate, and thus the Whig nominee for the Presidency closed the debate in a none too dignified fashion.

The necessary two thirds to override the veto could not be mustered, and Clay left Washington on the adjournment of Congress, July 16th, happy in the knowledge that "something had turned up" that would force the Bank and all its resources and influence to battle with a personal motive for his election.

And Jackson and his friends were jubilant.

Thus ended one of the longest and most bitter sessions the American Congress had ever known, "fierce in the beginning, and becoming more furious to the end." [1]

[1] Benton's *Thirty Years' View.*

CHAPTER IX

THE DRAMATIC BATTLE OF 1832

I

THE campaign of 1832 marked the beginning of many things that have come to be commonplace in American politics. For the first time the politicians were under the compulsion of cultivating and conciliating, not factions and groups, but the masses of the people. The day of Democracy had dawned, with all that means of good and evil. And in this struggle for the suffrage of the masses, Clay had unwittingly intrigued the Jacksonians into the advantage. Accustomed for years to relying solely on the wealthy and the influential, the great Whig leaders signally failed to appreciate that the very elements they had rallied to their support would tend to alienate the mechanics of the cities, the farmers of the plains, the pioneers struggling with poverty on the fringe of the forest. Thurlow Weed, who was one of the few practical Whig politicians, saw it, but he was then comparatively obscure. The clever politicians of the Kitchen Cabinet instantly sensed the opportunity and grasped it. A great moneyed institution, never popular with the masses, was seeking the humiliation of the most popular of Presidents. The most fortunate of that day were responding to the call of the Bank. The first battle at the polls between the "soulless corporation" and the "sons of toil" was on. For the first time in a presidential election the demagogue appeared with his appeals to class prejudice and class hate, and all the demagogy was not on the part of the Jacksonians. If these sought to arouse the masses against the prosperous, the prosperous, with gibes about the "mob," were quite as busy in prejudicing the classes against the masses.

And in this campaign the press played a more conspicuous and important part than ever before. The Jacksonians, who had tested the political possibilities of the press four years before, had perfected an organization throughout the country dependent on the editorial lead of the "Globe." If the political leaders of the Whigs were even now slow to grasp the potentiality of publicity, Nicholas Biddle of the Bank was more alert, and, through his agency, the powerful "New York Courier and Enquirer," edited by James Watson Webb, deserted the Democracy to espouse the cause of Clay and "the monster." That money played a part in the conversion was soon established in a congressional investigation; and when the "National Intelligencer," the Whig organ, joyously hailed the convert, Blair was able sarcastically to comment on its being "charmed with his [Webb's] honesty and independence in complying with his bargain with the Bank — and the bold, frank and honorable way in which he unsays all that he has said in favor of the President for the price paid him by Mr. Biddle." [1] Thus the editors in 1832 fought with a ferocity never before approached.

From the beginning Amos Kendall realized that the appeal would have to be made to the masses. He therefore conceived the idea of inaugurating the campaign with a more solemn and dignified appeal to the more intellectual element. The result was a carefully prepared campaign document reviewing the work of the first three years of Jackson's Administration. With a master hand he marshaled the triumphs of the Administration, and marched them — an imposing procession — before the reader. He anticipated and met all attacks. If parasites on the public service had been displaced by friends of Jackson, the new blood had injected new energy into the public offices. Business, long in arrears, had been brought up. Public accounts were more promptly rendered and settled. Scamps had been detected and scourged from

[1] *Globe*, Aug. 29, 1832.

office, and peculations to the amount of $280,000 had been uncovered. Economy and increased efficiency had resulted in the saving of hundreds of thousands.

In our foreign relations Kendall found nothing to be desired. Jackson had found Colombian cruisers depredating upon our commerce, and Colombian ports subjecting American cargoes to oppressive duties; he secured indemnities and the reduction of duties and the admission of American vessels to Colombian waters on the same footing as those of Colombia. He found no treaty with Turkey and the waters of the Bosphorus closed to us; he negotiated a treaty and our flag waved in the Bosphorus. He found no treaty with Austria — one was negotiated; a suspended treaty with Mexico — it was put in operation; the indemnity claims against Denmark for spoliation unpressed — he collected $750,000; the British West Indian controversy entangled by unskilled diplomacy — he untangled it with skillful diplomacy, and won a victory for American commerce; the French spoliation claims held in abeyance — and he triumphed there.

This brilliant foreign policy, he continued, had breathed new life into our domestic and foreign commerce, until "a commercial activity scarcely equaled in our history" was enjoyed. The hammers were heard in the shipyards, laborers were employed at high wages, prosperity pervaded every class and section. At Boston alone fifteen vessels were fitting out for trade in the Black Sea.

Despite these achievements Kendall complained that the President's political foes had devoted their energy and ingenuity to obstruction alone. Congress had refused or delayed the necessary appropriations, denied him the means to maintain a mission to France, refused to confirm the appointment of his Minister to England, trumped up charges of fraud against his friends, resorted to childish investigations, charged the President with sending bullies to attack members of Congress and to spy upon them, and capped the climax of insufferable impudence with resolutions to inquire into the private conversations of the hero of New Orleans.

This campaign document, the first of its kind, was sent broadcast over the country to awaken the indignation of the faithful and to revive and intensify the cry, "Hurrah for Jackson." [1] And it had the effect intended. The Jacksonians became all the more militant, ready to pounce upon and rend their enemies. Even the courageous Tyler, unfriendly to Jackson, cautioned his daughter in a letter home — "Speak of me always as a Jackson man whenever you are questioned." [2] With this document in the hands of the intellectual, the Kitchen Cabinet turned with their appeal to the masses on the Bank issue. This speedily became paramount. But Clay and the Whigs were busy with intrigues with groups, and, to understand the remarkable campaign in its ramifications, it is necessary to pause for a peep behind the scenes where Clay may be seen in a light other than that of a man who "would rather be right than President." We shall find him as willing, in Virginia, to unite with the champions of the Nullification he abhorred, as, in New York, with the party of the Anti-Masons he despised.

II

After the fashion of the old school politician of his day, Clay relied upon intrigue, upon the cultivation of groups with special interests and grievances. During the winter in Congress he had devoted himself to the consolidation of business and the ultra-conservative elements behind his candidacy. The bitterness of the contest was foreshadowed in the spring when Blair announced the publication of an extra weekly issue of the "Globe"; and in August, Duff Green made a similar announcement as to the "Telegraph." While Clay planned to win on the Bank issue, he very early began a

[1] This document is in Amos Kendall's *Autobiography*, 296–303.

[2] *Letters and Times of the Tylers*, I, 429.

furious flirtation with the Nullifiers and the Anti-Masons, thus injecting side issues that the Jacksonians were quick to accept. In April, Clay was writing a Virginia friend [1] of a possible coalition with the Nullification forces in three or four Southern States where extreme State-Rights views were prevalent. Governor Floyd of Virginia, destined to receive the electoral vote of the South Carolina Nullifiers, and for a time alienated from Clay, was making overtures for a conciliation. Duff Green, a messenger in Calhoun's livery, had made a remarkable proposition. The purport of this proposition was that Calhoun's friends would present his name for the Presidency if assured of three or four of the Southern States; that about August he would be announced as a candidate; that if arrangements could be made with Clay to place no electoral ticket in the field in Virginia, and to throw the support of his friends to Calhoun, the latter could carry the Old Dominion; that carrying Virginia, he would have a fair chance of carrying North Carolina, Georgia, and South Carolina, with a fighting chance in Alabama and Mississippi; and, accomplishing that, he could defeat the reëlection of Jackson, and force the determination of the issue upon the House of Representatives where Clay would no doubt be elected to the satisfaction of Calhoun. The wily editor made it clear to Clay that he was to have no ticket in the States mentioned, and should actively coöperate with Calhoun in Virginia.

And Clay was not shocked! But he had not "assumed that Calhoun had much political capital anywhere outside South Carolina," and doubted the practicability of abandoning a ticket in Virginia because of the imputations that would follow. And yet, if Calhoun could, by any chance, carry three or four of the Southern States, it was a consummation devoutly to be wished. "Let me hear from you, my dear friend, upon this matter," he wrote, "and particularly

[1] Judge Brooke.

your views as to the strength of the party of Mr. Calhoun in Virginia. Has it not relapsed into Jacksonism? Can it be brought forth again in its original force to the support of Mr. Calhoun? Suppose Mr. Calhoun is not put forth as a candidate, what course, generally, will his friends in Virginia pursue? Could our friends be prevailed upon to unite upon a ticket favorable to Mr. Calhoun? Or, in the event of no ticket being put up, would they not divide between Jackson and Calhoun, the larger part probably going to Jackson?"[1] The pet plan of the Calhoun conspirators failed, and in August, Duff Green set forth on a tour of investigation into New York and Pennsylvania, returning to Washington encouraged in the conviction that the defeat of Jackson could be accomplished through the unification of all the hostile elements against him. In announcing the campaign extras of the "Telegraph" — could he by chance have visited the marble bank building in Philadelphia? — he declared that "we believe that our duty requires us to demonstrate that General Jackson ought not to be reëlected." There was no mistaking the meaning of this move, and the Jacksonians were instantly on their toes. Under the caption, "Consummation of the Coalition," Blair vigorously denounced it in the "Globe." "If Mr. Clay were elected," he wrote, "Mr. Calhoun is well aware that it would instantly establish the Southern League, which is looked to by him as his only hope of ever attaining political power. This is the basis of the coalition between Mr. Clay and Mr. Calhoun. It is like that of Octavius and Anthony which severed the Roman empire."[2]

That Blair had not misinterpreted was immediately evident in the response of the Whig press. The influential Pleasants, of the "Richmond Whig," warmly commended Green's action and promised, "on the part of the 'Telegraph,'

[1] Clay to Brooke, Clay's *Works*, IV, 332–33.
[2] *Globe*, Aug. 25, 1832.

a luminous exposé of the misrule of Jacksonism." "Ah," wrote Blair, "the 'Richmond Whig' upon the appearance of Duff Green's proposals for a joint opposition leaps into its embrace." [1] And from that moment the "Globe" kept before its readers constantly the Calhoun heresy and the coalition with the Whigs. Early in September he began to discuss pointedly the Nullification meetings in South Carolina addressed by "Mr. Calhoun's leading partisans," warning that the sinister doctrine was "subversive of the Union," and that "by forcing a clash between the Government and South Carolina, Calhoun hopes to arouse the sympathy of the entire South." And he continued with a prescience that is now startling: "The Vice-President, as his prospect closes upon the elevated honors of the Federal Government, is exerting all his influence to place South Carolina in a position which shall compel the other Southern States to unite in a new system, or confederacy, which may open new views to his ambition." [2]

Thus, burning all bridges as far as the Nullifiers were concerned, the Jacksonian leaders, in the interest of the President, concentrated on capitalizing their connection with the Whigs and the Bank. When Whig and Bank papers warmly recommended the "Telegraph" to the patronage of the Clay supporters, Blair gave the recommendation publicity, with the suggestion that "that paper is the open advocate of Calhoun and Nullification." Thus he forced the coalition into the open. "Are not the Bank party turning to the Nullifiers?" he asked. "If not, why do they circulate the extra of Duff Green which is devoted to Nullification?" [3] Thus, by boldly repudiating and defying the Nullification element and Calhoun, the Jackson leaders more than neutralized any benefit that Clay and the Whigs might receive from their sympathy and support.

[1] *Globe*, Aug. 29, 1832. [2] *Ibid.*, Sept. 5, 1832. [3] *Ibid.*, Sept. 7, 1832.

III

But more important to Clay than the attitude of the Nullifiers was that of the Anti-Masons. Strangely enough, he had, at first, looked upon the growing movement, not only with complacency, but with approval. After the failure of the new party in New York in 1830, he had written to a friend: "If they had been successful they would probably have brought out an Anti-Masonic candidate for President. Still, if I had been in New York, I should have given my suffrage to Granger.[1] I will not trouble you with the reasons."[2] In the same letter, however, he expresses the opinion that such strength as the proscriptive party might muster would ultimately go to the Whigs, in general, and himself in particular, because "it is in conformity with the general nature of minorities," when they have no candidate of their own, to support the strongest opposition party. Then, too, they were protectionists, had been abused by Van Buren's organization in New York, "and General Jackson has, as they think, persecuted them." At any rate, wrote the intriguing politician, "there is no occasion for our friends to attack them."

But a new light broke for Clay when, in the spring of 1831, the Anti-Masons called a national convention, to meet two months before the Whigs'. His close friends became apprehensive. The sounding of the Anti-Masons disclosed no Clay sentiment. Quite the contrary. Much distressed at this revelation, one of the leaders of the movement urged him to exert his well-known powers of conciliation.[3] By the latter part of June he had concluded that the new party might not prove so advantageous after all. Writing to his bosom friend, Francis Brooke, he found that "Anti-Masonry seems to be the only difficulty now in the way of success, both

[1] Anti-Mason candidate for Governor.
[2] Clay to Bailbache, Clay's *Works*, IV, 289.
[3] Richard Rush to Clay, Clay's *Works*, IV, 299.

in Pennsylvania and New York." [1] By the middle of July he was convinced that "it would be politic to leave the Jackson party exclusively to abuse the Antis." [2] A few days later he had concluded that "the policy of the Antis is to force us to their support," and that "ours should be to win them to ours." [3]

As the time for the convention approached, the Antis were split on Clay, a small portion wishing the nomination of one who would later withdraw in his favor, but the majority hoping for the nomination of one who would be acceptable to the Whigs in their convention two months later. The problem was finally solved by the nomination of William Wirt.

That this brilliant man would have scorned the honor on any other theory than that his nomination would be acceptable to both the Whigs and Clay, with whom he had served in the Cabinet, and for whom he entertained an affection, is shown in his correspondence.[4] But, while resting at Ashland and still ignorant of the convention's action, Clay was writing to Brooke that "if the alternative is between Andrew Jackson and an Anti-Masonic candidate with his exclusive proscriptive principles, I should be embarrassed in the choice." [5]

In the interval between the two conventions, the Anti-Masons clung desperately to the hope that Clay would do violence to his dominating, domineering disposition by sacrificing himself. He was an intimate friend of Wirt's. Their views on fundamentals were alike. With Wirt elected, Clay would be the power behind the throne. With a divided opposition, Jackson's election would be inevitable, and Clay hated him with a consuming hate. For identical reasons the Whigs hoped that, on the nomination of Clay, Wirt would retire in his favor. As the Whig convention approached, Wirt abandoned all hope of his own nomination. "There seems

[1] Clay's *Works*, IV, 304. [2] *Ibid.*, 306. [3] *Ibid.*, 307–08.
[4] See Kennedy's *Life of Wirt*. [5] Clay's *Works*, IV, 316.

to be no doubt of Mr. Clay's nomination in the convention next week," he wrote to Judge Carr. "So be it. In a personal point of view I shall feel that I have made a lucky escape." [1] After the nomination of Clay, it was the ardent wish of Wirt to withdraw. His intimations to his party's leaders only brought the assurance that were the party dissolved there "were not enough Clay men among them to touch New York or Pennsylvania, nor consequently to elect Mr. Clay," and he was reluctantly forced to the conclusion that "there [was] no more chance for Mr. Clay with the Anti-Masons than for the Pope of Rome." [2] But the absurdity of his situation annoyed him, and he was soon wishing for "a little villa in Florida, or somewhere else, to retire to, and beguile the painful hours, as Cicero did, in writing essays."

If he remained in the field, it was because Henry Clay preferred it. The relations of the ostensible rivals were close and confidential throughout the campaign. Clay feared that Wirt's withdrawal would be ascribed to his influence, and would intensify the Anti-Masonic feeling against him. Then, again, the Whig board of strategy planned to deprive Jackson of the electoral vote of New York and Pennsylvania through an ingenious combination of the two opposition parties in those States. In New York the proscriptive party, meeting first, endorsed its national nominees, and nominated leaders of their own for Governor and Lieutenant-Governor. With great cunning they selected an electoral ticket, including Chancellor Kent, an idolater of Clay. The Whigs followed, and accepted the Anti-Masonic ticket, and thus the Opposition was consolidated in the Empire State. There was no mystery as to the intent in regard to the State ticket — it was to have the united support of both parties. The weakness, with the public, was the absence of any indication as to the intended disposal of the electoral vote. The plan of the conspirators was to throw the electoral votes to Wirt pro-

[1] Kennedy's *Life of Wirt*, II, 314. [2] *Ibid.*, 318.

vided there was a possibility of his election, or no possibility of the election of either Wirt or Clay; and for Clay in the event Wirt could not win and the Whig nominee could with the electoral vote of New York.[1] The plan met with the hearty approval of Clay, who entertained high hopes of its success in depriving Jackson of the electoral vote upon which his election depended.[2] Thus, before the campaign had fairly started, the politicians of these two parties were working in close coöperation with a complete understanding, while the rank and file of both parties were left entirely in the dark. Wirt, with no faith in the coalition, was doing nothing to advance his candidacy.[3] Thus the nominee of one party was secretly planning to deliver the prize to the man his own party had repudiated. Not only did he write no letters to advance his party's cause, but he "refused to answer whenever such answers could be interpreted as canvassing for office." [4]

Meanwhile the Jacksonians were merely amused at these intrigues of the old school politicians. The secret of their strength, here as always, was in their daring. Not only did they ignore the Anti-Masons and refuse to conciliate them, but they cast them off as completely as they had the Nullifiers. The highest member of the Masonic order in America was at the head of Jackson's Cabinet, and John Quincy Adams gave the utmost publicity to the fact by addressing his attacks on Masonry to Edward Livingston. Jackson himself sought and found an opportunity to go on record against the proscriptive hysteria. In this manner the Jacksonian managers rallied the Masons to their banner, and they held in their hands the ammunition with which to blow to atoms the plan of the coalition leaders to deliver the rank and file of the enemies of Masonry to Clay.

Early in October Blair published in the "Globe," without

[1] William H. Seward's *Autobiography*, 100.

[2] Clay to Brooke, Clay's *Works*, IV, 339.

[3] Wirt to Carr, Kennedy's *Life of Wirt*, II, 328–29.

[4] Kennedy's *Life of Wirt*, II, 331.

comment, Clay's manly letter to some Anti-Masons in Indiana refusing to be drawn into sectarian quarrels. "If a President of the United States . . . were to employ his official power to sustain, or to abolish, or to advance the interest of Masonry or Anti-Masonry," he had written, "it would be an act of usurpation and tyranny."[1] That was enough. The Democratic press of the country, taking the cue from the "Globe," reproduced the letter, and thus the rank and file of the party everywhere was strengthened in its determination not to support its author.

While Clay was intriguing with the Nullifiers and the Anti-Masons, the Democrats were audaciously denouncing both, and were gaining rather than losing by their temerity.

IV

THERE was but one issue — and that the Bank. Clay had made it the issue with the officers of the institution and their allied business interests; the clever leaders of the Jackson forces made it an issue with the masses of the people, who had always looked with suspicion and dislike upon the powerful financial institution.[2] And then, perhaps, the "Emperor Nicholas" bitterly regretted having yielded to the blandishments of Clay. If he had not considered the cost in money to the institution when he yielded, Clay understood it as well as Webster. They knew that a fight against the "weak old man," as they foolishly called Jackson, would be "no holiday affair." Satisfied of the support of the business element, they had calculated the cost of reaching the people generally — and they had the work of Biddle cut out for him.[3] And almost immediately, Biddle was as deeply involved as Clay himself.

The campaign plans of the two parties differed, since their special appeals were to different elements. The Clay men

[1] *Globe*, Oct. 8, 1832. [2] McMaster, IV, 145.
[3] Van Buren's *Political Parties*, 323.

relied on the distribution, with Bank money, of the printed speeches of Clay, Webster, and Calhoun, of tracts and pamphlets. These, falling into the hands of the masses, were thrown aside. They were sympathetically perused by the bankers, merchants, manufacturers, preachers, professors, and lawyers who were in no need of conversion.[1] The Bank made desperate efforts to win to its support the press of the larger cities and towns. It was notoriously willing to prove its appreciation of such support with the coin of the realm.[2] That Webb's paper had been won over with Bank money was common knowledge after the congressional investigation, and Amos Kendall, in the "Globe," charged that the "Evening Post" had been "approached," and that the "Standard" of Philadelphia had been offered five hundred dollars and a new set of type, and the inducement had been increased by five hundred dollars two days later.

Thoroughly frightened, Biddle spent lavishly for the printing and distribution of speeches and articles. Mailing the president of the Kentucky Bank [3] Webster's speech on the Veto, and an article reviewing the Message, he instructed that these, "as well as Mr. Clay's & Mr. Ewing's speeches on the same subject," be "printed and dispersed." [4] More than $80,000 — an enormous sum for those days — was spent by the Bank under the head of "stationery and printing" during the period of the campaign. Thousands of friendly newspapers were bought in bulk and scattered broadcast, and Blair announced the discovery that "about four bushels of the 'Extra Telegraph' is sent to New York to a single individual for distribution." [5] An analysis of Benton's speech and a reply was printed in pamphlet form, and thousands flooded the country and burdened the mails.

But more sinister still was the appearance, for the first

[1] McMaster, IV, 146.

[2] See Biddle to James Hunter, *Correspondence of Nicholas Biddle*, 127.

[3] John Tilford. [4] *Correspondence of Nicholas Biddle*, 197.

[5] *Globe*, Sept. 26, 1832.

time in American politics, of the weapons of intimidation and coercion. In New Orleans a bank commenced discounting four months' paper at eight per centum — "because of the veto." An advertisement appeared in a Cincinnati paper offering $2.50 per hundred for pork if Clay should be elected, $1.50 if Jackson won — a bribe of one dollar a head on each hundred pounds of pork. From Brownsville, Pennsylvania, went forth the disturbing report that "a large manufacturer has discharged all his hands, and others have given notice to do so," and that "not a single steam boat will be built this season at Wheeling, Pittsburg or Louisville." From Baltimore: "A great many mechanics are thrown out of employment by the stoppage of building. The prospect ahead is that we shall have a very distressing winter." And so the work went on, with the Bank and its political champions holding the sword of Damocles over the heads of the masses who dared to vote for Jackson.[1] Jackson was held before the conservative and timid as rash, dangerous, destructive. Webster's State convention speech at Worcester, expanding on the unfortunate sentence from the Veto Message as to the finality of Supreme Court decisions, was given general circulation. Even the brilliant Ritchie, of the "Richmond Enquirer," lived in constant terror of some rash act of Jackson's that would wreck the country.[2]

For the benefit of the ardent Jacksonians who disliked and distrusted Van Buren, the nominee for Vice-President, the Whig and Bank press gravely quoted some mysterious "Philadelphian" to whom Jackson had said, "with his own lips," that a reëlection would satisfy him as a vindication, and that he would resign and go home, leaving Van Buren in the Presidency. Even the "National Intelligencer" referred to the rumor as "the disclosure of an important fact . . . going to confirm our own impressions." And Blair had been forced to notice and denounce the story with the comment that "we

[1] Benton's *Thirty Years' View*, I, 281. [2] Van Buren's *Political Parties*, 323.

had always thought Simpson the most depraved of all the miscreants purchased by the Bank, but certainly now Gales [1] deserves to be put below him." [2] Earlier in the campaign the Whigs had attempted to serve the same purpose by circulating alarming reports regarding Jackson's health. And Blair, in denouncing this canard, announced that the President "receives from 50 to 100 persons daily, is incessantly engaged in the despatch of the duties of his office, and joins regularly at table his large dinner parties of from 40 to 50 persons twice a week." [3]

For the benefit of the preachers, teachers, and moral forces, the old stories of Jackson's bloodthirstiness were revived, apropos of the attack by Sam Houston on a member of Congress. At first the President had merely instigated the assault — and then the imaginative Whig scribes worked out a bloodcurdling, circumstantial story. After the brutal attack, the swaggering Houston had met Postmaster-General Barry at the theater, and the two had talked it over at the theater bar, and, after being congratulated by the Cabinet member, he had called on Jackson and been heartily commended for his act.

Thus the Whigs used every weapon that came into their hands — money, subsidized and bought papers, the hostility to Masonry, the hate of the Nullifiers, the fear of Van Buren, intimidation, coercion, and slander. And something comparatively new to politics — the cartoon — soon became a feature of the fight. Here the Democrats were at a disadvantage, and the pictorial editorials that have come down to us are largely anti-Jackson. Here we find the President pictured as a raving maniac, as Don Quixote tilting at the pillars of the splendid marble bank building in Philadelphia, as a burglar attempting to force the bank doors with a battering ram, while the most popular cartoon among the friends of

[1] Editor of the *Intelligencer*.

[2] *Globe*, Sept. 15, 1832.

[3] *Ibid.*, Feb. 1, 1832.

Clay pictured Jackson receiving a crown from Van Buren and a scepter from the Devil.[1]

V

But all the while the consummate politicians of the Jackson party were reaching and arousing the masses. Long before the opening of the campaign, Amos Kendall, Lewis, Hill, and Blair were cunningly appealing to the interests, the prejudices, and the hero worship of the voters of the cornfield and the village. These forerunners of the modern politician were keenly appreciative of the fact that between 1824 and 1832 a great body of voters, previously proscribed because of their poverty and lack of property, had been newly enfranchised. With the Whigs these were non-existent. The journalistic training of Kendall, Hill, and Blair pointed to the press as the surest way to reach the masses with their propaganda. The old-fashioned politician still affected a contempt for the press, and particularly for the little struggling papers of the country. The genius of Kendall immediately seized upon these, and, long before the campaign began, the sallow, prematurely gray young man of mystery, shut up in his petty office in the Treasury, was busy night and day, and especially at night, preparing articles and editorials laudatory of the Jackson policies, denunciatory of the Opposition, and these, sent to editors all over the country, were printed as their own. Thus the followers of Jackson in every nook and corner of the country were constantly supplied with ammunition in the shape of arguments they could comprehend and assimilate.

The center and soul of the Democratic organization was the office of the "Globe." Among the papers of national reputation, but two others were supporting Jackson, the "New Hampshire Patriot" of "Ike" Hill, and Van Buren's

[1] Parton's *Jackson*, III, 423; McMaster, IV, 147. Some of these cartoons may be seen at the Congressional Library.

organ, the "Albany Argus." But the "Globe" was equal to the demand upon it. Doubling the number of issues, the ferociously partisan Blair sat in the office writing feverishly, with Kendall gliding in and out with copy. Both possessed a genius for controversy. Both had mastered a style combining literary qualities, attractive to the educated, with the "pep" and "punch" that impressed, interested, delighted, the multitude. Blair dipped his pen in vitriol. In satire and sarcasm he had few equals. He was no parlor warrior, and he struck resounding blows like a boiler-maker. And he wrote in a flowing style that, at times, approached real eloquence. Having the average man in mind, his editorials, filling the greater part of the paper, were concise and brief. When language seemed weak, he resorted to italics. The longer and more sustained argumentative articles were written by the more brilliant Kendall. Through July, August, September, and October he wrote a series of articles on "The Bank and the Veto," beginning in an argumentative vein, and gradually growing personal until he was devoting one issue to the financial connections between the Bank and Duff Green, another to similar connections of Webb, of the "Courier and Enquirer," and another to Gales, of the "Intelligencer."

Infuriated by the gibes, taunts, and attacks, the Whigs charged that the "Globe" was being distributed gratuitously — the business manager replied with an affidavit as to the legitimacy of its circulation.[1] News of the deepest import was crowded out by the exigencies of the campaign, and with the cholera scourge taking a heavy toll of lives in Washington, the only mention of it in the "Globe" was in the official reports of the Board of Health. But there was room for columns of quotations from Democratic papers on the Veto, all striking the exultant key — "The Monster is Destroyed."

[1] *Globe*, Sept. 26, 1832, affidavit of John C. Rives.

Only the persistent hammering of the Whigs on the unfortunate sentence of the Veto Message caused acute distress in Democratic circles. Webster's Worcester speech was annoying. Here a sneer, there a gibe in the "Globe," but sneers and gibes did not quite satisfy the editor, who finally made a laborious effort to explain,[1] and, finding the effort tame, Blair countercharged with the publication of Clay's bitter anti-Bank speech of 1811 with appropriate comments upon it from the Jacksonian papers of the country.

As the campaign approached the end, Blair stressed the theory that the real fight was between Jackson and the Bank, with Clay a mere pawn in the game. "We see," he wrote, "the most profligate apostasies invited and applauded — the grossest misrepresentations circulated — the worst forgeries committed — open briberies practiced, and all for what? Not avowedly to elect Henry Clay or William Wirt, but any 'available candidate' [2] — in other words, any candidate with whom, in the end, the Bank directors can make the best bargain." [3] And a week later, under the caption, "The Gold," Blair announces that through private advices "we learn that certain heavy trunks, securely hooped with iron, have arrived at Lexington [4] from the East." [5] Such was the character of the publicity with which the Jacksonians appealed to the masses of the people.

But the practical minds of the leaders of the Kitchen Cabinet were not content with creating public opinion — they systematically organized and directed it. In every community, no matter how obscure, some Jackson leader, with a genius for organization work, was busy welding the Jackson forces into a solid mass. Here Major Lewis took charge. He anticipated the card-index system of the modern politicians. There was scarcely a county in the country in which he did not know the precise man or men upon whom absolute reli-

[1] *Globe*, July, 28, 1832.
[2] Duff Green's expression.
[3] *Globe*, Oct. 17, 1832.
[4] Clay's home.
[5] *Globe*, Oct. 23, 1832.

ance could be placed. And "Ike" Hill, now a United States Senator, made an extensive organizing tour through Ohio and Pennsylvania in early August.

In both publicity and organization, the greater part of the ability and all the genius was with Jackson.

VI

THE Jacksonians depended also to a greater extent than the Opposition on appeals to the people, face to face. A creature of another world, looking down from the skies upon the United States in the late summer and autumn of 1832, would have concluded that its people moved about in enormous processions on horseback, with waving flags, branches and banners. Great meetings were held in groves, addressed by fiery orators, furiously denouncing "The Monster" and the "Corporation" and calling upon the people to "stand by the Hero." Men left their homes, bade farewell to their families as though enlisting for a war, and rode from one meeting to another for weeks at a time.[1] Nor was this hysterical enthusiasm confined to the more primitive sections of the country. A French traveler sojourning in New York City was profoundly impressed by a Jackson parade there. "It was nearly a mile long," he wrote. "The Democrats marched in good order to the glare of torches; the banners were more numerous than I have ever seen in any religious festival; all were in transparency on account of the darkness. On some were inscribed the names of Democratic societies or sections; others bore imprecations against the Bank of the United States. Nick Biddle and Old Nick here figured largely. . . . From farther than the eye could reach came marching on the Democrats. The procession stopped before the houses of the Jackson men to fill the air with cheers, and halted at the door of the leaders of the opposition to give three, six or nine groans. These scenes

[1] Sargent's *Public Men and Events*, I, 248.

belong to history and partake of the grand; they are the episodes of a wondrous epic which will bequeath a lasting memory to posterity."[1]

And into these amazing demonstrations the campaign glee club, also new to American politics, entered, to play a conspicuous part, with pretty girls, and children gayly dressed, singing round the hickory poles that were raised wherever there were idolaters of Jackson. And so they sang:

"Here's a health to the heroes who fought
And conquered in Liberty's cause;
Here's health to Old Andy who could not be bought
To favor aristocrat laws.
Hurrah for the Roman-like Chief —
He never missed fire at all;
But ever when called to his country's relief
Had a ready picked flint and a ball.

"Hurrah for the Hickory tree
From the mountain tops down to the sea.
It shall wave o'er the grave of the Tory and knave,
And shelter the honest and free."[2]

Even where the Whigs were strongest, the militant Democrats poured forth in defiant demonstrations. When Jackson, returning to Washington from the Hermitage in the closing days of the campaign, approached Lexington, the home of his rival, a multitude streamed down the road five miles to meet him, with over a thousand on horseback and in carriages, and before he reached his lodging the throng extended back two miles along the road "with green hickory bushes waving like bright banners in a breeze."[3]

It was inevitable that in such a campaign personalities should intrude. In the winter of 1831–32, while Congress was in session, Jackson took advantage of the presence of Dr. Harris, an eminent Philadelphia surgeon, to have the bullet from Benton's pistol, long lodged in his shoulder, removed.

[1] M. Chevalier, as quoted by Sargent, *Public Men and Events,* I, 249.
[2] From the *Globe.* [3] Description in the *Globe.*

When the surgeon appeared at the White House, he was engaged with company, but excused himself with the explanation that he would have to submit to an operation; and a few hours later he reappeared among his friends with his arm in a sling. "Precisely," wrote Blair, "as he had appeared with it in battle among the enemies of his country." [1] This gave the Whigs their cue, and their press teemed with references to the "disgusting affair" in which the shot had been fired. And Blair himself was able to retaliate in kind with the story of a wound received by Clay in a personal conflict. "He was taken to a kind friend's house," he wrote, "he was treated with the utmost tenderness and courtesy by that friend's wife and family, and while enjoying their hospitality, he amused himself . . . by winning the money of his kind host at Brag."

If Jackson was a brawler, it was given out thus that Clay was not only a brawler, but a gambler and an ingrate. Both stories made their way through the country.[2]

If the cholera was not of sufficient importance for the news columns of the party press, it was rich in suggestion to the politicians. The Dutch Synod requested Jackson to set a day aside for prayer. He replied that he had faith in the efficacy of prayer, but that the special day to be set aside should be designated by the State authorities. Whereupon Clay arose to offer a resolution in the Senate setting a day aside and fixing the day. Aha, cried Blair, he wants a veto on a religious subject. "It is not the cholera that makes them so pious; it is the hope to steal a march on the old Hero. . . . What whited sepulchers some of these partisan leaders are!" he wrote.[3]

And when, a little later, the "Pittsburgh Statesman," a Clay paper, suggested that "the only effectual cure, under existing circumstances, for genuine Jacksonism is the equally genuine Asiatic Spasmodic Cholera," the "Troy Budget,"

[1] *Globe*, Jan. 14, 1832. [2] *Ibid.*, Jan. 18, 1832. [3] *Ibid.*, July 21, 1832.

supporting Jackson, was not surprised at "such political depravity," coming from the "editorial slanderers and ruthless murderers of Mrs. Jackson." And "Ike" Hill, in the "New Hampshire Patriot," was reminded that Clay himself had prayed "for war, pestilence and famine" in preference to the reëlection of Jackson. When the President left the capital for the Hermitage, the "Troy Sentinel," Whig, with its eye on the church vote, announced with emphasis that he had left Washington "at eight o'clock on Sunday morning." Blair, denouncing the story as "a lie," declared that "he did not leave the city until Monday morning and spent the Sabbath in religious duties as usual." When "Ike" Hill, speaking at a complimentary dinner at the Eagle Coffee House, in Concord, assailed Clay and Senator John Holmes, and referred to some Senators as "low and blackguard," the "National Intelligencer" protested, and Blair replied with a description of Holmes as a "besotted Senator who had indulged in indecent and ribald slang throughout the session," and as one given to "low buffoonery" — the "mere Thersites of the Senate." [1] Charges of impropriety touching on the personal integrity of political leaders were commonplace. The "Globe," centering its fire upon the activities of the Bank, charged it with subsidizing and seducing the press by paying for the publication of political speeches at advertising rates.[2] "Every press in Philadelphia," it said, "is closed by its influence, against the admission of anything unfavorable to its pretensions. The 'Mechanics' Free Press' broke ground against it in conformity with the principles of its party, when lo! a shower of gold, amounting to $1700 for publishing Mr. McDuffie's report, silenced it, and for good reasons, doubtless, it has ever since held its peace about the Bank." And the Whig press was equally shocked to find that officers

[1] *Globe*, Aug. 22, 1832. The *Globe* published Hill's speech in full, the only one thus noticed in the campaign except Forsyth's tariff speech attacking Clay, and C. K. Ingersoll's tribute to Jackson at Philadelphia.

[2] That this was done is disclosed in the *Correspondence of Nicholas Biddle*.

high in the Government were sending the "Globe" all over the country under their official frank. "A lie!" screamed Blair. And so the battle of personalities went on. From Hill's "New Hampshire Patriot" came the resurrection of the long-discredited "bargain" story against Clay.

Meanwhile, what had become of the candidates and what were their feelings as to the prospects? While scarcely due to the strain of the campaign, all three, Jackson, Clay, and Wirt, were threatened with serious illness. As we have seen, Clay was threatened with paralysis about the time of his retirement from the Cabinet. During the summer and autumn of 1832 the old trouble returned. His friend, Brooke, who became concerned over his health, urged him to caution, and Clay, much moved by his friend's solicitude, promised to be more careful of his diet, to abstain from wine, and to reduce his consumption of tobacco to "one form." [1] At times, during the summer session, he had been forced to leave Washington for a brief period of rest at his friend's home at St. Julien, Virginia; and as soon as Congress adjourned, he hastened to White Sulphur Springs for two weeks in hope of relief from the waters. Skeptical at first of his election, his confidence increased until he and Webster were exchanging letters of congratulation on its certainty.

Wirt, who had a serious attack, and was in a weakened condition, was forced by his physician to leave Baltimore, rather than take a chance with the cholera. After a brief sojourn at Bedford Springs, he went with his family to Berkley Springs where he remained through September. Here, with no thought of his own election, but with ardent hopes for Clay, he ignored the clamor of the campaign. Riding and lounging about the grounds during the day, regaling company with ghost stories in the evening, he bore no resemblance to a presidential candidate. [2]

Soon after Congress adjourned, the scourge reached Wash-

[1] Clay's *Works*, IV, 337. [2] *Life of Wirt*, II, 378.

ington, taking heavy toll of the Irish and Swedish laborers engaged in the first macadamizing of Pennsylvania Avenue, and spreading rapidly from the poorer parts to the White House section. Because of Jackson's weakened condition, his physicians insisted that he spend three months at the Hermitage, and near the middle of August, accompanied part of the way by Amos Kendall, Frank Blair, "Ike" Hill, Major Lewis, Lewis Cass, and Benton, he left the sweltering and infected capital and went down the Ohio. He was in high glee. Never for a moment had he doubted the result of the election. During the congressional fight over the recharter bill he had not punished those who had withheld their support by denying them patronage, except in the case of his most bitter foes. Just before the vote in the House, an Ohio Representative solicited an appointment for a constituent, and, upon being granted the favor, he explained that he thought it due Jackson for him to know that the favor was being granted a member who would vote for the Bank.

"I can't help that, sir, but I already knew it. See here — I can take a roll of the House and check off every Democrat who will vote for the Bank. In fact I have one here."

Turning briskly, he produced it, and the Representative, running over the list, indicated one name as that of a man who would vote with Jackson.

"How do you know?" demanded Jackson.

When told that this Congressman had been so unmercifully berated by his constituents that he had felt compelled to change his tack, the old warrior smiled grimly.

"He is a lucky fellow," he said, "to get the views of his constituents beforehand. There are several other Democrats in the House who will not get similar notice until next fall, sir." [1]

Nothing occurred after that incident to alter his opinion of the sentiment of the people. As Hill left the boat bearing

[1] This story was related by William Allen of Ohio to Buell, who uses it in his *Life of Jackson*.

the presidential party down the Ohio, at Wheeling, Jackson said, as he clasped his hand: "Isaac, it'll be a walk. If our fellows did n't raise a finger from now on the thing would be just as well as done. In fact, Isaac, it's done now."

That his friends shared his confidence we have ample evidence. Hill, writing to a friend, advised him to bet all he could on Pennsylvania and Ohio for Jackson — "not on stated majorities, but hang on to the general result." And he added frankly, "I am on the turf myself. Benton and his friends out West are picking up all they can get." John Van Buren, the son of Martin, and popularly known as "Prince John," made a small fortune with his ventures on the election, and Hone, commenting on the manner and appearance of Martin Van Buren, the nominee for Vice-President, thought it indicated a feeling of absolute security.

The result was a notable victory for Jackson and his policies — an unmistakable rebuke to Clay. In electoral votes Jackson received 219, Clay 49, and Wirt 7, and the popular vote gave Jackson 124,392 over the combined strength of Clay and Wirt, thus proving the absurdity of Thurlow Weed's theory that if Clay had acquiesced in the wishes of the Anti-Masons he could have been elected. The only State carried by Wirt was Vermont — as he had predicted. Clay carried Massachusetts, Rhode Island, Connecticut, Delaware, and Kentucky, and five out of the eight electoral votes of Maryland. All the other States went to Jackson but one — South Carolina, with childish petulance, threw its vote away at the behest of Calhoun.

Nothing could have been more ominous than this action. Going entirely outside the regularly nominated candidates, and acting in conformity with the views of the Nullifying party, which insisted on placing the State outside the Union, she gave her vote to Governor Floyd of Virginia. And Jackson, getting the returns, instantly caught the significance of the act, and girded his loins for a life-and-death struggle with Calhoun and Nullification.

CHAPTER X

THE POLITICS OF NULLIFICATION

I

CALLERS at the Hermitage about the first of October were surprised to find Jackson's thoughts remote from the election. Instead of a jubilant politician, they found an old man frothing with fury over the news from South Carolina that the Nullifiers had won a majority of seats in the Legislature and were arranging for an early summoning of a Nullification Convention. His indignation was so intense that his friends were shocked at the ferocity of his mood. The crisis had not crept upon him unaware. With keen, far-seeing eyes he had watched its advance, hoping that something would intervene to divert his native State from its mad course, but determined, if the issue came, to crush it with an iron hand. His hatred of Calhoun had, by this time, become an obsession, and when he threatened to "hang every leader . . . of that infatuated people, sir, by martial law, irrespective of his name, or political or social position," there was no doubt as to whom he referred.[1] Taking no further interest in the election, he put the campaign behind him and hastened to the capital. Blair, the politician always, hurried to the White House with some papers relating to the election. After a hasty and perfunctory glance, Jackson returned them to the editor, with a "Thank you, sir," and launched into a denunciation of the Nullifiers. The date set for the Nullification Convention had just reached him. Even Blair, accustomed to his fits of temper, was startled. He was in the presence of a Jackson he had never seen or known before. "The lines in his face were hard drawn, his tones were full of

[1] Letters to Hamilton, *Reminiscences*, 231.

wrath and resentment. . . . Any one would have thought he was planning another great battle."[1] Even the announcement of victory at the polls scarcely interested him. Blair and Kendall called with a table showing the electoral vote. Glancing at it indifferently for a moment, his face brightened. "The best thing about this, gentlemen, is that it strengthens my hands in this trouble." Such was the spirit with which Andrew Jackson faced the gravest crisis the Nation had yet known.

Beginning with an intensely nationalistic spirit,[2] South Carolina commenced to veer about with the tariff of 1816, and every succeeding tariff measure had been a provocation. Two years before Jackson's inauguration, the "Brutus" articles on the "Usurpations of the Federal Government," eloquent, fiery, defiant of the "Monster of the North," had created a profound impression, commanding the adherence of McDuffie, the Mirabeau of the disaffected, Hamilton, Preston, and Chancellor William Harper, described by Houston as "scarcely inferior to Calhoun as an exponent of metaphysical doctrines."[3] The principles of "Brutus" only awaited the authoritative sanction of Calhoun to place upon them the stamp of the State's approval.

The tariff of 1828 was the last straw, and sedition was openly talked by the greater part of the South Carolina congressional delegation at the home of Senator Hayne. One week later, Calhoun, at his home at Fort Hill, finished his "Exposition," enunciating the principles of Nullification, which the committee of seven of the State Legislature presented as its own. During the summer, politicians made numerous pilgrimages to Fort Hill for conferences, but not the scratch of a pen remains to indicate the character of the discussions. Calhoun was still "under cover." He was about to enter upon his second term in the Vice-Presidency, and his friends were

[1] Blair, as quoted by Buell.

[2] See Houston's *Nullification in South Carolina*, 27–28.

[3] *Ibid.*, 70.

looking forward to the Presidency in 1832. The world was to wait awhile for the openly avowed views of the Master.

With the publication of the "Exposition," the battle royal began, Cavalier against Cavalier, the Union cause brilliantly led by the elegant Joel R. Poinsett. In the early stages of the fight the Nullifiers did not scruple to represent Jackson as friendly to their cause. "I had supposed," wrote Jackson, in reply to a letter from Poinsett, "that every one acquainted with me knew that I was opposed to the Nullifying doctrine, and my toast at the Jefferson dinner was sufficient evidence of that fact." [1] Having no reason, after that, to doubt Jackson's position, the Unionists invited Jackson to attend one of their public dinners, and he sent a letter settling beyond all possibility of dispute his position on Nullification. The Nullifiers, dining at a rival banquet, and learning of the reading of the Jackson letter, reminded the writer that "old Waxhaw still stands where Jackson left it, and the old stock of '76 has not run out." After that the drama hurried to a climax. The tariff of 1832 was but oil on the flames. The fight was carried to the polls and Nullification won by a majority of 6000 out of 40,000 votes cast.

The most portentous feature of the campaign was the appearance in August of Calhoun's famous letter to Hamilton, decisively accepting as his own, and urging upon his people, the doctrine of Nullification. It was intended and timed to serve the purposes of the campaign. Unhappily Calhoun must ever remain more or less a steel engraving. His private life was carefully screened. Jefferson prowling among the brickmasons at the University, Jackson with his clay pipe on the veranda of the Hermitage, Webster among his cattle at Marshfield, Clay meditating speeches under the trees at Ashland, are possible of contact by future generations, but Calhoun at Fort Hill seems hopelessly remote and cannot be

[1] Stillé's *Life and Services of Joel R. Poinsett.*

visualized. He stalks upon the stage, a dramatic and impressive figure, and plays his public part, but no one is admitted to the dressing-room. Thus all we know of the occasion of the preparation of the famous letter, which became the Magna Carta of the Nullifiers, is told in the letter itself.[1] The events of that summer and early autumn were intimately known to Jackson as he walked the grounds of the Hermitage, and lingered mournfully about the tomb of his beloved Rachel. In the spring of 1830 the brilliant Poinsett, fresh from his mission to Mexico, had been shocked, on his return to the drawing-rooms of Charleston, to find sedition poured with the tea, and had hurried to Washington to be closeted with Jackson at the White House. Before he emerged, he had been designated by the President as his personal ambassador in South Carolina,[2] and after calling upon Adams, in retirement, to tell him of his hopes and fears,[3] he made all haste home to combat, inch by inch, the growing madness, and prepared, if need be, to die with a musket in his hands. During the intervening three years his confidential reports had kept Jackson in close touch with all the movements of the enemy, and the grim old warrior, reëntering the White House on his return from Tennessee, entertained no illusions as to what he faced.

Three days after Jackson reached Washington, the South Carolina Legislature fixed November 3d as the date for the Nullification Convention. Silently, but sternly, soldier-wise, the President was clearing the decks for action. The day he left the Hermitage the Collector of Customs in Charleston received instructions as to his course; on reaching the capital, the commander in charge of troops there was warned of possible attempts to seize the forts; to his apprehensive friends he was sending reassuring messages. "I am well advised as

[1] For this letter in full see Calhoun's *Works*, or Jenkins's *Life of Calhoun*, 195–232.
[2] Poinsett's letter to Jackson, Oct. 23, 1830, Stillé's *Life of Poinsett*.
[3] Adams's *Memoirs*, May 13, 1830.

to the views and proceedings of the leading Nullifiers," he wrote Hamilton on November 2d. "We are wide awake here. THE UNION WILL BE PRESERVED; REST ASSURED OF THAT."[1] Five days later, Cass was ordering additional troops to Fort Moultrie, and Jackson was dispatching a secret emissary to Charleston, with instructions to communicate with Poinsett, and to report upon the conditions of the forts and the lengths to which the Nullifiers might go.[2] The day preceding the meeting of the Nullification Convention, Cass ordered General Scott to Charleston, with minute instructions.[3] With Scott hurrying to South Carolina, the convention met, the Nullification Ordinance was passed, and February 1st was set as the day for it to go into operation. Three days after the convention adjourned, the Legislature met and passed laws to put the ordinance into effect. The Unionist Convention immediately met, denounced Nullification, and began to organize their forces for a possible armed conflict.

Meanwhile Scott had performed his mission with a discretion and sound judgment which called forth the commendation of Jackson.[4] Five days before Congress met, five thousand stand of muskets with equipment had been ordered to Castle Pinckney, and a sloop of war with smaller vessels were on their way to Charleston Harbor.[5] "The Union must be preserved, and its laws duly executed, but BY PROPER MEANS," wrote the President to Poinsett.

Thus, in this real crisis, the "law," the "Constitution," and "public opinion" were uppermost in the mind of the man generally described as reckless in the use of power. Long after the event, but while the contest was still on, he wrote to Poinsett of his regret at the failure of the Unionist Convention to memorialize Congress "to extend to you the guarantees of the Constitution, of a republican form of gov-

[1] Hamilton's *Reminiscences*, 247.

[2] George Breathitt, brother of the Governor of Kentucky.

[3] Smith's *Life of Cass*, 269–71.

[4] Cass to Scott, Smith's *Life of Cass*.

[5] Jackson to Poinsett, Stillé's *Life of Poinsett*.

ernment, stating the actual despotism which now controls the State." This, he explained, "would have placed your situation before the whole nation, and filled the heart of every true lover of his country and its liberties with indignation."[1] While at work on his Proclamation, he wrote Hamilton in New York, urging that public opinion assert itself in an unmistakable manner. "The crisis must be, and AS FAR AS MY CONSTITUTIONAL AND LEGAL POWERS AUTHORIZE, will be, met with energy and firmness. HENCE THE PROPRIETY OF THE PUBLIC VOICE BEING HEARD; — AND IT OUGHT NOW TO BE SPOKEN IN A VOICE OF THUNDER."[2] Thus, when the gavel fell on the opening of the Congress, Jackson had the situation well in hand, had perfected his plans for vigorous action within the limits of the Constitution and the laws, but still hoped, through the pressure of public opinion and the returning good sense of the Carolinians, it would be unnecessary to resort to force.

II

ON the opening day of the Congress the great Carolinian was not in his Senate seat, to which he had been immediately elected on his resignation from the Vice-Presidency, but public interest centered in it, nevertheless. The Jackson Message was awaited with keen anxiety. In its recommendation of a reduction of the tariff was easily recognized a conciliatory gesture toward the South Carolinians. Even his discussion of the crisis was temperate and unprovocative. No one listening to the Message could have had the slightest notion of what was taking place at that very hour in Jackson's workroom in the White House.

Even before the Congress met, Edward Livingston was at work preparing the Proclamation which was to thrill the country like a bugle blast, perpetuate the memory of Jack-

[1] Letter to Poinsett, Feb. 7, 1833, *Life of Poinsett.*

[2] Hamilton's *Reminiscences,* 248.

son, and reflect glory on himself. It was no mere accident which led to the selection of the Secretary of State for this task. His views on the integrity and perpetuity of the Union were intimately known to his chief; and it was a duty upon which Livingston could enter with all his heart. But the first draft of the Proclamation was written by Jackson in a frenzy of composition, so hurriedly that he scattered the pages over the table to let them dry. The general tenor of the document was therefore his. If the wording was Livingston's, the document breathed the soul of Andrew Jackson. During the period of its preparation, Jackson was in constant touch. He was thinking of nothing else. Thus, on the day his Message was read to Congress, the iron man was meditating his appeal to public opinion. It was almost midnight. In his room in the southeast corner of the mansion, he sat before the fireplace smoking his pipe — thinking. Bitter as he was against Calhoun and the leaders whom he felt had seduced the people of his native State, he felt an affection for the confused masses who had been deluded; and, while prepared, if need be, to strike with the military arm of the Government, he passionately hoped that this would not become necessary. Going over to the table on which always stood the picture of his Rachel, and the Bible to which she had been devoted, he wrote a conclusion to the Proclamation in the nature of a touching appeal to the patriotic memories of the South Carolinians. Then he wrote to Livingston: "I submit the above as the conclusion of the Proclamation for your amendment and revision. Let it receive your best flight of eloquence, to strike to the heart, and speak to the feelings of my deluded countrymen of South Carolina."

Three days later, the night again found Jackson obsessed with the preparation of the Proclamation. Livingston, in his writing, was sending it as he proceeded to the White House, where Major Donelson, the private secretary, was engaged in copying it for the printer. At four o'clock in the afternoon the Secretary of State had sent a number of sheets, and Donelson had finished copying and was waiting for more. Jackson was impatient of the delay. The Message having gone forth, he thought it important that it should be followed immediately by the Proclamation for the effect on South Carolina. Again he wrote to Livingston explaining the reason for his anxiety. The Secretary would therefore please send over at once, "sealed, by the bearer," such sheets as were completed, and the harassed Livingston complied. Under these conditions of pressure the immortal document was written.[1]

On the day Jackson gave this Proclamation to the Nation he made his last appeal. A letter written to Poinsett that day discloses a determination to move sternly and unhesitatingly to what he conceived to be his solemn duty. This letter breathed the spirit of the battle-field. The act of the Nullifiers was sheer treason. He had been assured that he would be sustained by Congress. "I will meet it [treason] at the threshold, and have the leaders arrested and arraigned for treason," he wrote. He was only waiting for the Acts of the Legislature "to make a communication to Congress, ask the means necessary to carry my Proclamation into complete effect, and by an exemplary punishment of those leaders for treason so unprovoked, put down this rebellion, and strengthen our Government both at home and abroad." The Unionists of South Carolina need not fear. In forty days he could have 50,000 men in the State, in forty more another 50,000. "How impotent," he wrote, "the threats of resistance with only a population of 250,000 whites, and nearly double that in blacks, with our ships in the port to aid in the execution of the laws!"[2]

Thus hoping that necessity would not compel him to send

[1] These letters, in possession of the Livingston family, were used by Hunt in his *Life of Livingston*.

[2] Stillé's *Life of Poinsett*.

armed forces, determined to meet the issue, however, as it might present itself, careful to observe all the constitutional and legal limitations of his power, enraged to fury against the leaders and eager to lay his hands on Calhoun, he gave the country the Proclamation which instantly wiped out party lines with most, and rallied the patriotic forces of the Union to his support.

III

At the time of the writing of the Proclamation, Andrew Jackson was sixty-six, and Edward Livingston sixty-nine years old, but it breathes the fire, the passion, the enthusiasm, and the eloquence of impetuous youth. As an oration, it was to be treasured as a masterpiece; as a public document, it has taken its place alongside the Emancipation Proclamation as one of the greatest pronouncements of American history. Its publication appealed to the Unionists of the country like a charge on the battle-field. To no one did it give keener pleasure than to Webster, who read it in New Jersey on his way to the capital. In Philadelphia he met Clay, and a friend of the latter explained Clay's plan of concessions to the Nullifiers through a new tariff of gradual reductions. The martial call of Jackson aroused the fighting blood within Webster, and Clay's game of politics repelled him. He hastened to Washington determined to give his best blows for Jackson and the Administration.[1]

John Marshall, in gloomy mood, found in the Proclamation the elixir for his pessimism.[2] Justice Story, despite his deep-seated prejudice, could not withhold his commendation, coupled with an expression of strange surprise. "The President's Proclamation is excellent," he wrote, "and contains the true principles of the Constitution; but will he stand to it? Will he not surrender all to the guidance of Virginia?"[3]

[1] Lodge's *Life of Webster*, 208. [2] Beveridge's *John Marshall*, IV, 570–73.
[3] Letter to Richard Peters, *Life and Letters of Story*, II, 113.

Adams described it as a "blister plaster." [1] Among all his long-time political opponents, Clay alone withheld enthusiastic commendation, with the comment that, "although there are some good things in it, there are some entirely too ultra for me." In truth, the man who would "rather be right than President" seized eagerly upon the President's patriotic position to curry favor with the extreme State-Rights men of the South.

Thus we soon enter upon the party phase of the fight. The effect upon some of Jackson's State-Rights supporters was one of painful embarrassment. While the average Virginian had no sympathy with Nullification, he subscribed to the State-Rights doctrine and to the right of secession. The very point on which Clay cunningly and unscrupulously pounced was therefore the one which caused the greatest consternation among the Administration Democrats of the Old Dominion. It was to them that Clay was making his appeal. The Virginia Assembly, which had just unanimously elected W. C. Rives, a Jacksonian, to the Senate, instantly reversed itself by electing John Tyler, an enemy, to that body, to succeed Tazewell, who had resigned. W. S. Archer, writing to Cambreleng in New York, declared that it would be ridiculous to expect Virginia to endorse the Proclamation,[2] and Governor Floyd, who had received South Carolina's vote in the recent election, rejoiced to find "the poor unworthy dogs, Ritchie, Van Buren & Co. deserted." [3] To the momentarily embarrassed Ritchie, his cleverness pointed a way out. Penning a mild objection to some of the doctrinal points, he accepted it as primarily a denunciation of Nullification, and, as such, gave it the support of his great prestige and pen.[4]

Such was the position of many others among the Southern leaders of the Jackson party, but Ritchie found himself in a minority. John Tyler, never friendly to Jackson, now seized

[1] *Memoirs*, Dec. 25, 1832.

[2] Ambler's *Thomas Ritchie*, 152. [3] *Ibid.* [4] *Ibid.*, 153.

upon the Proclamation as a pretext for pushing to the head of the Opposition. Writing heatedly to Tazewell of the "servility" to party of many Southern statesmen supporting the President, he drew a gloomy picture of the future. The Proclamation, he thought, had "swept away all the barriers of the Constitution," had established "a consolidated military despotism." He "trembled" for South Carolina. "The war cry is up — rely upon it," he wrote. "The boast is that the President by stamping like another Pompey on the earth can raise a hundred thousand men." [1]

It is significant of Whig hopes, that, when Tyler wrote and Ritchie was supporting the President, John Hampden Pleasants, the editor of the "Richmond Whig," and an intimate of Clay's, was denouncing the principles enunciated by Jackson and Livingston.[2] Resolutions were adopted by the Legislature denouncing both Nullification and the Proclamation.

Nor was Jackson indifferent to the attitude Virginia might assume. He planned to isolate South Carolina, and he feared an alliance with Virginia more than with any other State. Wishing to reach the Virginians as speedily as possible, he called upon Lewis Cass to prepare a letter in the form of an appeal to be published in Ritchie's "Richmond Enquirer." Within a few days after the appearance of the Proclamation, Virginians were reading a letter described by Ritchie as from "one of the ablest men in the country." Making no defense of the tariff, but pointing out the impossibility of the radical changes demanded being made within the limited time allowed by the Carolina politicians, he suggested that "Virginia might interpose most efficaciously, and add another leaf to the wreath which adorns her civic chaplet," if her Legislature would appoint a committee to proceed to South Carolina and "entreat her convention . . . to recall its late steps, and at all events to delay her final action till another trial is made

[1] *Letters and Times of the Tylers*, I, 448. [2] *Ibid.*, 451.

to reduce the tariff."[1] This was to lead, a little later, to the adoption of a similar plan.

Strange as it may now seem, the position of Virginia prevented New York from endorsing the Proclamation unqualifiedly, through her Legislature — and thereon hangs a tale of the political cunning of Martin Van Buren. In the Empire State the Proclamation had been received with enthusiasm. Even so bitter a partisan as Philip Hone poured forth his admiration and commendation on the pages of his diary. "As a composition, it is splendid," he wrote, "and will take its place in the archives of our country, and dwell in the memory of our citizens alongside of the Farewell Address. . . . I think Jackson's election may save the Union. If he is sincere in his Proclamation, he will put down this rebellion. Mr. Clay, pursuing the same measures, would not have been equally successful."[2] We have seen, in Jackson's letter to Hamilton, his desire that every agency of publicity should be employed to focus the sentiment against Nullification. The New York Legislature being then in session, Hamilton wrote leading men in Albany urging the passage of a commendatory resolution. In the absence of definite encouragement, he then wrote Van Buren, his political and personal friend, suggesting that he bring pressure to bear upon his friends in the Assembly. The letter was returned, opened, but unanswered, and Hamilton lost no time in writing of the incident to Jackson, with the comment that "this unfriendly, nay offensive course, resulted from Van Buren's fear of offending the dominant political party in Virginia."[3]

That Van Buren was deeply embarrassed by the doctrinal features of the Proclamation, if not by the possible effect upon his candidacy for the Presidency and his popularity among the Virginia politicians, has been admitted and explained by himself.[4] The document was delivered to him at

[1] *Richmond Enquirer*, Dec. 13, 1832.
[2] *Diary*, Dec. 12, 1832.
[3] Hamilton's *Reminiscences*, 250.
[4] Van Buren's *Autobiography*, 545–53.

the home of a friend in Albany as the party was in the act of going in to dinner. Instantly his practiced eye caught the phrasing that would arouse the ire of the State-Rights element. The Whigs in Albany were just as keen, and proceeded, with celerity, to take advantage. William H. Seward immediately offered a resolution in the State Senate to the effect that "the President of the United States . . . had advanced the true principles upon which only the Constitution can be maintained and defended." With Van Buren on the ground, and with the Democrats in the majority, the Whigs hoped, not without reason, either to force the Jacksonians to accept the conclusions of the resolution, or to a rejection of the endorsement, which would be interpreted as a rupture of the relations of the President and Vice-President. The Democrats did neither — they postponed action. It was probably at this juncture that Van Buren received the letter from Hamilton and returned it unanswered. Realizing, however, the fatality of non-action, Van Buren prepared a resolution, together with an elaborate and laborious report, taking issue with "the history given by the President of the formation of our Government," and calculated to satisfy the State-Rights men of Virginia. These were adopted, and sent to the White House with an explanation. Just what Jackson thought of it will never be known, for he filed the letter without a word of comment to his secretary, in whose presence it was read.[1] Nor was the subject ever mentioned in future conversations between the two leaders.[2] That a copy was also sent to Rives and Ritchie in Virginia we may be sure.

Such were the cross-currents of party politics at the time, with Jackson playing a bold and straight game, thinking solely of the Union, and Clay and Van Buren, rival candidates for the Presidency, pussyfooting and conciliating on a vital issue.

[1] Van Buren's *Autobiography*, 553.
[2] For Van Buren's report, see *Autobiography*, 550–52.

Meanwhile what was the effect in South Carolina? Senator Hayne, now Governor, met the challenge of the President in an able document, bitter in its defiance, which fired the fighting blood of the Nullifiers. Preston described it as "a document whose elegance of diction, elaborate and conclusive argument, just and clear constitutional exposition, confuted all the show of argument of the President's Proclamation." [1] Outside of Nullification circles, the bitterness of this counterblast made a deep impression. Adams found it "full of bitter words," and, after reading it, sent it to James K. Polk, the Jackson leader in the House.[2] The Hayne defiance was echoed by the Nullifiers. The eloquent Preston, addressing a mass meeting in Charleston, declared that "there are 16,000 back countrymen with arms in their hands and cockades in their hats, ready to march to our city at a moment's warning to defend us. . . . I will pour down a torrent of volunteers that will sweep the myrmidons of the tyrant from the soil of Carolina." [3] But Calhoun was disappointed with the Proclamation. He had hoped for an intemperate, ranting denunciation of the Carolinians that would heat their blood and put them on the march. The sober dignity of the document and its impressive appeal to the better natures of the people interfered with his plans.

In the House of Representatives, the Carolinians were seething with wrath. The impassioned McDuffie, according to Adams, "could not contain himself," and declared that "if Congress should approve the principles of that proclamation, the liberties of the country were gone forever." Whereupon Archer rose to suggest that a communication "would very shortly be received upon which the gentleman would have an opportunity to express his opinion without restraint." [4]

[1] Jervey's *Robert Y. Hayne.* [2] *Memoirs*, Dec. 26, 1832.
[3] March's *Reminiscences of Congress.*
[4] Adams's *Memoirs*, Dec. 14, 1832.

IV

The excitement over the Proclamation found Calhoun remote from the turmoil and in the midst of his family at Fort Hill. There he lingered to enjoy the Christmas festivities, and the day following he started to Washington to take his place in the Senate. There was much drama in this winter journey to the capital. One of his biographers has compared it to "that of Luther to attend the diet of Worms."[1] The public was convinced of the temper of Jackson and realized the possibilities when the lion in him was aroused. To some Calhoun's journey suggested a death march. Looked upon as the prime mover, the instigator, the leader of the seditious movement, many thought that he would be arrested on the charge of treason before he crossed the Virginia border. Interest in his progress was intense, and even among those who abhorred the new doctrine there was no little sympathy for the grim, impeccably pure statesman who had the courage to beard the lion in his den. New Year's Day found him at Raleigh, where he rested. Here crowds gathered to welcome, or merely to observe him, and a public dinner was offered him by his admirers. This he politely declined. There was something of grandeur in the dignity of his demeanor. As he proceeded from town to town, his approach was announced and elaborate preparations were made for his reception, for both North Carolina and Virginia were devoted to State Rights, and not a few of their citizens sympathized with the Carolina doctrine, and looked upon secession as an inevitable result of the crisis. Unlike the case of Burr, nothing personally sinister clung to him. His worst enemies conceded his honesty, and this was in his favor. Mrs. Bayard Smith, echoing the sentiment of the Washington drawing-rooms, found herself wondering, on Christmas Day, if all the "high soarings" of "one of the noblest and most generous

[1] Jenkins, 246.

spirits" were to end "in disappointment or humiliation or in blood." [1] That this friendly atmosphere, through which he moved, was reassuring to Calhoun, we may assume from his letter to his son on reaching the capital. Here he found "things better than anticipated" and that it was beginning to be "felt that we must succeed."

On the day he took the oath and his seat in the Senate, the little semi-circular chamber was crowded with friends and foes, drawn by the dramatic features of the situation. Tall, erect, his face sternly set, his iron-gray hair brushed back, he walked into the chamber over which he had presided, slowly and with a deliberation which seemed as studied as that of an actor upon the stage. When he took his seat, some Senators hastened to clasp his hand, but it was noticed that others, who had formerly been friendly, held back, deterred perhaps by the frown of the White House. At length the great scene — the taking of the oath. This he did in a reverential manner, and his voice was serious and solemn when he swore to support the Constitution which Jackson contended he had flagrantly violated.[2] The leader of Nullification was in his seat.

V

THE day after Calhoun started on his journey to the capital, the Verplanck Tariff Bill, sanctioned by the Administration, was introduced in the House. This measure, it was thought, might go a long way toward preventing any accession to the ranks of the Nullifiers in that it went far toward meeting the objections to the revenue laws. It was a rather radical measure, providing for the immediate reduction of numerous duties, with further reductions a year later. The protection forces rallied at once for its defeat. Through all the parliamentary devices of delay, Jackson, keenly watching developments through the reports of Lewis and Donelson, was

[1] *First Forty Years*, Dec. 25, 1832. [2] March's *Reminiscences of Congress*.

convinced that the Nullifiers were as much interested in its defeat as the protectionists. An "insulting and irritating speech" of Wilde of Georgia he thought "instigated by the Nullies, who wish no accommodation of the tariff." [1] Long before it could be brought to a vote, it had been hammered beyond recognition by amendments and Jackson had lost interest in the reduction of the tariff, rather preferring first to whip Nullification without any preliminary concessions.

Meanwhile Jackson was awaiting developments before submitting his Message to Congress asking additional powers to put down the heresy. Through the latter part of December and the early part of January, Hayne was making open preparations for an armed resistance. Poinsett, reporting constantly, had abandoned hope of "putting down Nullification by moral force," and hoped that the "vain blustering of these mad-men" would not influence Congress on the tariff, as "such a concession would confirm the power and popularity of the Nullifiers." [2] He was anxious for the contest. "Is not raising, embodying, and marching men to oppose the laws of the United States an overt act of treason?" he wrote the Unionist Congressman from Charleston, who still hoped that the crisis could be passed without recourse to the Federal army.[3] Thus, early in January, Poinsett was anxious to have Federal troops sent into the State, while other Unionists still held back. In this controversy Jackson agreed with the conservatives that the Unionists of the State should first have an opportunity to demonstrate their ability to handle the situation.

On January 16th, Archer's promise to McDuffie was fulfilled, when Jackson laid all the facts relative to the crisis before Congress with a request for authority to abolish or alter certain ports of entry, and to use the army to protect the officers in the discharge of their duties. He also asked for

[1] Stillé's *Life of Poinsett*. [2] Letter to Jackson, Stillé's *Life of Poinsett*.
[3] Poinsett to Drayton, Stillé's *Life of Poinsett*.

the revival of the sixth section of the Act of March 3, 1815, and for a provision for the removal to the United States Circuit Court, without copy of the record, of any suit brought in the State courts against any individual for an act performed under the laws of the United States. A grim touch was added in the request for authorization for marshals to make provision for keeping prisoners.

Very late on the night of the day the Message was submitted, Jackson, worn out and wretched from a bad cold, sat in his room writing to Poinsett. The Message had been read. Calhoun, "agitated and confused," had "let off a little of his ire" against the President, and John Forsyth had replied "with great dignity and firmness." That night it seemed to Jackson that Calhoun had been placed "between Scylla and Charybdis," and was "reckless." The uncertainty of negotiations had passed, and the hour for action — the happy hour for Jackson — had struck. The conferences with Drayton were over. Poinsett, at the front, was now the man of the hour. The moment the Nullifiers were "in hostile array," this fact was to be certified to Jackson by the attorney for the district, or the judge, and he would "forthwith order the leaders arrested and prosecuted." And he added in his note to Poinsett: "We will strike at the head and demolish the monster Nullification and secession at the threshold by the power of the law." [1]

Thus, that night, the fingers of Andrew Jackson were itching for the throat of John C. Calhoun.

Five days later, Senator Wilkins, of the Judiciary Committee, presented the famous "Force Bill," and one of the most violent debates in history began. On the following day, Calhoun submitted a set of resolutions setting forth his views of the constitutional question involved, in the hope of thereby directing the debate into that channel. But the Senate was in no temper for such a discussion and pushed forward to the

[1] Letter to Poinsett, Stillé's *Life of Poinsett*.

debate on the main and pressing question. The Calhoun resolutions were speedily tabled. Wilkins led off in the debate, and others followed, one on the heels of the other, until at length John Tyler took the floor to deliver the speech which, after that of Calhoun, was the most forceful attack to be made upon the measure. Reading his speech to-day one wonders how the Republic outlived the Jackson Administrations. Dire calamity was predicted as a result of his every action. He saw Carolinians again driven "into the morasses where Marion and Sumter found refuge," with their cities and towns leveled to the dust, and their daughters clothed in mourning, with "helpless orphans" made of their "rising sons." But, he continued, "I will not despair. Rome had her Curtius, Sparta her Leonidas, and Athens her band of devoted patriots; and shall it be said that the American Senate contains not one man who will step forward to rescue his country in this, her moment of peril? Although that man may never wear an earthly crown or sway an earthly scepter, eternal fame shall weave an evergreen around his brow, and his name shall rank with the proudest patriots of the proudest climes."

With the closing sentence, Tyler turned significantly to Henry Clay, who sat an interested spectator. Throughout this memorable debate he was to remain mute. The great orator and party leader was making sympathetic gestures to the extreme State-Rights men of the South. Even at this time, and knowing Tyler's views, he was writing to his friend, Francis Brooke: "Will he [Tyler] reëlected? We feel here some solicitude on that point, being convinced that under all circumstances, he would be far preferable to any person that could be sent." [1] And such was his partisan hate of Jackson that the second leader of the party Opposition, John M. Clayton, in speaking in support of the Force Bill, could not refrain from an exhibition of boorishness and bigotry in

[1] *Letters and Times of the Tylers*, I, 460.

coupling his advocacy of the Jackson measure with a sneer at Jackson.

"My support of the measure," he said, "is predicated on no servile submission to any Executive mandate, on no implicit and unlimited faith in any man. . . . I will not be deterred from the adoption of this measure by any consideration of the source from which it has emanated."

Thus did Clayton contribute to the pleasure of the Nullifiers by the denunciation of the man who stood in their way, and in sneering at those Southern Democrats who stood squarely behind Jackson despite the gibes of the Calhoun followers that they were yielding a servile submission.

Meanwhile Jackson's supporters were giving the measure their undivided support, and none of them more heartily, and none so ably, as Senators from the South. Senator Felix Grundy of Tennessee, able lawyer, seasoned statesman, resourceful parliamentarian, took charge of the fight on the floor. Rives of Virginia, learned constitutional lawyer, scholarly, polished, heroically sacrificed a seat in the Senate to stand by the Union. And Forsyth of Georgia, "the greatest debater of his time," affected to look upon the Nullification doctrine as "the double distilled essence of nonsense."

As the fight developed and the certainty of defeat grew upon the Nullifiers, efforts were made to gain time, with the Administration forces pressing for action. Senator Willie Mangum of North Carolina, brilliant, and sacrificing a great career to drink, on securing the floor asked for an adjournment on the ground of indisposition. Ordinarily the request would have been granted. But Forsyth, Grundy, and Wilkins were instantly on their feet with objections. Calhoun, pointing out that Mangum was the only member of the Judiciary Committee opposed to the bill, begged that he be given an opportunity to explain his position, only to be told, none too graciously, by Wilkins, that he had no doubt of Mangum's capacity to speak then. When Calhoun reminded him of

Mangum's plea of indisposition, he was ignored. At this juncture, Webster, who had been silent, suggested that Mangum could easily speak on another day and the debate proceed. Whereupon Senator King of Alabama made a transparent effort to draw Webster's speech at once. The New England orator significantly replied that "the gentleman from Massachusetts fully understands the gentleman from Alabama; but he has no disposition to address the Senate at present, nor, under existing circumstances, at any other time, on the subject of this bill." This was taken as indicating Webster's conviction that up to that time the advocates of the bill needed no reënforcements, and that he would reserve himself for Calhoun.

It was during these proceedings that an exchange occurred between Poindexter and Grundy which illustrates the hair-trigger conditions in Carolina. A rumor had just spread through the chamber that Jackson had ordered a portion of the fleet to occupy Charleston Harbor, and had sent instructions to the military commander in Charleston, and Poindexter immediately offered a resolution calling upon the President for information as to his actions and intentions. Grundy calmly, if provokingly, suggested that perhaps some very respectable gentlemen of Charleston had furnished the President with information on which the secret orders had been issued, and that Poindexter would surely not ask the names of the gentlemen and all the circumstances of the disclosure.

"All — all — the whole of them!" cried Poindexter.

"But would not such disclosures lead to the immediate shedding of blood?" Grundy inquired.

"I care not if it does!" shouted the excited Mississippian. "Let us have the information no matter what the circumstances!"

Grundy smilingly took his seat.

Thus the debate dragged on — the two greatest figures still silent.

VI

MEANWHILE, as the debate proceeded, Jackson was watching South Carolina and making all his preparations. On January 24th, he wrote Poinsett that the Force Bill debate was about to begin, that he had done his duty, and if Congress failed to act, and he should be informed of the assemblage of an armed force, he stood ready for drastic measures.[1] There is something of the heroic mingled with pathos in the picture this letter presents of Jackson at this time. It was late at night. The House sat late. He had not heard since seven o'clock. "My eyes grow dim."

Two hours later he ordered General Scott to Charleston to repel by force any attempt to seize the forts.[2] Holding his rage in check, measuring every step by his constitutional and legal powers, determined to do nothing rashly to precipitate bloodshed, Jackson held himself in readiness, as the debate on the Force Bill proceeded, to meet any eventuality that might arise.[3] But Jackson and the Administration were not at all satisfied with the progress of the debate. None of the trio of genius, Clay, Webster, and Calhoun, had yet participated. It would be too much to expect that Clay would speak on behalf of any Jackson measure, and it was certain that Calhoun would deliver one of his characteristically powerful arguments against the bill. There was just one man strong enough to meet the impact of that argument, and that was Webster. It was a reasonable hope that he would prominently support the measure involving the principles he had made his own. Among his intimates, such as Story, it was expected that he would enter at the psychological moment, but the great orator kept his own counsels, and during the early part of the debate was absent from the Senate Cham-

[1] Stillé's *Life of Poinsett.*
[2] Instructions in letter of Cass to Scott, Smith's *Life of Cass.*
[3] Jackson to Poinsett, Feb. 7, 1833, Stillé's *Life of Poinsett.*

ber on other engagements. As Calhoun prepared his heavy artillery for action, the apprehension of Jackson and his supporters increased, and every effort was made, at first through Webster's friends, to learn his intentions.[1] Then, one day, a carriage halted before the lodgings of Webster, and the tall figure of Livingston emerged and entered the house. It was not a half-hearted welcome to the Administration camp that the Secretary of State offered. On the contrary, Webster was earnestly importuned to take the lead on the floor, and to frame any amendments he thought necessary.[2] If such importunity was unnecessary, it was none the less pleasing to the vanity of the orator, and Livingston was able to carry back to the White House the assurance that when Calhoun spoke he would be answered by Webster. On the 11th of February, Webster was ready and waiting.[3] Four days later, abandoning the hope that Webster might speak first, Calhoun began one of the most powerful speeches of his career. The Senate Chamber and the galleries were packed.

As the tall, gaunt figure, with slightly stooped shoulders, rose, the solemnity of his mien and manner, the fire in the wonderful eyes that "watched everything and revealed nothing," suggested, to some, the conspirator with his back against the wall, to others the austere patriot battling for the liberties of his country.[4] We need not concern ourselves with the general tenor of his remarkable argument — a reiteration and reënforcement of his constitutional views. But the general spirit of resentment, the passionate hate of Jackson, the defiance, constitute dramatic features that assist in the sensing of the atmosphere in which the mighty battle was waged. Almost in the beginning, in defending his support of the tariff of 1816, and explaining that he had spoken at the in-

[1] *Perley's Reminiscences,* I, 140.

[2] March's *Reminiscences of Congress,* and *Perley's Reminiscences.*

[3] Story to Brazier, *Life and Letters of Story,* II, 124.

[4] March, in his *Reminiscences of Congress,* gives the best description of the Force Bill debate.

stance of Ingham, the late Secretary of the Treasury, this spirit flared in an amazing tribute to that mediocre and unscrupulous politician, and an indirect attack upon Jackson for dismissing him. As he proceeded, he startled the Senate now and then by the injection of personalities. Here a contemptuous fling at Van Buren, there a hint at Mrs. Eaton, and everywhere references to contemplated "war" and "massacres" and "savages." "I proclaim it," he solemnly declared, "that should this bill pass, and attempt be made to enforce it, it will be resisted at every hazard — even that of death itself." It was two o'clock on the second day of the speech that Calhoun concluded, with a warning to Southern Senators that should the bill be enacted all of them would be excluded from the emoluments of the Government, "which will be reserved for those only who have qualified themselves, by political prostitution, for admission into the Magdalen Asylum."

The moment he sank into his seat, Daniel Webster rose.

The relations between Webster and the Administration leaders after the visit of Livingston had been intimate and confidential, and the orator had availed himself of the invitation to make desirable amendments. One stormy day during this period, the great opponent of the Democratic Party might have been seen rolling up to the Capitol in the White House carriage. On the floor, when he rose, were many of the Administration leaders, including Lewis, ready to hasten the news of the speech and its reception to the White House, where Jackson was anxiously, but confidently, waiting. It was late in the evening when the orator concluded his masterful argument on the proposition that "the Constitution is not a compact between sovereign States." Brushing aside the personalities, scarcely referring to any speech made during the debate, he took the resolutions Calhoun had submitted as embodying his views, and based his argument upon these. Speaking with his accustomed gravity, with more than his usual earnestness, without passion or personal feeling, he took up the sophistries of the Nullification school and crushed them, one by one. Nullification was revolution, and success meant the destruction of the Republic, chaos, the end of American liberty. To prevent these evils was the duty of the National authority; and the Force Bill was necessary for their prevention.

Long before he closed, the lights had been lit in the little Senate Chamber where the crowd was densely packed. With his conclusion the galleries rose and cheered, and Poindexter, outraged at the exhibition of feeling, indignantly demanded an immediate adjournment. The great word had been spoken in the Senate — the Proclamation reiterated on the floor. No one was more delighted with Webster's triumph than Jackson. "Mr. Webster replied to Mr. Calhoun yesterday," he wrote Poinsett, "and, it is said, demolished him. It is believed by more than one that Mr. Calhoun is in a state of dementation — his speech was a perfect failure; and Mr. Webster handled him as a child." [1]

Thus Webster entered upon more intimate relations with the White House, with Jackson personally thanking him for a great public service, and Livingston reiterating expressions of appreciation. The Jackson Senators, Isaac Hill excepted, joined in the assiduous cultivation of the orator, and he was invited to strike from a list of applicants for office the names of all displeasing to himself. Such was the enthusiasm of the President that overtures were unquestionably made to Webster, as set forth by Benton,[2] to gain his adherence to the Administration. It was a crisis in his life and in the politics of the Nation. He was then closer to Jackson's views on vital matters than to those of either Clay or Calhoun. His antipathy to the latter's doctrines was as pronounced as that of Jackson; and he had no respect for Clay's play to the

[1] Jackson to Poinsett, Feb. 17, 1833, Stillé's *Life of Poinsett.*
[2] *Thirty Years' View.*

seditious with his compromise tariff. His ideas were not remote from those of Livingston. Had he then broken with his old co-workers, and allied himself with the dominant party, he would have been advanced immeasurably toward the Presidency. Senator Lodge admits[1] that there was much truth in Benton's theory, but reasonably holds that the coalition would have been wrecked by the inevitable clashing of the conflicting temperaments.

VII

MEANWHILE, with the debate dwindling to an anti-climax, Calhoun and his friends were not nearly so indifferent to war as they pretended. It was generally understood that Jackson was ready and eager to strike the moment an overt act was committed. With Hayne urging caution, some irresponsible hothead might at any moment hasten the crisis. Then, all knew, Jackson would place South Carolina under martial law, arrest Calhoun for treason, and turn him over to the courts for trial. Some of the latter's friends began to interest themselves in a compromise tariff that would open a door of escape. The Whig protectionists, the Nullifiers, and the Bank were rapidly rushing together to make common cause against Jackson. Under Clay's leadership at the beginning of the session these elements united in electing Duff Green, of the "Telegraph," printer to the Senate, and Gales, of the "Intelligencer," to the House. Thus, through Clay, the Nullification organ secured a new lease of life, and flooded the South with circularized appeals for support. "If the people of the South deserve to be free they will not permit this press to go down," Green wrote — and this was known to Clay. The Bank party looked on approvingly, with John Sargeant writing enthusiastically to Biddle of the new political alignments. "The new state of parties," he wrote, "will be founded upon a combination of the South,

[1] *Life of Webster*, 214–15.

and the leaders of it are friends of the Bank upon principle, and will be more so from opposition to Jackson." [1] With this alignment in mind, John M. Clayton cynically observed to Clay that "these South Carolinians are acting very badly, but they are good fellows, and it would be a pity to let Jackson hang them." [2] When Representative Letcher of Kentucky, a boisterous partisan of Clay's, suggested the compromise plan to his chief, he "received it at first coolly and doubtfully." [3] Afterwards Clay reconsidered and broached the subject to Webster, who, holding the Jackson view, replied that "it would be yielding great principles to faction; that the time had come to test the strength of the Constitution and the Government." [4] Thereafter Webster was not included in the consultations.

Perhaps the true story of the compromise tariff of 1833 will never be known. One version credits the initiative to Clayton in calling a meeting of men primarily interested in the tariff, and only incidentally in the Nullification crisis, consisting of but half the New England Senators, and the two from Delaware, with Clay, Webster, and Calhoun all absent.[5] Many years later John Tyler accepted the responsibility. According to his version he "waited on Mr. Clay." They "conversed about the times." Clay "saw the danger." Tyler "appealed to his patriotism," and "no man appealed so in vain." The Virginian referred Clay "to another man as the only one necessary to consult, and that man was John C. Calhoun." It would not only be necessary for Clay to "satisfy his own party," but to "reconcile an opposite party by large concessions." Thus Clay and Calhoun "met, consulted and agreed." [6] This differs in some particulars from the Benton version.[7] Here we have it that Clay prepared his measure and sent it to Calhoun by Letcher, as the

[1] *Correspondence of Nicholas Biddle,* 201. [2] *Thirty Years' View,* I, 342.
[3] *Ibid.* [4] *Ibid.* [5] Comegys, *Memoir of Clayton.*
[6] *Letters and Times of the Tylers,* I, 467. [7] *Thirty Years' View.*

two negotiators were not, at the time, on speaking terms. Finding some objectionable features which he thought a personal interview would persuade the author to eliminate, Calhoun asked Letcher to arrange a conference, which was held in Clay's room. The meeting was "cold and distant." Clay rose, bowed, and asked Calhoun to be seated, and, to relieve the embarrassment, Letcher took his departure. Clay refused to yield.

The story here enters into the melodramatic although there is nothing impossible about it. Letcher, in another conference, this time with Jackson, found the grim old warrior hard set against any sort of a compromise, unwilling to discuss one, and determined to enforce the laws. The Kentuckian related the conversation to McDuffie; he to Calhoun. A little later Letcher was awakened from a sound sleep by Senator Johnston of Louisiana, an intimate friend of Clay, with the startling story that he had heard authoritatively that Jackson would admit of no further delay, and was preparing to arrest Calhoun for treason. It was agreed that the Carolinian should be immediately notified, and in the darkness of the night Letcher hastened to Calhoun's lodgings. As the gaunt statesman sat up in bed, the Johnston story was told him and "he was evidently disturbed."[1] That some such incident occurred is corroborated by Perley Poore,[2] who was an observer of events in the Washington of that day. Here we have some embellishments. Calhoun had heard some threats and had sent Letcher to Jackson to ascertain his intentions. The old man's eyes had been "lighted by an unwonted fire," and he had told the emissary that with the first overt act, he would try Calhoun for treason and "hang him high as Haman." Thereupon Letcher made all haste to Calhoun, who received him sitting up in bed, with a cloak thrown around him. "There sat Calhoun," wrote Perley Poore, "drinking in eagerly every word, and, as Letcher proceeded, he turned

[1] Benton's *Thirty Years' View*, I, 343.

[2] *Perley's Reminiscences.*

pale as death, and great as he was in intellect, trembled like an aspen leaf, not from fear or cowardice, but from consciousness of guilt." [1] Here we detect the professional journalist drawing perhaps on his imagination to dramatize the picture.

However, Calhoun, convinced of Jackson's grim determination, was ready to welcome a way out short of conflict or utter humiliation, and at the same time Clay and Clayton were not happy over the situation. The protective system had brought the country to the very verge of disintegration. With Nullification crushed by force, conservative public opinion might demand a complete reversal of the revenue policy and destroy the "American System." That Clay at this time was thinking primarily of the preservation of his protective system, and secondarily of currying favor with the extreme State-Rights party, including the Nullifiers, is plainly disclosed in the record. Thus the proposed combination of the Nullifiers and the protectionists to stay the arm of Jackson. In this combination no one was more prominent than John M. Clayton, the brilliant and bibulous, who frankly cared less about saving the Union than of saving the tariff, and who would "pause long before he surrendered it [the tariff] even to save the Union."[2] He was to prove himself as good as his word a little later.

Thus, in the midst of the discussion of the Force Bill, Clay, Calhoun, Clayton, Letcher, and Tyler were in constant communication on the compromise tariff. Webster was utterly ignored, as was Jackson, these two refusing to "compromise a principle" in any such fashion.[3] The fact that Clay and Calhoun had reached a general agreement was soon known, and it was accepted as an offensive and defensive alliance against Jackson. "They are partners in a contra dance," wrote Blair in the "Globe." "For some time they turned

[1] *Perley's Reminiscences,* I, 138.

[2] Clayton's speech on the compromise tariff.

[3] Van Buren thought Clay's action patriotic and Webster's "bloody." (*Autobiography,* 554–57.)

their backs on each other. They will make a match of it. In plain English, we have a new coalition." [1]

In due time the bill was introduced by Clay, much to the delight of Tyler. "I recall the enthusiasm I felt that day," said Tyler, almost thirty years afterwards. "We advanced to meet each other, and grasped each other's hands, midway of the chamber." [2] This measure, differing from Clay's original plan, provided that for all articles paying more than twenty per cent duty, the surplus above that rate should be gradually reduced, until in 1842 all should disappear. The manufacturers as usual had been summoned and consulted. At first dismayed and outraged, they soon realized that it was to their interest to fall into line. Certain features had been voted down in committee, but here Clayton asserted himself. He announced that these would be introduced as amendments on the floor, and that unless every Nullifier voted for them all, he would kill the bill himself by making the motion to table it. The most objectionable of these, to Calhoun, was that on home valuation.

Such was the situation when Clay presented the bill on February 12th, three days before Calhoun rose to speak on the Force Bill. Webster and Adams, thoroughly disgusted, at once announced their opposition, and Jackson could not restrain his contempt for the unholy alliance, which was almost immediately to become a triple alliance with the Bank as the third party. "I have no doubt," the President wrote Hamilton, "the people will duly appreciate the motive which led to it." [3]

In presenting the measure, Clay made no secret of his purpose. "I believe the American System to be in the greatest danger," he said, "and I believe that it can be placed on a better and a safer foundation at this session than next." Webster, however, was not impressed. "This may be so, sir,"

[1] *Globe*, Feb. 20, 1833. [2] *Letters and Times of the Tylers*, I, 467.
[3] Jackson to Hamilton, Hamilton's *Reminiscences*.

he replied. "This may be so. But, if it be so, it is because the American people will not sanction the tariff; and if they will not, then, sir, it cannot be sustained at all." Calhoun heartily approved the object of the bill. "He who loves the Union," he said, "must desire to see this agitating question brought to a termination." John Forsyth, representing the Administration, objected to the introduction of the bill fourteen days before the expiration of the Congress. Would it not be better to await the action of the House on the bill before it — the Verplanck Bill? And he objected, properly, on the ground that all revenue measures had to originate in the House. This constitutional objection, raised by Forsyth, was met on February 25th just as the House was about to adjourn for dinner, when the ever handy Letcher arose and moved the substitution of the Clay bill for the one then pending. The motion was carried and the bill passed the lower branch of Congress.[1]

Thus the two measures, the Force Bill and the compromise tariff, were pending in the Senate at the same time, with Clay making every effort, but without avail, to pass his measure first.

On February 24th the Force Bill was called up for final action. With the beginning of the calling of the roll, all the enemies of the measure, with the single exception of John Tyler, arose and filed from the Senate Chamber. Taken by surprise at such conduct, Tyler immediately moved an adjournment. Wilkins called attention to the fact that Calhoun and his followers had just that moment withdrawn, and the motion was defeated. The roll-call proceeded — and only the name of John Tyler appears on the list of the negatives. Such was always the courage of this much-belittled man — a courage which we shall meet again.[2] Five days later the tariff bill was called up, and Clayton offered his amendments

[1] Letcher's character and status are discussed by Adams, *Memoirs*, March 5, 1831.
[2] *Letters and Times of the Tylers*, I, 467.

which were so offensive to Calhoun and his followers, repeating his threat to kill the bill if Calhoun and all the Nullifiers did not vote for every amendment. Clay and Calhoun consulted, and Clayton was importuned to yield, but the stubborn protectionist was adamant. Thus confronted, Clay and Calhoun accepted the amendments, and, as Clayton presented them, voted for them, one by one, until the last and most distasteful, on home valuation, was reached.

Here the friends of Calhoun balked, and Clayton, never given to idle bluster, immediately made his motion to table the bill. Clay implored, and Clayton set his jaws and shook his head. The measure seemed doomed. Meanwhile, the Nullifiers, greatly alarmed, withdrew to the space behind the Vice-President's chair for consultation. Finally Clayton was requested to withdraw his motion to give Calhoun and his friends time for consideration. With the understanding that, unless the votes were forthcoming, the motion would be renewed, the request was granted, and the Senate adjourned for the night.

The morning found Clayton confronted with a plan devised during the night to spare Calhoun the humiliation of voting for the hated amendment, provided enough votes were assured to carry it through without his vote. The immovable Clayton sternly shook his head. Calhoun must vote for every amendment and for the bill. When the Senate convened, it was still uncertain what the Carolinian would do. At length, after all of his friends had first stated their objections, and yet reluctantly yielded, Calhoun arose, repeated the performance, and, having voted for the amendment at the dictation of Clayton, voted for the bill.[1] The unhappy plight of Calhoun was not lost upon his enemies, and Blair found in it an inspiration for his sarcasm. "A single night," he wrote, "was sufficient to change the settled opinion of the

[1] Benton makes the point that Clayton, and not Clay or Calhoun, was the master of the situation. (*Thirty Years' View*, I, 344.)

profound reader of the Constitution. We exceedingly doubt whether in the private interview in which Mr. Clay disposed of Mr. Calhoun's constitutional scruples, a word was uttered in relation to the Constitution."[1] Thus passed into law, under circumstances deserving of Benton's reprehension, the measure concocted by a combination of erstwhile foes.[2] The Nullifiers died hard, and Duff Green, the pen of Nullification, made printer to the Senate by this incongruous combination, in performing the hateful official duty of publishing the Force Bill in the "Telegraph," had the impudence to dress his paper in mourning. "This is the way," observed a Jacksonian paper, "this ungrateful wretch shows his gratitude to the Senate for his recent appointment."[3]

VIII

MEANWHILE, what of South Carolina?

The letter of Cass, published in the "Richmond Enquirer," had borne fruit, and Virginia had sent Benjamin Watkins Leigh, a lawyer of distinction and an orator of no mean ability, to Charleston to ask a suspension of the Nullification Ordinance until Congress had adjourned. An ardent devotee of State Rights, now a bitter enemy of Jackson, and soon to enter the Senate to make his opposition felt, he had much in his principles and personality to command a respectful hearing from South Carolina. The call of the Nullification Convention was consequently postponed until after the adjournment of Congress, and March 11th was fixed as the day for reassembling. By that time it was all over — the Force Bill in effect. The convention met at Columbia, with Hayne in the chair. Leigh was invited within the bar. The dominating figure of the scene, however, was Calhoun, who had gone post-haste to Carolina to urge the acceptance of the compromise. The tall, thin figure of the great Senator, seated among the delegates on the floor, was the star of the

[1] *Globe*, March 2, 1833. [2] *Thirty Years' View*, I, 345. [3] *Mohawk Gazette.*

assembly. A committee was named to consider the general course of action; and one week later the Ordinance of Nullification was rescinded, and by a vote of 153 to 4 the convention agreed that the threatened danger was over.

The political effect of the fight was to be felt throughout the period of the generation then living. The Secessionists and Nullifiers paraded, with much flapping of banners, out of the Democratic Party, to be joyously and effusively welcomed by Henry Clay into the Opposition. During the remainder of Jackson's Administration, the most bitter and persistent of his foes were to be men, once Democrats, who had left the party because Jackson was prepared to preserve the Union with the sword. Calhoun and Preston, McDuffie and Poindexter, Leigh and Tyler — these were to crowd Clay for the leadership of the party that now prepared to enter the lists against Jackson and his Administration, flying the flag, and posing as the real friends of the Republic and the Constitution. If they had been free with their characterizations of Jackson during the Nullification fight as "tyrant," "despot," "autocrat," they were to use the epithets more frequently in opposing him upon the Bank. If during this latter struggle they were to speak with almost convincing eloquence of the destruction of free institutions, they had learned the language when calling upon the people to defend their liberties against the author of the Nullification Proclamation. Out of this alliance, for which Clay had so cunningly planned, was to come a party to oppose the Democratic Party with indifferent success for twenty-two years; and, strangely enough, the only one of its leaders to become a beneficiary of the unholy alliance was John Tyler, who was to reach the White House. Poinsett, after the Nullification fight, retired to his rice plantation, where he lived with his books and enjoying the society of cultivated men and women, until called by Van Buren to enter his Cabinet. Serving throughout the Administration, he returned, at the expiration of his term, to his plantation, where he died ten years before the attack on Sumter.

The passage of the two important measures was not, however, to end the drama of the session — one of the most dramatic in American history. It was on the last night that Jackson, finding many of his friends had left the Capitol, "pocketed" Clay's Land Bill and his own veto. Naturally enough the session ended in bitter partisan wrangles and with much bad blood on both sides. Uproarious shouts of derision greeted the customary resolution of thanks to the Speaker. Many members were in a state of hopeless drunkenness. It was five o'clock in the morning when Adams invited Edward Everett to ride home with him. The drowsy driver touched the horses, and over the frozen ruts of the Avenue, the carriage jolted homeward. Almost immediately the driver was asleep, and the carriage, striking a rut in front of Gadsby's, the sleepy statesmen narrowly escaped a plunge into the snow. Soon, however, they reached the "macadamized part of the Avenue," without more mishaps; and having left Everett at his lodgings, Adams alighted and walked to his own home, with the thermometer registering six below zero. Thus the last figure of that historic and bitter session of whom we catch a glimpse is that of the short, blear-eyed ex-President, trudging homeward through the dark, ill-paved Washington streets at five o'clock on a frigid morning.[1]

[1] Adams's *Memoirs*, March 2, 1833.

CHAPTER XI

JACKSON VS. BIDDLE

I

Congress adjourned two days before the second inauguration of Jackson, which lacked the spectacular features of the first. His brief inaugural address revealed absolute confidence in the approval of the people. There was nothing on the surface to warn of his purpose to continue an aggressive war upon the Bank. The transfer of Livingston from the State Department to the Legation in Paris necessitated a reorganization of the Cabinet. Louis McLane, unsympathetic toward the President's Bank policy, was moved from the Treasury to the State Department. This left the secretaryship of the Treasury vacant, and it was of the highest importance that it be filled by one in complete harmony with the Executive plans.

The choice finally fell on William J. Duane of Philadelphia, variously described as "a distinguished lawyer" and as "the bottom of the Philadelphia bar." His selection had been recommended by Van Buren [1] and urged by McLane, who was Van Buren's intimate at the time.[2] He was at least known to Jackson as the son of the fighting editor of the "Aurora," which had led the fight against the Alien and Sedition Laws.[3] Assuming in the son the militant qualities of the father, and actuated partly, perhaps, by the thought that the appointment would strengthen the Administration in its fight upon the Bank, Duane was pressed to enter the Cabinet, and con-

[1] *Autobiography,* 600.

[2] Professor Bassett credits the appointment to McLane (*Life of Jackson*), and Parton has it that it was a personal appointment of Jackson's (Parton's *Life of Jackson,* II, 632).

[3] See George Henry Payne's *History of Journalism in the United States,* 176–89.

sented. The personality and character of Duane are dim on the page of history. The Democratic press was apparently hard put to explain the appointment. The "Harrisburg Chronicle" described him as possessing "a well disciplined mind, severe habits of business, which, combined with sound Democratic principles and unbending integrity, are the highest recommendations for office in a free popular government." Thomas Ritchie, of the "Richmond Enquirer," who made a more studied effort, feared that the appointment would "scarcely be hailed with the feeling of approbation which it so richly deserves." But Duane understood "the character of the Bank of the United States — its designs and dangers," and "on that cardinal subject we have no doubt he will deserve and command the confidence of the friends of the Constitution." The "Pennsylvanian" informed the National Democracy that "Stephen Gerard saw and appreciated his talents," and that he was "one of the most sagacious men of the age." [1] It was only after his break with Jackson that the champions of the Bank discovered his many virtues, and Administration circles his utter insignificance. One of Jackson's enemies, in berating him, referred to Duane as "that other darling whom you fished up from the desk of a dead miser, and the bottom of the Philadelphia bar." [2] At first, however, Jackson was much impressed with his discovery, and frequently referred to him as "a chip of the old block, sir."

Having reorganized his Cabinet, Jackson now concentrated on his plans for the invasion of "the enemy's country" — his New England tour. His remarkable popularity in that quarter, previously so hostile, grew out of his vigorous defense of the Union and his new relations with Webster. In the spring of 1833 these relations were most cordial, and never were to become personally bitter. At that time he was not on speaking

[1] These editorial comments were copied in the *Globe* by Blair.

[2] Henry Lee, quoted by Bassett, *Life of Jackson*, II, 633.

terms with either Clay or Calhoun, and when he met Adams on the street, by chance, he bowed stiffly, without a word. But whenever, in his meanderings about the dingy capital, he encountered Webster, the iron man would pause for a hearty greeting. And while Webster never ceased to consider Jackson temperamentally unfit for the Presidency, he never doubted his integrity or whole-hearted patriotism. "His patriotism," he was wont to say, "is no more to be questioned than that of Washington." [1]

It was early in June that Jackson set forth in company with Van Buren, Cass, Woodbury, Donelson, Hill, and the artist, Earle, who lived at the White House. From the moment the party reached Baltimore it was one continuous ovation. Received like a conquering hero in Philadelphia, with an enthusiasm bordering on idolatry in New York City,[2] the ovations he received in Massachusetts eclipsed them all. Harvard conferred upon him the degree of Doctor of Laws, Everett delivered an address of welcome at the foot of Bunker Hill, and while the multitude went wild at sight of him in the streets and on the Common, the gentry of Beacon Street refused him the homage of appearing at the windows,[3] and the crabbed Adams, hiding at his Quincy home, a few miles away, poured forth his spleen upon his journal and mourned the degradation of his Alma Mater.[4] Under the load of adulation, the old man's strength finally failed, and during the last part of his progress he dragged himself from his bed to the parade, and from the physician with his barbarous lancet to the master of ceremonies.[5] Throughout the tour his thoughts were centered on the Bank and his plans for the removal of the deposits, and but few suspected that the

[1] Thurlow Weed's *Autobiography*.

[2] Hone in his *Diary*, hostile, recorded, after witnessing the ovation, that he was "certainly the most popular man we have ever known." (June 13, 1833.)

[3] Josiah Quincy's *Figures of the Past*.

[4] *Memoirs*, June 17, June 18, June 27, July 2, 1833.

[5] See Quincy's *Figures of the Past* for graphic description of the Massachusetts ovations.

courtly old man, whose eyes moistened and beamed at the applause of the crowds, was meditating the step.

When Hamilton called upon him at his hotel in New York, he found him obsessed with the subject. When the son of the father of the first National Bank joined him in the presidential suite to accompany him to the banquet, Jackson placed in his hands papers by several people urging the removal of the deposits, with the request that he examine them carefully and give him an opinion. Promising a careful perusal, Hamilton ventured the suggestion that the proposed step was "a very questionable one" that would "lead to great disturbances in commercial affairs." [1] Meanwhile, when alone with Van Buren, the President was discussing the project with him to his keen distress.[2] Throughout the tour, sick or well, Jackson found time to work on the Vice-President and favorite, and when, at Concord, he finally won him over to the plan, the frail old man abandoned the tour and hastened back to Washington to begin a new battle.[3] And Adams, learning of the curtailment of the trip, wrote that "President Jackson has been obliged by the feeble state of his health to give up the remainder of his tour." [4] Just how feeble Jackson was we shall soon see.

II

It is impossible definitely to determine the time Jackson decided on the removal of the deposits. The activity of the Bank in the presidential campaign had not been lost upon him, and he probably had it under consideration at that time. The historian of the Bank is convinced that such was the case.[5] Immediately after the election these ru-

[1] Hamilton had been previously warned of the plan by McLane. (Hamilton's *Reminiscences*, 253.)

[2] Van Buren gives the impression that he actually helped Jackson work out his plans on this trip. (*Autobiography*, 602–03.)

[3] Hamilton's story in his *Reminiscences*.

[4] *Memoirs*, July 2, 1833.

[5] Catterall's *Second Bank of the United States*, 128.

mors multiplied, and Biddle was deluged with warnings, but without disturbing the sublime serenity of his conceit. The autocrat of the Bank was satisfied that the Calhoun following would thereafter be arrayed in favor of the recharter. About this time Dr. Thomas Cooper, then president of the College of South Carolina and one of the intellectual leaders of Nullification, wrote him of his allegiance to the cause.[1] Blair had already charged, in the "Globe," that there was a coalition between the forces of Clay, Calhoun, and Biddle, and made much of the fact that more Bank stock was owned in South Carolina than in all the other States of the Union south of the Potomac and west of the Alleghany Mountains.[2] The Democratic disaffection, together with the temporary alliance between Jackson and Webster, was quite enough to restore confidence to the ever sanguine Biddle,[3] who took no pains to conceal his satisfaction. This was water on the wheel of Blair, who, Iago-like, and always at Jackson's elbow, kept impressing him with the idea that the Bank planned and expected an ultimate triumph. In this work he was ably seconded by Amos Kendall and James A. Hamilton, who wrote from New York that "a gentleman whose knowledge of the views of the U.S. Bank is only second to that of its President" had informed him that it expected to get a new charter.[4] It was firmly believed by Amos Kendall that the Bank's purpose in adding $28,000,000 to its discounts, and multiplying its debtors and dependents, was to serve a political end in the campaign of 1836, and with characteristic persistency he urged the removal of the deposits to prevent their use for political purposes.[5] Jackson himself feared the effect of loans and legal retainers to members of the Congress. In all these suspicions

[1] Cooper to Biddle, *Correspondence of Nicholas Biddle,* 208.
[2] *Globe,* March 23, 1833.
[3] Catterall, *Second Bank of the United States,* 290.
[4] Hamilton's *Reminiscences,* 251.
[5] Kendall's *Autobiography,* 374–75.

there was ample justification.[1] It did not require much, knowing as he did the character of the banker, to persuade Jackson that his duty was plain, and during the winter and spring of 1833 he was in frequent consultation with Roger Taney, Amos Kendall, and Frank Blair, the three men responsible for the step he took.

During these days of mysterious conferences, the conservative members of the Cabinet, and Van Buren with the traditional timidity of the candidate, were gravely concerned. To none was the prospect more appalling than to Louis McLane, then Secretary of the Treasury, a conservative, a former Federalist, and a prospective candidate for the Presidency. In his anxiety he sent for Kendall, avowed his doubts, and asked for information. In the end he frankly confessed that he was not satisfied as to the wisdom of the step, but that he would execute the plan if called upon to do so by the President. The interview was friendly, and Kendall returned to his office and prepared, for McLane's edification, an elaborate argument in favor of the removal. It is characteristic of Kendall that, while the paper lightly touched upon the alleged insecurity of the deposits, the greater part of the paper was a discussion of the political effect. The hostility of the Bank to the Administration, he thought, could not be intensified. If the deposits were placed with the State banks, they would become partisans of the Administration. The people of the Southern and Western States would be pleased, and the New York banks, always jealous of the financial preëminence of Philadelphia, would at least secretly rejoice. The New England States were not concerned, one way or the other, and could be safely ignored. And in the end, Kendall insisted that a failure to remove the deposits would make a recharter certain. That this letter, written March 16, 1833, was promptly placed in the hands of Van Buren, who was McLane's sponsor in the Administration, there can be no doubt.

[1] See Theodore Roosevelt's *Life of Benton*, 103 and 110, on Biddle's character.

The aftermath of the letter came a few days later, when Van Buren, meeting Kendall at a White House dinner, warmly protested against the plans of the Kitchen Cabinet. The genius of that famous group rose from the table in his excitement, declared that failure to remove the deposits made a Whig victory certain in 1836, and that he was prepared to lay down his pen. "I can live under a corrupt despotism," he exclaimed, "as well as any other man by keeping out of its way, which I shall certainly do."[1] It was the Vice-President and not the auditor of the Treasury who afterwards apologized.

It was under these conditions that Jackson propounded a series of questions to his Cabinet, with a preliminary statement that he favored the removal. The first count of noses in the official household showed Livingston and Cass for the Bank, Barry and Taney against it, with Woodbury hedging. McLane, having greater responsibility as the head of the Treasury, took two months in the preparation of an exhaustive reply opposing the removal, and his argument was afterwards to be used against the Administration.

A month after Congress had adjourned there was a relaxation of tension in Bank circles and among the conservatives of the Administration party, who assumed that nothing would be done during the congressional recess. The hostility of a majority of the Cabinet had not abated, and Biddle thought that the deposits were safe.

But if the official Cabinet was to hear no more, for months, of the proposed removal, the Kitchen Cabinet went into almost continuous session for the consideration of this one subject. The disposal of the deposits, and the time for making the removal, were the principal subjects discussed during those spring days in the White House, and it required but little discussion to determine upon the time. Hugh Lawson White strongly urged the postponement of action until

[1] Kendall's *Autobiography*.

Congress convened, but this was instantly overruled by Taney and Kendall, who urged a recess removal for different reasons. The Attorney-General favored such action "because it is desirable that the members should be among their constituents when the measure is announced, and should bring with them when they come here, the feelings and sentiments of the people." [1] Kendall suggested another reason, also political. The conservatives had made some impression on Jackson's mind with the warning that, if he removed the deposits, Congress would order them restored, and he appealed to Kendall for his opinion. "If I were certain," said Kendall, "that Congress would direct them to be restored, still they ought to be removed, and any order by Congress for their restoration disregarded; for it is the only means by which this embodiment of power which aims to govern Congress and the country can be destroyed." And, to this militant advice, he added his reasons for favoring the removal during the congressional recess. "Let the removal take place so early as to give us several months to defend the measure in the 'Globe,' and we will bring up the people to sustain you with a power which Congress dare not resist." [2]

Meanwhile Duane had reached Washington and assumed his duties. Soon after his arrival, Kendall was surprised to find him loath to discuss the removal, and when the story of this reticence was carried to Jackson, he explained to his Secretary of the Treasury what was wanted. When Duane demurred, he was told to take his time and report on the President's return from New England. By this time Amos Kendall had assumed the leadership, and he was instructed to interview the head of the Treasury during Jackson's absence.

At this time Van Buren, waiting in New York to join his

[1] Taney's letter to Jackson at Rip Raps in August thus referred to this advice previously given. (Tyler's *Life of Taney.*)

[2] Kendall's *Autobiography*, 376.

chief on his tour, was blissfully ignorant of the embarrassments that awaited him until he received a letter written on the day Jackson set forth on his journey. "The Bank and change of deposits have engrossed my mind much," he wrote; "it is a perplexing subject, and I wish your opinion before I finally act." Three days later, while Jackson was receiving the plaudits of the multitude, Kendall made the situation clear, in a letter to Van Buren, announcing that the removal had been determined upon and outlining the tentative plans. Nothing could have been more painful to the Vice-President, who had strongly urged that, with the veto of the recharter bill, the Bank be permitted quietly to go its way to the termination of its charter.

III

WHILE Jackson between illnesses and ovations was bringing the power of his compelling personality to bear upon his protégé's timidity, Kendall was following instructions in Washington in attempting to ascertain the intentions of Duane. In this he was wholly unsuccessful. Time and again the subject was broached only to be brushed aside, and Jackson, constantly informed, had some savage moments while smiling urbanely upon the crowds.

Reaching the capital on July 4th, he immediately summoned Duane to a conference. The Secretary, who had been ill, rose from a sick-bed and presented himself at the White House looking pale and feeble. At the sight of his wan adviser, the impulsive Jackson penitently grasped both his hands, reproved him for venturing forth in such a condition, and kindly postponed the interview until he had recovered.[1] After an absence of eight days Duane appeared at the White House again, with a lengthy letter setting forth his reasons for objecting to the removal until after Congress had been informed. Three days later, or on July 15th, another con-

[1] Van Buren's *Autobiography*, 602.

ference between Jackson and his rebellious Secretary was held with Duane stubbornly holding his ground, and Jackson kindness itself. In truth, it appears that, with the aid of McLane, Duane had succeeded in arousing some misgivings in Jackson's mind as to the possibility of persuading the State banks to accept the deposits.

"Send me to ask them, and I will settle that question," said Kendall.

"You shall go," Jackson replied.

Summoning the unhappy Duane, the President announced a postponement of discussions until the attitude of the State banks could be ascertained. Kendall was to be the agent of the Treasury on a tour of investigation, and Duane was to prepare the necessary instructions.

When these instructions were delivered to Kendall, he was amazed. They merely asked the opinions of the banks on the general question, and, in view of their well-established hostility, it was clear enough what the answer would be. Wrathfully hastening to the White House, Kendall bluntly refused to carry instructions so framed, declaring the sole purpose of the investigation should be to learn whether State banks would accept the deposits. He was told to prepare his own instructions, and thus the head of the Kitchen Cabinet sallied forth on his own terms. About the same time, Jackson, in need of a rest and release from the sultry atmosphere of Washington, went to Rip Raps in Hampton Roads, where he was accustomed to relax in the summer, accompanied by Frank Blair. Thus, with one member of the Kitchen Cabinet making a tour of the banks on his own instructions, another was at Jackson's elbow in the unconventional environment of Rip Raps.[1] All these various moves were promptly reported to Biddle by some member of the Administration, and on the day Kendall was expected in Philadelphia, the

[1] During this time Jackson was deluged by propaganda letters on behalf of the Bank from "friends." (Blair to Van Buren, Van Buren's *Autobiography,* 607.)

financial autocrat was writing to Dr. Cooper, his new ally, in laudation of the firmness of Duane and the viciousness of the Kitchen Cabinet.[1]

Meanwhile, in his visits to the banks of Baltimore, Philadelphia, New York, and Boston, Kendall was pulled and hauled and mauled by both the servitors of the Bank and the conservatives of the Administration circle. At Philadelphia it was hinted that a fortune was within his grasp if he would but avail himself of the opportunity.[2] There, too, he fell foul of James Gordon Bennett, then editor of the "Pennsylvanian," whose mask of cordiality was dropped in the publication of Kendall's private letters showing hostility to the Bank — as though private letters were necessary to the proof.[3]

But more significant, and politically more important, was Kendall's interview with Van Buren and McLane in New York City. The three met by chance in the breakfast room of an hotel, and in an interview, then arranged, it was proposed by the hedging politicians that the removal of the deposits be postponed until January when Congress would be in session. This plan originated with McLane, and Kendall, who suspected it was proposed with the hope and expectation that Congress would interpose, replied that he would be satisfied provided McLane, Duane, and the other Bank Democrats would agree to use their personal influence with members of Congress to have the deposits removed.[4] It was agreed that all three should write Jackson at Rip Raps, and, in complying, Kendall said that the proposal was against his judgment, and Jackson instantly rejected it.[5]

Throughout July the Opposition and Bank papers were warning the public of the movement on foot, and the "In-

[1] *Correspondence of Nicholas Biddle*, 214.
[2] Kendall's *Autobiography*.
[3] Bennett soon afterwards established the *New York Herald*.
[4] Significantly enough, Van Buren overlooks this incident in his *Autobiography*.
[5] Kendall's *Autobiography*, 383.

telligencer" was especially alarmed, dwelling at length on the rumor that Kendall was in Philadelphia before he had even left Washington. Blair was moved to mirth. He admitted that Kendall had been seen taking a stage, carrying with him "a large black trunk," and that, while he "looked charitable, his intent may be wicked." Worse still, "the Editor of the 'Globe' left for the South two days before with baggage enough to last a man a lifetime." A mysterious, uncanny combination of events, he conceded, that "bodes to owners of U.S. Bank stock, who purchased at 50 per cent, no good." [1]

This facetiousness enraged and alarmed the Opposition, and its press began to threaten to impeach Duane if he removed the deposits. Kendall was scourged with excoriations, and State banks were warned against taking the deposits on pain of the displeasure of the Biddle institution. Papers under the influence of the Bank, but still posing as Jacksonian, were sure that Jackson "and his able Secretary of the Treasury" would "not be hurried or retarded in his important measure by the violent and indiscreet denunciations and threats of any set of men," and would "act on the deposits at the proper time and in the proper way." [2] And Blair, catching the subtle suggestion of Bennett, hastened to assail him as having been "smuggled into the confidence of an unsuspecting Democracy as a friend of the cause" and as a "treacherous instrument of Webb and Biddle," who had "the impudence to propose by praise to flatter the President and his Cabinet to adopt the views of the Bank." [3] From his sanctum in the office of the "Albany Journal," Thurlow Weed, wisest of the Whig journalists, sent forth the threat of panic. "We are impatient for the removal," he wrote. "Nothing short of a general ruin will cure the people of their delusions, and the sooner it comes, the better." [4]

[1] *Globe*, July 31, 1833. [2] *Pennsylvanian.* [3] *Globe*, Sept. 7, 1833.
[4] Blair carefully collected all such threats and published them in the *Globe*.

IV

MEANWHILE Jackson at Rip Raps was in daily conference with Frank Blair on the problems of the removal. All this time Blair was creating the impression in the "Globe" that the President's sole thought was the recovery of his health. The sea air was "proving advantageous," his appetite better, his strength returning. Nothing was more remote from the thoughts of Jackson. The situation was delicate and politically mixed. The Cabinet was, for the most part, hostile. Conservative Democrats were terrified at the thought of such radical action, and feared the complete disruption of the party and its defeat in 1836. Kendall does not misstate the conditions when he says that "the ambitious politicians who still surrounded General Jackson, trembled in their knees, and were ready to fly," and that "almost the only fearless and determined supporters he had around him were Mr. Taney, the editor of the 'Globe,' and its few contributors."[1] The brilliant, but ultra-conservative Ritchie, of the "Richmond Enquirer," feared that the party would "rue the precipitate step in sackcloth and ashes," and that it would "present nothing but a splendid ruin."[2]

Painful as the situation was to all conservatives, it was maddening to Van Buren, who thought he saw the Presidency slipping from his grasp. In his desire to get as far away as possible, he was planning a month's outing with Washington Irving among the Dutch settlements of Long Island and the North River, when a letter reached him from Jackson calling upon him to take a stand. His reply, under date of August 19th, would have pleased Talleyrand. Having great confidence in Silas Wright, Senator from New York, he wrote that he would confer with him and then formulate his views. A little later he wrote that he and Wright favored

[1] Kendall's *Autobiography*, 391.

[2] Letter to Stevenson, in Ambler's *Thomas Ritchie*, 160.

the McLane plan. The tone of sharp surprise in Jackson's response alarmed the hard-pressed heir apparent, and he hastily wrote that he would yield to the wisdom of Jackson. But his troubles were not over. Another letter from Jackson, more alarming still, pursued him to poison his vacation, summoning him to Washington for a consultation. The cunning politician never faced a more painful problem. He could not afford to break with the all-powerful party dictator in the White House — that would be to abandon the Presidency. Nor was he at all certain that he could afford to become intimately identified with the desperate enterprise upon which the chief was determined to embark. The one would deprive him of the nomination of his party; the other might make that nomination worthless. The campaign of 1836 was already in full swing, and the Opposition was insinuating a directing influence between the most unpopular measures of the Administration and Van Buren. Timid and cautious by temperament, his peculiar situation accentuated these traits in the candidate, and the summons to the seat of war sounded to him like the crack of doom.

But he was equal to the crisis. Writing at once of his willingness to respond if Jackson thought best, he feared his presence in Washington at the time of the withdrawal would dim the prestige of the act by giving it the appearance of having been inspired by the moneyed interests of New York.[1] Having painted this thought, he added some lines for the protection of Louis McLane, his friend. He was fearful that, on the resignation of Duane, McLane might feel that he should also tender his, and that would be a pity. Would it not be a good idea, in the event the resignation were offered, to reply that "you confide in him &c, notwithstanding the difference between you on this point, and that if he could

[1] Biddle was trying to make it appear that the real fight was "between Chestnut Street and Wall Street — between a Faro Bank and a National Bank,' as shown in his letter to Dr. Cooper. (*Correspondence of Nicholas Biddle*, 209.)

consistently remain in the Administration, you would be gratified?" That the suspicious Jackson was deceived is highly improbable, albeit where his affections were involved, as in the case of Van Buren, his vision was apt to be occasionally defective.

But Van Buren and his advice were not needed, for a stronger man, with courage and an iron will equal to his own, was moving to the side of Jackson. Throughout the months of conferences and discussions the one member of his official Cabinet who was in whole-hearted sympathy with the wishes of the Kitchen Cabinet was Roger Taney, the Attorney-General. Before leaving for Rip Raps, Jackson had discussed with him the steps to be taken in the event of a definite refusal from Duane to order the removal, and had intimated that he would transfer Taney to the office of the Secretary of the Treasury. Just about the time Jackson was puzzling over the peculiar hedging of Van Buren, he received a letter from Taney that delighted him. The latter reiterated his conviction that the deposits should be removed, and during the congressional recess. He was sure "the powerful and corrupting monopoly" would "be fatal to the liberties of the people" unless destroyed, and Jackson alone could encompass its destruction. The President had "already done more than any other man has done, or could do, to preserve the simplicity and purity of our institutions, and to guard the country from this dangerous and powerful instrument of corruption." He had "doubted" whether Jackson's friends and the country had the right to ask him "to bear the brunt of such a conflict as the removal of the deposits under present conditions is likely to produce." He had no desire for the secretaryship of the Treasury, but he "would not shrink from the responsibility" if, in the President's judgment, "the public exigency would require" him to undertake it.[1] Here was a man quite as persuasive in his flattery as Van Buren,

[1] Tyler's *Life of Taney*.

and prepared, as Van Buren was not, to stake his future upon an aggressive support of the removal.

For the time being, then, exit Van Buren.

Enter Roger B. Taney.

By this time Jackson's mind was thoroughly made up. The tour of Kendall had not been a complete success. The banks were timid and fearful of the power of "The Monster." Catterall credits the report that Kendall himself had concluded the plan unwise, and had admitted to Jackson that "the project of removing the deposits must be given up." [1] This advice, if given,[2] came too late. The old military leader was in the saddle, war was declared, retreat was defeat. Thus, a few days after receiving Taney's letter, Jackson wrote him that he had considered the probability that Congress would attempt to overawe him, and had determined that, when Duane withdrew, Taney should step into the place and conduct the affairs of the Treasury until toward the close of the next session of Congress, when the battle would have been won or lost, and the refusal of the Senate to confirm Taney's nomination would not interfere. He was only awaiting proof of the expenditure of $40,000 of Bank money in the campaign. With this proof, of which he had no doubt, he would feel justified in removing the deposits. The Bank might "rebel against our power, and even refuse to pay to the order of the Government the public money in its vaults, and lay claim to all the money that remains uncalled for on the books of the loan office." Everywhere he found the "assumed power of this monster." This pretension must be challenged and tested, and he had no doubt of being "sustained by the people." [3]

Thus the die was definitely cast at Rip Raps early in September, and Jackson returned to Washington determined to force the fighting.

[1] Catterall, *Second Bank of the United States*, 203.

[2] Kendall, in his *Autobiography*, gives no hint of such discouragement or advice.

[3] Letter in Tyler's *Life of Taney*.

V

As soon as he reached the capital, he began to press Duane more insistently, with the Secretary stubbornly refusing to budge. Some time before he had voluntarily given the assurance that if the President should determine upon the course outlined, and he should be unable to comply, he would promptly tender his resignation. The President's intentions were now thoroughly understood, but Duane gave no indication of a disposition to relinquish his post, and the pro-Bank papers were decorating him with laurels. The first covert attack upon him from Administration circles appeared in the "Globe" of September 12th, when Blair, taking cognizance of an article in the "Baltimore Chronicle," denounced it as a "slanderer of Mr. Duane." "Would the 'Chronicle' convert the Secretary of the Treasury into a Bank officer, and have him communicating to the corporation what belongs only to his relations with the President?" Even Duane could not have mistaken the implication. Five days after this article appeared, the Cabinet was convened, and Jackson took the opinion of his advisers. McLane, Duane, and Cass were against the step, with Taney, Barry, and Woodbury (who had previously hedged), favoring it.

On the following day the Cabinet was again convened to hear the President's reasons for his determination, set forth in the famous "Paper Read to the Cabinet." This document, as read, had been revised and rewritten from the notes sent by Jackson from his retreat at Hampton Roads to Taney, and was to become the storm center of congressional controversy, although it did not concern the Congress in the least. Beginning with a confession of a fixed hostility to the Bank on the conviction of its unconstitutionality and danger to the liberties of the people, he elaborately reviewed the charter controversy. The people had passed upon his conduct at the polls and he had been overwhelmingly vindicated.

The Nation, therefore, having definitely decided on the abandonment of the Bank as a place of deposit, some method should be devised for the future deposit of the public funds before the expiration of the charter. Under the law, the Secretary of the Treasury could withdraw the deposits whenever he saw fit, provided he informed Congress of his act at the earliest opportunity. To leave the deposits with the Bank until the day of the expiration of the charter with the expectation of making the transfer to some other depository at once would mean "serious inconvenience to the Government and people." Such work, he thought, "ought not to be the work of months only, but of years," for otherwise "much suffering and distress would be brought upon the people." These considerations alone, he thought sufficient to justify the step he proposed.

But in the conduct of the Bank additional and more pressing reasons could be found. Knowing of the Government's decision to appropriate the greater part of its deposits during 1832 to the payment of the public debt, the Bank, in the sixteen months preceding May, 1832, had extended its loans more than $28,000,000, and the maximum of the extension had been made in May. And two months before that, the Bank had so perfectly understood its inability to pay over the public deposits when called upon, that it had secretly negotiated with foreign holders of the three per cent stock a year's postponement of a demand for payment after notice should be given by the Government. "This effort to thwart the Government in the payment of the public debt," he said, "that it might retain the public money to be used for their private interests, palliated by pretenses notoriously unfounded and insincere, would have justified the instant withdrawal of the public deposits."

Since the congressional report in favor of the Bank, other things had occurred that would surely alter the opinion of the lawmakers. "The fact that the Bank controls, and in some cases substantially owns, and by its money supports, some of the leading presses of the country, is now more clearly established." Extravagant sums had been loaned to editors on unusual time and nominal security in 1831 and 1832. And the proceedings and management of the Bank had been unusual and indefensible. The terms of the charter had been violated; and when Government directors undertook to restore methods in conformity with the terms of the charter, they had been disregarded. Worse still: the most important transactions involving the credit of the Bank had been turned over to Biddle, and the committees left in utter ignorance of what he was doing. He had been given unlimited authority in the use of the Bank's money for propaganda purposes. Thousands of dollars had been squandered in the printing of speeches and pamphlets, not only defending the Bank, but attacking the chosen representatives of the people. If, as claimed, the Bank could bring distress and chaos in retaliation, all the more reason for breaking the power of the tyrannical institution. And he closed by fixing October 1st as the day for action.

As the members of the Cabinet sat in the White House that day under conflicting emotions, all appreciating the seriousness of the step, and some contemplating the closing of a career, there could have been none unmindful of the fact that the Paper was intended less for them than for the public. It was characteristic of Jackson in preparing his ground for a fight to speak over the heads of both Cabinet and Congress to the people. That Kendall and Blair were in large part responsible for the original draft which reached Taney for revision, there can be no doubt.

Knowing the real purpose of the Paper, Duane requested a postponement of publication until he could definitely decide. While the Paper was being put in type at the "Globe" office, McLane and Cass threatened to resign rather than accept any responsibility for the act, and Lewis suggested that they be publicly relieved of responsibility. When Blair hastened to Jackson with Lewis's suggestion, the grim man of iron added the concluding paragraph assuming full personal responsibility — much to the chagrin and disgust of Taney.[1]

The crisis had now been reached, and the action of Duane was awaited by the Kitchen Cabinet with the keenest interest, not unmixed with fear lest Taney decline to take the vacant place and face the bitter fight. Taking counsel of his fears, Kendall rushed to the Attorney-General and was reassured. Confessing his fear that his acceptance would mean the end of his lifelong hopes for a place on the Supreme Bench, Taney declared himself in the fight to the end.[2]

On September 21st, the "Globe" authoritatively announced that "the deposits would be changed to State banks" as soon as the necessary arrangements could be made; and in anticipation of the nature of the war the Bank would wage, Blair stressed the fact that the deposits would not be immediately withdrawn, and that the process would be gradual. "It is believed," he wrote, "that by this means the change need not produce any inconvenience to the commercial community."

Four days later the "Paper Read to the Cabinet" appeared in full in the "Globe."

VI

Two days after this publication, Major Lewis wrote Hamilton that "if Mr. Duane cannot or will nót make the order," he would be superseded by Taney. "who has been decidedly with the President in relation to this matter from the beginning to the end," and discrediting rumors of other Cabinet resignations.[3] Whatever may have been the feelings of Hamilton, who looked upon the plan as fraught with possibilities of disaster, the effect of the "Globe's" announce-

[1] The story of the added paragraph is told in Tyler's *Life of Taney*.

[2] Kendall's *Autobiography*, 386.

[3] Hamilton's *Reminiscences*, 266.

ment on Thomas H. Benton, sojourning with relatives in Virginia, was that of a bugle blast to a war charger. He felt "an emotion of the moral sublime at beholding such an instance of civic heroism," and that "a great blow had been struck, and that a great contest must come on, which could only be crowned with success by acting up to the spirit with which it was commenced." He "repaired to Washington at the approach of the session with a full determination to stand by the President." [1]

The day after the reading of the Paper, Jackson called upon Duane for a decision, and the Secretary begged for time to confer with his venerable father, then *en route* to Washington. The same day Major Donelson, the President's secretary, informed him of the decision to publish the Paper in the "Globe" on the morrow, and the hard-pressed Minister protested against such precipitancy. This protest was followed with a letter to Donelson reiterating his plea for time, with the assertion that if he were President he would "consult at least reasonably the feelings of a man who has already anxiety enough." [2] Jackson had, in fact, exercised a most unnatural restraint of his temper, and had been remarkably considerate of his Minister's feelings. Even before the reading of the Paper, and before Duane had made his choice for martyrdom, Jackson had opened a graceful avenue of escape to the Legation at St. Petersburg, but the offer had been declined.

On the 21st, Duane appeared at the White House and left his written decision with Jackson personally. It is a letter of many words, evidently prepared for publication. After asserting that the Secretary of the Treasury is, by the terms of the charter, the sole custodian of the public funds, he finally reached his reasons for refusing to "carry your di-

[1] Benton's *Thirty Years' View*, I, 379.

[2] These notes are incorporated in the 5th Exhibit accompanying Duane's *Address to the People of the United States.*

rections into effect." It would be a "breach of public faith," would appear as "vindictive and arbitrary," and "if the Bank has abused or perverted its powers, the judiciary are able and willing to punish." The House of Representatives had declared the funds safe, and, if anything had happened since its report, "the representatives of the people, chosen since your appeal to them in your veto message, will in a few weeks assemble." Again, "a change to local and irresponsible banks will tend to shake public confidence," and "it is not sound policy to foster local banks." And so on with other reasons, including the charge that "persons and presses known to be in the confidence and pay of the Administration" had tried to intimidate him. There could be no misunderstanding of the purpose of the letter. It was written in a spirit bitterly hostile to the Administration, and in the hope of serving the moneyed institution and having the service rewarded.[1] Having thus insulted the President, he withdrew his promise of July to resign if unable to meet his chief's views, and carefully pointed out that Jackson had the power of dismissal. Here was a martyr zealously seeking the cross.

Jackson immediately wrote a brief, dignified reply to the effect that he could not receive such a communication, nor "enter into further discussion of the question." Rather sharply, the grim old man reminded his subordinate that the imputation in the latter's letter had no place in a correspondence between a President and a member of his Cabinet, that the letter of July offering to resign was before him, and brusquely demanding a final answer. Early in the afternoon Duane again took his pen in hand. The result was another tiresome letter concluding with a distinct refusal to issue the order or to resign, and impudently protesting against the interference of the Executive in the affairs of a member of the Cabinet. This second letter could hardly have reached the

[1] Kendall charges that Duane hoped to "feather his nest." (*Autobiography*, 385.)

White House when Duane, seized with a perfect passion for self-expression, wrote a third "to present another view." The burden of this epistle was that he had been treated unkindly by the "Globe." Having started this upon its way by messenger, the superheated Secretary grasped his pen for another effort, consisting of painful reiterations. All these letters, thousands of words, and pages of paper, were written on the 21st, but with the exception of the reply to the first, Jackson ignored them. Then, two days later, Jackson wrote a short note, returning the last two letters as containing inaccuracies and being inadmissible, and closing with a curt dismissal. Thus Duane laid down his pen, packed his belongings, and passed out of public life.[1]

The day following Duane's dismissal, written by Taney, Cass and McLane consulted Jackson as to the desirability of their resignations. This was almost too much for the old warrior's patience, and he irritably reminded them that they had been released from responsibility, and could remain unless they preferred to join the Opposition. The fire of battle was now in his blood, and he had no intention of parleying with the timid in his official household. Three days later, Taney issued his famous order, McLane and Cass tendered their resignations, and Jackson, in replying, followed Van Buren's suggestion, and they remained.

On the publication of the Paper in the "Globe," the Bank summoned a meeting of the directors and a committee was appointed to take action. Writing from Boston to Biddle, Webster made the suggestion, which was adopted, of a memorial to Congress.[2] This memorial, which referred to the President of the United States as "Andrew Jackson," indicated a disposition to consider the approaching struggle as between "Andrew Jackson" and Nicholas Biddle, between the Bank and the Administration, and the ill-advised arrogance of the

[1] He served the Bank feebly during the fight that followed.

[2] *Correspondence of Nicholas Biddle,* 216.

paper showed all too clearly that the financiers felt that in such a contest the power and the victory would be on the side of the Bank. And such was the prestige of that powerful corporation that not a few Democrats, including friends and supporters of Jackson, shared in the feeling. When Van Buren was authorized by Jackson to offer the attorney-generalship to Daniel of Virginia, that timid lawyer admitted that his fears of Jackson's rashness and situation dissuaded him.[1] It was not until early in November that Benjamin F. Butler, yielding to the personal persuasion of Van Buren, accepted the post. And to obtain his consent it was necessary to appeal to personal friendship, private interest, pecuniary benefit, and the allurements of fame.[2]

And almost immediately the storm broke.

VII

"The times will be hard, and the struggle a great one," wrote Van Buren to Hamilton, "but the patriotism and fortitude of the people will triumph." [3] And Nicholas Biddle did not propose that the inconvenience should be slight. He was delighted with the order for the removal. He was convinced that out of the distress in business circles would come an irresistible demand, not only for the restoration of the deposits, but for the rechartering of the Bank. This last act of Jackson's was the golden opportunity. The advantage would be followed. The public, which had sustained Jackson at the polls, was to be punished, or "disciplined," as Webster mildly described the process. "This discipline," wrote the orator to Biddle, who was his client as well as his party colleague, "it appears to me, must have very great

[1] Van Buren's first choice was John Forsyth, or some Southerner, "if he is a speaking man." (*Autobiography*, 606.) He tells of Daniel's timidity in his *Political Parties in the United States*, 322.

[2] See Van Buren's letter to Butler, in William Allen Butler's *A Retrospect of Forty Years*, 39–43.

[3] Hamilton's *Reminiscences*, 280.

effects on the general question of the rechartering of the Bank."

The "disciplining" of the people began with the Bank's first curtailments on August 13, 1833; and practically ended on July 11, 1834, although it continued to some extent until September. The first move — a proper one — was to issue an order that the amount of money loaned on discounts was not to be increased, and that bills of exchange should be drawn only at short dates and on the Eastern offices. These orders meant inevitable contraction, but of the sort that could be justified. But immediately after Taney had issued his order, the Bank adopted additional measures — the reduction of discounts, the application of the order of restriction on the drawing of bills to all the offices of the Bank, the collection of the balances against the State banks, and the restriction of the receipt of State bank notes. The historian of the Bank truly says that "on the whole, nothing but peril to the Bank could excuse such measures."[1] But even this second step seemed all too mild to the officers and directors in the marble front building on Chestnut Street, and three weeks later a third step was taken. The branch banks in the West were ordered to persevere in "the course of measures already prescribed," and instructed that an extraordinary effort should be made to keep down circulation, and to avoid drafts on the northern Atlantic offices.[2] One month later, Philip Hone, the New York banker and business man, was recording in his diary that the "ill-advised and arbitrary step of the President" was "producing an awful scarcity of money, with immediate distress and melancholy forebodings to the merchants and others who require credit to sustain them"; and that "stocks of every description have fallen — Delaware and Hudson from one hundred and twenty-five to one hundred and fourteen, Boston and Providence from one hundred and fifteen to one hundred and three," and that

[1] Catterall, *Second Bank of the United States*, 318. [2] *Ibid.*

"money cannot be had on bond and mortgage at 7 per cent, and I am told that good notes will hardly be discounted at 9 per cent." [1]

Just about the time Hone was recording these conditions, Biddle was offering the notorious Samuel Swartwout, the Jacksonian Collector in New York, whose irregularities in office were to be unmercifully exploited by the Whigs, a directorship in the Bank, and the latter, declining because of the onerous duties of his office, advised that since "the Bank's power has been shown" in the distress, it might be well now to manifest mercy.[2] Where Niles had found money scarce in September and October without being able to conceive a reason, he wrote in November of "a most severe pressure for money" and the prospect of a "collapse of business." That month State bank notes began to depreciate and loans were at eighteen per cent per annum. With the convening of Congress and the President's uncompromising Message in December, Biddle increased the pressure for the purposes of "discipline." Business men were unable to get credit. Factories were shutting down because of the inability of manufacturers to get loans, and laborers were thrown out into the street. The Christmas season found New York "gloomy" with "times bad," stocks still falling, and a panic prevailing "which will result in bankruptcies and ruin in many quarters where, a few short weeks ago, the sun of prosperity shone with unusual brightness." [3] And three days later the Lord Holland of the American Whigs, in his misery and apprehension, was beginning to suspect that politics and the Bank, as well as Jackson's "ill-advised and arbitrary step," might be playing a part, and concluding that "between them both the community groans under the distress which these misunderstandings have created." "A plague on both your houses," he wrote, his impartial cas-

[1] *Diary*, Nov. 18, 1833. [2] *Correspondence of Nicholas Biddle*, 218.
[3] Hone's *Diary*, Dec. 27, 1833.

tigation springing, perhaps, from the fact that he had lost $20,000.[1]

In January the crash came. Business houses began to fail in New York, Philadelphia, and Washington, and by the end of the month loans could not be had in New York and Baltimore at less than one and a half per cent discount per month. Wages decreased, along with prices, with laborers out of employment and the real estate values on the slump. And at this time, with the Opposition in Congress working in hearty coöperation with the Bank to create the fear that fed the panic, Jackson sat in the White House one Sunday morning writing to Hamilton: "There is no real distress. It is only with those who live by borrowing, trade on loans, and gamblers in stocks. It would be a godsend to society if all such were put down . . . I must stop. The church bells are ringing and I must attend." [2] This theory that it would be a "godsend" to rid the country of the men who live on borrowing was to be used with considerable effect against Jackson by his congressional enemies.

And at the same time, Biddle was writing to the president of his Boston branch [3] that "the ties of party allegiance can only be broken by the actual conviction of existing distress," and that "nothing but the evidence of suffering abroad will produce any effect in Congress"; and to Major Jack Downing in New York that "if the bank were to suffer itself to be misled into the measure of making money plentiful, it will only give to its enemies the triumph of having robbed it with impunity." [4] Thus the evidence is abundant that the Bank exerted its power to the utmost to bring the country to the verge of ruin, and so compel it to consent to a recharter. The fact that the majority of its victims were among its most zealous supporters did not interest Mr. Biddle.[5] Two days

[1] Hone's *Diary*, Dec. 30, 1833.

[2] Hamilton's *Reminiscences*, 270.

[3] William Appleton.

[4] *Correspondence of Nicholas Biddle*, 219.

[5] Catterall severely criticizes the banker for this attitude; for Catterall's righteous sentence on this state of mind, see *Second Bank of the United States*, 229.

after writing the letter to Downing, Biddle determined upon a further contraction in discounts to the amount of $3,320,000, with orders that this should be made within thirty or sixty days, and the largest reductions were to be made in the Western and Southwestern banks. Not content with this, he made another increase in the rates of exchange, and here again discriminated frankly against the West. Thus, in eight months the Bank planned a reduction in discounts to the amount of $13,300,000, which Catterall describes truly as "a preposterously large sum." [1] When to this is added the further restrictions of as much as $5,000,000 through the breaking up of the exchange dealings of the Bank, the contraction in eight months amounted to at least $18,300,000.

Had the Bank acted honorably, there would have been an inevitable depression for the time because of the removal order, but the panic was the Bank's panic, deliberately conceived, and cruelly produced, with the frankly avowed purpose of blackmailing the American people into granting another charter. In his letter to the president of the Boston branch, Biddle had bluntly confessed his purpose. "I have no doubt," he wrote, "that such a course will ultimately lead to a restoration of the currency, and the recharter of the Bank." [2]

During this time there were certain unscrupulous speculators, the buzzards of the panic, whispering commendation into Biddle's ear while feathering their own nests through the distress of the people.[3] But Webster, alarmed at the havoc, had urged Biddle, through Horace Binney, "that the Bank ought to reduce as slowly and moderately as they can — and occasionally to ease off — where it is requisite to prevent extreme suffering." [4] This advice aroused the banker's ire and resulted in no good. It was Biddle's idea that the

[1] *Second Bank of the United States*, 321.

[2] *Correspondence of Nicholas Biddle*, 219.

[3] Notably James Watson Webb.

[4] Binney to Biddle, *Correspondence of Nicholas Biddle*, 220.

Bank's senatorial champions, instead of suggesting a policy of moderation, should be using the distress as an argument for a new charter. "The relief," he wrote Joseph Hopkinson, the distinguished lawyer and jurist, "to be useful or permanent, must come from Congress, and from Congress alone. If that body will do its duty, relief will come — if not, the Bank feels no vocation to redress the wrongs of these miserable people. Rely upon that. This worthy President thinks that because he has scalped Indians and imprisoned Judges, he is to have his way with the Bank. He is mistaken." [1]

VIII

MEANWHILE the Bank was encouraging, inspiring, arranging indignation meetings of the people, where Jackson was arraigned for bringing ruin upon the community, and petitions were drawn asking for the restoration of the deposits. Clay, eager to lash the people into fury, had suggested the plan. "It would be well," he wrote, "to have a general meeting of the people to memorialize Congress in favor of a restoration of the deposits. Such an example [in Philadelphia] might be followed elsewhere; and it would be more influential as it might be more general." [2] The artificial nature of many of the petitions was well understood by the Jackson leaders, and the usually elegant John Forsyth had referred to them in the Senate as "these pot-house memorials," much to the astonishment of Adams.[3] These petitions, according to the plan, were, in many instances, taken to Washington by committees that waited upon the President before presenting them to Congress. Here they were presented in lugubrious speeches calculatingly designed further to fan the fears of the people and keep the panic going. When the New York merchants adopted a memorial and secured the signatures of three

[1] *Correspondence of Nicholas Biddle*, 222. [2] *Ibid.*, 218.
[3] *Memoirs*, April 14, 1834.

thousand people, Tammany Hall ordered meetings in every ward in the city to approve of Jackson's actions.[1] A few days later, between twelve and fifteen thousand friends of "sound currency by means of a national bank" met at noon in the park. When Hone, selected to preside, reached the park, he found an "immense crowd" composed in large part "of the most respectable mechanics and others of the city — men of character, respectability, and personal worth, with a few miscreants who went, perhaps, of their own accord, but were probably sent there to excite disturbances." In truth, "the rabble had gotten possession of the chair," and it required "some hard thumps" from the men of character, respectability, and personal worth to clear the way sufficiently for the presiding genius of the Whig dinner table to reach the platform. When he attempted to speak, the "yells of the mob" rendered all the chairman's efforts "unavailing"; so he "put the question upon the resolutions which were carried by an immense majority," and the meeting adjourned. Unhappily the "mob" did not disperse for some time afterwards.[2]

When these committees, composed of bitter enemies of the President, began to pour into the capital and knock at the White House door, they were received, at first, with urbanity and heard with patience. The committeemen, however, carried back "grossly colored" stories of the interviews, and Jackson thereafter decided to hear and dismiss them without discussion.[3] In these stories Jackson is pictured as raving and ranting, spluttering and spouting imprecations and profanity. McMaster, however, accepts as true that he received these committees "with that stately courtesy for which he was so justly distinguished," and concludes from the evidence that he "soon began to lecture them."[4] In these lectures Jackson is reported to have told the committees to "go

[1] Hone's *Diary*, Jan. 28, 1834.

[2] *Ibid.*, Feb. 7, 1834.

[3] Kendall's *Autobiography*, 411.

[4] *History of the United States*, IV, 201.

to the Bank" or to "go to Biddle" for relief. No less an authority than Catterall has concluded that he was not far wrong. On one occasion he did use extreme language to a committee which implied the threat of rebellion. "If that be your game," he exclaimed, "come with your armed Bank mercenaries, and, by the Eternal, I will hang you around the Capitol on gallows higher than Haman."[1] There is no doubt that he did harangue the committees with bitter denunciations of "The Monster" and properly ascribed a large part of the distress to the deliberate purpose of the Bank to "discipline" the Nation. Some historians have suggested that these outbursts were staged, and it is recorded as a fact by Henry A. Wise, the brilliant Virginia Whig. "When a Bank committee would come . . ." he writes, "he would lay down his pipe, rise to the full height of his stature and voice, and seem to foam at the mouth whilst declaiming vehemently against the dangers of money monopoly. The committee would retire in disgust, thinking they were leaving a mad man, and as soon as they were gone, he would resume his pipe, and, chuckling, say, 'They thought I was mad,' and coolly comment on the policy of never never compromising a vital issue."[2] This interpretation of Jackson's tempests and whirlwinds of passion, coming from a severe critic of his Bank policy, is the most dependable of all the opinions that have been expressed by friend or foe.

IX

And while the committees may have hooted the idea that the Bank was responsible for the severity and continuance of the panic, it very slowly began to dawn upon the New York merchants that possibly the "Emperor Nicholas" might be able to alleviate conditions without in the least compromising the safety of the Bank. Some of his champions were slow to realize or loath to concede this declining popularity. In

[1] Kendall's *Autobiography*, 412. [2] *Seven Decades of the Union*, 107.

February the bankers and merchants of New York appointed a committee to wait upon him and urge a suspension of the contraction, and Albert Gallatin, former Secretary of the Treasury, pointedly warned him that the committee was satisfied of his ability to grant relief, and would so report to the New York merchants. Thus cornered and threatened with the desertion of its friends, the Bank finally agreed that up to May 1st there should be no further contraction. This was a fatal concession in that it was a confession that relief had been previously deliberately denied.[1] Even such champions of the Bank as James Watson Webb found real cause for melancholy complaint in heavy losses in Bank stock, and we find him whining that he had lost all except his paper, and that other speculators, including Alexander Hamilton, Jr., had been among the victims.

Thus the drift against the Bank, which began when Governor Wolf of Pennsylvania denounced its actions in his Message to the Legislature, increased alarmingly. The fact that the Governor had been a firm supporter gave tremendous weight to his act. The friends of the institution were stunned, and, as we shall see a little later, the Governor was bitterly denounced and warmly defended in the Senate. Thus the advice of Jackson to "see Biddle," so mirthfully related by the committees at the time, and so much ridiculed by some historians since, was demonstrating its wisdom. One month after Wolf acted, Governor Marcy of New York imitated his example with the recommendation of a State plan of relief. His proposal to issue $6,000,000 of five per cent State stock to be loaned to State banks was adopted.

The Bank, in its game of "disciplining" the people, had vastly overplayed its hand, and, by its cruel, implacable policy of ruining friends as well as foes, had begun to lose ground in the late winter and early spring. Even among the ultra-conservatives of business, the feeling was germinating

[1] Catterall's view, *Second Bank of the United States*, 344.

that Jackson was not far wrong in the conclusion that a moneyed institution possessing the power to precipitate panics to influence governmental action, was dangerous to the peace, prosperity, and liberty of the people.

X

But the politicians in the Congress were the last to see the drift. Long after the bankers and merchants had lost interest in the fate of Biddle's Bank, they continued their fight in its behalf throughout the most bitter congressional session the Republic had ever known. The actions of the Bank, the tumult of the market-places, the proceedings of the merchants, are all intimately interwoven with the activities of the Bank's champions in House and Senate. There the last stand was taken, there the battle was definitely lost. And there the most dramatic feature of the fight was staged. It was at this juncture that three important figures, not hitherto intimately identified with or against the Administration, moved to the firing line. Thomas H. Benton assumed the leadership of the Jacksonian forces, and Clay's fighters were brilliantly augmented by the advent of two Senators, William Campbell Preston of South Carolina, and Benjamin Watkins Leigh of Virginia.

The complete harmony between Benton's views and Jackson's actions in the Bank controversy has given an overshadowing prominence to his leadership. For thirty years he was a constructive force in legislation, associating his name with more important measures written into law than Clay, Webster, and Calhoun combined. In the Senate his faults of mannerism, his arrogance, and stupendous conceit, together with the interminable length of his speeches and his diffusive tendencies, served to overshadow his very substantial contributions to the discussions. The fact that the Chamber emptied and the galleries cleared when he arose did not disturb him in the least. He spoke from the Chamber to the country, and his carefully prepared speeches, especially during the Bank fight, were treatises intended for the education of the people. His personal life was above reproach. His austerity, his imposing dignity, discouraged attempts at intimacy in a day when men loved conviviality and were a trifle lax in their morals. He was one of the colossal figures of American politics and he never loomed larger than in his fight for Jackson.

William C. Preston, fresh from oratorical triumphs in the Nullification contest, entered the Senate at the age of thirty-eight. Few have made a more favorable début in that body. His fame as an orator had preceded him, and Clay's plans had dedicated the panic session to perfervid oratory. It is impossible to understand, from his speeches in the "Congressional Globe," the extravagant enthusiasm of so stern a critic as Adams. But we cannot discount the common verdict of his contemporaries who considered him one of the most consummate of orators, and "one of the greatest rhetoricians and declaimers of his generation."[1] From another we learn that "many thought him the most finished orator the South had produced," and that he "could arouse his audiences to enthusiasm, and then move them to tears."[2] Not least among the truimphs of his art was his power to sway a mob in the street as well as move the case-hardened critics of the Senate house. Poet and painter, as he was, it is not surprising that in the heat of advocacy his feelings often predominated over his judgment, and his superheated imagination sometimes led him beyond the realms of reality, but these very weaknesses were to delight the enemies of the Jackson Administration, led to the daily assault by Clay. Thus, in his first year in the Senate, he took his place, far in advance of most of his colleagues, and side by side with Clay, Webster, Calhoun, and Clayton.

In addition to Preston, the Opposition was to be further

[1] Laborde. [2] Wilson's *Washington the Capital City*, I, 244.

strengthened by the arrival with the panic session of Leigh. Intellectually, he was one of the strongest men in a State of strong men, and at the bar he was recognized as a great constitutional and civil lawyer. As an orator, he was fluent, fiery, intense, impressive. Wise, who was himself no mean master of English, has described him as "a purist in his Anglo-Saxon," and as having a style "equal to that of the Elizabethan age of English literature." [1] Like Prentiss, he was a small man who loomed large when speaking, and, like him, too, he had one short leg and wore a cork on the sole of his shoe. Unlike Prentiss, he capitalized his infirmity oratorically. Wise found that, while his mannerisms were not graceful, they "always excited sympathy for his infirmity." His voice, which was no small part of his oratorical equipment, has been described as "clear, soft, flute-like, not loud, but like murmuring music." [2] His manner, his speaking method, his very appearance, fitted in well with Clay's programme of dramatic, lugubrious oratory, and he at once moved to his place beside the panic orators, and played a conspicuous and theatrical part.

Thus, with the panic at its flood, with Benton moving to the front of the Administration forces, and with Clay's oratorical battery strengthened, it is time to look in upon the Senate.

[1] *Seven Decades of the Union.* [2] *Ibid.*

CHAPTER XII

THE BATTLE OF THE GODS

I

FROM the moment Congress convened, it was evident that the session was to witness the most bitter party battle ever waged. This was inevitable because of the realignments of the previous session, and the spirit of the Bank. The coalition between Clay and Calhoun gave the Opposition a clear majority in the Senate. It was common gossip four days after Congress was called to order that "the understanding between Mr. Clay and Mr. Calhoun" gave the Opposition all the numerical advantage.[1] This was thoroughly understood by Jackson, Taney, Kendall, and Blair, and all public papers regarding the removal of the deposits were accordingly framed as appeals to the people, rather than to the bodies to which they were addressed. The Presidential Message, in touching upon this topic, was a campaign document and a challenge. Taney's forceful report submitting reasons for the removal was a defiance, and a clarion call to the people in the corn rows, the villages, and the factories. Thus Jackson and his friends forced the fighting from the beginning.

Clay led the onslaught with a resolution calling upon Taney for a report on the new depositories. "I want to inquire where the Treasury of the United States is," he explained ironically. The bristling Benton instantly moved a reference to committee. The Secretary of the Treasury had "charged the Bank distinctly with interfering with the purity of elections, with corrupting and subsidizing the press, with dishonoring its own paper and that of its branches," and these "charges of great criminality" should be investi-

[1] Adams's *Memoirs*, Dec. 6, 1833.

gated. Affecting to ignore Benton, Clay followed with another resolution calling upon the President to say whether the Paper, "alleged" to have been read to the Cabinet, was genuine, and if so, to lay a copy before the Senate. This was a stupid tactical blunder, and John Forsyth, with his suave courtesy, which was not always as innocent as it seemed, inquired the purpose of the "unusual" call. Clay's reply was a quibble. The Paper had been published as having been read by the President, and even promulgated through the press, and he, for one, refused to assume that it was genuine.

"If I understand the gentleman from Kentucky," pressed the courtly Forsyth, "he admits that with the intercourse between the President and his Cabinet we have nothing to do."

"I make no admission," snapped Clay.

It was then that Forsyth revealed the theory on which the Administration forces were to proceed. Why could not Clay indicate the purpose which impelled him? he asked. Was it for the purpose of impeachment? Then the call should have originated in the House, not the Senate. "When the President should be brought to our bar, and put on trial for his violation of the Constitution, that paper would be produced in support of the charge," he continued. But why should the Senate call for it? It was accessible for all purposes of argument. He could understand the resolution only "as a desire to prompt the other House to proceedings by impeachment, and to condemn the President in advance." But after Clay had reiterated the absurd explanation that he merely sought authentic verification of the genuineness of the Paper, the resolution was adopted.[1] The response of Jackson was immediately made in a dignified and unanswerable note of refusal. "As well might I be required to detail to the Senate the free and private conversations I have held with those officers on any subject relating to their

[1] *Cong. Globe*, I, 20–21.

duties," he said.[1] It was a sharp rebuke, richly merited, and left Clay in an unenviable position.

The next brush came in the prompt rejection by the Senate of the nominations of the Government directors who had furnished the report on which Jackson had based his charge of wrongdoing. The moment their names were sent to the Senate, Biddle began to deluge his senatorial friends with demands for their rejection. "They are unfit to be there [on the board]," he wrote Webster; "unfit to associate with the other members." [2] In the Bank circles they were denounced as "spies," and thus, in response to the demand of Biddle, they were rejected. Such was the intimacy of the relation between the party of the Opposition and the Bank of the United States. The sinister nature of this relationship is painfully illustrated in the case of Daniel Webster, who, two weeks after the opening of the session, had written Biddle of his rejection of a professional employment against the Bank, with the bald suggestion that "I believe my retainer has not been renewed or refreshed as usual," and that "if it be wished that my relation to the Bank should be continued, it may be well to send me the usual retainers." [3]

Thus the first days of the session were passed in maneuvering for position, with frequent incidents of a petty nature indicative of the rancorous party spirit of the times. Having observed the unobtrusive figure of Major Lewis, that most consummate of politicians and presidential reporters, moving about the floor of the House, Richard Henry Wilde, poet and politician, Nullifier and Whig, framed a resolution to exclude him, but it was defeated.[4] Meanwhile Clay was busy mapping his campaign, preparing the resolutions on which he proposed to make the issue. The Opposition leaders were clearly embarrassed in determining their course of action.

[1] *Cong. Globe,* 23. [2] Written Dec. 30, 1833, and quoted by Catterall.
[3] Webster to Biddle, *Correspondence of Nicholas Biddle,* 218.
[4] Adams's *Memoirs,* Dec. 19, 1833.

Webster appealed to Justice Story, the scholarly associate of John Marshall, for an opinion on the legal phases; and writing from Cambridge that great jurist would not advise that the deposits could not be legally withdrawn unless danger to their security was involved, but he advanced the theory on which the Bank champions acted — that the Secretary of the Treasury did not become custodian of the funds by virtue of his position in the Cabinet, but held them as a "personal trust, and as much so as if confided to the Chief Justice of the United States." Thus he furnished the Opposition with the opinion it required. The President had no right to interfere; more — if he did interfere, and the Secretary submitted against his own judgment, he violated his trust; and the State banks had no proper authority to take over the deposits.[1] Unhappily, the learned jurist failed to take the next necessary step, and conclude that the President had no power to remove a Secretary of the Treasury.

And it was just this queer opinion that Clay was zealously seeking. About the time Webster was appealing to Story for the elucidation of legal points, Clay was writing to former Senator Tazewell at Norfolk, a great constitutional lawyer, inquiring as to whether or not Jackson had transcended his power in dismissing Duane. It must have been with some embarrassment that he read the Virginian's reply, that to him it was "manifestly absurd to regard the President as responsible for the acts of subordinate agents, and yet to deny him the uncontrolled power of supervising them, and removing them from office whenever they had lost his confidence."[2] This opinion, however, did not deter some statesmen from advancing the idea that Tazewell had contemptuously rejected.

But the position of Story was accepted, and Clay submitted his resolutions censuring the President, and holding

[1] Story to Webster, *Life and Letters of Story*, II, 156–58.
[2] Clay's *Works*, v, 379.

the reasons given by Taney for the removal "unsatisfactory and insufficient." Thus the decks were cleared for action. The real fight began in the debate that day upon these resolutions, and upon these, and others growing out of them, the verbal battle, which at times threatened to be other than bloodless, raged with intemperate fury for seven months.

II

NEVER up to that time, nor again for more than a generation, did Congress so completely hold the interest of the country. The great orators of the Opposition never shone with greater luster, and by their impassioned eloquence, and not a little of consummate histrionics, they persuaded their followers, if not themselves, that they were actually fighting the battle of liberty against despotism. The Democrats contended, on the defensive, that Jackson had the right to dismiss Duane, and that Taney had the legal right to order the removal.

It is not surprising that the little city of Washington, with all its interests revolving about the performances at the Capitol, should have poured forth its people daily to pack the galleries and crowd the lobbies. The Senate Chamber became the peacock alley of fashion — they who met at the dinner or the dance the night before mingled there in the daytime. The debate drew many from other sections, and the belles of country places and remote towns helped to crowd the Chamber to suffocation.[1] In the fashionable character of the gallery audiences we catch the hostility of the aristocracy to the President and his party. The distress committees with their petitions were wont to pack the galleries "applauding the speakers against the President — saluting with noise and confusion those who spoke on his side."[2] Confirmation of such scenes are to be found in the official

[1] Mrs. Smith, in *First Forty Years,* touches on this feature.
[2] Benton's *Thirty Years' View,* I, 424.

report of the proceedings.[1] It has been the fashion to refer to the Jacksonians as the "rabble" and the "mob," and as partaking of the nature of the Jacobins, but throughout the Bank fight the "mob" in the galleries, resorting to the Jacobin methods of hissing and cheering the proceedings on the floor, were largely confined to the enemies of the President.

The debate on the Clay resolutions had scarcely begun when the daily arrival of distress petitions furnished a diversion in the Senate. The memorials were lugubrious recitals of wreck and ruin, and pathetic appeals for the restoration of the deposits. Frequently presented by committees, the bearers repaired to the gallery to give sympathetic ear to the mournful speeches of the Senators to whom their petitions had been entrusted. There was a marked similarity in the petitions, and an even more striking resemblance in the speeches. The burden of both was that the happiness of a prosperous community had been struck down by a tyrant, and that nothing but the restoration of the deposits could end the agony. That the action of such men as Clay, Webster, and Calhoun, in picturing in lurid and exaggerated colors the distress of the moment, and predicting even greater calamities, was calculated to frighten the timid and create panic must have been understood by them. At any rate, these petitions were part of the leaders' plan.[2] This phase of the fight developed with the presentation of Clay's resolution to "inquire into the expediency of affording temporary relief to the community from the present pecuniary embarrassments by prolonging the payment of revenue bonds as they fall due." This resolution opened the way for Clay's first "distress speech." And Forsyth, who was something of a cynic in his way, saw no objection to the resolution, provided it were amended by instructing the committee "to inquire into the extent and causes of the alleged distress of the

[1] *Cong. Globe*, I, 74 and 123.

[2] Van Buren vividly describes these scenes, in his *Autobiography*, 726–27.

community, and into the propriety of legislative interference to relieve them." The proposal of the amendment gave Forsyth the opportunity to present the Administration's opinion of the panic. He had no doubt that there was distress, but it had been greatly exaggerated. "Whence does it arise?" he asked. "From the conflict — the war that the Bank is waging to get the deposits back. The deposits have been removed. The Bank stands still to see what will follow, and it stands still, too, that its power may be felt in every nerve and fiber of the community — and every man shall feel the necessity of the institution." [1]

Thus the panic speeches began. "There sits Mr. Biddle," rather stupidly exclaimed one Senator, presenting a petition, "in the presidency of the Bank, as calm as a summer's morning, with his directors around him, receiving his salary, with everything moving on harmoniously; and has this strike reached him? No, sir. The blow has fallen on the friends of the President and the country." [2] Thus did one Opposition leader rejoice in the serenity of the Bank and its president in the midst of the distress of his country.

Very early the friends of the Administration took their cue from its enemies, and began to flood the Senate with memorials against the Bank. Thus day by day the proceedings were opened by the reading of petitions, followed by speeches on the "distress," and replies belittling the panic. Mr. Clay's heart was wrung by news of the distress in Savannah and Augusta; whereupon Mr. Forsyth rose to deny that there was distress in those cities. "I know the individuals," he said. "They are highly respectable men — merchants and members of the Bar. They are friends of the Bank of the United States." [3] A New Jersey Senator, opposed to the Administration, presented conflicting petitions from his State, with the Jackson petitions numerically the

[1] *Cong. Globe*, I, 101.
[2] Senator Frelinghuysen, *Cong. Globe*, I, 129.
[3] *Cong. Globe*, I, 203.

stronger. Ah, laughed Forsyth, "from the State of New Jersey we have three cheers for one groan."[1] When an Opposition Senator presented a petition from Portsmouth with a doleful tale, Senator Isaac Hill killed the effect by explaining the dubious manner in which the signatures had been obtained. And when, a little later, Hill undertook to present a petition of the New Hampshire Legislature against the Bank, Webster moved to lay it on the table. In truth the actions of legislatures were beginning to annoy the panic-breeders. Maine, New York, New Hampshire, and other States had spoken in support of Jackson's policy. It became necessary to devote more attention to that end of the petition business. "What is doing in your legislature about the deposits?" Clay wrote to his friend, Judge Brooke of Virginia. "We want all aid here on that subject which can be given us from Richmond."[2] And when the Legislature acted, John Tyler lost all patience with the Governor for not sending the petition on at once. "The resolutions of the legislature have not yet reached me," he wrote impatiently to Mrs. Tyler, "nor can I conceive what Floyd is after that he does not forward them."[3] They arrived in time, and Webster did not move to lay them on the table.

Then, with the effect of a bomb exploding among the Bank champions, came the message of Governor Wolf of Pennsylvania, denouncing the Bank for responsibility for the depression. Clay lost no time in denouncing him as a man worshiper, albeit the Governor had previously favored the Bank. Another Bank Senator rushed forward with a resolution "disapproving the vacillating or time-serving policy of the Governor of Pennsylvania," while Forsyth and others criticized the taste of the proceedings.[4]

Thus the battle of the petitions went merrily on, some spontaneous, most inspired by the Bank agents, while the

[1] *Cong. Globe*, I, 228.

[2] Clay's *Works*, v, 377.

[3] *Letters and Times of the Tylers*, I, 484.

[4] *Cong. Globe*, I, 344.

conflicting memorials were conceived to offset the intended effect. As the weeks extended into months, and the depression began to lift, extraordinary efforts were made to reawaken the country against the "tyrant in the White House." Webster harangued a crowd in New York City; but the major part of the platform propaganda work was assigned to McDuffie, who better than most men knew how to "ride on the whirlwind and direct the storm"; to Preston, who could arouse men to frenzy or move them to tears; and to Poindexter, who was a veritable fire-eater. These three consummate mob-baiters set forth on a journey that took them to Baltimore, Philadelphia, and New York. The orators reached Baltimore on Sunday. But no matter; as a minister of the Gospel piously said, "in revolutionary times there were no Sabbaths," and the meeting was held. It was on this occasion that McDuffie, with the true spirit of the demagogue, solemnly discussed the "rumor" that Jackson, the tyrant, might attempt to dismiss Congress at the point of the bayonet, and promised that "ten days after the entrance of the soldiers into the Senate Chamber, to send the Senators home, 200,000 volunteers would be in Washington." [1]

Meanwhile the Kitchen Cabinet was capitalizing all the intemperate attacks upon Jackson, and Blair was publishing letters in the "Globe" threatening the life of the President if he did not restore the deposits. One of these recited that three young men in New York had been selected to "proceed in the course of the present month to the capital, there to put in execution the design entrusted to their hands." [2]

III

Such, however, were the side issues of the session. The real fight was waged on Clay's resolutions to censure, and later on the President's Protest. Clay opened the debate on the censure resolutions in a three-days speech bristling with

[1] Benton's *Thirty Years' View*, I, 422. [2] *Washington Globe*, Feb. 13, 1834.

extravagant invective — a tremendous philippic, not only against Jackson's Bank policy, but against his entire presidential career. Intended to serve outside the Senate Chamber in alarming the people, his appeal was to the passions and the fears of the multitude. The central idea of it all was that all power was being concentrated in one man. The constitutional rights of the Senate had been outraged. The public domain was threatened with sacrifice. The Indian tribes had been miserably wronged. Even the tariff was in danger. An "elective monarchy" was all but established. On every hand was depression, suffering, gloom. The power over the purse had been lodged with that over the sword — a combination fatal to free government. The President's conduct had been lawless. Such, in brief, was the tone and temper of one of the greatest philippics that ever poured from the lips of Clay.[1] As he sank into his seat, Benton instantly began his three-days reply, meeting the attack with a counter-offensive. "Who are these Goths?" he demanded — referring to Clay's call upon the people to drive the Goths from the Capitol. "They are President Jackson and the Democratic Party — he just elected President over the Senator himself, and the party just been made a majority in the House — all by the votes of the people. It is their act which has placed these Goths in possession of the Capitol to the discomfiture of the Senator and his friends."

Calhoun followed in a speech of an hour and a half in support of the resolutions, proclaiming the coalition. "The Senator from Kentucky anticipates with confidence," he said, "that the small party who were denounced at the last session as traitors and disunionists will be found on this trying occasion in the front rank, and manfully resisting the advance of despotic power." But Calhoun's intellectual self-respect deterred him from contending that the removal of Duane was an act of Executive usurpation.

[1] Clay's *Works*, VII, 575–620.

Then followed Rives in a manly defense of the Administration which he well knew would force his retirement from the Senate under the instructions of the Virginia Legislature. And then the new orator of the Opposition, William Campbell Preston, entered the lists, attacking Government directors for furnishing the President with a report of the Bank's activities. The President had no right to ask information, and the directors no right to comply. The galleries were moved to applause, and the Carolinian took his place among the popular orators of the day.[1] Forsyth followed Preston, to be succeeded by Grundy, who was trailed by Frelinghuysen for the resolutions.

Meanwhile Webster was impressively silent. Unwilling longer to make the Bank the football of party politics, he looked disapprovingly upon the war of personalities. He knew that no constructive measure had been proposed, and that Biddle's frenzied pressure on the people was driving supporters from the institution. He had no heart at this time for an attack on Jackson — recalling the "reciprocal kindnesses" of the last few months.[2] He realized that a senatorial censure and exterior pressure would never drive Jackson to such a recharter measure as had been proposed. And yet, in January, Calhoun was positive that the Administration had been mortally wounded.[3] Preston was exuberantly proclaiming that the removal of the deposits would force a recharter on the Bank's terms.[4] In February, when the Bank was losing ground with the people and making no congressional converts, Clay was writing to Brooke that "we are gaining, both in public opinion and in number in the House of Representatives."[5] That Clay was supremely selfish in his relations with the Bank is generally conceded by historians now,[6] and was keenly felt even by Biddle, who preferred a

[1] Adams's *Memoirs*, Jan. 23, 1834; Mrs. Smith's *First Forty Years*, 353.
[2] March's *Reminiscences of Congress*.
[3] Catterall, *Second Bank of the United States*, 333. [4] *Ibid.*
[5] Clay's *Works*, v, 377. [6] Such is Catterall's view.

joint resolution ordering the restoration to wasting months in wrangling over a vote of censure. This plan he urged upon Webster, through Horace Binney of the House. But Clay scoffed at the idea. He was more interested in making Jackson obnoxious for party reasons than in serving his friends in Philadelphia, and he actually felt that he was succeeding in his purpose.

At length Webster determined to strike out for himself.

IV

Early in March he came forward with his compromise recharter measure providing a renewal for six years only; for an abandonment of the monopoly features to the end that Congress might, in the meantime, if it saw fit, grant a charter to another company; for the restoration of the deposits only after July 1st; and for the issuance of no note under the $20 denomination. This compromise had been discussed with friends of the Administration, who were ready to support it provided the friends of the Bank would unite upon it. Three days later Webster addressed the Senate on the virtues and purposes of the measure, carefully refraining from personalities or denunciation of the President. The most militant of Jackson's friends could have found no fault with the orator's treatment of their idol. Nor did he imitate his party colleagues in an intemperate discussion of the removal. He traced the origin of the distress to Taney's order; showed the relation between commerce and credit, and between credit and banking, and effectively disposed of Jackson's fallacy that men who operate on credit are undeserving of consideration. It was only in his affectation of indignation over the charge that the Bank was deliberately contributing to the distress that he departed from the high ground of statesmanship, and played the hypocritical politician. But the Senators listening eagerly to his words did not know of the letter he had written to Biddle predicting that the "disciplining" of the people would result in a renewal of the charter, or that he had urged upon Biddle, through Binney, that he ought to "occasionally ease off, where it is requisite to prevent extreme distress." No one knew better than he that the Bank not only possessed, but exerted, the power charged by the Administration. This aside, Webster's was the most dignified, impersonal, and statesmanlike speech of the session.

But the moment he resumed his seat, the schism among the leaders of the Opposition was emphasized when Leigh arose to announce that the Virginia view of the unconstitutionality of the Bank would make it impossible for him to support the bill. Three days later Calhoun criticized the measure as only a temporary expedient, and proposed, instead, a bill of his own providing a recharter for twelve years. The only extensive attack on the Webster compromise, however, was that of the "Cato of the Senate," Hugh Lawson White, who had not up to that time wholly broken with his old friend in the White House. Respected as a financier, he was always heard with profound respect. He vigorously defended the removal of the deposits on the grounds set forth in Jackson's Message. His speech was all the more impressive because he had advised against the removal and his letter had been read to the Cabinet. The day before taking the floor, he wrote of his embarrassment, but later developments having changed his opinion, he felt it would be censurable to remain silent.[1]

But in the end it was not the opposition of Democratic Senators that suddenly terminated the consideration of the Webster compromise. It was soon found that the friends of the Bank were hopelessly divided on any constructive programme. Even in the inner Bank circles there were clashing views. Biddle favored the Webster plan; Sergeant, the chief counsel, and Binney, leading spokesman in the House, preferred the Calhoun measure. Even these differences might

[1] *Memoir of Hugh Lawson White*, 143.

have been reconciled but for the selfishness of Clay, who persisted in his determination to use the Bank for party purposes. "If Mr. C [Clay] and Mr. C [Calhoun] would go along with us," Webster wrote Biddle, "we could carry the compromise bill through the Senate by a strong two thirds majority. Can you write through anybody to talk with Mr. Calhoun?"[1] In the meanwhile Calhoun was attempting the conversion of such Administration Senators as Benton and Silas Wright, without success.

While these negotiations were in progress, the fury of Clay over the independence of Webster increased in intensity, culminating in the threat that, if the New Englander failed to move to lay his own motion on the table, he would make the motion himself. Thus, one week after the delivery of his speech, Webster killed his own measure. When, with the explanation that he had been disappointed in his hopes, he made the motion to table, John Forsyth demanded the yeas and nays to show that Webster's bill had not been killed by the Administration Senators, but by his own party friends. The roll-call showed practically all the Bank Senators voting to table, with Benton, Forsyth, White, Hill, Wright, and Grundy voting against the motion. Thus the only practical and constructive attempt made by the friends of the Bank to save the institution was slaughtered in the house of its friends.[2]

V

With the accumulating evidence of impatience in the country, Clay at length determined to bring to a vote the resolutions, submitted merely to irritate and provoke a debate that would give the panic time to act. So firmly was Clay convinced that the "disciplining" of the people was working the destruction of Jackson's popularity, that he sought to transfer a portion of his fancied resentment to Van Buren,

[1] Catterall, *Second Bank of the United States*, 336. [2] *Cong. Globe*, I, 264.

who was all but certain to be the Democratic nominee in 1836.[1] There has probably never been a more transparent bit of histrionics perpetrated upon a deliberative body than that of Clay in his pathetic appeal to Van Buren, seated in the chair, and with a padlock on his lips, to hasten to Jackson with a plea for the suffering people.

"To you, sir, in no unfriendly spirit, but with feelings softened and subdued by the deep distress which pervades every class of our countrymen, I make this appeal," he exclaimed, his eyes moist with tears. "... Depict to him, if you can find language to portray, the heartrending wretchedness of thousands of the working classes cast out of employment. Tell him of the tears of helpless widows, no longer able to earn their bread, and of unclad and unfed orphans, who have been driven by this policy, out of the busy pursuits, in which, but yesterday, they were gaining an honest livelihood.... Tell him that he has been abused, deceived, betrayed by the wicked counsels of unprincipled men around him. Inform him that all efforts in Congress to alleviate or terminate the public distress are paralyzed and likely to prove totally unavailing, from his influence upon a large portion of its members who are unwilling to withdraw their support, or to take a course repugnant to his wishes and feelings. Tell him that in his bosom alone, under actual circumstances, does the power reside to relieve the country; and that unless he opens it to conviction, and corrects the errors of his Administration, no human imagination can conceive, and no human tongue can express the awful consequences which may follow."

With this piece of play-acting, Clay, looking as much distressed as one of his petitioners, sank exhausted in his seat. Throughout the ludicrous scene, Van Buren "maintained the utmost decorum of countenance, looking respectfully and

[1] "Our city is full of distress committees. The more the better." (Clay to Brooke, *Works*, v, 377.)

even innocently at the speaker all the while as if treasuring up every word he said to be repeated to the President." [1] But all the while the more astute Red Fox was thinking that the speech "would tend to strengthen greatly the attachment of his friends; would warm up their sympathies in his behalf and concentrate their regard." [2] With the eyes of all upon him — and the Senate had been really affected by Clay's voice and manner — Van Buren called a Senator to the chair, placidly descended to the floor as though he were not the object of interest, deliberately walked to Clay's seat, and, in his most courtly manner, and with his most courtly bow, asked for a pinch of his snuff. The startled orator gave him his snuffbox. Van Buren took a pinch, applied it to his nostrils, returned the box, bowed again, and resumed the chair as though nothing had happened. And the Senate smiled. Clay's appeal had hovered dangerously near the ridiculous, and Van Buren pushed it over. No single incident so well illustrates the political purpose of Clay's activities on the removal of the deposits.

But even panics and politics cannot go on forever, and the discussion on the Clay resolutions had covered "the longest period which had been occupied in a single debate in either House of Congress since the organization of the Government." [3] Thus, on March 27th the Senate, by a vote of 26 to 20, placed the stigma of a censure upon the action of the President.

Jackson was now to have his inning.

VI

WITH mass meetings being organized against him in all sections, with the capital crowded with hostile delegations, and with the Senators thundering their extravagant philippics

[1] Benton's *Thirty Years' View*, I, 420.
[2] Van Buren's statement to Senator Foote, as given in the *Casket of Reminiscences*.
[3] Clay's speech, *Cong. Globe*, I, 269.

at the tyrant responsible for the widows' and the orphans' woes, Jackson remained serene and unafraid.[1] But with the adoption of the resolutions of censure, he determined to strike back in such a way as effectively to reach the people. There were men in those days who thought that a senatorial censure would wreck any reputation. They had not yet sensed the spirit of the times. Three weeks after the Senate acted, Major Donelson appeared in the Chamber with the famous Protest. Nothing could have been more merciless than the cold logic with which the iron man pounded the resolutions of condemnation; nothing more biting than his reference to those Senators supporting them, who had thus "deliberately disregarded the recorded opinion of their States." He solemnly protested "against the proceedings . . . as unauthorized by the Constitution, contrary to the spirit and to several of its express provisions, subversive of that distribution of powers of government which it has ordained and established, destructive of the checks and safeguards by which those powers were intended on the one hand to be controlled and on the other to be protected, and calculated, by their immediate and collateral effects, by their character and tendency, to concentrate in the hands of a body, not directly amenable to the people, a degree of influence and power dangerous to their liberties and fatal to the Constitution of their choice."

Not only had his public character been assailed, but imputations had been cast upon his private character. "In vain do I bear upon my person," he continued in a passage of no little eloquence, "enduring memorials of that contest in which American liberty was purchased; in vain have I since periled property, fame, and life in defense of the rights and privileges so dearly bought; in vain am I now, without a personal aspiration or the hope of individual advantage, encountering responsibilities and dangers from which by mere

[1] Benton's *Thirty Years' View*, I, 424.

inactivity in relation to a single point I might have been exempt, if any serious doubts can be entertained as to the purity of my purpose and motives. If I had been ambitious, I should have sought an alliance with that powerful institution which even now aspires to no divided empire. If I had been venal, I should have sold myself to its designs. Had I preferred personal comfort and official ease to the performance of my arduous duty, I should have ceased to molest it. In the history of conquerors and usurpers, never in the fire of youth nor in the vigor of manhood could I find an attraction to lure me from the path of duty, and now I shall scarcely find an inducement to commence the career of ambition when gray hairs and a decaying frame, instead of inviting to toil and battle, call me to the contemplation of other worlds where conquerors cease to be honored and usurpers expiate their crimes." And he closed with the request that the Protest be entered upon the journals of the Senate.[1]

Whatever else may be said of this remarkable document, its effect upon the masses of the people, idolizing Jackson as they never had another American, was certain to be tremendous. The ideas were largely Jackson's. Attorney-General Butler, a brilliant lawyer, worked out the legal end, while Amos Kendall devoted his genius to those portions intended for political effect. The Protest appeared immediately in Blair's "Globe," and was soon published in all the Administration papers of the country.

VII

THE effect on the Senate may be better imagined than described. Poindexter, whose private grudge was the inspiration of his renegadism, could not "express the feeling of indignation" the paper had excited in his bosom, and he would "spurn it from the Senate" — "that body which stands as a barrier between the people and the encroachments of execu-

[1] See Richardson's *Messages and Papers of the Presidents.*

tive power." It was not a Message — merely "a paper, signed 'Andrew Jackson,'" and "nothing else."[1] Sprague of Maine, who had been pilloried, spoke "more in grief than in anger," and while the President had referred to "his Secretary" and felt that this was "his Government," he, the Senator, "never bowed the knee to Baal." And while the tyrant was appealing to the people, look about. "Behold your green fields withered; listen to the cries of distress of the widows and orphans, rising almost in execration of the exercise of that power which has blasted their hopes and reduced them to despair."[2] Frelinghuysen of New Jersey, another pilloried statesman, next arose to discuss "this most extraordinary proceeding — one which would form an era in American history." What a spectacle! "When the busy hum of industry was silenced, when the laborer was in want of employment, when banks were breaking in every direction, and the cries for relief from the unrelenting hand of power were heard everywhere around us," the Senate had listened to a lecture of an hour and a half. And why refer to the New Jersey Legislature? He had "dared to meet the frowns of his constituents" because of his zeal for his country.[3] Southard of New Jersey, also pilloried by Jackson, hoped that he might "school himself into that degree of moderation necessary for the occasion." He could find no excuse for Jackson's indignation. And yet "we have received, not from Charles I, Cromwell, or Napoleon Bonaparte, but from a man combining the characters of the whole of them, a warning to cease our further proceedings."[4] And Leigh closed the day's events by declaring "before God that upon the fate of these resolutions, and the disposition of this question, depends the permanency of the Constitution, handed down to us by our fathers."[5]

To get the right perspective upon these speeches, it should be borne in mind that at the time of their delivery the busi-

[1] *Cong. Globe*, I, 317. [2] *Ibid.*, 318. [3] *Ibid.* [4] *Ibid.*, 321. [5] *Ibid.*, 323.

ness men were openly charging Biddle with responsibility for the panic. Niles's "Register" had admitted that the Bank's power was too great, and the "St. Louis Republican," a stanch supporter of the Bank, had turned upon it with a bitter denunciation of its course.[1] Thus, however, the debate began, and in this spirit was it continued for a month — a month of fierce invective. On the second day, following the philippic of Leigh, the crowds in the packed galleries clashed with cheers and hisses. Especially pleased were the galleries when, apropos of Jackson's reference to his gray hairs, the fiery cripple compared him to Mount Ætna, "whose summit was capped with eternal snow, but which was always vomiting forth its liquid fire." [2] The discussion finally revolved around the Poindexter resolutions not to receive. A few days later Calhoun attacked the Protest with great bitterness, and amendments were offered by both Calhoun and Forsyth. That of the Carolinian declared the President had no right to send, and the Senate no right to receive, such a document. Then the Administration disclosed its hand in the Forsyth resolution providing that "an authenticated copy of the original resolution [Clay's] with a list of the ayes and nays, of the President's Message and the pending resolution be prepared . . . and transmitted to the Governor of each State of the Union to be laid before their legislature at the next session, as the only authority authorized to decide upon the opinions and conduct of the Senators." [3] Here was a declaration, by indirection, from the leader of the Administration that the President was not authorized to pass upon the opinions and conduct of Senators. Had the resolution stopped there, it would not have differed materially from those of Poindexter or the resolution of Calhoun. But it declared that there was an authority to pass upon the conduct of Senators — the people who elected them to the Senate; and that, with the facts before them, they should pass upon

[1] Feb. 10, 1834. [2] *Cong. Globe*, I, 328. [3] *Ibid.*, 368.

the conduct of the public servants. This was an impressive proclamation that the Jacksonian Senators were convinced that the people sustained them; and the fact that the Forsyth resolution was defeated by a party vote was an admission from the Opposition that it lacked such faith.

When in early May the Poindexter resolutions were called up for final consideration, the debate was closed by Webster in a constitutional argument pitched upon a higher plane than that of personalities, and interspersed with passages of eloquence seldom equaled even by him.[1] Nothing reveals the inability of the senatorial oligarchy to understand the altered spirit of the people so well as his contention that the Senate was expected to stand between the people and the tyranny of Executive power. The fact that the peaceful revolution of 1828 was a rising of the people against the aristocracy of the old congressional clique does not appear to have occurred to Webster or his party friends at any time during the Jacksonian period.

When Webster concluded, the last word for the Administration was spoken by its most eloquent spokesman, who, better than any other, was temperamentally fitted to meet the New England orator upon the high plane he had chosen, John Forsyth. Webster rejoined, briefly, the vote was taken, and the resolutions passed with a margin of eleven votes.

VIII

MEANWHILE the battle over the deposits was being fought in the House, albeit with less vituperation and abuse. John Quincy Adams, one of the Bank's leaders, looked upon the proceedings in both Houses with cynical amusement as being the mere ebullitions of party politics with no terminal facilities. Though a talkative member, his name appearing ninety-three times during the session, he made none of the

[1] Especially the famous passage inspired by memories of his emotions on the ramparts of Quebec.

principal speeches on the leading questions; but whenever his vote was required, it was cast for the Bank, and whenever his advice was solicited, it was given. The more active leadership of the tempestuous McDuffie, whose partiality for the Bank had displaced him in the chairmanship of the Ways and Means Committee, was more in evidence. But more impressive than either in the front rank of the Bank champions was a new member whose extraordinary ability placed him immediately with the foremost of congressional orators. When Horace Binney entered the House, he was in his fifty-third year, at the height of his forensic fame, and at the head of the Philadelphia Bar. He was, perhaps, the sole figure among the Bank leaders in House or Senate who was not moved in the slightest degree by political considerations. He had overcome his distaste for political controversy and entered the House with the sole purpose of protecting, as best he could, the interest of the institution of which he had, but the year before, become a director. He was as much the attorney and special pleader of the Bank in the House as he could have been in the courts. His physical appearance alone would have distinguished him in any assembly. Tall, large, and perfectly proportioned, he has been described by one who observed him during the Bank fight as "an Apollo in manly beauty." [1] As an orator he was of the Websterian mould. He spoke with great deliberation, and with perfect enunciation and modulation with a voice that was full and musical. Unlike McDuffie, he was incapable of tearing a passion to tatters. Never noisy, even in moments of great excitement, he was always graceful and easy in his manner. He spoke the language that Addison and Swift wrote. He addressed the House with the same scrupulous care and the same lofty dignity with which he would have addressed John Marshall on the Supreme Bench, or conversed with Mrs. Livingston in her drawing-room. In social relationships, his

[1] Sargent's *Public Men and Events,* II, 213.

innate refinement could not be marred by the free-and-easy manners of the cloak-room; his suavity could not be disturbed by the ferocity of attack; his dignity could withstand any circumstance. Such was the Bank's most perfect champion in its greatest crisis. He left his profession to serve its cause, and that cause defeated, he gladly bade farewell to public life and returned to his profession and his habitual peace of mind.

As chairman of the Ways and Means Committee, the burden of the battle for the Administration fell on James K. Polk. History has settled on the verdict that he was a man of mediocre ability, with nothing to commend him to the admiration, and little to the respect, of posterity. But he managed the fight for the Administration with consummate parliamentary skill. Beset on all sides by tremendous onslaughts, he remained cool, courteous, and fair throughout, and won the open commendation of McDuffie for the manliness of his methods. It is impossible to turn the yellowing pages of the "Congressional Globe," recording the day-by-day story of the fight, without a growing feeling of admiration for Polk. He was never diverted from the question, never excited by attacks, patient, and yet always pressing courteously for action. In the midst of the frenzied partisans, he looms large.

The fight began over the reference of the Taney report and Polk's motion that it be referred to his committee. In explaining his reasons the latter avowed a purpose to investigate the Bank, and the forces rushed into action. "Why investigate," cried McDuffie, "when admissions would be made without an investigation?" Had Bank money been used in the campaign? Admitted! "State your sum," he shouted, "fifty, sixty, or a hundred thousand." The Congress had named a depository for the public money; it had been removed; it must be restored — that was the subject for debate.[1] Binney immediately arose to supplement McDuffie's

[1] *Cong. Globe*, I, 24.

suggestion. "What is the object of the inquiry asked for?" he demanded. "Is it to suggest reasons for the Secretary's act . . . ? If you bring in other facts, other judgments, other reasons, you annul the judgment of the Secretary, agree that it was wrong, and assume to exercise an original instead of a derivative power." If Taney had acted on sufficient reasons, "it was for the House, on behalf of the people, to pronounce their judgment; and if they were sufficient, then there was an end to the question." More: "What knowledge have we of the condition of the banks selected by the Government?"

The State banks not safe? Polk retorted. Very well, "this constitutes one of the chief objects of the investigation proposed." A "question of public faith?" as Binney had hinted. "Is it not proper, then," asked Polk, "for a committee . . . to inquire by which party the contract was violated?" And only to inquire into the sufficiency of Taney's reasons? Why, "some of the reasons given may involve the charter of the Bank." [1]

After a week of wrangling, the Administration won on the reference, but the moment the vote was announced, McDuffie moved instructions to the committee to report a joint resolution providing for the depositing of all revenues thereafter collected in the Bank of the United States — and this was the peg on which the main discussion hung.

The impetuous McDuffie was the first to rush into the arena. His was a bitter, brilliant excoriation of Jackson, a fulsome glorification of the Bank, and he thundered on for two days,[2] impassioned, in a state of constant volcanic eruption, but little more than "a fierce attack upon the President." [3] One week later Polk consumed two days in a reply which, in its moderation of tone and language and its argumentative character, was in striking contrast to that of the vituperative Carolinian. Defending in detail the position

[1] *Cong. Globe*, 25. [2] *Ibid.*, 43. [3] Adams's *Memoirs*, Dec. 23, 1833.

of Jackson, discussing the legal and constitutional phases, citing precedents and authorities, he built up a case for the Administration which could not have been other than impressive in view of the attempt of most of the Bank's champions to answer him.[1] Another week elapsed before Horace Binney rose to reply, in a masterpiece of parliamentary oratory. In musically flowing sentences he described the prosperity preceding the attack upon the Bank, the nature of the currency and credit, the effect of the shaking of confidence, the necessity for the Bank's curtailments, and argued that "the control of the public deposits is inherent in the Congress." But had the Bank been charged with exercising political power? "Granted — granted — the charge is granted, but the Bank has not succeeded in this exercise of political power. . . . The late election proves that it did not succeed. The force of array, legislative and executive, is against the Bank; and it did not succeed. The act of removal was not, therefore, an imperative and retributive act; but an act of malignant dye — an act vindictive." In all his historical researches he knew of only one instance where a charter had been destroyed "on the alleged ground of the assumption of political power." That was in the reign of Charles II, when, on that ground, he obtained possession of the charter of London. "But it was restored when constitutional liberty dawned." Thus he approached his conclusion — a demand for the immediate restoration of the deposits, and, speaking with a rapidity that the reporter could not follow, launched upon his peroration, with the plea that the question be not considered in the spirit of party, but "rather as one affecting the general interest of the community; as one involving the integrity of the Constitution, the stability of contracts, and the permanence of free government; as a question involving public faith, national existence, and the honor and integrity of the country, at home and abroad." [2]

[1] *Cong. Globe*, I, 68.

[2] *Ibid.*, 84–94.

Thus, refraining from personalities, and frowning upon the party aspect of the controversy, the most clever of the Bank's champions, speaking with the cunning of the proverbial "Philadelphia lawyer," attempted, too late, to undo the work Clay had done to serve a selfish end. The night after the conclusion of the speech found him at the White House, one of numerous guests, and Jackson sought him, devoted himself to him with an embarrassing assiduity, and thanked him for advocating his cause without indulgence in personal abuse.

But it was not every Philadelphia lawyer that was to be looked upon so kindly in Jacksonian circles. In the midst of the struggle in the House a series of Bank articles began to appear in the "National Gazette" over the signature of "Vindex." It was just at the time Joseph Hopkinson, the Federal Judge for eastern Pennsylvania, began to haunt the floor and lobby of the House — a privilege he enjoyed by virtue of previous membership in that body. His activity among the members became so open as to create comment, and the "National Gazette" made a laborious attempt to explain his presence. It was a purely social visit. He had come on the invitation of the Judges of the Supreme Court. It was natural that he should delight in renewing old friendships. This explanation gave Blair his opportunity, in a column editorial, to assail the Philadelphia jurist as a lobbyist, to insist that he had disqualified himself to sit on any Bank case, and to challenge the "National Gazette" to deny that he was the author of the "Vindex" articles.

"But further we would inquire," wrote Blair, "whether the judge is not a debtor of the Bank as well as its anonymous vindicator? We believe he is — and it is difficult to say whether the judge's extreme solicitude and activity in behalf of the Bank arises from its pecuniary favors, the bonds of family affection which bind him to Mr. Biddle, his son having married Mr. Biddle's sister, or the old Federal feeling which always distinguished him, and which inclined him against his country during the last war, and prompted his speech after its close, declaring the Nation was disgraced by the peace." [1] Such was the bitterness and such were the blunt weapons in evidence in the contest even in the House.

Early in March, Polk submitted his report justifying every step of the Administration, and including the sensational resolution providing for an investigation of the Bank at Philadelphia. Binney submitted a minority report favoring the restoration of the deposits, and the debate took a fresh start. The outstanding speech of this phase of the debate was that of Rufus Choate, described by Adams, on the evening of its delivery, as "the most eloquent speech of the session, and, in a course of reasoning, altogether impressive and original." [2] Still young, and his public career but brief, his great intellectual labors had already undermined his health, and even thus early in life he presented to the House when he arose the "cadaverous look" which confronts us to-day in the portraits of his later life.[3] With all the consummate skill which so distinguished his advocacy in the courts, he sought to divert the discussion from the channels it had followed. "As to the Bank itself," he said, "I shall go throughout on the supposition that it will not be rechartered. I call on gentlemen to look upon the proposition to restore the deposits merely as a temporary measure of relief." The crying need of the immediate hour was the use of the public money, and this could be had in a beneficial way at the time only through the Bank of the United States. Like Binney, he won the respect of Administration forces, and the succeeding speaker, hostile to the restoration, found the views expressed "new and interesting, and delivered in a tone and spirit becoming the representatives of a free people." [4] But the debate dragged on without any high lights until in early

[1] *Washington Globe*, June 3, 1834.
[2] Adams's *Memoirs*, March 28, 1834.
[3] Adams refers to his "cadaverous look."
[4] *Cong. Globe*, I, 272.

April, when McDuffie returned to the attack, still in a superheated condition, and seeing swords and daggers gleaming in the air. Never in all history, he thought, had "the progress of the usurpation of the Executive been more rapid, more bold, or more successful than in the United States in the last fifteen months." As he sat down, the previous question was moved, and with the appointment of tellers there fell a deep silence with the contending forces "glowering upon each other."[1] The roll was called — and victory fell to the Jacksonians with an overwhelming majority.

In pursuance of the resolutions providing for an investigation, a committee was appointed, and with no thought of meeting opposition, it repaired to Philadelphia, sent Biddle a copy of the resolutions, informed him of the committee's presence and its readiness to visit the Bank on the following day at any hour that he would indicate. Then followed days of struggle, with the committee obstructed at every turn by the technical barricades thrown up by John Sergeant. It was not for nothing, in the old days, that men characterized the cunning as "smart as a Philadelphia lawyer." Having exhausted their resources, the committeemen returned to Washington and prepared reports to the House. The minority report, submitted by Edward Everett, excused the Bank. The majority charged contempt of the House, and asked that warrants be issued for the arrest of Biddle and the directors. A few days later Adams offered his resolution to discharge the committee from further duty, setting forth that there had been no contempt, and characterizing the proposed arrest of Biddle and his directors as "unconstitutional, arbitrary, and an oppressive abuse of power." If this resolution was novel, under the circumstances, the speech in which it was supported was even more remarkable. "The House has sent a committee to investigate the affairs of the Bank," Adams said. "Have they not done it? Not one

[1] Jenkins, *Life of Polk*.

word on that subject is to be found in the report. It contains no information on the affairs of the Bank." [1] And how could the House enforce its decrees? he asked. "We have not a soldier to enforce our orders." And Adams was more laudatory in his references to the bankers, "distinguished for their talents," than he ever was to political friend or foe.

Thus nothing came of the resolutions. Perhaps nothing was expected. If the Bank's curt treatment of the committee amused the business element and the Whig politicians, it delighted Kendall and Blair, for they knew how effectively the incident could be used with the masses.

IX

After the adoption of the Poindexter resolutions no further steps were taken in the Senate until Clay, three weeks later, presented his resolution ordering the restoration of the deposits. This was in the midst of the difficulties of the House committee with the Bank. Why, demanded Benton, had it not been presented in the early part of the session? Why now with no possibility of concurrence in the House? And why now in the midst of a controversy between the House and the Bank, with contempt proceedings pending against the Bank, and the House awaiting the report of its investigation? What right had the Senate to interfere in behalf of the Bank? He hoped the Senate would postpone the consideration of the resolution for a week to permit the House to decide the question of contempt.[2] Nevertheless, the Senate, by a party vote, passed the futile resolution.

But the senatorial champions of the Bank were to encounter embarrassments other than those growing out of the action of the House. In May, Mr. Clay had called upon Taney for a report upon the finances. At the time this was done, the Senate was being deluged with distress petitions,

[1] The report very clearly explained the reasons. (*Cong. Globe*, I, 446–48.)

[2] *Cong. Globe*, I, 409.

mass meetings were being held, and the doleful senatorial descriptions of wreck and ruin were falling mournfully upon the Senate Chamber, day by day. It was the middle of June when Taney's report reached the Senate. The facts as set forth were in such startling contrast with conditions as they had been depicted by Clay and his followers that the Administration leaders, always clever, and always thinking more of the voters in the country than of the politicians in the Senate house, determined that it should have the greatest possible publicity. The day before, Taney had summoned Benton to the Treasury, and had gone over the report with him, furnishing him with all the data, and preparing him for a speech that could be sent to the country. As anticipated, the reading in the Senate had not proceeded far when Webster arose to move that further reading be dispensed with, and the report sent to the Finance Committee. Benton objected. The report was read. Then Benton, in his most flamboyant mood, arose to comment upon it.

"Well, the answer comes," he exclaimed with the Bentonian flourish. "It is a report to make the patriot heart rejoice, replete with rich information, pregnant with evidences of national prosperity. How is it received — how received by those who called for it? With downcast looks and wordless tongues. A motion is made to stop the reading." But he did not propose that such a report should be disposed of "in this unceremonious and compendious style." No, "a pit was dug for Mr. Taney; the diggers of the pit have fallen into it: the fault is not his; and the sooner they clamber out, the better for themselves." And, regardless of the embarrassment of the conspirators, he proposed that the country should know that "never since America had a place among nations was the prosperity of the country equal to what it is this day." [1]

In this exordium he did not exaggerate the story of the figures of the report; and the report did not misrepresent

[1] *Cong. Globe*, I, 454.

the condition of the country. The Bank panic had run out. Only its friends were now suffering, and even Philip Hone in New York was secretly cursing the name of Biddle.

But the enemies of the Administration in the Senate were to have their revenge. Andrew Stevenson, for almost seven years Speaker of the House, one of the most courtly and talented men in public life, had been nominated for the English Mission. He resigned from the Speakership and from Congress, and his name was sent to the Senate for confirmation. And the political combination that, in a spirit of proscription, had refused to confirm Van Buren, declined to confirm the man selected as his successor. This act was too flagrant even for John Tyler, who voted to confirm.[1] As a result of this petty policy, America was unrepresented in England from 1832, when Van Buren was humiliated, until 1836, when a Democratic Senate confirmed Stevenson.

As the end of the session approached, Jackson sent to the Senate the nominations of Taney and Butler, as Secretary of the Treasury and Attorney-General. The latter was confirmed; the former rejected. But the rejection of Taney had been considered more than probable by Jackson, who had refrained from sending the nomination to the Senate until the last minute. This was the first time, however, in the history of the Government that a Cabinet officer had failed of confirmation. It was in no sense, however, a reflection upon the man; it merely reflected the insane bitterness of the time. On his return to Maryland, Taney was greeted with a series of ovations. At Baltimore he was met by a multitude and conveyed in a barouche drawn by four white horses, escorted by a cavalcade of several hundred horsemen, and given a dinner. Another dinner awaited him at Frederick, and another at Elkton, and each was made the occasion for a powerful speech which made an impression on the country.

Thus the prolonged session of Congress, lasting almost

[1] *Letters and Times of the Tylers.*

seven months, had accomplished nothing for the Bank. The anti-Jackson Senate had censured the President and ordered the restoration of the deposits. The Jacksonian House had declared against the restoration of the deposits, against the renewal of the charter, and had summoned Nicholas Biddle to its bar for contempt. The politicians had fought the battle in Congress to a deadlock, and the next and final fight was to be waged at the polls.

We shall now note the effect of the sham battles of the Congress on the people.

CHAPTER XIII

POLITICAL HYDROPHOBIA

I

Philip Hone, seated in the little Senate Chamber, and still entranced with Clay's theatrical appeal to Van Buren, was awakened from his reverie by observing Webster beckoning him out of the room. The entertainer of the Whig celebrities followed the god of his idolatry to one of the committee rooms, where, for more than an hour, the orator "unburdened his mind fully on the state of affairs and future prospects." The burden of it all was the importance of carrying the spring elections. When Hone called on Clay, he found him of the same opinion. "He says that the only hope is the election in our State and in Pennsylvania." Meeting John Quincy Adams, "that sagacious man," he found that the former President shared the belief that "our only hope lies in the elections in New York and Pennsylvania, particularly our charter election." [1] That the Administration forces and the Kitchen Cabinet were equally impressed with the strategic value of victories in New York City is disclosed in a letter from Major Lewis to James A. Hamilton, "Have you any doubt of succeeding at your election?" he wrote. "I hope not; yet I confess I have my fears. The strongest ground to take with the people is the fact, that under the existing arrangements with the State banks, the whole revenue collected through your customs house is left to be dispensed in your own city, instead of being transferred to a neighboring rival city. Our friends should ring the changes upon this view in every quarter of the city." [2] It is thus evident that the contending forces were concentrating for the election of

[1] Hone's *Diary*, March 4, 5, 6, 1834. Hamilton's *Reminiscences*, 282.

aldermen and a mayor in a city then numbering few more than 200,000 people.

Early in March the Opposition deliberately made the Bank the issue by nominating Gulian C. Verplanck, driven from Congress by the Democrats because of his fidelity to the Bank, and planning for a popular vindication of that institution. Two days later the Democrats nominated Cornelius W. Lawrence, who had been exceedingly bitter against the Bank while in Congress. Accepting Hone's opinion that "the personal characters of both the gentlemen is above reproach," [1] the election would definitely determine the drift of public opinion on the contest then in its most bitter stage. The election returns were confusing. The mayoralty candidate, who had been ousted from his seat in Congress because of his support of Biddle, was defeated by the man whose bitterness against the Bank while in Congress had been notable. The Democrats won here, and the Opposition lost. The fact that the latter elected a majority of the aldermen was loudly hailed as a vote against Jackson on the Bank question, although, in the more spirited contest for the more important office, the Bank champion was overwhelmed by the Democrat. The Opposition was jubilant, or pretended to jubilation. A great celebration was held at Castle Garden, and the faithful poured forth by the tens of thousands to sit about the tables "spread in a row" and to do full justice to the "three pipes of wine and forty barrels of beer placed in the center under an awning." Full of fire and froth, the exuberant partisans, learning that Webster was the guest of a lady at her home, moved thence *en masse*, where the orator, who had declined to appear among the beer kegs in the Garden, presented himself at the window and delivered "an address full of fire" which "was received with rapturous shouts." [2] All over the Eastern country the Whigs insisted on accepting the defeat of the Bank candidate for mayor as

[1] Hone's *Diary*, March 21, 1834.

[2] *Ibid.*, April 15, 1834.

a victory for the Bank, and the Philadelphians had "a grand celebration at Powelton on the Schuylkill"; the Whigs of Albany "fired one hundred guns"; the Whigs of Buffalo "made a great affair of it with guns and illuminations"; those of Portsmouth "received the news with one hundred guns" and "had a town meeting and made speeches."[1] Meanwhile the Democrats were proclaiming the election of Lawrence a Jacksonian triumph. After the various salutes from Portsmouth to the Battery of a hundred guns, and the celebration in the Garden among the beer kegs, the Democrats arranged their celebration for the day that Lawrence was to make his triumphant entry. A steamboat went down to Amboy to receive the mayor-elect, and "with colors flying and loud huzzas," the Jacksonians sat down to a dinner on board, "where Jackson toasts were drunk and Jackson speeches were made." Landing at Castle Garden, the new mayor was conducted in a "barouche drawn by four white horses, and paraded through the streets."[2]

But the desperate Opposition, hard pressed, and requiring encouragement for its followers, succeeded, through exaggerations and red fire, in convincing the rank and file that an anti-Jackson wave had swept the Nation. Rhode Island, never a Jackson State, went against the Democrats, and this was celebrated with as much enthusiasm as though a stronghold of the enemy had been taken. The triumph of the Whigs in the Philadelphia ward elections was exploited as a signal triumph. Virginia, anti-Bank as well as anti-Jackson, was lost to the Democrats, and the Opposition interpreted it as a pro-Bank as well as an anti-Jackson verdict. In Louisiana the Whigs won on the tariff, but the impression was given that the result reflected a popular resentment of the mistreatment of Nicholas Biddle. As a matter of fact, no intelligent politician could have attached any particular significance to the results of the spring elections, and the leaders immedi-

[1] Hone's *Diary*, April 23, 1834.

[2] *Ibid.*, May 12, 1834.

ately began their preparations for the congressional elections in the fall.

II

In these elections the Opposition to Jacksonian Democracy was to fight for the first time under its new party name. In February, 1834, James Watson Webb, the unscrupulous speculator in Bank stock, and editor of the "Courier and Enquirer" of New York City, had proposed that the combination against the policies of Jackson should be known as the Whig Party. "It is a glorious name," said John Forsyth, "and I have no doubt they will disgrace it." Within six months the National Republicans and the Anti-Masons disappeared — united under the Whig banner. In September, 1834, Niles records, in his "Register," that, "as if by universal consent, all parties opposed to the present Administration call themselves Whigs." And all who called themselves Whigs denounced the Jacksonians as Tories. It was a pretty conceit. The Whigs of England had fought the battles of the people against the usurpations of the throne, and the Whigs of America were fighting the usurpations of Jackson. The Constitution against anarchy, the people against the Power — such was the fight of Nicholas Biddle, Henry Clay, and John C. Calhoun against Jackson.

A more incongruous combination of contradictions and a more sinister and unholy alliance than that of the Whigs of the Jacksonian period has never appeared in the political life of the Republic. These men held common opinions on none of the fundamental principles of government. A few years, and few of the leaders and founders could agree as to the character of the combination.[1] The only plank in the platform of this ragged array on which all could stand was a hatred of Andrew Jackson. That was the open sesame to

[1] Professor Tyler, in *Letters and Times of the Tylers*, I, 478, graphically shows the hotchpotch nature of the alliance.

the temple. Beyond that no questions were asked. Born with the seed of inevitable disintegration, it was to stagger along through twenty years, to end without a mourner, and to leave no record worthy of an epitaph. And about the time of its birth, and after its insignificant successes in the spring elections, that astute journalist and politician, Thomas Ritchie, of the "Richmond Enquirer," foresaw its future with the clear light of a prophet. "When it comes to act upon any policy or principle," he wrote, "not connected with a hatred of Jackson, it must fall to pieces and commence a war *inter se.* It contains all the elements of dissolution, and is destined to share the fate of other monstrous alliances." [1]

But its creators were not concerned in 1834 with anything further than the overthrow of Jackson and his followers. Not daring to advance a constructive programme, for the very effort would have wrecked the party, they confined themselves to extravagant and absurd denunciations of Jackson as a tyrant usurping power and clambering to a throne. The congressional campaign opened with a rush. All over the land the Whigs were raising liberty poles — because they were fighting the battle of liberty against the despot. And Nicholas Biddle and his Bank, as usual, wore the liberty cap. When Congress adjourned in June, the moneyed institution was in a dying condition, and the money market was again about normal. Only a signal Whig triumph could now save the institution on Chestnut Street.

III

With the adjournment of Congress, Jackson, with his customary complacency and confidence in the support of the people, set forth for the Hermitage for a much-needed rest. He had just again reorganized his Cabinet because of the fail-

[1] Ambler's *Thomas Ritchie.*

ure of the Senate to confirm Taney and the resignation of Louis McLane. The motive for the latter's retirement is only conjectural. That he had never felt at home in the Cabinet circle, we may well believe. While in the Cabinet, he was not of it. But for the constant friendship and support of Van Buren, his position would have been delicate indeed. He was out of sympathy with Jackson at every stage of the Bank fight. He would have renewed the old charter without a change; would have renewed it with concessions from the Bank; but he would have renewed it. With the removal of the deposits he was entirely out of sympathy. He would not have removed them at all; but, if removed, he would not have removed them until Congress had convened. His social affiliations were largely with the old official aristocracy. That he entertained presidential aspirations was generally understood, and it is quite possible that he considered a complete separation from the Administration advantageous to his interests. His associations were such that he could not have heard much that was not venomously hostile to Jackson and the Jacksonians. But, a gentleman of dignity, he withdrew gracefully, plunging into no undignified recriminations.[1]

In appointing his successor, Jackson turned to John Forsyth, whose services as Administration floor leader in the Senate had been of immense value, and whose urbanity, wisdom, conservatism, diplomatic experience, fitted him for the post better than any of his Jacksonian predecessors. To the place left vacant by Taney, he transferred Mr. Woodbury, and to the navy he appointed Mahlon Dickerson of New Jersey, a gentleman of extensive public experience as a Senator for sixteen years. Just previous to his appointment, he had declined the Russian Mission. This was the only Cabinet upheaval of Jackson's time which had not been accompanied with much bitterness, with charges and countercharges.

[1] Van Buren, finding his friend treacherous, discusses the resignation and the character of McLane at length in his *Autobiography*, 611.

Thus, with affairs in Washington in capable hands, with victory in the Bank fight on his side, with the delights of the Hermitage just beyond, the iron man set forth in high spirits and with no regrets or fears. The Biddle threat of more "discipline" for the people during the summer and autumn, because of the failure of Congress to recharter the Bank, had not disturbed him so much as it had alarmed the Whigs. Those in Boston met the threat with a counter-threat of denunciation, and those in New York warned Biddle that more distress would certainly prove disastrous to the Whigs in the fall elections. Biddle deeply resented the criticism of the Whigs, who, under the leadership of Clay, had practically blackmailed him into using the Bank's power against the Democrats. When those of Boston warned that more discipline of the people might "even create a necessity for the Whigs, in self-defense, to separate themselves entirely" from his institution, he wrote in defiant mood to the president of his Boston branch that "if . . . any political party or association desires to separate itself from the Bank — be it so." He had not read the letter to the board of directors lest the members favorable to the Democrats might use it to the disadvantage of the Whigs.[1] But he was to find that his frown had lost its force. Another Whig from New York wrote of much dissatisfaction in that city and State among the Bank's friends and "those of influence in the Whig Party — and sure I am that it is increasing every day." The feeling was prevalent, encouraged by the views of Albert Gallatin, that the Bank could have relieved the distress had it so desired. And Alexander Hamilton, the brother of Jackson's friend, and son of the father of the National Bank, wrote a little later to a correspondent that "it has been found expedient to abandon the Bank in our political pilgrimage." He found that "the people are now familiarly acquainted with the immense power of a national bank and apprehend all

[1] Biddle to Appleton, *Correspondence of Nicholas Biddle*, 240.

kinds of terrible consequences from its exercise."[1] Thus, instead of more "discipline," the Bank found it possible to take steps, which, according to Catterall, justified Jackson, the following December, in saying in his Message that "the Bank . . . announced its ability and readiness to abandon the system of unparalleled curtailment . . . and to extend its accommodations to the community."

Just, as in 1832, when floating down the Ohio on his last visit to the Hermitage during the presidential campaign, Andrew Jackson was at peace with himself and the world. But his friends had given orders to take nothing for granted and to open the fighting along the whole line. They had a twofold purpose — to hold the line in Congress, and to defeat, wherever possible, any senatorial enemies who were candidates for reëlection. Blair, of the "Globe," began to issue special editions and to send them broadcast all over the country.

The fight, as it was waged in New York, Virginia, and Mississippi, will suffice to illustrate the general character and method of the campaign. In all three States the Bank was the issue. Even the most hopeful of the Whigs entertained no illusions as to Pennsylvania, where the most powerful financial and commercial interests were arrayed with the Bank. The two parties in the Empire State were mobilized, organized on a military footing, and ready and eager for the fray.[2] The elections in New Jersey and Pennsylvania were held in October, a month before those in New York, and the first shock to the Whigs came in the returns from these two States. That Pennsylvania, the home of Biddle, Sergeant, and Duane, should have gone against the Bank and for Jackson, was not disappointing, for little had been expected there. But much was expected in New Jersey. There the issue was distinct. The two Senators from that State had

[1] Hamilton to Woodworth, *Correspondence of Nicholas Biddle*, 244.
[2] Hone's *Diary*, Oct. 4, 1834.

voted with the Bank on the deposits question. The Legislature had adopted resolutions commendatory of Jackson's actions, and in his Protest the fighting President had not scrupled to quote these resolutions to prove that the Senators had deliberately misrepresented their people. Senator Frelinghuysen, in commenting upon these instructions, had boasted that he and his colleague had "dared to meet the frowns of their constituents," and would not "bow the knee to these instructions."[1] Now he was before the people for reëlection, and the issue was plain. The people's verdict was unmistakable. The little State swept into the Jackson column with a substantial majority, and Frelinghuysen was retired.

Goaded by the sting of the New Jersey defeat, the New York Whigs redoubled their efforts. "The Whigs are raising liberty poles in all the wards," wrote Hone. "I went to one of these ceremonies yesterday at the corner of the Bowery and Hester Street. The pole, a hundred feet high, with a splendid cap and gilt vane with suitable devices, was escorted by a procession of good men and true."[2] Thus, if the "mob" could make the welkin ring at Democratic meetings, the more aristocratic Whigs could sally forth from their counting-rooms and libraries to rub shoulders with the common herd at Hester Street and the Bowery and shout approval of the raising of a pole. But all was in vain. By nine o'clock on the evening of the first day, Hone and his fellow Whigs realized that "enough was known to satisfy us to our hearts' content that we are beaten — badly beaten; worse than the least sanguine of us expected."[3] The jubilant Democrats, however, were determined that the Whig leaders should not feel utterly deserted, and a crowd of them surged before Hone's house with hisses and catcalls which kept him awake all night. The Lord Holland of the American Whigs, who was sick at the time, was inclined to resent it, but the

[1] *Cong. Globe*, I, 318. [2] *Diary*, Oct. 31, 1834. [3] *Ibid.*, Nov. 5, 1834.

next evening he found consolation in dining with Webster who "was in a vein to be exceedingly pleasant." [1]

Such was the intensity of feeling and the bitterness of the struggle that enthusiastic partisans partook of the nature of mobs in the larger centers. Nowhere were the Democrats so intense as in Philadelphia, where, on election day, the warring partisans exchanged shots, the headquarters of the Whigs was sacked and burned by a mob which drove back the firemen that attempted to quench the flames. A number of houses were completely reduced to ashes. Such was the panic of Nicholas Biddle that the day before the election he sent his wife and children into the country, filled his house with armed men, and prepared for a siege. The Bank building bristled with the bayonets and muskets of guards. But when the gray dawn came, the one-time financial dictator found that none of his property had been molested. It was blow enough to him to learn that the Whigs, the country over, had gone down before the popular uprising.

But the bitterest fight was waged in Virginia, where the situation was mixed to the point of chaos. The State was anti-Bank, but it was anti-Jackson. Opposed to the Bank, it had been equally opposed to the removal of the deposits. The feeling in Richmond was so inflamed that only personal respect for Ritchie saved the "Enquirer" from mob violence, for the courageous editor stuck to his guns and tried to divert attention to the Bank itself. Administration papers were established throughout the State with instructions to follow the lead of his pen. The Virginia plan was twofold: to make the most of the unpopularity of Leigh, who was again a candidate for the Senate, and to divide and distract the Whigs by playing Clay against Calhoun. Nowhere did the Democrats appreciate, as they did in Virginia, the impossible nature of the Whig combination, and they dwelt upon its inconsistencies from the beginning. Clay announced

[1] *Diary*, Nov. 6, 1834.

that he was not a candidate for the presidential nomination in 1836. "But Mr. Clay knows not himself," wrote Ritchie. "But ambition does not burn so intensely in his bosom as it does in the heart of another leader of the Senate (Mr. Calhoun). If recent signs do not deceive us, this extraordinary man (extraordinary every way for the vigor of his mind, the variety of his principles, and the intensity of his ambition) will soon take the field, with feeble hopes of winning the votes of the South, as well as the support of the Bank. Then we shall see under which king the various members of the opposition will range themselves."[1] This irrepressible conflict of Whig ambitions and interests was played upon by the Democratic press of Virginia all through the summer and autumn of 1834.

But the immediate purpose of the Virginia Democrats was to humiliate Leigh, who was unpopular with the masses because of his bitter fight in the Constitutional Convention against the extension of the suffrage. And he was as strongly with the Bank as Virginia was against it. A house-to-house canvass was made, and in districts where a majority were found against him it was proposed to evoke the right of instructions to Assemblymen. The plan succeeded to the extent of disclosing a majority hostile to the reëlection of Leigh, but the Whigs, who carried the State, succeeded after a bitter struggle in returning him through a flagrant disregard of the expressed will of the constituencies. The battle was thus but half lost. The Democrats were supplied with ammunition they were to use with deadly effect, and within little more than a year they were to drive the two anti-Jackson Senators of Virginia into private life. Ritchie began the next year's battle without delay. The "Enquirer" was flooded with resolutions and letters protesting the election of Leigh over the instructions of the majority of the people.[2]

In Mississippi the Jacksonians determined to prevent the

[1] Ambler's *Thomas Ritchie*, 160. [2] *Ibid.*, 166.

reëlection of Senator Poindexter, long the idol of the Mississippi Democracy, who had turned upon Jackson with a virulence scarcely equaled by any old-line Federalist, and cast his lot with Clay. With the adjournment of Congress, the Mississippi Senator hastened home, where the enemies of the Administration had planned a series of banquets at which he was to denounce the President and vindicate himself. The Whigs were with him. The Democrats, delighted with a slashing and brilliant assault on Poindexter by Robert J. Walker, put that able publicist in the field, and within a week he was engaged in one of the most spectacular canvasses Mississippi had ever known, firing enormous open-air meetings of frenzied Jacksonians. The outcome was the election of Walker — a victory sweet to Jackson, for it was the vanquished who had sponsored the resolution attacking his Protest.[1] And the triumph was all the sweeter from the fact that, while Poindexter had supported the Nullifiers, Walker had taken the lead against them in Mississippi, on the platform, and through the press.

Thus the elections of 1834 were more than pleasing to Jackson and his party. Two of his strongest senatorial opponents had lost their seats as a result of their opposition, and Leigh had been saved only by a disreputable betrayal of the people. In the Senate the Administration was strengthened; and in the House the Democratic majority was reduced but eight votes, leaving it a clear majority of 46 out of 242 members.

Strangely enough, so reliable an historian as McMaster has described these elections as a triumph of the Whigs. Such was not the interpretation of the Whigs themselves. Hone thought that they were "badly beaten — worse than the least sanguine of us expected."[2] Webster accepted the

[1] The story of the Mississippi contest is told by Senator Foote in *A Casket of Reminiscences*, 217–18.

[2] *Diary*, Nov. 5, 1834.

verdict as final, and, much to the distress and indignation of Biddle, announced that he was through. But the most conclusive evidence of the contemporary opinion of the Whigs comes from Thurlow Weed, the sagacious Whig journalist of the "Albany Journal." More prescient than most of the Whig leaders of the time, he had foreseen the inevitable result of an attempt to win upon the Bank issue. Quite early, when Webster's keynote speech on the Bank, delivered at a mass meeting in Boston, was sent for publication to all the party papers, the copy that reached Weed never found its way into the "Albany Journal."[1] And immediately after the election in 1834, he editorially expressed the feeling which appears to have taken possession of the party generally. "There is one cause," he wrote, "for congratulations, connected with the recent election, in which even we participate. It has terminated the United States Bank war. . . . We have from the beginning deprecated the successive conflicts in defense of the Bank. . . . But we have gone with our friends through these three campaigns, under a strong and settled conviction that in every issue to be tried by the people to which the Bank was a party, we must be beaten. After struggling along from year to year with a doomed Bank upon our shoulders, both the Bank and our party are finally overwhelmed."[2] Nor is it surprising that Clay, whose selfishness had forced Biddle into making the recharter a campaign issue, was glad to dump the doomed Bank from his shoulders. It is impossible to follow his course, pointing as every act does to a purely party purpose, without arriving at the conviction that he really cared little about the institution on Chestnut Street. As the fight became more hopeless, he found the importunities of Biddle more irksome. Viewed purely as a political or party contest, the clever politicians who dominated the Jacksonian camp had shown far more prescience and sagacity than the wisest of the Whigs. Amos Kendall had a

[1] Weed's *Autobiography*, I, 372.

[2] *Albany Journal*, Nov. 15, 1834.

better understanding of the psychology of the masses than Clay or Webster. Among the Whigs, Weed alone saw the end from the beginning. The attempt to arouse the people in behalf of a great moneyed institution against the attacks of a popular hero was in itself a grotesque and ghastly absurdity. But after the decision had been made to undertake it, the methods of Biddle and his political allies made defeat a certainty. Frank Blair, of the "Globe," was evidently sincere in his assertion that had he been permitted to dictate the policy of the Whigs, he could not have hit upon a plan more satisfactory to the Democrats.

That Jackson knew little of banking and advanced some strange theories in the course of the fight; that he resorted to methods of violence in some instances; and that he fought to kill, rather than to reform, may be admitted. But the very nature of the fight he waged compelled the Bank to disclose its tremendous power over the prosperity of the people. No matter what they may have thought in the beginning, no one could have doubted toward the end that the Bank did have the power to precipitate panics, to punish the people for legislation it resented, to dominate, in the end, the legislation of the future by the threat of reprisal upon the business of the Nation. No one, in 1834, doubted that the National Bank, in the hands of a man like Biddle domineering over pliant directors, and assuming dictatorial authority over the members of Congress, possessed powers incompatible with the preservation of the rights and liberties of the people. From that day on, the Bank has had its apologists among historians, and Jackson has been excoriated as an ignorant usurper, but there has never been a time since when the American people would have tolerated a return to the system that was destroyed. Through several years the country was to be disturbed by the sometimes stumbling processes of transition from the old to the new system, but the Bank fight ended with the verdict of the polls in 1834. Only the censure of the Senate remained to poison the mind of the iron man in the White House. The Bank lingered on, a little while, under the laws of Pennsylvania, and then crashed to the earth, ruining many of its supporters.[1] And on the banker's death, Hone copied into his diary the comment of William Cullen Bryant in the "New York Evening Post," that Biddle "died at his country seat where he passed the last of his days in elegant retirement, which, if justice had taken place, would have been spent in the penitentiary."[2]

The prolonged battle has left a lasting impression upon the political life and methods of the Republic. It aroused, as never before, that class consciousness, to which politicians have ever since appealed; it gave dignity to demagogy, and made it pay. It marked the beginning of the active participation of powerful corporations, as such, in the politics of the country, witnessed the adoption of the methods of intimidation and coercion, of systematic propaganda, of the subsidization of disreputable newspapers. From that day on, the powerful corporation has been anathema to the masses, monopoly has been a red rag, and the contest between capital and labor has been a reality. If this has been unfortunate, the fault has been no less with Clay, who sought and made the issue, and with Biddle and his arrogant reliance on the power of money, than with Jackson and the Kitchen Cabinet who challenged the political pretensions of the Bank

IV

The Whig leaders entered upon the congressional session of December in a bitter mood. Calhoun was especially vicious and in a chronic rage against the President and the Administration. The fury of the Whigs was not moderated by the fact that State Legislatures were beginning to demand the expunging from the records of the resolution of censure. Benton, in the previous session, had served notice of his in-

[1] Hone's *Diary*, April 17, and Dec. 14, 1841.

[2] *Ibid.*, Jan. 18, 1844.

tention to move to expunge, and the Kitchen Cabinet in the meanwhile had been busy in building backfires against the offending Senators among their constituents. The first State to act was Alabama. The day before Senator King presented the Alabama resolutions, during a running discussion of the revelations of mismanagement and crookedness in the Post-Office Department, Senator Preston suggested that the Senate should censure some one. Just whom he would censure was not made clear, but he did refer to the previous declaration of Jackson that he was responsible for the Executive departments. "Does any one doubt the turpitude of the Post-Office?" asked Preston. "When hardly the age of man, it is found steeped in corruption the most foul, the most melancholy. If the President is responsible, and the officers acted improperly, is this the house to present the subject? And shall we stand by without saying or doing anything in regard to the present state of things in that department?"

Calhoun was instantly on his feet. He had listened to the report on the Post-Office "with sorrow and deep mortification." After twenty-two years of connection with the Government he was able to say that "in all that time the charges of corruption against all the departments of the Government that he had ever heard of were not equal to the disclosures here made." In truth he thought that "the exhibition would disgrace the rottenest age of the Roman Republic." He hoped some resolution would be presented.

This implied threat was not lost on the ever alert Benton, and on the following day he took the floor, reminded the Senate of his promise, declared that nothing less than the expurgation of the offensive censure would suffice, and served notice of his intention to present the resolution. This opened the first debate on expurgation. Clay, with a personal fling at Benton, saltily expressed the hope that before acting the Missourian would carefully examine the Constitution, and concluded that he would "oppose such a resolution at the very threshold." Preston conceded that his party had been "beaten down," and demanded to know whether "everything that we have done shall be expunged." Calhoun would "like to see a resolution which proposed to repeal the journal — to repeal a fact." If the thing could be done, "the Senate itself could be expunged," and the Government itself was at an end. He was "anxious to see who would attempt to carry out the doctrines of the Protest of last year — doctrines as despotic as those which were held by the autocrat of all the Russias."

To this, King took vigorous exception. The resolution of censure was not "a fact." "The Democracy of this land has spoken and pronounced its condemnation of the proceeding." He had hoped, when Calhoun declared on a previous occasion that he would act for the country, he would have little more to do with party, but he had since manifested a very different feeling. Stung by the taunt, Calhoun made no half-hearted denial of partisan bias. "I have no purpose to serve," he said. "I have no desire to be here." And then, with evident insincerity, he added, "Sir, I would not turn upon my heel to be entrusted with the management of the Government." [1]

When, a few weeks later, the day before the expiration of the session, the discussion was renewed, Hugh Lawson White, now rapidly cooling to frigidity toward Jackson, moved to amend Benton's resolution by striking out the word "expunge" and substituting "rescind, reverse, and to make null and void." This incident has been given an historical importance beyond its due by many who have attributed to the motion the final break between Jackson and White. The action of the Tennessee Senator unquestionably outraged the Jacksonians, who ascribed it to hostility, but such was not the dominating motive. He took the position that he could not vote to "obliterate and deface the journal

[1] *Cong. Globe*, I, 176.

of the Senate." Benton protested that the word "expunge" was strictly parliamentary. To his astonishment and chagrin, he discovered that White was not the only Democrat who objected to his phrasing of the resolution, as others crowded about him to urge the acceptance of the amendment. Finding himself almost deserted, he afterwards said that he "yielded a mortifying and reluctant consent." [1] All this the proud Missourian could stand. But when Webster immediately arose, and, after sounding the pæan of triumph, moved that the resolution be laid upon the table; and after Clay and Calhoun had spoken with bitterness and contempt, the spirit of compromise died out in his heart, and he then and there promised himself to continue the battle. The debate was acrimonious in spirit, and in the midst of "great excitement." [2] This was the preliminary battle which was to have a spectacular ending in a Jacksonian triumph a short time before the expiration of the iron man's Presidency.

V

To the Jacksonians, the most distressing feature of the short session was the disclosure of the utter incompetency, blackened by positive crookedness, in the rapidly growing Post-Office Department, which called for the management of a man of more than ordinary organizing and business ability. Major Barry possessed neither qualification. An honest man himself, without the slightest business sense, easily imposed upon, surrounded by subordinates who were scamps, and forced to deal with mail contractors who were criminals, he lost control early in his administration. When the Clayton investigation was completed, the department was found honeycombed with fraud, plastered with forgeries, and in a hopeless financial condition. And yet no one seriously suspected Barry of complic-

[1] *Thirty Years' View*, I, 550.

[2] The words of the official reporter of the *Congressional Globe*.

ity. Clay, who had lost the support of Barry, his neighbor in Lexington, on the "bargain" story, did not hesitate to exonerate him from culpability. But there was no defense for the conditions, and Jackson, in his Message, had recommended a complete reorganization of the department better to safeguard the public interest. The two parties stood together on the Reorganization Bill, and no member of either party attempted any justification of the conditions. But the Democrats were on their toes throughout the session to prevent any personal condemnation of either Barry or Jackson. The Whigs lost no opportunity to capitalize the scandal. The public money had been squandered. Crooked contractors had been permitted to loot the Treasury. They did not know the extent of the corruption, nor the responsibility of the head of the department, but they did know that the putridity of the thing had never been approached in American history. The majority report of the investigating committee found a deficit of $800,000; the minority placed the amount at $300,000; but both agreed that it was due in part at least to maladministration.[1] Felix Grundy, who had charge for the Administration, rejoiced in the fact, "to the honor of his countrymen," that no one "had been found to accuse the Postmaster-General of corruption";[2] and Senator Bibb of Kentucky, a supporter of Clay, paid tribute to the personal qualities of Barry and ascribed the failure to "the good disposition and kindness" of the head of the department, which had been imposed upon by "interested and selfish persons to further their own private interests." Thus, in the Senate, the debate on the Reorganization Bill was conducted with decorum and without exciting personalities. An utter lack of system, a director deficient in business sense and over-credulous, and all preyed upon by

[1] Professor MacDonald, in *Jacksonian Democracy*, p. 246, says that "a large part of the deficit, however, was fairly chargeable to the cost of the large number of post-offices and post-routes established in 1832."

[2] *Cong. Globe*, I, 206.

dishonest subordinates and criminally inclined speculators — such was the sense of the Senate.

But in the House, Barry's personal integrity was not to go unchallenged. In the lower branch he was unfortunate in friends who loved, not wisely, but too well, who thought to prevent assault by challenging it. Some of these had avowed a disposition to consider such an assault a personal offense. During a night session, William C. Johnson of Maryland, a promising and eloquent young Whig of imposing personal appearance, sought an opportunity to affront Representative Hawes of Kentucky, a member of the special dueling club. An insignificant incident during the discussion of a post-route bill sufficed. On obtaining the floor, Johnson looked significantly at Hawes, and with sinister deliberation began: "It has been broadly hinted by some gentlemen . . . that he who shall have the temerity to criticize the acts of the Postmaster-General must answer therefor elsewhere than in this hall. . . . Sir, I come from a portion of the country where the law of personal responsibility is recognized among gentlemen. I hold myself amenable to that law . . .; and now, in the face of those menaces which have been thrown out on this floor, and intending to be responsible for what I am about to say, I declare that the Post-Office Department is corrupt from head to foot, through and through, and I believe that the head of the department, William T. Barry, is as culpable as any officer under his control."

The House was instantly in an uproar as Hawes rose to ask if Johnson meant that the department was corrupt from Barry down. The young blade from Maryland jauntily replied in the affirmative. Hawes said that Barry was "as honest and honorable as any man who has a seat on this floor," and asked Johnson for the grounds for his charge. In the spirit of swashbuckler he had set out to be, the latter merely reiterated what he had said. There was no misunderstanding the meaning of the situation — it meant a duel unless Johnson would agree to a qualification of his statement. To all such appeals he was adamant. When, as a result, he was challenged by Barry's son, he began to hedge with the demand that the duel take place "immediately." He would not even consent to a day's delay, and young Barry withdrew the challenge. The incident proved nothing except that in the Thirties young men carried chips on their shoulders, and bandied words lightly.

The contemporaries of Barry exonerated him, and history has acquiesced in their verdict.[1] But it was apparent that his usefulness in the Cabinet was over. He had never been qualified. While the debate on the Reorganization Bill was still in progress, Jackson summoned Amos Kendall to the task of assuming charge and placing the department on a business basis. At that time, the wizard of the Kitchen Cabinet, in ill health, and without private means, was planning to retire from the public service to serve his family more satisfactorily in a financial way. He demurred — Jackson insisted — and in the end, like the good soldier that he was, he yielded.

Barry, gracefully let out with the mission to Spain, sailed away, to die in London on the way, and Kendall took charge. It is amazing that the party prejudices of ninety years ago should still persist and refuse justice to the genius of this exceptional man. Professor MacDonald does not overstate when he describes him "as a man of remarkable administrative power." [2] Nor is it probable that so seasoned an observer of public men as Senator Foote was unduly impressed when he described him as "discoursing upon the gravest and most important questions with a profundity and power which left a lasting impress."[3] Brilliant with the pen, sagacious beyond almost any man of his time as a poli-

[1] *Cong. Globe*, I, 283, merely refers to the excitement. Sargent's *Public Men and Events* gives the details.

[2] *Jacksonian Democracy*, 51.

[3] *A Casket of Reminiscences*, 65.

tician, wise in counsel, and yet capable of managing the dry-as-dust details of the most practical of departments, Amos Kendall is probably one of the greatest all-around publicists the Republic has produced.

His first step on taking charge was thoroughly to familiarize himself with the minute details of his office, with the special functions of each subordinate, and the character of the man. He soon discovered the secret of the good-natured Barry's undoing, when a clerk, suspected of having relations with a contractor as agent, approached him ingratiatingly with the announcement that he "had control of funds and would be happy to accommodate him with loans." He was promptly discharged.[1] After a thorough survey, Kendall concluded that "a few powerful mail contractors, through favors to the officers and more influential clerks, had really controlled the department, and for their own selfish ends, and been the cause of all its embarrassments." [2] He adopted stringent rules for the guidance of employees. The acceptance of a gift was to mean dismissal. So, too, with free rides on stage-coaches, steamboats, or railroad cars carrying mail. Applying the rules as rigidly to himself as to others, he promptly returned all presents and free tickets, and thenceforward the Postmaster-General paid his way. But the task confronting him was tremendous. The department was deeply in debt and was sinking deeper. Not satisfied with the showing of corruption by the congressional committee, he went over the ground and uncovered crookedness it had overlooked. The postmaster of New York was caught in the net and instantly dismissed. Some powerful and influential contractors who had carried the mail between Washington and Philadelphia were suspected, and Kendall made a searching investigation. Major Barry, still in Washington at this time, became seriously disturbed, and conceived the notion that his successor was bent on embarrassing him,

[1] Kendall's *Autobiography*, 337. [2] *Ibid.*

and Kendall, who had no suspicion of his predecessor, sent for him and personally reassured him. But there were other embarrassments within the Administration household. Mrs. Eaton, then in Washington, and intimate with the family of one of the contractors who was pressing a claim that Kendall was examining, called one day on Mrs. Kendall with the bald proposition that if the claim were allowed, the contractor would present the wife of the Postmaster-General with "a carriage and a pair of horses." The incident was promptly reported to Kendall, who recorded the story many years later.[1] Applying himself and his administrative genius diligently to his task, driving out the incompetent and corrupt, practicing economy while extending the scope of the department's services, he soon put it on a paying basis, and before the expiration of Jackson's Administration, less than two years later, wiped out the deficit. This is the man some historians have described as a vulgar politician and a "printer."

VI

No incident of this session so well illustrates the partisan bitterness and the venomous nature of the hates engendered by the struggles of the preceding years as the attempt on the life of Jackson at the Capitol on January 30, 1835.[2] Under normal conditions and in ordinary times the incident would have been dismissed, and, properly, ascribed to the insanity of the assailant. But it was the first time an attempt had been made upon the life of a President — and it was a President who had been intemperately denounced as a tyrant, despot, and wrecker of American institutions and liberties. Just as John Tyler had instantly thought of "political effect,"[3] the ardent friends of Jackson caught

[1] *Autobiography*, 351.

[2] Miss Martineau graphically describes the attempt in her *Retrospect of Western Travel*, I, 161.

[3] *Letters and Times of the Tylers*, I, 509.

the same idea from the opposite angle. And two days later, Frank Blair in the "Globe" threw out the suggestion of a conspiracy. "Whether Lawrence [the assailant] has caught, in his visits to the Capitol, the mania which has prevailed the last two sessions of the Senate," he wrote, "whether he has become infatuated with the chimeras which have troubled the brains of the disappointed and ambitious orators who have depicted the President as a Cæsar who ought to have a Brutus; as a Cromwell, a Nero, a Tiberius, we know not. If no secret conspiracy has prompted the perpetration of the horrid deed, we think it not improbable that some delusion of intellect has grown out of his visits to the Capitol, and that hearing despotism and every horrible mischief threatened to the Republic, and revolution and all its train of calamities imputed as the necessary consequence of the President's measures, it may be that the infatuated man fancied that he had reason to become his country's avenger. If he had heard and believed Mr. Calhoun's speech of day before yesterday, he would have found in it ample justification for his attempt on one who was represented as the cause of the most dreadful calamities of the Nation; as one who made perfect rottenness and corruption to pervade the vitals of the Government, insomuch that it was scarcely worth preserving, if it were possible." [1]

The intimation here thrown out was bitterly resented by the Opposition leaders, and particularly by Calhoun, who was mentioned. The very fact that the intemperate and insincere denunciations of high officials as responsible for the distress of the people, acting upon the diseased brain, can very easily persuade the madman to constitute himself the executioner, served to infuriate the orators who had given themselves full play. Stung to the quick, Calhoun denounced the "Globe" as "base and prostitute," and described it as "the authentic and established organ" of Jackson, "sus-

[1] *Washington Globe*, Feb. 2, 1835.

tained by his power and pampered by his hands." "To what are we coming?" he exclaimed. "We are told that to denounce the abuse of the Administration even in general terms, without personal reference, is to instigate the assassination of the Chief Executive. . . . I have made up my mind as to my duty. I am no candidate for any office — I neither seek nor desire place — nothing shall intimidate — nothing shall prevent me from doing what I believe is due to my conscience and my country." [1] Mr. Calhoun sat down — and Mr. Leigh immediately rose to present a report from the Committee on Revolutionary Claims.

But Mr. Calhoun's attack on the "Globe" was not unnoticed by Blair, who replied by quoting from the most venomous portions of Calhoun's and Preston's tirades on the Post-Office report. A week later the Administration organ was still harping on conspiracy. "Every hour," wrote Blair, "brings new proof to show that Lawrence has been operated on to seek the President's life, precisely as we had supposed from the moment we learned that he had been an attendant on the debates in Congress." [2]

Very soon the capital was startled with the connection of Senator Poindexter's name with that of the assailant. The obsession took possession of Jackson that his Mississippi enemy had instigated the attempt at assassination. The examination of Lawrence had clearly established his insanity; just as clearly shown that he had taken to heart the charges of Jackson's enemies that he was responsible for the distress of the people. Finding himself hard pressed by fate, and ascribing his unhappiness to the tyranny of Jackson, he had determined to kill him. That explanation was convincing and sufficient. But the suggestion that Poindexter had planned the deed fell on receptive soil. Affidavits had been placed in Jackson's hands to the effect that "a gentleman who boarded in the same house informed him that Mr. Poin-

[1] *Cong. Globe*, I, 183–84.

[2] *Washington Globe*, Feb. 7, 1835.

dexter had interviews with Lawrence but a few days before the attempt on the President's life." Some time before the attack, "a captain in high standing in the navy" had said that Poindexter, on a voyage to New Orleans, had threatened to demand personal satisfaction of Jackson, and if he refused "he would shoot him wherever he saw him." This had caused such anxiety to Jackson's friends that the Reverend Mr. Hatch, chaplain of the Senate, had personally informed Jackson of the threat. All this, followed, after the assault, with an affidavit that Lawrence had been seen to "go repeatedly to Poindexter's residence," thoroughly convinced Jackson, who appears to have been in a morbid condition like his enemies.[1] He excitedly charged it in conversation with callers at the White House. Miss Martineau, who was friendly with the Poindexters, and apparently fond of the Senator, was literally forced to leave the White House by the abusive denunciation of the Mississippian. She became his ardent partisan, and took pains to record in her book that, on visiting the Poindexters on the night of the assault, she had "greatly admired the moderation with which Mr. Poindexter spoke of his foe."[2]

Hearing from many quarters of Jackson's charges, Poindexter wrote him that he would discredit the reports unless confirmed by the President, but that a failure to reply would be accepted as a confirmation. Jackson displayed Poindexter's letter to visitors, but made no response. Thus a perfectly foolish notion of Jackson's was forced to an issue. To understand the feeling behind it all, and to appreciate the bitter hostility of Poindexter, to which frequent reference has been made, it is necessary to know more of the character and career of this really remarkable but tragic figure.

George Poindexter was something of a genius, and, until his break with Jackson, an idol of Mississippi. From the

[1] *Washington Globe*, Feb. 23, 1835, sets forth all these facts.
[2] *Retrospect of Western Travel*, I, 163.

beginning he had been accorded the leadership of the Democratic or Jeffersonian Party in that Territory. His early congressional career was a justification of his leadership. One who knew him in those days tells us that "his mind was logical and strong; his conception was quick and acute; his powers of combination and application were astonishing; his wit was pointed and caustic, and his sarcasm overwhelming."[1] These qualities made him a tremendous power upon the stump with the then primitive people of his State. In the gubernatorial office he rendered invaluable service which strengthened his hold upon the masses. On the bench, he was noted for his ability and justice, and, among the lawyers, he was conceded to have few equals before a jury. During the War of 1812 he had further endeared himself to the Mississippians by his patriotic appeal for preparation, and, after he had aroused the Territory to fever heat, and Jackson had appeared upon the scene, he became a volunteer aid upon the staff of the future President. It was to Poindexter that the negro or soldier carried the infamous British countersign, "Booty and Beauty," and it was Poindexter who conveyed it to Jackson. Later his enemies charged that he had forged it to win the favor of the General. That such a man should have made enemies was inevitable. So bitter were his denunciations of his political enemies, so unscrupulous his use of terms, that at one time a conspiracy was formed to force him into a duel and kill him. The opportunity came after a peculiarly vitriolic attack upon a wealthy merchant who affiliated with the Federalists. The merchant challenged and was killed. Then Poindexter's enemies charged that he had fired before the word was given.

Nowhere in the campaign of 1828 did Jackson receive more ardent support than in Mississippi where his old friend Poindexter directed his forces, and one year after his inauguration, the lieutenant entered the Senate, and almost

[1] Sparks, *Memories of Fifty Years*, 335.

immediately the feud between the erstwhile friends began. The sordid feature of the story is the fact that it grew out of a patronage controversy. Jackson had determined on the appointment of a Tennesseean, a neighbor of the Hermitage, to the land office of Mississippi. Poindexter protested that this patronage belonged to his State and to him. Jackson refused to yield. Poindexter prevented the confirmation of the Tennesseean. Jackson made a recess appointment, and thenceforward the two comrades of 1812 were at swords' points. Thus far Jackson was manifestly in the wrong. His loyalty to friendship cannot explain his disloyalty to Poindexter — who was also a friend, and a friend in need. But such was the Mississippian's prejudice and hate that he abandoned, not only the President and purely Administration measures, but the principles he had espoused and advocated for a generation. He crossed the Rubicon, burned the bridges, and became a special favorite of Clay's. In every great fight of the Jackson period, Poindexter was found arrayed with the Opposition. He stood with the Bank, favored the censure, and offered the resolutions denunciatory of the Protest. In the Nullification contest, he had essayed to lead the Nullifiers, and became more offensive than Calhoun.

Unfortunately for Poindexter, in the fighting that followed he was far from invulnerable on the personal side. Having been unfortunate in his domestic relations, he had divorced his wife, denied the paternity of his children, and plunged into the most reckless dissipation.[1] His indecent reflections upon the purity of his wife drove her family, extensive and influential, to his enemies; his intemperate tirades against Jackson alienated the dominant Democratic sentiment of the State; and while he fought boldly and bitterly to sustain himself, he failed, and, at the time of the attack on Jackson by the madman at the Capitol, was so discredited in Mississippi that he was planning to leave the

[1] Sparks, *Memories of Fifty Years.*

State, with his second wife, on the expiration of his term. A man of genius whose morals failed to sustain his mentality — such the epitaph of George Poindexter.[1]

Three weeks after Lawrence had fired and failed, Poindexter called the Senate's attention to an anonymous letter stating that affidavits were in the hands of the President charging that interviews had taken place between the assailant and himself a few days before the attempt on Jackson's life, and asking the appointment of a special committee of investigation. Henry Clay, avowing that the rumors "inspired him with nothing but the deepest mortification and regret," and that it was "impossible to credit the statement that affidavits should have been procured at the instance of the Chief Executive for the purpose of implicating a Senator of the United States in so foul a transaction," reluctantly consented to an investigation. Without further discussion, a committee, consisting of John Tyler, chairman, Smith, Mangum, King, and Silas Wright, was appointed, with permission to sit during the sessions of the Senate; and three days later it unanimously exonerated Poindexter from suspicion. Webster asked for the yeas and nays on its acceptance; every Senator voted yea, and thus ended the most unfortunate incident in the career of Andrew Jackson. The "Washington Globe," which had published the affidavits, wholly discredited them about the same time.[2]

VII

The Calhoun inquiry "into the extent of federal patronage, the circumstances which have contributed to its great increase of late, the expediency and practicability of reducing the same, and the means of such reduction," served further to fan the flames of partisan madness during this session.

[1] Sparks, *Memories of Fifty Years*, 336–41; also, Foote's *Casket of Reminiscences*, 218–20.

[2] *Washington Globe*, Feb. 28, 1835.

Persisting in the fallacy that he was not moved by partisan or political considerations, he suggested that the committee be composed of two members of each party. The Senate, however, was not deceived as to his purpose, and selected four enemies of the Administration, Calhoun, Webster, Southard, and Bibb, and two Democrats, Benton, and King of Georgia. In due time an elaborate report was submitted. It set forth that 60,294 persons were in the employ of the Government; that together with the pensioners this meant more than 100,000 dependent on the Treasury. Implying that these constituted a federal machine, Calhoun added all engaged in business who wished to furnish supplies as part of the organization, influenced by patronage. Worse — there were thousands who wished to get upon the pay-roll who would willingly play the part of pliant tools to curry favor with Executive power. And how was this to be remedied? Since one of the causes contributing to the enlargement of the President's patronage was the increase in governmental expenditure, the statesmanlike thing to do would be to reduce the revenue. A great amount of public land had been thrown upon the market, calling for an army of receivers, registers, and surveyors — all of whom were tools of Jackson. The Jacksonian policy of removing men from office to make way for henchmen had reduced the efficiency of the public service by making reappointments dependent on something other than faithful service. This, by making the officials dependent upon the President, tended to make them all subservient to his will, and little better than his slaves. More: the power assumed by the President to select the banks for the public deposits made them a part of the presidential machine. If the public revenue could be reduced, and the Government thus starved, many would be forced from the public crib, but unhappily this could not be done. He proposed, therefore, a constitutional amendment permitting the annual distribution of the surplus till 1843 by a division of it into as many shares as there were Senators and Representatives, with ten shares for each Territory and the District of Columbia. And in addition to all this, he would enact a law to regulate the deposits of public money, and another to repeal that part of the Act of 1820 which limited the terms of customs officers.

When the report was submitted to the Senate, Poindexter made it the occasion for mournful and indignant reflections upon the growing tyranny of Jackson. He was profoundly moved by the revelations. Surely as many as thirty thousand extra copies of the report should be published for distribution. "The question now submitted to the Nation," he said, "is whether power is to be perpetuated in the hands of him who now wields it, and the one he may select as his successor." It was most unfortunate that the people would not awaken to the sinister attacks upon their liberties and institutions. The thoughtful, however, could not but see the trend.

But why print thirty thousand copies, asked King of Georgia, if not to serve a party purpose at the expense of the taxpayers? "What a spectacle we do present from day to day!" he exclaimed. "The Senate has been a week making war on the extras of the Post-Office Department. We are now warring against the extravagance of the Executive; and whilst brandishing the sword in one hand in defense of the public Treasury against the ravages of the Executive, we are, with the other, slipping it into our own pockets, or scattering it in profuse and wasteful extravagance."

The Senate compromised on ten thousand copies, and a rather dull debate, in which the Bank question was revived, resulted. The bills proposed by the Whig committee passed the Whig Senate to be promptly rejected in the Democratic House. These measures merely served as pegs on which to hang further denunciations of Jackson and his policies.

And the Democrats countered with an enthusiastic banquet in celebration of the wiping-out of the national debt for the first time in history. This had been one of Jackson's ambitions — a consummation Clay had determined should not come before the presidential election of 1832. But it could not be prevented; and while the Whigs were expanding on extravagance and the crowded public crib, the Jacksonians were pointing to the extinguishment of the public debt as an answer to the attacks. Benton, who presided as toastmaster at the banquet, was in flamboyant mood.

"The national debt is paid," he said. "This month of January, 1835, in the fifty-eighth year of the Republic, Andrew Jackson being President, the national debt is paid, and the apparition, so long unseen on earth — a great nation without a national debt — stands revealed to the astonished vision of a wondering world. Gentlemen, my heart is in this double celebration, and I offer you a sentiment, which, coming directly from my own bosom, will find its response in yours: President Jackson: may the evening of his days be as tranquil and as happy for himself as their meridian has been resplendent, glorious, and beneficent for his country."

Such was the partisan madness of this short session that a resolution, offered and urged by Preston, the Whig, for the purchase of some pictures for "the President's house," was promptly voted down, and Preston's efforts to have the vote reconsidered were unavailing. It was into this madhouse of partisan rancor that the French crisis, threatening war, involving the world prestige of the Republic, had been thrown by Jackson; and we shall now note how nearly partisanship came to compromising and weakening the Nation in the face of a foreign antagonist.

CHAPTER XIV

WHIG DISLOYALTY IN FRENCH CRISIS

I

The most important battle of the short session of 1834–35 was waged over Jackson's determination to compel France to observe her obligations under the treaty signed in Paris and Washington in July, 1831. After futile efforts by the four preceding Administrations to bring France to the payment of an indemnity for losses to American vessels during the Napoleonic wars, Jackson succeeded in negotiating a treaty in which France stipulated to pay the United States five millions in six annual installments, and we agreed to the reduction of duties on French wines. We immediately conformed to our agreement, but the French manifested no such respect for their obligations. Several sessions of the French Chamber failed to make appropriations for the payments, notwithstanding the earnest remonstrances of Washington. Thoroughly vexed at the contemptuous indifference of Paris, Jackson withdrew Livingston from the State Department, and sent him to the French Court to insist upon the discharge of the treaty obligations. Before the crisis came, he had summoned to his side as Secretary of State the courtly and able John Forsyth, concerning whom the American people know all too little. In view of the tendency to picture the Jackson of the French crisis as a bull in a china shop, it is worth while to consider the characters of the men who were, at this time, his advisers in foreign affairs. The character of Livingston has been described.

In the Washington of the Thirties no public man was more generally respected and admired for ability and elegance of manner than the new Secretary of State. This courtliness of demeanor was an inheritance from his French ancestors.[1] In person he was notably handsome, well built, with classical features; and his manners were those of the drawing-room and the Court. One who knew him has written that "in the times of Louis XIV he would have rivaled the most celebrated courtier; and under the dynasty of Napoleon he would have won the baton of France." [2] Another has described him as "Lord Chesterfield, minus his powdered wig and knee buckles," and as "all duke and all democrat." [3] Even-tempered, seldom giving way to passion, rich in a sense of humor, he was one of the few statesmen of his time who could find an equal welcome in the drawing-rooms of Whigs or Democrats. He was intensely social, and prone to fritter away valuable time in polite conversation with the pretty women of the capital, albeit a perfect husband, ardently devoted to the accomplished daughter of Dr. Josiah Meigs, whom he had married.[4] Cultivated, polished, graceful, he was the perfect gentleman and conversationalist.

As an orator, he was one of the most consummate of his time, singularly free from the then prevailing vice of tearing a passion to tatters. With a glance of the eye, a movement of the finger, a mild gesture of the hand, he could convey subtle meaning, and in his expressions of contempt he required nothing more than a twitch of the Roman nose or a scornful curl of the lip.[5] His voice, rich and musical, was as carefully trained as that of a prima donna. One writer compared it to a trumpet, "clear and piercing in its tones, and yet as soft as an organ." [6] Another, referring to "the constant stream of pure vocalization,' described it as "clear and resonant, al-

[1] *Forsyth of Nydie*, by Forsyth de Fronsac.

[2] J. F. H. Claiborne, in *The Cabinet: Past and Present.*

[3] Knight's *Reminiscences of Famous Georgians.*

[4] In a letter written Mrs. Forsyth on board the U.S.S. Hornet bearing him to the Court of Spain, now in possession of Waddy Wood, a descendant, Washington, D.C., the beautiful relations of the Forsyths are impressively disclosed.

[5] Miller's *Bench and Bar of Georgia.* [6] *Ibid.*

ways pleasant to the ear, and perfectly modulated." [1] A contemporary writer for the "Boston Post" recorded that "the rhythmic accents of his voice suggested the musical notes of the Æolian harp." [2]

By the common verdict of all contemporaries he was the most powerful debater of his day, and as the floor leader in the Senate, he was a tower of strength to the Administration before entering the Cabinet. A competent critic wrote that "as an impromptu debater to bring on an action or to cover a retreat, he never had a superior"; was "acute, full of resources, and ever prompt — impetuous as Murat in charge, adroit as Soult when flanked and outnumbered," "haughty in the presence of enemies, and affable and winning among friends." [3] Another thought him as adroit a debater as ever lived — "the Ajax Telamon of his party." [4] When the fight was made against the confirmation of Van Buren, the Administration rested its case against the attacks of Clay and Webster on his presentation. In the campaign of 1832, it summoned him to make the one speech upon the tariff, and then dismissed the topic definitely. When, at a critical moment in the Nullification movement, Georgia was about to be swept into the fallacy under the leadership of Berrien, in a convention called specifically for that purpose, it was Forsyth who was dispatched to take charge of the Administration forces, and, under his brilliant management, the Nullifiers were defeated in the presence of Chancellor Harper, who had been summoned from South Carolina to witness the triumph of the sinister doctrine.[5] During the panic session, it was upon his sarcasm that the Jacksonians largely relied to minimize the effect of the exaggerated speeches and the lugubrious petitions and memorials.

[1] Northern's *Men of Mark in Georgia.*

[2] Knight's *Reminiscences of Famous Georgians.*

[3] Claiborne's *The Cabinet: Past and Present.*

[4] Sparks, *Memories of Fifty Years.*

[5] See Foote's *Casket of Reminiscences;* Miller's *Bench and Bar of Georgia;* and Northern's *Men of Mark in Georgia.*

And yet, ardent though he was in his partisanship, he commanded the affectionate esteem of his opponents by his manliness and fairness. When the "bargain" charge was made against Clay, it was Forsyth who demanded an investigation in the interest of justice, thereby incurring the displeasure of many of his associates. Even Adams found him fair.

In many respects he fails to fit in with the Jacksonian picture. He was temperamentally an aristocrat, like Livingston, rather cynical toward the masses, and not at all enamoured of the Kitchen Cabinet. The letter from his son-in-law during the first Cabinet dissensions, expressing the hope that Jackson would "send off Lewis and Kendall," was doubtless written in the confidence that the sentiment would meet with the approval of the recipient.[1] But Forsyth was too much the man of the world to quarrel over details or personalities, and in the company of Van Buren and Livingston, he was able to forget the Kendalls and the Blairs.

When he entered the Cabinet, he assumed tasks that were to his taste. He prided himself particularly upon his diplomacy, and his experience as Minister to Madrid to negotiate the purchase of Florida justified his confidence. This position called for great address, finesse, a knowledge of human nature, and infinite patience, persuasiveness, and tact. The cunning Ferdinand, who needed the money, but was loath to part with his possession, was inclined to haggle, and, while history has given credit for the success of the negotiations to the instructions of Adams, it was the ingratiating qualities of Forsyth that finally overcame the scruples of the King.

That a President so impetuous as Jackson should have been served in foreign affairs by men of the conservatism and caution of Van Buren, Livingston, and Forsyth seems providential. One day, after dinner, Jackson sat before the fire in the White House smoking his pipe and outlining plans for

[1] This letter from Arthur Schaaf to Forsyth, written from Georgetown, June 25, 1831, is in possession of Waddy Wood, Washington, D.C.

radical action on the Oregon boundary dispute that would have made war inevitable. Forsyth, to whom he was speaking, observing his dangerous mood, simulated sympathy with his indignation. Then he began with quiet suggestions. Perhaps Jackson's plan would seem to be a plan to force a fight. It might put the country in the wrong light. Then, too, he recalled that the offensive action proposed in Parliament had been dropped on the request of the British Minister for Foreign Affairs. Possibly the London Government did not sympathize with the faction seeking trouble. Again, a year's notice would have to be given, preliminary to any action by the United States, and Jackson's Administration would then be drawing to a close. Possibly it might be best to do nothing. The President sat a few moments looking into the fire, and then, slowly refilling and lighting his pipe, he concluded — "I reckon you're right, Forsyth; at least you're right now."

Such was the man who, with the assistance of Edward Livingston, was to grapple with the French crisis.

II

On presenting his credentials, Livingston was warmly received by Louis Philippe, and assured that the necessary laws for the immediate execution of the treaty would be passed at the next meeting of the Chamber.[1] The French Government then understood the certain effect on American public opinion of a contemptuous treatment of its obligations. The peculiar action of the Chamber had been the subject of a conversation between the Duc de Broglie and James Buchanan, then in Paris, *en route* from his mission to St. Petersburg and this had been stressed.[2] Thanks to the clever Count Pozzo di Borgo, Russian Minister to France, Buchanan had been able to convey to Jackson an accurate idea of the

[1] Livingston to McLane, *Messages and Papers*, III, 130.
[2] Buchanan's diary, Sept. 12, 1833, Buchanan's *Works*, II, 388.

difficulties — the weakness of the King's Government and the hostility and cupidity of Dupin, the President of the Chamber.[1] Nor did it take Livingston long to discover the secret of the apathy of the King and his Ministers. Louis's throne was a keg of dynamite, and he ruled in constant fear of the Deputies. He hoped to postpone an unpleasant duty until an auspicious moment. The treaty was described by the enemies of the dynasty as a bad bargain; the supporters of the old régime hated America because of the Revolution, and the Republicans hated the King because he was King. With Jackson manifesting more and more irritation, Livingston importuned the King, remonstrated with the Ministers, and labored with the members of the Chamber, and in all this he had the active coöperation of Lafayette. But after six months of conferences, the Chamber took adverse action.

The Government was seriously concerned. The King expressed his deep regret, and a French war vessel was sent to America with instructions to Serurier the French Minister, to assure Jackson that, as soon after the elections as the charter would permit, the Chamber would be summoned, the appropriation would be pressed, and the President informed of the result in time for him to communicate the facts to the Congress at the beginning of the session of December, 1834. This held Jackson's impatience in check. But the elections passed, the Chamber convened, nothing was done, and the next session would not convene until three weeks after the Congress would meet.

As the congressional session approached, Livingston informed Forsyth that only a manifestation of strong national feeling in America would force action in Paris. "This is not a mere conjecture," he wrote. "I know the fact." And he reiterated that the moderate tone of the President's Messages had convinced the French politicians that he would not be

[1] Buchanan's *Works*, II, 290–91.

supported in vigorous measures, and closed with the significant comment that "from all this you may imagine the anxiety I shall feel for the arrival of the President's Message."[1]

The indignation of Jackson over this trifling, intensified by the conviction that France would not have dared thus in the case of a European Power, can be imagined. Many of his friends who lived in constant terror of his temper were beside themselves at the prospect.[2] But he had put his hand to the plough, and it was unlike him to turn back. In the preparation of his Message a futile effort had been made to persuade him to the employment of less emphatic language, but the Cabinet members thought to change slightly the phrasing without his knowledge. Forsyth, who was a master in diplomatic wording, made slight changes in a paragraph, and the Message was sent to the "Globe" to be put in type. When the proof reached the White House, John C. Rives[3] was with Jackson, and Donelson, a party to the plan to moderate, began to read as Jackson, with his pipe in his mouth, paced the floor. All went well until the altered paragraph was reached, and Donelson tried so to slur his reading that the change would not be noticed. Vain hope! Jackson stopped short.

"Read that again, sir."

This time the secretary read distinctly, and Jackson, the lion in him thoroughly aroused, thundered:

"That, sir, is not my language; it has been changed, and I will have no other expression of my own meaning than my own words."

And then and there he rewrote the paragraph, making it stronger than originally. Then, placing it in the hands of Rives, he forbade him to print anything else "at his peril."[4]

[1] Livingston to Forsyth, *Messages and Papers*, III, 130.

[2] Ambler's *Thomas Ritchie*, 163.

[3] Associated with Blair in the publication of the *Globe*.

[4] Wise's *Seven Decades of the Union*, 145–46.

Reading the Message to-day it seems moderate enough in tone, without a trace of bluster, and, compared with Cleveland's Venezuela Message, positively mild. The greater part is a calm, accurate, dispassionate recital of the facts, but it closed with the request for authority for making reprisals on French property should the next session of the Chamber fail to make the required appropriation. "Such a measure," he said, "ought not to be considered by France as a menace. Her pride and power are too well known to expect anything from her fears, and preclude the necessity of a declaration that nothing partaking of the character of intimidation is intended by us."

The tone of the Message, appealing to the pride and self-respect of the people, was embarrassing to the Whigs, who for a time hesitated as to their course. To support Jackson might only tend to enhance his popularity, already too great to suit; to attack his course would certainly be disadvantageous to the country in an international controversy.[1] Hone, the Whig diarist, however, was quite sure that the Message "will weaken our cause with the lookers on in other nations."[2] A month later he was still depressed because of Jackson's "unnecessary threats," but, being a praying Whig, he had hopes that Congress would still save the country.[3] Justice Joseph Story was quite as mournful. "The President," he wrote, "is exceedingly warm for war with France if he could get Congress to back him. The Senate, in these days our sole security, it is well known, would steadily resist him."[4]

Meanwhile, with the Whigs of the Senate laying their plans to repudiate the President's position in the face of a foreign adversary, events were moving in France. The Chamber met in the midst of excitement, the Ministry successfully putting their popularity to the test of a vote of confidence.

[1] Lewis to Hamilton, Hamilton's *Reminiscences*, 283.
[2] Hone's *Diary*, Dec. 3, 1834. [3] *Ibid.*, Jan. 1, 1835.
[4] Letter to Judge May, *Life and Letters of Story*, II, 192.

Livingston was encouraged.[1] But a very little later his optimism vanished, and he awaited hopefully the arrival of the Presidential Message.[2] Thus concerned over the tone of the Message, he arranged for couriers to hurry it to him on its arrival at Havre. It reached Paris in an American newspaper at two o'clock in the morning. The excitement was intense. Even Livingston was momentarily stunned. "The feeling," he wrote Forsyth, "is fostered by the language of our Opposition papers, particularly by the 'Intelligencer' and the 'New York Courier,' extracts from which have been sent on by Americans, declaring them to be the sentiments of the majority of the people. These, as you will see, are translated and republished here, with such comments as they might have been expected and undoubtedly were intended to produce, and if hostilities should take place between the two nations those persons may flatter themselves with having the credit of a large share in producing them." He felt, however, that "the energetic language of the Message" would "have a good effect." And contrary to the fear of Hone that it would degrade us in the eyes of the onlookers, he found that "it has certainly raised us in the estimation of other Powers if we may judge by the demeanor of their representatives here." He was sure that "as soon as the excitement subsides it will operate favorably on the counsels of France." Already "some of the papers have begun to change their tone." As soon as the Message was known, "the funds experienced a considerable fall, and insurance rose." [3]

In compliance with the request of Comte de Rigny, the Minister for Foreign Affairs, Livingston personally delivered to him a copy of the Message, and stressed the point that, under our governmental form, the Message was a consultation between departments of our Government, and was not directed to France. Then shifting to the offensive he added

[1] Livingston to Forsyth, *Messages and Papers*, III, 132.
[2] *Ibid.* [3] *Ibid.*, 135–36.

that it was most unfortunate, in view of Serurier's promise, that there had not been an earlier call of the Chamber. De Rigny seemed to attach the most serious importance to the intimation of bad faith, but the interview was friendly. That evening, at the Austrian Minister's, Livingston found him all suavity; and the next night a curt note from him announced the withdrawal of Serurier from Washington, and a readiness to give the American diplomat his passports on application![1] He made much of Jackson's comments on the failure to convene the Chamber when, as a matter of fact, the Chamber was then actually assembled in virtue of a royal ordinance. This, while true, could not have been known to Jackson in those days of slow communication. He only knew the original purpose. But it pleased de Rigny to assume an unexplainable offense, and to announce that "His Majesty has considered it due his own dignity no longer to leave his Minister exposed to hear language so offensive to France."[2] Resisting an impulse to demand his passports, lest such action seem unnecessarily provocative, Livingston replied in a dignified note that unless de Rigny's letter was intended as a dismissal, he would await instructions from his own Government.

III

MEANWHILE the Whigs were planning to make political capital out of the crisis. The "Intelligencer," the organ of the Senate Whigs, had assumed an attitude which, as we have seen, had given much comfort to the French enemies of the treaty. "We trust," it said, "that it will be universally understood, not only at home, but everywhere abroad, that the recommendation of the President is his own act only, and is not likely . . . to receive the approbation of the Congress or the people of the United States." And Blair, in the "Globe," hotly replied that "if she [France] shall shed American blood

[1] Livingston to Forsyth, *Messages and Papers,* III, 137–38.
[2] De Rigny to Livingston, *ibid.*, 138–39.

in this controversy, and push her injustice to actual war, the responsibility for all the destruction of human lives . . . will justly rest upon the heads of the editors of the 'National Intelligencer.'"[1] The "National Gazette," another Opposition paper, compromised with the thought that Jackson "did well to present the subject to Congress . . . though we would earnestly dissuade Congress from giving him a discretion so important as that of reprisals." Which, interpreted by Blair, meant that the mercantile class and bankers were interested in French claims, and it would be well to enforce them, "but if the national rights and honor, implicated in a refusal to execute the treaty, should be vindicated by President Jackson, it would add renown to the man whom it was the editors' business to traduce."[2]

The first act of the Whigs was to pack the Foreign Relations Committee of the Senate with the President's enemies, three of the five, Clay, Mangum, and Sprague, being virulent foes. "There are certainly not three men in the French Chamber," wrote Blair, "more anxiously bent on thwarting the measures of General Jackson's Administration."[3] Into the hands of these was delivered that portion of the Message dealing with the French affair, and a month later Clay offered his resolution that "it is inexpedient at this time" to grant authority to the President to make reprisals. In presenting his report, Clay made the startling statement that if France was prudent "she will wait to see whether the Message should be seconded by the Congress." Thus, in the face of a prospective foreign foe, patently in the wrong, the leader of the Whigs attempted to create the impression that Jackson stood alone. This was the cue to the politicians. The Clay report was extravagantly praised. Poindexter, in ecstatic mood, moved that twenty thousand copies be printed for circulation — as propaganda to isolate the President. Calhoun favored "the largest number." The report had delighted him. "War

[1] *Washington Globe*, Dec. 6, 1834. [2] *Ibid.* [3] *Ibid.*, Dec. 17, 1834.

was at all times to be avoided." [1] Only two Whigs objected to twenty thousand copies, and these on the ground that the printing of so many would require four months.[2] Hill demanded the yeas and nays, and by a party vote the "largest number" of Clay's campaign document was ordered. Thus, from the beginning, the divisions in the Senate on an international crisis were along party lines.

On the day Livingston received the curt note from de Rigny, Clay, in opening the discussion of his resolution, threw out the suggestion twice that France might make the appropriation conditional on an "explanation" from the President of the United States. He felt sure that France would understand that Congress did not share the President's views. The Democratic members of the committee, in a minority report, differed from the majority in explaining the reason for finding it "inexpedient" to grant authority — the fact that the Chamber had been called a month earlier than anticipated. The only vigorous attack on the majority report, and the sole unapologetic American speech, was that of Buchanan, who, better than any other member of the Senate, understood the conditions in Paris. He called for an unqualified assertion of our determination to demand the observance of the treaty. "I hope I may be mistaken," he concluded, "but I believe it never will be paid before." [3] The brief debate, heard by the fashion of the capital packed in the galleries, was conducted with decorum, but quite discernible beneath the surface one may read the party feeling which even an international crisis could not obliterate. The Clay resolution was adopted. The "National Intelligencer," now finding its way regularly to Paris, expressed the hope that "with this unquestionable proof of the pacific temper of the Senate . . . it will now be understood at home and abroad that there is no morbid appetite for war among the grave and considerate portion of the American people."

[1] *Cong. Globe*, II, 95. [2] Leigh and Preston. [3] *Cong. Globe*, II, 125.

Several weeks were to intervene before the House took action. Meanwhile in Paris, Livingston, in seclusion, prepared his masterful and spirited formal reply to the impudent note of the French Minister. He loftily rebuked him for referring to the President as "General Jackson" in official language, firmly reiterated and proved the charge of broken faith in the matter of the Serurier pledge, and pitilessly exposed the hypocrisy of the complaint that Jackson had misrepresented, purposely, regarding the time of the calling of the Chamber. Had not de Rigny himself informed him that it was constitutionally impossible to call the session earlier when protest had been made as to the date? And yet it had been called. When a copy of this note reached Forsyth, he summoned Van Buren and the two repaired to the White House, where it was read and warmly approved.[1] By this time Jackson was in no mood to compromise or conciliate. Forsyth instructed Livingston that, if the French Chamber again rejected the appropriation bill, a frigate was to be immediately sent to convey him home. Ten days after these instructions were written, Serurier was recalled, and Forsyth, in refusing an audience, coolly informed him that he was "ready to receive in writing any communication the Minister of France desires to have made to the Government of the United States."[2]

Meanwhile the French papers reaching the United States were noisily militant. War-clouds lowered. James A. Hamilton tendered his services to Jackson for duty "civil or military, at home or abroad."[3] Major Lewis, gravely concerned because of his daughter's marriage to M. Pageot of the French Legation, hastened to reassure Hamilton with extracts from personal letters from governmental officials in Paris — and thus threw an interesting side-light on the

[1] Hunt's *Life of Livingston; Messages and Papers*, III, 202–08.

[2] Notes exchanged between Forsyth and Serurier, *Messages and Papers*, III, 144–45.

Hamilton's *Reminiscences*, 283.

romance and tragedy of international marriages, for these letters had been translated, for the benefit of Jackson, in the French Legation by Madame Pageot, the wife of the First Secretary![1]

IV

UNDER these ominous conditions, with offers of military service pouring into the White House, with the French Minister on the ocean *en route* to Paris, and with additional letters in the diplomatic duel before it, the House of Representatives began its discussion of the crisis. With the majority report and resolutions declaring against further negotiations and in favor of contingent preparations, the House was immediately engaged in an animated and acrimonious discussion indicative of the excitement of the times. Edward Everett, the pacifist of the session, offered a substitute coupling a declaration of adherence to the treaty with a request for the renewal of negotiations. Adams, in ugly temper, threw out the hint that it appeared that "the supporters of the Administration were the only ones to be heard upon the subject." With some feeling, Cambreleng, in charge for the Administration, assured the former President that he was ready to enter upon a free accommodation of differences that a united front might be presented to the Nation's adversary. This little storm cleared the atmosphere, and on the next day when the debate began in earnest it was wholesomely free from purely partisan rancor. Then it was that Adams explained his dissent from the phrasing. He objected to the assertion that negotiations should be discontinued. "The only alternative compatible with the honor of nations is war," he said. If a continuance of the negotiations failed, he was ready for the "hazard of war." He realized that "the interest and honor of the Nation" were at stake. The pledge of France had been given, and the sole question was

[1] Hamilton's *Reminiscences*, 284.

"whether we shall suffer the nation that made this treaty to violate it." We could not afford to compromise to the extent of a penny.

"What will be the consequences," demanded the fiery old man eloquent, "if you give it up? Why, every nation will consider itself at liberty to sport with all treaties that are made with us."

And then Adams startled the Democrats, and broke with the Whigs, in his reference to Jackson. "Whatever may be said of the imprudence of that recommendation," he exclaimed, "the opinion of mankind will ever be that it was high-spirited and lofty, and such as became the individual from whom it emanated. I say it now, and I repeat, that it is the attitude which the Chief Magistrate will bear before the world, and before mankind, and before posterity." [1]

Quite different the feeling of William S. Archer, a Virginia Whig, who looked with fear and trembling to a contest with France. Think, he cried, of the commercial loss! Why sacrifice this with so little involved? "It would be quixotic, and even romance scarcely presented a precedent, unless that of Sir Lucius O'Trigger." And even if right, why take the chance? He had been surprised that Adams had said nothing about fear.

"No," shouted Adams, "the gentleman's whole argument is fear!"

The Virginian closed by offering a resolution "that in the just expectation that the Government of France will have made provision . . . this House will forbear at the present time to adopt any measure in relation to that subject." [2]

With flaming indignation, James W. Bouldin, a Virginia Democrat, replied to Archer's timorous speech. "The gentleman asks if we would really go to war for five million dollars," he said. "Will a man fight if you spit in his face?" Already the French Chamber was boasting that we had taken

[1] *Cong. Globe*, II, 309–10. [2] *Ibid.*, 310–11.

the like from others, and declaring that we were "a money-making, money-loving people, and would never spend a hundred million to obtain five." And, continued Bouldin, "I have heard as much praise of foreign nations as I want to hear. . . . All I want to hear at this time is whether we intend to hold upon the treaty or give it up entirely." [1]

Cambreleng, aroused by the sordid character of the Archer appeal, sharply warned that "the honor and welfare of the Nation is involved, and the measure will no longer be sacrificed to gratify the spirit of party." [2] To which Tristam Burges, a Rhode Island Whig, responded with the amazing assertion that "France would be cowardly indeed if she should pay the money under such circumstances." [3]

Edward Everett followed with a typical pacifist appeal for peace, but it was reserved for the eloquent Horace Binney to present the most novel reasons for America's consent to her humiliation. In the President's Message he had found "the President's design . . . impossible to fathom." [4] The action of the French Chamber was none of our business. In the meantime we should not close the door on negotiations. The French Republicans were using the treaty as a club upon the monarchy, and should this country "strengthen the hands of a constitutional monarchy?" [5]

Then Adams, in no conciliatory temper, rose again. "Whence come these compliments to France?" he asked. "Are they elicited by her virtues? Is it because she has refused the payment . . . due us? Is it because she has violated her plighted faith? Is it from the style of the dignified debates . . . where we are characterized as a nation of mercenaries — where the basest and meanest of motives are attributed to the American people — those of sordid avarice, speculation, and gain?. . . Is it on this that the gentleman from Virginia bases his 'just expectations'?" And, turning

[1] *Cong. Globe*, II, 312. [2] *Ibid.*, 312–13. [3] *Ibid.*, 313.
[4] Binney's *Diary; Life of Binney*, 126. [5] *Cong. Globe*, II, 320.

to Everett: "We have heard much of war and its horrors. No man can entertain a greater abhorrence of war than I. I would do anything but sacrifice honor and independence to avoid it. But when I hear it advanced that there is no such thing as national honor, that it is merely ideal, I must take leave to say that I do not subscribe to such a doctrine." [1]

But the next speaker, Benjamin Hardin, though hailing from the fighting State of Kentucky, was not impressed. Randolph had compared his wit to "a coarse kitchen butcher knife whetted upon a brickbat," [2] but he now purred gently to the harsh strokes of the French Chamber. "What would we go to war for?" he demanded. "The paltry sum of five million dollars!" In one year war would "sweep from the ocean at least fifty millions of our commerce." And where would the expense fall? "Upon the hard-working and industrious farmer." [3]

The outcome was the adoption of a resolution which was a compromise between that of the committee and the ideas of Adams, insisting on the maintenance of the treaty and in favor of preparations. This was adopted at a night session on the 2d of March, and the session was then thought to expire at midnight on March 3d.

V

An occurrence on the last day of the session, due to partisan madness, left the Republic all but naked to its prospective foe. Early in the evening, during the consideration of the Fortifications Bill, an amendment was offered in the House, appropriating three millions to be used at the discretion of the President for emergency work in the event France should strike during the congressional recess. It met with no opposition in the House, but the moment it reached the Senate it

[1] *Cong. Globe*, II, 322.

[2] General Linder's *Early Bench and Bar of Illinois*, 48.

[3] *Cong. Globe*, II, 322.

was pounced upon by the Whig leaders as another proof of Jackson's itch for power. Webster, assuming the leadership in the sorry business, proposed instantly to dispose of the amendment with a motion to "adhere" to the Senate measure. This harsh, unusual course was intended as a notice that the Senate would not even meet the House in conference upon the subject.

Then followed a most amazing spectacle, with the Whigs assailing Jackson and his alleged contempt for the Constitution and determination to declare war without an Act of Congress. Senator Buchanan, protesting against the Webster motion, pointed out the necessity for the appropriation — the possibility of a blow from France during the recess, the frankly expressed apprehension of Livingston. "In that event," he continued, "what will be our condition? Our seacoast from Georgia to Maine will be exposed to the incursions of the enemy; our cities may be plundered and burnt; the national character may be disgraced; and all this whilst we have an overflowing Treasury." [1]

King of Alabama earnestly pleaded with Webster to withdraw the harsh motion. "In what way," he asked, "does it violate the Constitution? Does it give the President the power to declare war? This power belongs to Congress alone, nor does the bill in the slightest degree impair it. Does it authorize the raising of armies? No, not one man may be enlisted beyond the number required to fill up the ranks of your little army."

But Webster was deaf to the appeal. The "autocrat" and "tyrant" was again making an onslaught on the Constitution, and he would have none of it. And by a strict party vote, for White of Tennessee had by now definitely joined the Opposition, the motion to adhere was adopted.

When this surprising action reached the House, it swallowed its pride and asked for a conference. The conferees

[1] Buchanan's *Works*, II, 439–41.

met and remained in deadlock until midnight. Forsyth and Van Buren were at the Capitol trying without avail to get action. Meanwhile in the Senate something very like a filibuster was begun. Benton was impressed by the number of the speakers, their vehemence, perseverance, provocative attacks on Jackson, and indirectly on the House.[1]

All this time, Jackson was patiently waiting in his room at the Capitol to sign the bill when passed. At midnight he put on his hat and returned to the White House. The conference and debate continued, with many, who considered the session dead at midnight,[2] leaving the Capitol, until repeated calls of the House failed to secure a quorum. At a late hour some of the Whig members of the House were insisting that the amendment be abandoned, with the Democrats refusing to yield and placing the responsibility upon the Senate. Partisan bitterness became more pronounced as the end approached. "There are men who would willingly see the banner of France waving over your Capitol, rather than lose an opportunity to make a thrust at the Administration," bitterly exclaimed Jesse Bynum of North Carolina. "This is not a miserable Administration or anti-Administration question," protested Henry A. Wise, the Whig who favored the amendment. The danger of war was real and if it came "every fortification on your coast is liable to fall into the hands of a strong maritime power," he warned.[3] At intervals, motions to recede were offered and overwhelmingly defeated.

It was two o'clock in the morning when Cambreleng returned to the House with a compromise — $300,000 for arming the fortifications, $500,000 for repairs and the equipping of war vessels, "an amount wholly inadequate if it should be required, and more than necessary if it should not." As he entered the House, he found no quorum, and no possibility

[1] *Thirty Years' View*, I, 594.
[2] The then prevalent belief.
[3] *Cong. Globe*, II, 330.

of getting one. On a motion to adjourn, only 111 members were present and voting; a few moments later but 75; and at three o'clock, Speaker Bell rose, delivered a brief valedictory, and the House stood adjourned without day. The Nation was naked to the foe, and in the midst of negotiations.

Far from weakening Jackson's determination to maintain the dignity and rights of the Nation, the failure of the Fortifications Bill but strengthened his will, and two days after Congress adjourned, Forsyth instructed Livingston to demand an explanation or qualification of an insinuation in Serurier's note of withdrawal that the President had knowingly misrepresented in his Message to Congress.[1]

Meanwhile, in France, the Whigs' campaign to picture Jackson as isolated in his position from both Congress and the people was having its effect, and there were Whigs in America who rejoiced in the fact. Scanning the French newspapers, Philip Hone was delighted to find that Clay's report and the Senate resolution had had the effect he anticipated. He rejoiced to find that they convinced the French that the proposal of reprisals "are only the acts of the President" and "would not be sanctioned by the legislature of the Nation."[2]

And Hone was not mistaken as to the effect of Jackson's firmness and the Senate's action. The money was appropriated by the Chamber with the payment contingent on an apology or explanation from Jackson. In the discussion of the appropriation measure, Jackson was roundly denounced, and ridiculed as one repudiated by his own people. Boasts were made of the ease with which France could crush the United States. "The insult from President Jackson comes from himself alone," said M. Henri de Chabaulon. "This is more evident from the refusal of the American Congress to concur with him in it.... Suppose the United States had

[1] Serurier to Forsyth, *Messages and Papers*, III, 211; Forsyth to Livingston, *ibid.*, 210.

[2] Hone's *Diary*, March 14, 1835.

taken part with General Jackson, we should have had to demand satisfaction, not from him, but from the United States; . . . and we should have had to . . . entrust to our heroes of Navarino and Algiers the task of teaching the Americans that France knows the way to Washington as well as England." And this insulting speech was received with applause. "When the Americans see this long sword," exclaimed M. Rance, "believe me, gentlemen, they would sooner touch your money than dare to touch your sword." [1] Left to his own resources by the absence of instructions on the proviso of the measure of the Chamber, Livingston informed the Duc de Broglie that an attempt to enforce the proviso would be repelled "by the undivided energy of the Nation." [2] And four days later he left Paris, with Barton, his son-in-law, at the American Legation as Chargé d'Affaires.

From this time on to the crisis, the American Legation in Paris and the French in Washington were under Chargés d'Affaires, and strangely enough the wives of both were prime favorites of Jackson and intimates of the White House circle. The beautiful and exquisite Cora Livingston, daughter of the Minister, was long the reigning belle of the American capital. Josiah Quincy had been infatuated with her, and the story has come down of Van Buren trying to get her under the mistletoe. In the White House she had come and gone with the informality of a member of the household, and many an evening she had spent with Mrs. Donelson in one of the private rooms of the President's house, with Jackson sitting at one side smoking his pipe. She had married Barton a short time before Livingston's departure for Paris, and it had pleased the man of iron, with so much of tender sentiment where women were concerned, to appoint the bridegroom Secretary of the Legation that Cora might be in Paris with her mother. Enclosing his commission in a letter to

[1] Quoted by Benton, *Thirty Years' View*, I, 592.
[2] *Messages and Papers*, III, 178–79.

"My Dear Cora," he had asked her to "present it to him with your own hand."

Quite as closely connected with the White House circle was Madame Pageot, known to Jackson as little Delia Lewis, daughter of one of the members of the Kitchen Cabinet. He had known her as a child in Tennessee where her father dwelt close to the Hermitage, and she had known and loved the sainted Rachel. When her engagement to Pageot was announced, Jackson had insisted that the marriage should take place in the White House, and when her first child was born and called "Andrew Jackson," the christening had been in the President's house. It was on this occasion when the Minister, following the form, asked the infant, "Andrew Jackson, do you renounce the Devil and all his works?" that the President with great fervor responded, "I do most indubitably," to the delight of all.

Thus there was a touch to the closing days of the crisis that probably has no parallel in the history of diplomacy.

VI

HAD the French politicians been able to witness the popular ovation accorded Livingston on his arrival in New York, they might have changed their opinion concerning Jackson's isolation from the people. An immense crowd greeted him at the wharf, followed him to his lodgings, clamored for a speech, and thronged the City Hall at the public reception. Philip Hone, one of the Whigs who rejoiced in the demand of a foreign nation for an apology from the American President, was gravely concerned because he had returned in "a bad humor," and might "infuse some of it into the mind of the obstinate and weak old man at the head of the Government, and so prevent an amicable arrangement." [1] But the Whig diarist's greatest disgust came with Livingston's ovation at the dinner of the Corporation on July 4th, when at the con-

[1] Hone's *Diary*, June 23, 1835.

clusion of his brief speech the room rang with cries of "No explanations!" "No apology!" — dividing, as Hone records, "the echoes of the spacious dome with equally inspiring shouts of 'Hurrah for Jackson!'"[1] At Philadelphia, *en route* to Washington, Livingston was the guest of honor at an equally enthusiastic dinner, and, thus acclaimed by his countrymen, he reached Washington and went into conference with Jackson, Forsyth, and Van Buren.

Calm and determined, Jackson waited patiently until in September when he proposed to press the issue to a decision. Forsyth sent instructions to Barton. If nothing indicative of a purpose to pay the indemnity had been done, the Chargé was to call upon the Duc de Broglie and ask for a definite answer with the view to the regulation of his conduct. If the Minister should fix a day for the payment, Barton was to remain in Paris; otherwise he was to demand his passports because of the non-execution of the treaty. And this step was to be taken in time to permit the result to be communicated to Jackson before he prepared his Message for the opening of Congress. In the latter part of October, Barton had his audience with de Broglie, and handled himself with consummate tact and caution. With studied impudence the French Minister announced that the money would be forthcoming when an explanation or apology had been received, and a few days later, Barton sailed for the United States.

Meanwhile the Congress convened, and Jackson in his Message reported progress, soberly reviewing the course of the negotiations up to the passage of the indemnity bill by the French Chamber with its offensive proviso, and bluntly concluding that the French Government has "received all the explanation which honor and principle permitted." He informed Congress of his final instructions to Barton and of his purpose to communicate the result when ascertained.

It was while awaiting the report of the American Chargé

[1] Hone's *Diary*, July 4, 1835.

d'Affaires that M. Pageot received notice of his recall, and by the time he was able to sail the two nations were on the verge of war. Hone, noting the departure of the Poland bearing M. Pageot and "the odds and ends of the French Legation," could not restrain his mirth over the prospective discomfiture of the French Chargé in bearing back to the French Court a young heir, bearing "the august name of Andrew Jackson." [1]

When Barton reached New York, he hastened with all speed to Washington, where Livingston awaited him. It was with no little anxiety that Van Buren, Forsyth, and Livingston accompanied him to the White House. The three older men, all devoted to Jackson, and all at some time at the head of his Department of Foreign Affairs, were greatly concerned over the possible effect of the report on the thoroughly aroused President.

Observing their solemnity, Barton turned upon them:

"Well, gentlemen, shall it be oil or water?"

"Oh, water, by all means," they answered in a chorus.

To none of these, not even to Livingston, had Barton indicated the nature of the report he had to make. Pressing the former Minister's hand as a token of appreciation of his confidence, Barton led the way into the iron man's presence.

The moment the conference was over, Jackson began the preparation of his Message to Congress, and, on its completion, submitted it to Livingston. In view of Hone's fear, it is interesting to note that it was the former Minister of State who persuaded Jackson to a moderation of its tone. Drawing a substitute, he sent it to the White House with an ingratiating letter.

"The characteristics of the present communication," he wrote, "ought, in my opinion, to be moderation and firmness. Our cause is so good that we need not be violent. Moderation in language, firmness in purpose, will unite all hearts

[1] Hone's *Diary*, Jan. 26, 1836.

at home, all opinion abroad, in our favor. Warmth and recrimination will give arguments to false friends and real enemies, which they may use with effect against us. On these principles I have framed a hasty draft which I enclose. You will, with your usual discernment, determine whether it suits the present emergency. At any rate, I know you will do justice to the motive that has induced me to offer it." [1]

Jackson took the advice in good part, destroyed his declaration of war, and prepared, with the assistance of Forsyth, another, which was submitted to Congress on January 15th. It was an excited body of men that listened that winter day to the reading of the Message that might mean war. But three days before, an acrimonious debate had been precipitated by Benton, charging the partisanship of the Senate with responsibility for the failure of the Fortifications Bill; and only the day before, Webster, in a spirited reply, had attempted to shift responsibility to the Democratic House. John Quincy Adams, enraged at Webster's reflections upon the House, was meditating his sensational reply. In this atmosphere the Message was read.

After reviewing the controversy up to the hour of the Message, with the declaration that "the spirit of the American people, the dignity of the Legislature, and the firm resolve of their Executive Government forbid" an apology or explanation, he called upon Congress to "sustain Executive exertion in such measures as the case requires." This included, according to his idea, reprisals, the exclusion of French products and French vessels from American ports. But there was more to be done. Naval preparations of the French intended for our seas had been announced. He knew not the purpose. But, "come what may, the explanation which France demands can never be accorded, and no armament, however powerful and imposing, at a distance or on our coast, will, I trust, deter us from discharging the high

[1] Hunt's *Life of Livingston.*

duties we owe to our constituents, our national character, and to the world"; and he called upon the Congress "to vindicate the faith of treaties and to promote the general interest of peace, civilization, and improvement." [1]

VII

NOTWITHSTANDING the seriousness of the crisis the memory of the failure of the Fortifications Bill in the last session would not down. Throughout the spring, summer, and autumn of 1835, the press and politicians were engaged in bitter criminations and recriminations as to the responsibility. It was manifestly the fault of the Senate Whigs, but their harassed leaders bitterly retaliated on the Democratic House, and drew upon their imagination in an effort to place responsibility upon the Jacksonian leaders. A fantastical article, once attributed to Daniel Webster, appeared in the "National Gazette," charging that Van Buren and John Forsyth had expressed the wish to Cambreleng, the Democratic leader in the House, that the bill should fail, that the calamity might be ascribed to the Whigs of the Senate. The people had been thoroughly outraged at the base prostitution of the Nation's interest to the pettiness of party politics. During the summer, Blair called attention in the "Globe" to Serurier's action in sending to Paris with Jackson's Message the criticism of the "National Intelligencer," with the comment that the French Minister for Foreign Affairs would do well to read the two together! Paris was assured by Serurier that the Whig paper had "pretty considerable influence," had "under the presidencies of Madison and Monroe been the official paper," and "has spoken energetically against the measure" the President had proposed. The President's sharp reference to the unfortunate situation created by the failure of the bill, in his Message of December,

[1] The naval activities in France are set forth by Benton, in *Thirty Years' View*, I, 592–93.

1835, had shown a determination, on the part of that consummate politician, to turn the popular indignation upon the Opposition. However, with the passion of the parties smouldering beneath the surface, there was no open fight until, on January 12th, the pugnacious Benton, speaking on the national defense, reviewed the failure of the Fortifications Bill, and laid the responsibility at the Senate's door. He closed his biting comments with an effective reference to the approach of the French squadron, sent on the supposition of our helplessness, and the suggestion that the Senate should then act "under the guns of France and under the eyes of Europe." [1]

That was the call to battle. The irate Webster sprang to his feet to announce that a little later he would be able to exonerate the Senate, and the fiery Leigh of Virginia protested that "the objection to the appropriation was not because of any distrust of the President," but because of the unconstitutionality of the amendment: this in delicious disregard of the plain record of the debate. But Preston, who followed, exposed the cloven hoof of the partisan animus. If the French fleet was coming, why had the President kept Congress in the dark? Why had he withdrawn our representatives from Paris? Why had we no representative at the Court of England? — an audacious question in view of the refusal by the Whig Senate to confirm either of two excellent appointments to that post. Why assume that the French fleet came with hostile motives? "It may be that this fleet is coming to protect the commerce of France," he thought. From this it was an easy step to the reiteration of the Whig apologies for and defense of the action of the French Government.[2]

But the last word in defense of the Senate was reserved for Webster, who rose twenty-four hours before the Special Message reached the Senate and while it was being prepared. It

[1] *Cong. Globe*, II, 91–92. [2] *Ibid.*, 92.

was a laboriously wrought attempt. The amendment to the Fortifications Bill had been offered at the eleventh hour. The President had not requested the additional appropriation in a Message. No department had recommended it. Nothing of which Congress was cognizant had occurred to justify it. The Senate had passed a resolution "reminding" the House of the bill in the closing hours. The conference report had not been passed upon by the House. And "the bill therefore was lost. It was lost in the House of Representatives. It died there, and there its remains are to be found." Had not the President announced at one o'clock that he would receive no further communications from the Congress? What right had he to interfere with the time Congress should fix for adjournment?[1] And what constitutional right had Congress to make an appropriation when there was no specification of the precise use to be made of the money? And with true Websterian eloquence he closed with mournful meditations on the encroachments of Jackson upon the Constitution, and the prediction that, unless checked, men, then living, would "write the history of this government, from its commencement to its close."[2]

That the Jacksonians were not impressed with the danger was shown in the brief reply of Cuthbert of Georgia, that the great danger to Rome was not in the kingly name they feared, but "in the patrician class, a moneyed aristocracy, a combination of their political leaders, seeking to establish an aristocratical government, regardless of the welfare of the people." But the answer to Webster was not to come from a Democrat, but from a Whig — and that, too, a Whig from Massachusetts, who had been defeated for reëlection to the Presidency by Andrew Jackson!

[1] At that time it was generally believed that a Congress died at midnight on the 3d of March rather than at noon on the 4th, as now assumed.

[2] Webster's *Works*, IV, 205–29.

VIII

THERE had long been an undercurrent of hostility between Daniel Webster and John Quincy Adams. Webster had gladly left the House during the Adams Administration to escape the necessity of defending the President; and the comments on the great orator, running through the famous "Diary" of Adams, are often sarcastic, usually unfriendly, and seldom fulsome. That this spirit of animus alone should have impelled Adams to make his notable reply — a reply which has been strangely ignored by historians — cannot be reconciled with his character as a public man. The fact that Webster had assailed the House of which Adams was a leading member, and the amendment with which Adams had had something to do, may explain the bitterness of his retort. But no one can read the speeches of Adams on the French controversy without being impressed with the robust Americanism of the man, and his utter impatience with a partisan thought in the presence of a foreign adversary.

The opportunity for Adams's reply came one week after the Webster speech, six days after the President's Special Message, and when the international crisis seemed most menacing. The "National Intelligencer" had made an attack upon the House of Representatives, along the line of the Webster speech, and Cambreleng, who had been personally assailed, in resenting the article had said that "more than one member of the House, not only on this side, but on both sides, will vindicate the proceedings of the House in relation to the bill." Immediately afterwards Adams presented his resolution for an investigation, and launched into one of the most bitter, dramatic, and sensational speeches ever heard in the American Congress. He rose in fighting armor. Scarcely had he begun his attack upon the Senate when he was called to order for mentioning that body; whereupon he jauntily observed that he would "transfer the location of the place where these things had happened from the Senate to the office of the 'National Intelligencer'" — and thus proceeded to the castigation of that journal. In explaining the reasons for the three-million-dollar amendment, he recounted the story of the resolution adopted in the House.

"In all the debates in the 'National Intelligencer,'" he said, "there is no more trace of such a resolution having passed the House than if it had never existed; no more trace than can be found on the journal of the Senate of what they would do for the defense of the country, or to insist on the execution of the treaty of July. But in the debate in the 'National Intelligencer,' I find a prodigious display of eloquence against the constitutionality of the section appropriating $3,000,000 for the defense of the country, because it had not been recommended by the Executive."

The House was instantly in an uproar, and Adams was again called to order for his reference to the Senate. The old man stood listening calmly to the excited observations of some of his colleagues, and was finally permitted to proceed.

"Observe, sir," he continued, "the terms, the object, and the conditions of that appropriation. It was to be expended, in whole or in part, under the direction of the President of the United States — the executive head of the Nation, sworn to the faithful execution of the laws; sworn especially, and entrusted with the superintendence of all the defenses of the country against the ravages of a foreign invader; it was to be expended for the military and naval service, including fortifications and ordnance and increase of the navy. These, sir, the natural and appropriate instruments of defense against a foreign foe, were the sole and exclusive objects of the appropriation. Not one dollar of it could have been applied by him to any other purposes without making himself liable to impeachment; not by that House of Representatives, but by us, their successors, fresh from the constituent body, the people; yet before the same Senate for his judges, a majority of whom were surely not of his friends; not one dollar of it could have been expended without giving a public account of it to the representatives of the people and to the Nation. Nor was this all. Thus confined to specific objects, it was to be expended, not unconditionally, but only in the event that it should be rendered necessary for the defense of the country prior to the then next session of Congress — an interval of nine months — during which no other provision could have been made to defend your soil from sudden invasion, or to protect your commerce floating upon every sea from a sweep of a royal ordinance of France.

"And this is the appropriation, following close upon that unanimous vote of 217 members of the House, that the execution of the Treaty of 1831 should be maintained and insisted upon. This is the appropriation so tainted with man-worship, so corrupt, so unconstitutional, that the indignant and patriotic eloquence of the 'National Intelligencer' would sooner see a foreign foe battering down the walls of the Capitol than agree to it."

If this reference to the declaration of Webster caused the members of the House to catch their breath, the next sentence brought the Democrats to their feet with prolonged cheers and shouts.

"Sir," Adams continued, "for a man uttering such sentiments there would be but one step more, a natural and an easy one to take, and that would be, with the enemy at the walls of the Capitol, to join him in battering them down."

With the Whigs dazed, and the Democrats shouting their approval, James K. Polk, in the chair, was forced to hammer vigorously with his gavel before he could restore any semblance of order — and the old man lunged again at Webster's argument.

"Are we to be told," he asked, "that this and the other House must not appropriate money unless by recommendation from the Executive? Why, sir, the Executive has told us now that that appropriation was perfectly in accord with his wishes. Yet here the charge is inverted, and unconstitutional conspiracy and man-worship are imputed to this House on account of that appropriation because it was approved and desired by the Executive. Where was the possibility of a recommendation from the Executive; of statements from the departments; of messages between this and the other House, when the resolution of the House had been passed but the day before?. . ."

And man-worship? Here Adams refused to follow his fellow Whigs in withholding commendation from the patriotism of the President.

"I will appeal to the House to say whether I am a worshiper of the Executive. . . . Neither the measure of issuing letters of marque and reprisal, nor the measures of commercial interdict or restriction — neither had that House approved; but the House, and, thank God, the people of the country, have done homage to the spirit which had urged to the recommendation, even of those measures which they did not approve. Why must the House be charged with man-worship and unconstitutional conspiracy, because they passed an appropriation of three millions for the defense of the country, at a time when imminent danger of war was urged, as resulting from that very resolution, which, but the night before, passed by a unanimous vote? Because, forsooth, that appropriation had not been asked for by the Executive; and yet because it was approved by the Executive."

In reviewing the action of both Senate and House on the President's recommendation, Adams scornfully and contemptuously dismissed the Clay resolution in a few words: "A resolution not only declining to do that which the President had recommended to vindicate the rights and honor of the Nation, but positively determining to do nothing — not even to express a sense of the wrongs which the country was enduring from France."

"And now, sir," he continued, "where is all this scaffolding of indignation and horror at the appropriation for specific purposes, for the defense of the country, because, forsooth, it had not been recommended by the Special Message of the Executive? Gone, sir, gone! You shall look for it and you shall not find it. You shall find no more trace of it than, in the tales of the 'National Intelligencer,' you shall find of that vote of 217 yeas — which was the real voucher for the purity and patriotism of that appropriation of $3,000,000 — denounced to the world by the eloquent orators of the senatorial press as so profligate and corrupt, that an enemy at the gates of this Capitol could not have justified a vote in its favor to arrest his arm, and stay his hand in battering down these walls. You shall find no more trace of it upon the journals of the Senate than you shall find of sensibility to the wrongs which our country was enduring from France."

The old man eloquent thence passed to the complaint that the Senate was ignorant of the reasons impelling the House to the adoption of the amendment, and tore it to shreds; and then on to the responsibility for the failure of the bill. This, he contended, was due to the very spirit of the Senate — its temper an insult to the President and the House. The Webster motion to adhere, he said, was always considered a "challenge," and had never before been made at such an early stage of a difference between the Houses. "It was a special disposition," he said, "to cast odium on the House, a special bravado that induced the Senate thus to draw the sword, and throw away the scăbbard — and they adhered."

Turning then to the willingness of the Senate, when it was too late, to accept an amendment for $800,000 instead of $3,000,000, he continued:

"Thus, sir, this horrible conspiracy against the Constitution melted down to a mere question of dollars and cents." And when this agreement was reached by the Senate, the House was dead — the hour of midnight having passed. He did not himself believe that a Congress died at midnight, but others did, and they were conscientious. And the Senate, knowing of that situation, had the insolence to adopt its resolution of reminder and send it to the House. "But to complete the true character of that message we must inquire at what time it was sent. It was sent at two o'clock in the morning; it was sent at a time when it was known, both in the House and the Senate, that no quorum was to be found. When that message was delivered, I must confess, if ever a feeling of shame and indignation had filled my bosom, it was at that moment. I felt it was an insult to the immediate representatives of the people; and if it had been sent at a moment when the House existed, with the power to resent unprovoked insult, I verily believe, that, imitating the example of our Congress in a somewhat similar case during the Revolutionary War, I should have moved that a message be sent by two members of the House to cast the Senate message on their floor, and tell them it was not the custom of the House to receive insolent messages." [1]

Thus did Adams the Whig stand forth as the special champion of the President and the Democratic House, and tear the Webster sophistry to tatters; thus did he serve notice that, outside the more selfish politicians of the Whig Opposition, the Nation applauded the spirit of Jackson and was prepared to follow him against any foreign foe. The speech was the sensation of the day, and Adams was never forgiven. Henry A. Wise, the brilliant Virginia Whig, followed in a remarkable medley of gossipy charges against his colleagues, but his effort was so novel in its irregularities that it destroyed itself — and the fight over the loss of the Fortifications Bill is told in the speeches of Webster and Adams. The Whigs pursued the latter with their resentment to the polls in the autumn of that year, and he was able to record, after the

[1] *Cong. Globe,* II, 130–32. Reference is also made to the debate in Sargent's *Public Men and Events,* I, 309.

election, that he was "reëlected to the next Congress without formal opposition, but almost without Whig votes." And looking back at the end of the year, and recording his impressions, he referred to his reply to Webster with evident relish. "It demolished the speech of Webster," he wrote, "drove him from the field, and whipped him and his party into the rank and file of the Nation in the quarrel with the French King." [1] It did something more; it disclosed the fact that the Whig leaders, in their hate of Jackson, approached perilously near disloyalty to their country. If Jackson won his fight, it was after battling against, not only the Government of France, but against the party Opposition at home. And fighting this double battle, he won.

IX

Adams spoke on January 21, 1836, while Congress was considering the recommendations of the Special Message. Alphonse Pageot, and his wife and son, Andrew Jackson, were in New York awaiting passage back to France; and two days after the French Chargé left New York, Charles Bankhead, the British Chargé d'Affaires at Washington, acting on instructions from his Government, offered the mediation of England in the settlement of the Franco-American dispute, in a letter to Forsyth. Jackson and his Secretary of State took six days to deliberate on the proposal before giving a formal answer. The note, signed, and no doubt prepared by Forsyth, is a strong and polished review of the controversy, a reiteration of Livingston's contention that no nation has the right to attempt an interference with the "consultation" of the departments of the American Government, and an explicit reservation that the American Government would not make the explanation or apology prescribed by the Government of France. There is no single sign of weakening, absolutely nothing new in the way of a concession, and

[1] Adams's *Memoirs*, Dec. 29, 1836.

only a repetition of the Livingston notes to the Duc de Broglie.

Twelve days later, Bankhead informed Forsyth of the success of the mediation. "The French Government," he wrote, "has stated . . . that the frank and honorable manner in which the President has, in his recent Message, expressed himself in regard to the points of difference between the Governments of France and the United States, has removed those difficulties, upon the score of national honor, which have hitherto stood in the way of the prompt execution by France of the treaty." [1] This was a complete reversal. The President had "expressed himself on the points of difference" through Livingston, in conversation, and through notes to both de Rigny and de Broglie, and he had expressed himself to them precisely as in "his recent Message." And it was after he had thus expressed himself that France had insisted that an explanation or apology prescribed by her should be made as a condition to the execution of the treaty. Jackson added nothing; France accepted what she had scornfully refused before, and the triumph of Jackson was complete. On May 10th Jackson was able to inform Congress that France had paid the four installments due. Thus, after the failures of the Administrations of Jefferson, Madison, Monroe, and Adams to get a settlement with France, Jackson had negotiated a treaty within two years of his first inauguration, and had enforced the observance of the treaty almost a year before the expiration of his last term.

The theory of some historians that Jackson, in his dealings with foreign nations, was lacking in finesse and success, is manifestly colored by blind prejudice. The prestige of the Nation abroad was never so high as after his stern insistence that a treaty with the United States could no more be disregarded than one with any of the European Powers. John Fiske touched the real significance of the result of the con-

[1] *Messages and Papers*, III, 221–22.

troversy when he wrote that "the days when foreign powers could safely insult us were evidently gone by." [1] And the same historian discloses the necessity for the position assumed by Jackson. "In foreign affairs," he writes, "Jackson's Administration won great credit through its enforcement of the French spoliation claims. European nations which had claims for damages against France on account of spoliations committed by French cruisers during the Napoleonic wars, had no difficulty after the Peace of 1815 in obtaining payment; but the claims of the United States had been superciliously neglected." [2] And so pronounced a partisan as John W. Foster, Secretary of State under the second Harrison, has recorded the deliberate judgment that "in its foreign relations his Administration maintained a dignified and creditable attitude." [3]

The Whig leaders in the Senate and the press, the Clays and Websters and the Gales, had permitted their bitterness against Jackson to lead them to the verge of disloyalty to country, and the indignant protest of Adams was a true reflection of the popular opinion. The clever politicians of the Kitchen Cabinet were not slow to see the opportunity again to picture Jackson as the patriotic hero, for the second time leading his people in a fight against a foreign adversary.

[1] Fiske's *Historical Essays*, I, 308. [2] *Ibid.*, 307.

[3] Foster's *A Century of American Diplomacy*, 273.

CHAPTER XV

THE BATTLE OF THE SUCCESSION

I

FROM the adjournment of Congress in March, 1835, until it convened in December, the political leaders concerned themselves with presidential politics, and the struggle for position was desperate and unscrupulous. From the hour in the first year of his first Administration, when Jackson, fearful of an early death, wrote his celebrated letter to Judge Overton expressing a preference for Van Buren, the latter had been looked upon as the crown prince. From that hour the master political manipulators surrounding Jackson made no move not intended to advance the "magician" toward the goal of his ambition. In the summer of 1833 Major Lewis was disturbed over the prospective candidacy of Justice McLean,[1] but it failed to materialize, and, within a year after the Major's trepidation, the White House circle realized that the most serious challenge to the plans for the succession would come from Hugh Lawson White of Tennessee, considered a renegade from the Jackson camp. The close attachment of the President and the Senator from his State had perceptibly cooled in less than a year after the inauguration. The latter was of a proud and sensitive temperament, and the growing intimacy of his old friend with the new school of practical politicians was enough to estrange him. Had he hoped in the beginning to become the legatee of Jackson, we should have a plausible explanation of his bitter resentment of the President's failure to observe his one-term pledge. We only know that he drifted, first into the position of an independent supporter of the Administration, and later into one of frank

[1] Lewis to Hamilton, Hamilton's *Reminiscences,* 259.

hostility. His imagination began early to play pranks with his judgment. He began to seek evidence of slights. In all the new school of Jacksonian leaders he saw enemies. He carefully scrutinized the "Globe" for discriminations against him. That there was no conscious effort on the part of the paper to ignore him is shown in the action of Blair, on learning that the Senator was offended. In a cordial letter he assured the suspicious Senator that he felt "the most perfect consciousness" that he had "done nothing to offend — certainly not intentionally," and begged him to "frankly state the offense that it may be righted." The curt, ungracious reply of White was overlooked and an appeal made for a personal interview, but the response was so repellent that further attempts at a reconciliation were abandoned. There is some justification for the conclusion that White had early determined upon a quarrel with the view to placing himself at the head of the opposition wing of the Democratic Party. In 1833 the Opposition began to claim him as its own when he supported Calhoun's bill on Executive patronage in a powerful speech, and joined Clay in opposing the Administration plan in the Nullification fight.

It is not surprising that under these conditions the small faction of the Democratic Party should have turned to him as the logical man to pit against the pretensions of Van Buren. The former was a Southerner, the latter a Northerner, and the slavery controversy had become acute. The fact that White was a Tennesseean was expected to embarrass and handicap Jackson in his support of the New Yorker. To the Whigs he not only presented the best prospect for a schism in the party in power, but for a time the leaders actually considered the wisdom of making him their own candidate. Clay was fearful that his candidacy would fail to infuse among the Whigs "the spirit and zeal necessary to insure success," but thought he might, as an independent candidate, "obtain the undivided support of the South and

South-West," and thus throw the contest into the House and defeat Van Buren.[1] Thus all the elements were present to make his disaffection probable. Hurt by what he conceived to be Jackson's ingratitude, jealous of the new friends that haunted the White House, importuned by the anti-Administration Democrats, and cleverly encouraged by the Whigs, he was gradually pushed into the attitude of a candidate. To all of these, the gossips of the day, malignant as always, added a new reason, which they insisted was the predominant one — the ambition of his wife.[2]

Just before he decided upon the plunge, the Whigs had been assiduous in their cultivation of him, and ardent in their expressions of sympathy because of the harsh treatment accorded him by his old friend in the White House. One of the most persistent of the tempters was Clay's intimate and reflector, R. P. Letcher, Representative from Kentucky, who had maintained the most constant social relations with the Whites during the preceding winter, ingratiating himself into the old man's confidence, and frequently enjoying the hospitality of his home. The hollow mockery of Letcher's attachment appeared in a letter to a friend, written a little later, in which he galloped over the gossip of the capital, and announced that "Judge White is on the track running gaily, and won't come off; and if he would, his wife would n't let him."[3] A more suspicious man than the Tennessee Senator might have found, in this, evidence of treachery and duplicity. The slur on Mrs. White was resented by Blair, in a stinging editorial in the "Globe," but his excoriation of Letcher does not appear to have given White a more favorable impression of the editor.[4] The intimation regarding Mrs. White was basely false, the slur wholly unjustified.

By the spring of 1834, White had announced his candidacy

[1] Clay's *Works*, v, 393–94. [2] Benton's *Thirty Years' View*.

[3] This letter was published in the *Frankfort Argus* and copied by Blair into the *Washington Globe*, Nov. 28, 1835.

[4] *Washington Globe*, Nov. 30, 1835.

and the gage of battle was thus thrown down to Jackson in Tennessee, which became the battle-ground. In the autumn of that year, while on a visit to the Hermitage, Jackson, on learning of the partiality of many for the Senator, had entered into a warm defense of his favorite, ridiculed the prospects of White outside his own State, and, in more conciliatory mood, proposed the nomination of the Tennesseean for Vice-President with a view to the succession on the expiration of Van Buren's term. Learning of these interviews, White wrote to James K. Polk, knowing his intimacy with the President, inquiring as to his information on the presidential position, but the only satisfaction he received was a warning to give no credence to any such gossip unless from an unquestionable source.[1] But if Polk was not then familiar with Jackson's uncompromising hostility to White's aspirations, he was not to remain long in doubt. It was the plan of the Jackson organization in Tennessee, led by Polk and Felix Grundy, to simulate sympathy with the Senator's ambition, and persuasively lead him into the shambles of the Baltimore Convention. But when he refused to go passively to the slaughter, and a meeting of the Tennessee congressional delegation was called in the interest of his candidacy, Polk and Grundy refused to attend, threw off the mask, and declared open war. Thus the fight was extended into the congressional elections in Tennessee in the summer of 1835, with Polk assuming the leadership of the Administration forces, taking the stump in opposition to White's candidacy, and throwing the weight of his Nashville paper into the scale. Henceforth Polk's attitude was courageous. He would be glad to see a son of Tennessee elevated to the Presidency if it could be done in regulation manner by the Democratic Party, but he would not countenance any attempt to divide the party in the interest of the Whigs. The National Democracy favored Van Buren, and it was the duty of Tennessee not to separate from the party in the Nation.

[1] Polk to White, *Memoir of Hugh Lawson White*, 254.

The elections resulted in the triumph of White's followers, with casualties among Jackson's congressional followers, but Polk was triumphantly reëlected, and he redoubled his efforts. At a series of banquets he denounced the attempt of Democrats to create a schism in the face of the common enemy. But immediately afterwards the Legislature, through the adoption of resolutions, formally nominated White for the Presidency.

II

Although the fame of Hugh Lawson White has been obscured by the years, he was familiarly known to his generation as "the Cato of the Senate." Without sparkle or magnetism, the purity of his character, the soundness of his common sense, his fidelity to duty, and assiduous application commanded respect if not admiration. His senatorial speeches were noteworthy because of their temperate tone — rare in his generation. Clarity and strength characterized his every utterance. If his speeches lacked eloquence, they smacked of statesmanship and substance. No member of the Senate more impressively looked the part. Tall, slender, and well-proportioned, with a broad forehead and deep-set, serious, penetrating blue eyes, he was the embodiment of senatorial dignity. With long gray hair, brushed back from his forehead, and curling at some length on his shoulders, he appeared the patriarch. In repose, he was sad and stern. Because of the rarity and thoroughness of his speeches, he commanded the respect and confidence of his colleagues. He looked upon his duties with the solemnity of the Roman Senator of the noblest period of the Roman Republic. Always heard with attention, he was attentive to others, and he was frequently the one listener to an uninteresting speech. Even in familiar conversation, he rarely jested outside the domestic circle, and, while an interesting and instructive conversationalist about his own fireside, he was apt to be taciturn and retiring in company. Had fate ordained that he should have reached the Presidency, he would have made a safe, conventional Executive, and he would be remembered as a pure, patriotic public servant. Such was the man who was to give Jackson, in the election of his successor, his only uneasy hours.

III

THE concern of the Jackson organization over White's candidacy may be read in the persistency of Blair's vigorous denunciations in the "Washington Globe." Beginning in the early spring and continuing throughout the summer, the Administration organ teemed with attacks on the Tennessee Senator and his most ardent champion, John Bell, Speaker of the House of Representatives. The ill-advised announcement of White's followers that his candidacy was intended to destroy the landmarks of party gave the editor his cue. "This artifice," wrote Blair, "has been so frequently attempted, and in vain, by those seeking to divide and destroy the Republican [Democratic] Party in this country, that we would have supposed the design would not have been confessed on the part of those supporting the interests of a man, who, up to the age of sixty, at least has made it his boast to support his party firmly, as the only means of maintaining his principles. But he now seeks office at the hands of the Opposition, and like all new solicitors for the favor of Federalism, becomes a no-party man." [1] The fact that White had voted with the Whigs on the Fortifications Bill was made the text of many discourses on the questionable character of his patriotism; his connection with Calhoun offered the opportunity to picture him as a half-disguised friend of Nullification. The encouragement given his candidacy by the Whig leaders was interpreted as a desertion of the house of his friends to do the work of the enemy. Tying him up tightly

[1] *Washington Globe*, April 2, 1835.

with the Whigs and the Nullifiers, attacking the no-party idea as a wooden horse of Troy in which discredited Federalism planned to reënter the Capitol, Blair smote the Tennesseean hip and thigh throughout the summer.

But scarcely less offensive to the "Globe" than White was John Bell, and the determination of the organization to prevent his reëlection to the Speakership was evident in the systematic attacks upon his record. Beginning in May, and continuing through the summer, there was scarcely an issue of the "Globe" that did not deal with some phase of Bell's alleged perfidy, in a special article.[1] The virulent hostility to Bell, of the Kitchen Cabinet, was not due in whole to his relations with the candidacy of White. Following his election over Polk to the Speakership, Duff Green, in the "Telegraph," ascribed Polk's defeat to his support by the Kitchen Cabinet, and described "Kendall, Blair, and Lewis parading the lobby" in attempts to drum up votes for their favorite. This had been bluntly denied by Blair, who insisted that he had spoken to no one on the Speakership, and that Lewis was "known to have been inclined to Mr. Bell's election."[2] But the charge in the "Telegraph" had been accepted by many and the pride of the Jackson leaders had been aroused. The White candidacy, Bell's espousal of it, and Polk's determined stand against it, made it imperative that Bell should be retired in the interest of Polk.

Meanwhile the Baltimore Convention assembled on May 20, 1835 — an assembly that no more deserves the popular reproach of being a convention of office-holders than the average convention of the dominant party ever since. The absence of delegates from South Carolina and Illinois was

[1] May 28th, "Mr. Bell and the Speakership"; May 30th, "Mr. Bell and Judge White"; June 1st, "The Bank President and Mr. Bell"; June 2d, "Mr. Bell and the Bank"; June 3d, "Mr. Bell — His Banking Facilities"; June 4th, "The Result of Mr. Bell's Machinations"; July 3d, "Bell and Gales"; July 10th, "John Bell and Davy Crockett"; August 21st, "Mr. Bell's Preparation to Bargain Off Judge White's Party in the House of Representatives."

[2] *Washington Globe*, June 5, 1834.

tolerable to the Jacksonians, but the failure of Tennessee to appear, notwithstanding the personal importunities of the President, was painfully embarrassing. That had to be corrected. A comparatively unknown Tennesseean, E. Rucker, was found in the city, and literally pushed into the convention to cast the unauthorized vote of Tennessee — and thus the word "Ruckerize" was added to the vocabulary of practical politicians. The polished Andrew Stevenson, who had resigned the Speakership to accept the diplomatic post in London, only to share the fate of Van Buren, was called upon to deliver the "keynote" address in the capacity of chairman. But this honor, bestowed upon the Virginians, was more than neutralized by New York's desertion of her Virginia allies in the nomination of the vice-presidential candidate.

Never had the Old Dominion been dominated by a more powerful machine than that led by Judge Spencer Roane, a man of great intellectual force, who had been favored by Jefferson for the Chief Justiceship. He had a powerful colleague in his cousin, Thomas Ritchie, the forceful editor of the "Richmond Enquirer." Stevenson was an important member of the clique, and no one was closer to its leader than the scholarly Senator William C. Rives, who had, as Jackson's first Minister to France, negotiated the indemnity settlement. The Virginians had early pledged themselves to the political fortunes of Van Buren. The alliance of the two States, Virginia and New York, was one of the significant facts in the politics of the day. Never doubting the loyalty of their ally, Roane and his organization determined to dictate the nomination of Rives for the Vice-Presidency with a view to the succession. It was not until the eve of the convention that the Virginians learned, to their dismay, that the New Yorkers had other plans. Almost incredulous, chagrined, disturbed, Ritchie hastened to write Rives of the new developments. He had heard that "some of our strongest friends in Washington" were looking with favor on Richard M. Johnson of Kentucky. Van Buren's preference was a mystery. However, Ritchie had been pressing Rives's claims and had written letters, not only to delegates, but to "a gentleman in Washington, who can, if he thinks fit, exercise a sort of potential voice." But unhappily for the Virginians, Lewis, Kendall, Blair, Silas Wright, and Hill were opportunists, with their eyes upon the West, in view of the candidacy of both Harrison and White. It was clear to them that expediency demanded the nomination of a Westerner for the Vice-Presidency. The stubborn, and now thoroughly outraged, Virginians refused to acquiesce in the reasoning of the Kitchen Cabinet, and Rives went down before the first of the "steam rollers" that have become so commonplace in national conventions.[1] Thoroughly disgusted by what they conceived to be a betrayal, the Virginia organization declared open war on Johnson, and Van Buren was much perturbed. But that wily diplomat, assisted by Silas Wright, immediately took personal charge of the work of conciliation, writing numerous letters to Rives and Ritchie, and the storm was stilled for the time when Van Buren made a journey to Castle Hill, the country home of the defeated candidate, where the fatted calf was killed and the leaders of the Roane organization were invited to participate in the feast and to accept the apologies and pledges of the presidential nominee.

IV

MEANWHILE the Whigs were in a quandary as to what to do, with their greatest popular leader, noting a tendency to set him aside, spending the summer at Ashland in bitterness of soul. In a letter written in July he had unbosomed himself to a friend, with the confession that he had thought it probable that his party would again turn to him, but had noted a tendency to "discourage the use of my name." In Ohio,

[1] Ambler's *Thomas Ritchie*, 170.

where he was popular, the Legislature had discredited his possible candidacy by its endorsement of Justice McLean. In the spirit of an Achilles sulking in his tent, he discussed the various names canvassed, pointing out their weaknesses. White would be intolerable as a Whig candidate because "he has been throughout a supporter of the Jackson Administration and holds no principle, except in the matter of patronage, as to public measures, in common with the Whigs." While he thought Webster's attainments greatly superior to those of any other candidate, "it is to be regretted that a general persuasion seems to exist that he stands no chance." Harrison was damned with the faint praise that he "could easier obtain the vote of Kentucky than any other candidate named." The only rift in the clouds that he could see was in the nomination of three candidates, with White as one of the three, to draw off the Democratic strength in the South and portions of the West, and the defeat of Van Buren by thus throwing the contest into the House.[1] That this plan was uppermost in the minds of the Whigs is shown in a letter to Clay from James Barbour of Virginia, in August. Because of the slavery question, he thought White the strongest candidate to be pressed against Van Buren in Virginia. Webster was out of the question. McLean, not even considered. Harrison, after White, would make the strongest appeal. "It seems to me," he continued, "that we have no prospect of excluding Van Buren but by the plan you suggest, of selecting two candidates who will be the strongest in their respective sections. White, I apprehend, for the South, Webster for the East, North and West, or whomsoever Pennsylvania prefers." [2] Thus, in the correspondence of the Whig leaders, we have the proof that White was intrigued into the race by the Whigs with the view to furthering their own interest, and not his.

By September, Clay, having met Harrison in Cincinnati,

[1] Clay's *Works*, v, 393–95. [2] *Ibid.*, 397–99.

and finding him "respectful and cordial," was more cordial toward his candidacy, although he preferred any choice Pennsylvania might announce. The Rhode Island and Connecticut elections had shown that "it is in vain to look even to New England for the support of Mr. Webster." [1] Out of this confusion of counsels, Harrison ultimately emerged with the general support of the Whigs, but, like the Democrats, the Whigs were to be embarrassed by a double tail to their ticket. With the popular sentiment favoring Tyler, the politicians, with their eyes on the Anti-Masons, nominated Granger. It was the contention of contemporaries that Clay, who had engineered the move against Tyler, feared that the concentration of the Whigs on some strong candidate for the Vice-Presidency might result in his election with Van Buren, because of the dissatisfaction of the Virginia Whigs with Johnson; and that a Whig Vice-President, under a Democratic President, would become a formidable rival for the presidential nomination in 1840.[2] Both Tyler and Granger, however, remained in the field, thus dividing the vote in the election.

The Massachusetts Whigs, nothing daunted by the turn of affairs, remained faithful to Webster, who was placed in the field; and in South Carolina, where Calhoun's followers made a point of separating themselves from all parties and all other States, Senator Willie P. Mangum was nominated. Thus, in the campaign of 1836 there were five candidates, with the Democrats united behind Van Buren, and the Opposition dividing its strength between Harrison, White, Webster, and Mangum. Nothing could have been more to the liking of the Democracy. It entered the campaign in solid ranks except in Tennessee, where even the magic name of Jackson was unable to prevent a schism which was to result in the humiliation of the venerable chief.

[1] Clay's *Works*, v, 399.

[2] *Letters and Times of the Tylers*, I, 519.

V

During the summer of 1835 the militant methods of the Abolitionists forced the slavery question to the front to the embarrassment of the politicians and the candidates. The Nation was still on edge because of the anti-slavery and anti-abolition riots of the year before, when George Thompson, the Abolition firebrand from England, arrived in America with exhortations to the Northerners to end slavery at once. The South was outraged, the North, shocked. Coincident with Thompson's mad crusade, the American Anti-Slavery Society, having collected a large sum of money for the purpose, began to circularize the country, and especially the South, with literature calculated to arouse the slaves to insurrection.[1] The defense of the abolitionists was that the literature was sent to the whites alone; but much of it fell into the hands of the blacks, and excitement reached fever heat. In Philadelphia a pouch of these tracts was confiscated by a mob, and sunk in the Delaware River. In Charleston the mail was searched for them, and three thousand citizens assembled at night to witness their destruction in a bonfire. Mass meetings were held in all the larger Northern cities to denounce the desperate enterprise of the abolitionists, and in Boston the citizens packed Faneuil Hall to hear Harrison Gray Otis denounce them in a spirited address. When Thompson, in one of his inflammatory speeches, proposed that the slaves should arise and cut their masters' throats, the bitterness in the North was as pronounced as in the South, and after Garrison had narrowly escaped the rope through the intercession of the Mayor of Boston, whom he had scathingly attacked in his paper, the English orator went into hiding until he could be spirited out of the country. The most important effect of this miserable blunder of the abolitionists was to force

[1] John Quincy Adams could see no other object.

the slavery question into politics, and from that hour on, the slave-owners of the South became dominant in the politics of the Republic.

It is certain that Jackson, like all other responsible leaders, abhorred these appeals to the slaves to rise and cut their masters' throats. The burden of dealing with an important phase of the problem, the transmission of such matter through the mail, fell upon the Administration, and in the absence of any law to prevent it. But when the postmasters of New York and Charleston wrote Postmaster-General Kendall for instructions, that astute politician replied that the United States should not carry such matter in the mail; and, acting upon the hint, the postmasters threw all such matter out with the tacit consent of the Government.

The Opposition, however, planned to turn the hatred of the abolitionists against Van Buren, who was hostile to the extension of slavery. Writing to Clay in the late summer of 1835, Senator Barbour rejoiced in the injection of the slavery question as certain to injure the Democratic nominee.[1] The close political associates of Van Buren were keenly alive to the danger, and John Forsyth wrote him that unless something should be done in New York he "should not be at all surprised at a decisive movement to establish a Southern Confederacy," and suggested that "a portion of the Magician's skill is required in this matter . . . and the sooner you set the imps to work the better." [2] Whether the wily politician "set the imps to work" we do not know, but within a month of the writing of the letter the New York postmaster publicly announced that he would refuse to forward the objectionable literature. This was given the widest publicity; so, too, the letter of Amos Kendall accepting and endorsing the action of the New York official. And about the same time, whether due to the Van Buren "imps" or not, one of the

[1] Clay's *Works*, v, 378.
[2] Forsyth to Van Buren, Butler's *Retrospect of Forty Years*, 78, 79.

greatest meetings ever held in New York was held in the park to denounce the methods of the abolitionists. Nothing was done by Van Buren personally, in a public way, to divorce himself from all sympathy with the abolition movement.

The Whig nominee, determined publicly to repudiate the abolition methods, found an opportunity at a dinner in his honor at Vincennes, Indiana, in a speech intended as a friendly gesture to the slave-holding States, and for the cultivation of such of those in Virginia as were prone to associate Van Buren with the abolition sentiment in portions of New York.[1] The position of White was as clearly fixed on slavery as that of Calhoun, and we shall observe a little later how the latter sought to place Van Buren in a position hostile to Southern interests.

VI

MEANWHILE Van Buren serenely went his way, undisturbed by the storm, and in the best of humor. Soon after the Baltimore Convention, the most unconventional campaign biography ever published in America was issued by a Philadelphia publishing house and given an extensive circulation. The present generation scarcely realizes that there were two Davy Crocketts — the man of the woods and the fight, and the less admirable creature who made a rather sorry figure in the Congress. It was the latter who was persuaded to write a part, and to father all, of this scurrilous biography of Van Buren, although it is generally accepted that Hugh Lawson White, the man of ponderous dignity and lofty ideals, was the man behind this questionable literary venture.[2] The personal references to Van Buren are crudely and coarsely offensive throughout.

"He is about fifty years old," he wrote, "and notwithstanding his baldness, which reaches all around and half

[1] See Montgomery's *Life of Harrison*, 308–10.
[2] This is Shepard's view in his *Life of Van Buren*, 256.

down his head, like a white pitch plaster, leaving a few white floating locks, he is only three years older than I am. His face is a good deal shriveled, and he looks sorry, not for anything he has gained, but what he may lose." [1] In describing his subject's mental operations, he found that "his mind beats round, like a tame bear tied to a stake, in a little circle, hardly bigger than the circumference of the head in which it is placed, seeking no other object than to convert the Government into an instrument to serve himself or his office-holding friends." [2]

In explaining Van Buren's rise, the hero of young Texas proceeded: "He has become a great man without any reason for it, and so have I. He has been nominated for President without the least pretensions; and so have I. But here the similarity stops. From his cradle he was on the non-committal tribe. I never was. He had always two ways to do a thing; I never had but one. He was generally half bent; I tried to be as straight as a gun barrel. He could not bear his rise; I never minded mine. He forgot all his old associates because they were poor folks; I stuck to the people that made me." [3]

And in a superb bit of demagogy, Crockett described Van Buren as traveling through the country in an English coach with "English servants dressed in uniform — I think they call it livery"; refusing to mix "with the sons of the little tavern-keepers," forgetting "his old companions and friends in the humbler walks of life"; eating "in a room by himself," and carrying himself "so stiff in his gait and prim in his dress, that he was what the English call a Dandy." The reader was assured that "when he enters the Senate Chamber in the morning, he struts and swaggers like a crow in a gutter," that he "is laced up in corsets such as women in town wear, and if possible tighter than the best of them." Indeed, Crockett found it "difficult to tell from his personal

[1] Crockett's *Life of Van Buren*, 26. [2] *Ibid.*, 58. [3] *Ibid.*, 27.

appearance whether he was a man or a woman." [1] The Eaton scandal was salaciously served anew, the fight between Jackson and Benton was described in detail, and, unfortunately for his candidate for President, a chapter was devoted to a hot defense of White on the Bank and on the Fortifications Bill.

The book, now happily forgotten, is only interesting and historically important in indicating the tone of the political contests of the time, and the scurrility of the attacks on Van Buren in the campaign. If the Little Magician enjoyed the queer concoction, it was not without the realization of its possibility for doing harm. At any rate, a little later, another and a friendly biography by Holland was published, seriously reviewing Van Buren's public career. While not written in bad taste, it aroused the ire of John Quincy Adams who took the time to read it. "A mere partisan electioneering work," he wrote in his diary. "Van Buren's personal character bears, however, a stronger resemblance to that of Mr. Madison than to that of Mr. Jefferson. These are both remarkable for their extreme caution in avoiding and averting personal collisions. Van Buren, like the Sosie of Molière's 'Amphitryon,' is 'l'ami de tout le monde.' This is perhaps the secret of his great success in public life, and especially against the competitors with whom he is now struggling for the last step on the ladder of his ambition — Henry Clay and John C. Calhoun. They, indeed, are left upon the field for dead; and men of straw, Hugh L. White, William Henry Harrison, and Daniel Webster, are thrust forward in their places. Neither of these has a principle to lean upon." [2]

If these intrigues and attacks disturbed Van Buren in the least, he gave no sign. During a ten-day sojourn in New York in October, Philip Hone, who vainly sought an open date to entertain him at dinner, found "his outward appearance like the unruffled surface of the majestic river

[1] Crockett's *Life of Van Buren*, 80. [2] Adams's *Diary*, April 13, 1835.

which covers rocks and whirlpools, but shows no marks of the agitation beneath." [1] In this same good temper, he faced the ordeal of presiding over the Senate, dominated by his political foes, in the long session preceding the election. We shall here find him threading his way among pitfalls provided by his enemies with such skill as to conceal all effort.

VII

The halls of Congress in the session of December, 1835, were used as the hustings, and there, largely, the presidential battle was fought. The first blow was struck by the Jacksonians in the election of Polk to the Speakership, over Bell. The latter was a man of much capacity, considered by Van Buren as the intellectual superior of White, and he had been elected to the Speakership, on the resignation of Stevenson, through a combination of the Whigs and anti-Administration Democrats. In seeking a reconciliation with the Jacksonians, he had hinted at a desire for a confidential conference with Van Buren, and the two were finally invited to dine with a mutual friend. Unhappily for Bell, a severe toothache, real or diplomatic, forced the candidate of the Jacksonian Democracy to retire the moment the ladies left the table. When a few days later the two found themselves together on the speakers' rostrum on the occasion of the delivery of Adams's oration on Lafayette, Bell had attempted to discuss the differences of the factions, but the canny Red Fox "put a civil end to the conversation with a few general remarks in regard to the duty the friends of Judge White owed" to the party, and soon afterward the Tennessee Senator had entered the field, and Bell was forced to espouse his cause.[2] Thus the course of history may have been changed by the toothache of a politician. At any rate, it was enough, to the Jacksonian leaders, to know that Polk had risked his

[1] Hone's *Diary*, Oct. 26, 1835. [2] Van Buren's *Autobiography*, 225–26, n.

popularity and future by taking the offensive in favor of Van Buren, and he was rewarded with the Speakership.

The Whigs instantly accepted the challenge by bitterly opposing the confirmation of Roger B. Taney as Chief Justice of the United States. No one questioned his professional ability or his eminent fitness for a high judicial position. Bitterly hostile as he was to Jackson's Bank policy, John Marshall had recognized Taney's qualifications for the bench when the President had previously made an unsuccessful attempt to elevate his former Secretary of the Treasury to that tribunal. At that time the venerable Chief Justice had quietly interested himself in his successor's behalf, and among the papers of Senator Leigh, still in possession of the family, is the brief but significant note from Marshall: "If you have not made up your mind on the nomination of Mr. Taney, I have received some information in his favor which I would wish to communicate." [1] But after Marshall's death and Taney's appointment, the Whig and pro-Bank politicians attempted to array all the late jurist's friends and admirers against the confirmation by picturing Jackson as not only hostile to the trend of his decisions, but to the perpetuation of his memory. The "Richmond Whig" announced that "he [Jackson] thinks undue honors have been rendered to the memory of General Marshall, and predicts that the attempt to build a monument to his memory in Washington will fail." This was a willful perversion of a comment actually made to the editor of the "Southern Literary Messenger" at Rip Raps, that, in view of Jackson's inability to interest Congress in an appropriation for a monument to Washington, he was afraid that it would be impossible to build one to Marshall.[2] But the idea of the fighting Secretary of the Treasury in the seat of Marshall was maddening to the Whig leaders, and

[1] Tyler's *Life of Taney*.

[2] Blair gives the details of the conversation, in which he participated, in the *Globe* of August 12, 1835.

the nomination was attacked with intemperance and even scurrility by both Webster and Clay, and it was not until in March, three months after the nomination was sent to the Senate, that it was confirmed.

But the appearance of resolutions from legislatures, instructing Whig and pro-Bank Senators to vote to expunge the resolution of censure against Jackson, was the most bitter pill of all. Not only did it further embitter the Whigs against the Administration, but it put them at loggerheads with each other. This was especially true of the Whig Senators from Virginia, Tyler and Leigh, who took opposite views as to the inviolability of instructions. Throughout his entire career, Tyler had stoutly insisted upon the right of the people, speaking through their legislatures, to instruct their representatives in the Senate. This position had been adopted by the Virginia Whigs, and accepted by the people of the State. Because of this, Leigh now sat in the Senate, in the seat from which Rives had been instructed. But when a resolution was introduced in the Virginia Assembly, instructing the Senators from that State to vote to expunge, the Whigs began to divide on the question of compliance in the event of its adoption. There was never any question as to the attitude of John Tyler. Pilloried in history as a second-rate politician and a weakling, it is impossible to study his career without being impressed with his consistency, which was all too rare in his generation, and the unfaltering courage with which he lived up to his principles, regardless of the effect upon his personal fortunes. But Leigh, who owed his seat in the Senate to the principle of instructions, was made of less heroic clay. With the encouragement of Virginians, including Judge Brooke, who always reflected the views of Henry Clay, he began to hedge. Senator Barbour, another of Clay's intimates, urged upon Tyler sophisticated reasons for ignoring the instructions.[1] When the resolutions were adopted in

[1] *Letters and Times of the Tylers,* I, 527.

the lower branch of the legislature, the pressure of the Whigs to ignore them met with a gracious yielding on the part of Leigh, and the unscrupulous partisans were able to concentrate their efforts on Tyler. Such was the logic of party bigotry in 1836 that the Maryland Legislature, which had nominated Tyler for the Vice-Presidency, threatened to rescind the nomination if he complied with the instructions, and the future President, the truckling, tricky politician of historical caricature, expressed his disgust in a letter to his son: "These incidents look almost like a political romance in these days when everything is surrendered for office. . . . Give me the assurance that history will do me justice . . . and I will go to my grave in peace."[1] When the resolution was passed by both branches, and certified to the two Senators, Tyler, without a moment's hesitation, resigned in a dignified letter to Van Buren, and retired to private life. Leigh ignored the instructions and retained his seat, but resigned in July. This contradiction sadly crippled the Whigs in Virginia; and when, during the spring, a dinner was given the two Senators by their fellow partisans, and Tyler was lauded for his act, the spicy Thomas Ritchie, of the "Richmond Enquirer," insisted that two of the toasts were:

"John Tyler: Honor to him, because he could not, with honor, retain his seat."

"Senator Leigh: Honor to him, because he could not, with honor, relinquish his seat."

Thus Tyler passed from the ranks of the Opposition in the Senate, and William C. Rives, the friend of Jackson and Van Buren, vindicated by events, returned to strengthen the forces of the Administration.

The attitude of Ewing of Ohio toward similar resolutions by the legislature of his State was that of Leigh.[2]

All these manifestations of popular approval of the Admin-

[1] *Letters and Times of the Tylers*, I, 537.

[2] *Cong. Globe*, 1st Session, 24th Congress, 308.

istration, and dissatisfaction with the Whigs and their allies in the Senate, tended to infuriate the Opposition which found itself helpless before the tide. In Tennessee, however, the Administration was unable to secure instructions aimed at White, and the attempt merely furnished the opportunity for laudatory speeches on the Tennessee Senator, and bitter denunciations of the proposal to expunge. This defeat in Tennessee was the only hopeful sign that reached the Whigs in Washington.[1]

The greater part of the congressional session was devoted to some phase of the abolition agitation, and Calhoun bent all his efforts toward arraying the North and South against each other. He seemed determined to have it that the Northern people were in sympathy with the methods and purposes of the radical followers of Garrison. The mobs that had all but lynched Garrison, and forced the friends of Thompson to spirit him away, were Northern mobs. If the obnoxious literature had been burned by the people of Charleston, it had been thrown into the river by the people of Philadelphia and denounced by the people of Boston. No Northern statesman or politician had raised a voice in defense of the abolitionists, and most of them vied with Calhoun in their denunciation of them. But when, on January 7th, an abolition petition was presented, and Calhoun moved that it be not received and supported his motion in an intemperate speech, some of the most pronounced pro-slavery Senators took alarm. The great Nullifier declared that an irrepressible fight had been forced and should be met. "We must meet the enemy on the frontier — on the question of receiving," he said. "We must secure that important pass — it is our Thermopylæ. The power of resistance, by the universal law, is on the exterior. Break through the shell, penetrate the crust, and there is no resistance within." When, four days

[1] For story of the attempt see Foster's letter to White, *Memoir of Hugh Lawson White*, 337–38.

later, Buchanan presented a petition for the abolition of slavery in the District of Columbia and moved that it be received and rejected, Calhoun demanded that the question be put first on receiving, and a debate was precipitated which dragged along for weary weeks, ending in the defeat of Calhoun's plan.

During the period of these intermittent discussions, the "Telegraph," reflector of Calhoun, teemed with articles bitterly attacking, not so much the abolitionists as the North. This determination to treat the Northerners as enemies of Southern institutions was so apparent that a number of pro-slavery Southern Senators were moved to protest and to criticism of the Southern leader. Whether he was actuated, that early, by a desire to lay the foundation for a Southern Confederacy, or merely used this method to create feeling in the Southern States against the candidacy of Van Buren, can never be determined. But the Democrats supporting Van Buren had no doubt that the latter was the dominating motive. The sharp-tongued Isaac Hill, of New Hampshire, in a fierce assault on Calhoun's position, directly charged that the "Telegraph" had been exerting itself from the time of the Nullification movement to drive a wedge between the sections, and warned Calhoun that the agitation he was forcing on Congress played directly into the hands of the abolitionists. But the latter had determined upon his course, and appeared not only willing, but anxious, actually to break with the friends of the South among the Northerners in Congress.

If he expected, however, in his fight against receiving the petitions, to prove Van Buren hostile to the interest of the South, he failed. The ten votes he mustered were recruited from both parties. Five were Whigs,[1] three were Democrats supporting the Administration,[2] and two were against the

[1] Black of Mississippi; Leigh of Virginia; Nicholas and Porter of Louisiana; and Preston of South Carolina.

[2] Cuthbert, Moore, and Walker.

Administration and hostile to Van Buren.[1] Thus, with the exception of three Senators, all the supporters of Van Buren and the Administration voted to receive the petitions. The vote of White was unquestionably political, intended to strengthen his candidacy among the pro-slavery radicals of the Southern States.

But Calhoun was not discouraged. His political motive was more apparent in the battle over his bill to regulate the transmission of the mails, and exclude therefrom all abolition literature intended for the slave-holding States. We have noted the excitement of the preceding summer, and the attitude of Kendall. In his Message at the opening of Congress, Jackson had recommended the enactment of such a law "as will prohibit, under severe penalties, the circulation in the Southern States, through the mail, of incendiary publications intended to instigate the slaves to insurrection." Calhoun had eagerly seized upon this recommendation to move its reference to a special committee, instead of to the regularly organized Committee on Post-Offices. Buchanan opposed the suggestion on the ground that the unusual course would tend to increase the excitement of the people.[2] Grundy of Tennessee held that the very fact that the majority of the Committee on Post-Offices came from a section not directly interested would give more weight to its recommendations.[3] King of Alabama took advantage of Calhoun's queer disclaimer of a political motive to insinuate its existence, and favored the regular course for the reasons advanced by Buchanan.[4] Leigh supported Calhoun's plan on the fantastic ground that since the obnoxious mail could not be excluded by the existing post-office regulations, the Committee on Post-Offices was clearly not the proper body.[5] But it was left to Preston of South Carolina to explain bluntly the mo-

[1] Calhoun and White.
[2] *Cong. Globe,* 1st Session, 24th Congress, Dec. 21, 1835.
[3] *Ibid.* [4] *Ibid.* [5] *Ibid.*

tive of Calhoun. Since the South was especially interested, the committee should be composed of Senators from the slave-holding States. The Senate good-naturedly consented to Calhoun's plan, and a special committee was named with Calhoun as chairman.

A little later, an extreme bill, professing to meet the views of the President, was submitted, accompanied by an inflammatory report, reiterative of the compact theory of the Constitution, and calculated further to fan the excitement on the subject of abolition. Both the Administration and Whig leaders were hostile to the measure, but it best served the purpose of Calhoun to ignore the Whigs and to harp incessantly upon the opposition from Senators close to the Jackson-Van Buren organization. The report, according to the interpretation of Calhoun, set forth three propositions: that the National Government had no right to prohibit papers, no right to say what papers should be transmitted, and that these rights belonged to the States.[1] The bill provided that it should be a crime for a postmaster knowingly to receive and put into the mail any written, printed, or pictorial matter concerning slavery, directed to any post-office in a State which prohibited the circulation of such matter; that such literature, if not withdrawn from the mails within a given time, should be burned; and it made the Postmaster-General and all his subordinates responsible for the enforcement of the law.

Early in the debate the political motive appeared when King of Alabama again charged Calhoun with being moved by hostility to Jackson. What, exclaimed the bristling Carolinian, "I have too little respect for General Jackson's judgment, and if he were not President of the United States, I would say for his character, to place myself in such a position." [2] On the following day we find him striking the same note: "I cannot but be surprised at the course of the friends

[1] Calhoun's speech, *Cong. Globe*, April 12, 1836. [2] *Ibid.*

of the Executive," he said. "I have heard Senators denounce this measure, recommended by the Executive, as unconstitutional, as tyrannical, as an abuse of power, who never before dared whisper a word against the Administration. Is it because the present Executive is going out of power that his influence is declining?"[1] This constant harping on the attitude of the Administration Senators, whether so intended or not, was looked upon by them as an attempt to make political capital against Van Buren in the slave States. "I wish the gentleman would restrain the frequent repetition of such expressions," said Cuthbert of Georgia, "as they necessarily bring on him a suspicion of his sincerity. Why should this be a party question? It would show a wickedness, a recklessness of the welfare of our common country for any man to endeavor to make it so."[2]

But Calhoun persisted in his attempt to maneuver the friends of Van Buren into an attitude offensive to the Southern States. Benton notes, significantly, that it was rather remarkable that three tie votes occurred in succession, two on amendments, and one on the engrossment of the bill. His clear implication is that this was done to force Van Buren to cast a deciding vote, never doubting that it would be hostile to the measure. When the bill came up for engrossment, Calhoun demanded an aye and nay vote. When three men appeared to make a majority, three on the other side instantly appeared. At the time the vote was being taken, Van Buren had left the chair and was pacing up and down, concealed by the colonnade, behind the rostrum. Benton says that "his eyes were wide open to see what would happen."[3] He observed the keen eyes of the excited Calhoun searching the chamber for his anticipated prey. He heard him ask "eagerly and loudly" where the Vice-President had gone, and demand that the sergeant-at-arms look for him. But Van Buren had heard and seen all, and, when the

[1] *Cong. Globe*, April 13, 1836. [2] *Ibid.* [3] *Thirty Years' View*, I, 587.

time came, he calmly took the chair, and with his characteristic serenity cast the deciding vote in favor of engrossment. Benton was positive that had he voted otherwise the Calhoun faction, with the aid of the "Telegraph," would have inflamed the South against him. This would have been all the easier because Hugh Lawson White, who was playing openly for the extreme State-Rights and pro-slavery support, voted for the bill. But Van Buren and his friends were not blind to the conspiracy, and the two Democratic Senators from New York, intimate political friends of the presidential nominee, ascertaining first that their votes were not needed to defeat the measure, cast expediency votes in its favor, and thus robbed Calhoun and White of the opportunity to make political capital out of the bill. It was defeated by a vote of 25 to 19.[1]

Thus the session dragged on into June, with none of the parties gaining any material advantage for the purposes of the campaign. As the session was drawing to a close, Senator White, who took his candidacy more to heart than any of the other candidates, made a discussion of the resolution to expunge the occasion for an acidulous attack upon Jackson in the presence of Van Buren, who serenely presided. He charged that Jackson had "made up his mind who should be his successor," and had used all the power of patronage to destroy him (White). With great particularity, he went over the part the President was taking in the canvass then on, the letters he had written, the copies of the "Washington Globe" he had personally franked, the material he had furnished White's enemies upon the stump in Tennessee.[2] The personal tone of the attack appears to have made a painful impression even upon White's friends, and certainly did not disturb

[1] Charles. H. Peck in *The Jacksonian Epoch,* implies (p. 281) that the tie vote was arranged by Van Buren's friends, but Benton, who was one of the most intimate, takes the opposite view. In his *Autobiography,* Van Buren makes no reference to the incident.

[2] *Memoir of Hugh Lawson White,* 340–42.

the smiling complacency of Van Buren, who listened with courteous attention. The "Congressional Globe" of the session is filled with such assaults on Jackson and his Administration, but the Big-Wigs of both parties, with the exception of Calhoun and White, maintained an unusual reserve. But Calhoun did his part in full measure. Not only did he abuse Jackson with indecent invective, but, in the presence of Van Buren, sneered at the latter's character and ability. Jackson had "courage and firmness; is warlike, bold, audacious; but he is not true to his word and violates the most solemn pledges without scruple." He had "done the State some service, too, which is remembered greatly to his advantage." But Van Buren "has none of these recommendations." No, as Senator Mangum [1] had said, he "has none of the lion or tiger breed about him; he belongs more to the fox and the weasel." [2]

With nothing better to offer than this, the tired statesmen adjourned on July 4th, and hastened to their homes, some to sulk in their tents in disgust, others to take the field to wage the fight.

VIII

In 1836 the issues of the campaign were not so clearly defined by conditions as in 1832, nor by platform declarations, as in more recent years. The party declarations of principle had no meaning. That of the Democrats could have summed up all in the endorsement of the Jackson Administration and a pledge to continue the Jacksonian policies; that of the Whigs in a denunciation of the principles and policies of Jacksonian Democracy.

The platform of Senator White is found in his letter in reply to that of a committee informing him of his nomination — a personal protest. "When an attempt is made," he wrote, "to create a party not founded upon settled politi-

[1] South Carolina's candidate for President. [2] *Cong. Globe*, Feb. 17, 1836.

cal principles, composed of men belonging to every political sect, having no common bond of unity save that of a wish to place one of themselves in the highest office known to the Constitution, for the purpose of having all the honors, offices, and emoluments of the Government distributed by them among their followers, I consider such an association, whether composed of many or a few, a mere faction, which ought to be resisted by every man who loves his country, and wishes to perpetuate its liberties." [1]

The most influential leaders of the Whigs were not enthusiastic over any of the Opposition candidates, with the exception of Webster, who manifestly had no chance. "White and Webster are now the golden calves of the people," wrote the caustic Adams, "and their dull sayings are repeated for wit, and their grave inanity is passed off for wisdom. This bolstering up of mediocrity would seem not suited to sustain much enthusiasm." Such as there was, the cynical Puritan ascribed to the fact that "a practice of betting has crept in," and "that adds a spur of private, personal, and pecuniary interest to the impulse of patriotism." [2] Naturally, Adams was not enamoured of Van Buren, who impressed him as a "demagogue of the same school [as "Ike" Hill] with a tincture of aristocracy — an amalgamated metal of lead and copper." [3]

There was no hero worshiping of the candidates in 1836, but the worship of Jackson continued, and the Whigs contemplated the phenomenon with melancholy misgivings. Philip Hone, that faithful chronicler of Whig sentiment, found the political aspect of the country "worse than ever." Indeed, "General Jackson's star is still in the ascendant and shines brighter than ever." A month before the nomination

[1] *Memoir of Hugh Lawson White*, 333–34.

[2] Adams's *Memoirs*, Nov. 11, 1836.

[3] *Ibid.*, Oct. 9, 1834. As we have noted, however, Adams in other parts of his diary is cordial to Van Buren, and Van Buren's *Autobiography* shows the latter to have admired Adams.

of Van Buren, the Whig diarist had been forced to admit that business conditions had vastly improved.[1] In truth the Whigs were without an issue they dared advance, and could hope for success only through the amalgamation of all the disgruntled with the Whigs — the Anti-Masons, Nullifiers, State-Rights extremists, and disappointed office-seekers — and this was manifestly impossible.

The campaign was not so exciting as that of 1832, and lacked the hysteria of the stump which characterized that of 1840. The newspapers were relied upon largely for propaganda, and the "Globe" was summoned to herculean efforts. To meet the work of Blair, a campaign paper, called the "Appeal," was established in Washington to advocate the claims of White. The "Telegraph," edited by the frenzied Duff Green, viciously attacked both Jackson and Van Buren. And the work of these papers colored that of all the minor papers of the country. But the people remained calm and indifferent. The attacks upon the candidates, many bald slanders, stirred no one but the politicians. The custom of interrogating candidates had now become fixed, and the three aspirants were bombarded with questions covering a multitude of subjects.

The followers of Calhoun feverishly continued their efforts to embarrass Van Buren on the abolition movement. From North Carolina came a demand for his position on the right of Congress to abolish slavery in the District of Columbia. His answer was not as definite as the questioner had hoped. There was no question as to the right of Congress to act in the District, but the wily candidate had no intention to give a curt reply. His answer was that Congress had no right to interfere with slavery in the States — a question not put; and that he was opposed to the abolishment of slavery in the District by congressional action — which was not a reply at all.

[1] Hone's *Diary*, April 8, 1836.

Then followed the questions of the Equal Righters, or Locofocos, as they were dubbed in New York by the "Courier and Enquirer," as to Van Buren's position on their "declaration of rights." The reply of the Red Fox, that his long public career furnished a sufficient illumination of his position on the general principles of the new party, was considered by the Locos as an "evasion," and denounced as unsatisfactory "to any true Democrat."

Meanwhile Clay was exercising an unnatural restraint on his partisan zeal, remaining in strict retirement at Ashland, tending his cattle, looking over his fields, writing an occasional letter, and meditating a retirement from the Senate before the next session. During the preceding winter, the death of a favorite daughter had crushed him to the earth. He keenly felt the apparent neglect of his party. In the canvass he took no part. It was not until the campaign was nearing its close, in October, that he appeared upon the platform to discuss the candidates, and then with evident reluctance. A barbecue had been arranged at Lexington, within sight of Clay's home, and a declination to participate would have given deadly offense. He spoke, however, with unusual temperance, urging a unification of the opposition against Van Buren. This was to have been expected. Paying tribute to the civic worth of White, he announced his intention to vote for Harrison, not because he was his first choice — for he pretended to prefer Webster — but because he thought that Harrison "combined the greatest prospects of defeating Mr. Van Buren." [1]

If Clay was indifferent, his old rival, Andrew Jackson, was not. Assuming the certainty of his favorite's election, his personal pride was touched by White's challenge of his own leadership in Tennessee, and as soon as Congress adjourned, he started on the long and tiresome journey to the Hermitage.

[1] Clay to White, *Memoir of Hugh Lawson White*, 367. Clay's real dislike of Webster is discussed by Van Buren in his *Autobiography*, 677–79.

Passing through eastern Tennessee, he appeared frankly in the rôle of a canvasser for votes. With old-time fire, he denounced his erstwhile friend, the Senator, as a Federalist — a discovery he had but recently made; and with all the fervor of Jacksonian friendship he held Van Buren up as the purest and most uncompromising of Democrats. The domineering quality of his leadership flared in his declaration that no friend of White's could be other than his own enemy. At Blountville, Jonesboro, Greenville, Newport, Lebanon, and Nashville — every point he touched — he delivered political harangues in conversations with the friends and admirers who flocked to greet him.[1] Thus he employed every method known to electioneering, short of actually taking the stump.

This effort of the President was met by White with a powerful speech at Knoxville, where a banquet in his honor was arranged for the purpose. "It is not I who am to be put down and disgraced in this controversy, if Tennessee is either coaxed or coerced to surrender her choice," he said. "The Saviour of the World, when upon earth, found among the small number of His disciples, one Judas, who not only sold but betrayed him for his thirty pieces of silver. It were vain for one of my humble attainments, who has nothing to offer but his best efforts to promote the public welfare, to hope that all who professed to be his friends must continue to act up to that character. Already have I found more than one Judas, who, by parting with their interest in me, have received, or expect to receive, more than twice their thirty pieces." [2] Thus, however tame the campaign elsewhere, it was a hand-to-hand struggle in the President's own State — and here Jackson was to meet the greatest humiliation of his career.

[1] For Jackson's activities in Tennessee see *Memoir of Hugh Lawson White,* 356.

[2] White's speech, *Memoir of Hugh Lawson White,* 346–55.

IX

The elections in 1836 were not held on the same day in all the States, and from November 4th, when Pennsylvania and Ohio voted, until November 23d, when the election was held in Rhode Island, the politicians were kept in suspense, and it was not until the first week in December that the Democrats were able to rejoice in the certainty of their victory. Massachusetts, which then idolized her Webster, gave him her electoral vote, and stood alone. South Carolina, which had encouraged White to enter the contest, again sulked, and, going outside the list of avowed candidates, gave hers to Senator Willie Mangum, of North Carolina. White greatly disappointed the Whigs, who had expected him to get enough votes in the Southern and Western States to throw the contest into the House of Representatives, by carrying only Tennessee and Georgia. Harrison received the electoral votes of Delaware, Indiana, Kentucky, Maryland, New Jersey, Ohio, and Vermont — a total of 73; while Van Buren won Connecticut, Maine, New Hampshire, and Rhode Island in New England; Alabama, Arkansas, Louisiana, Mississippi, Missouri, North Carolina, and Virginia in the South; Illinois and Michigan in the West; and both the most important States in the Union, Pennsylvania and New York. With only 124 electoral votes divided among his four opponents, Van Buren had 170, a majority of 46.

However, in the results the more prescient of the Democratic leaders could find ample justification for concern as to the future. The votes of Georgia, Indiana, New Jersey, Ohio, and Tennessee, which had gone to Jackson four years before, had been lost by Van Buren, and he had gained only Connecticut. But the electoral vote does not indicate the full extent of the Democratic slump. The popular vote in some of the States he had carried had fallen off woefully from the previous election. The Democratic majority in Virginia had decreased from 22,158 to 6893; in Illinois from 8718 to 3114; in North Carolina from 20,299 to 3284. As compared with Jackson's popular majority of 157,293 in 1832, Van Buren won only on a popular majority of 24,893 out of a total of 1,498,205 votes cast. In his own State of New York, however, he increased Jackson's popular majority of 13,601 in 1832 to 32,272.

In White House circles there were some painfully humiliating features in the results, and to none more than to Jackson. The people of Tennessee gave White a majority of 10,000, and even in the President's own precinct, White received 43 votes to 18 for Van Buren. In Georgia, the home of the President's Secretary of State, John Forsyth, the people turned from the candidate of the Georgian, who was so intimately identified with Van Buren's political fortunes that he was to be retained at the head of the Cabinet through the new Administration, to give their vote to White. In Tennessee, the result was not unnatural. The President overestimated his strength in assuming that he could persuade the people to reject their neighbor and fellow citizen, who had served them well, for a New York politician. In Georgia the turnover was political, due to the ascendancy of the radical State-Rights party, and the strength of the Nullifying element which Forsyth had courageously fought.

The result of the congressional elections even more impressively indicated the drift away from the Jacksonian policies. The Democratic majority in the House during the Twenty-Fourth Congress, of 46, was reduced in the next Congress to a plurality of 2 over the Whigs, with 10 independent members holding the balance of power. Whether this was due to a reaction against the Democratic Party, or merely measured the loss of the personal prestige of Jackson as the candidate, was the problem that gave concern to the Democracy. If Van Buren looked forward with any misgivings to his Administration, however, he gave no sign; and

Jackson, if chagrined over his loss of Tennessee, was masterful in dissimulation. There was as much jubilation in the Democratic camp as though the victory had been as decisive as that of four years before. When the electoral votes were being counted, Clay turned to Van Buren with the observation: "It is a cloudy day, sir." "The sun will shine," replied the smiling Red Fox, "on the 4th of March, sir." [1]

[1] *Perley's Reminiscences*, I, 198.

CHAPTER XVI

TWILIGHT TRIUMPHS

I

JACKSON returned to the White House after the election in a serious physical condition. The exertions of the hot summer, the long and wearisome journey, the keen disappointment over the loss of Tennessee, and his humiliation over his defeat in the Hermitage precinct, had greatly weakened the old lion. The return journey to the capital had increased his debility, and soon after reaching the White House he was driven to his bed by a hemorrhage of the lungs. Ill almost to death, no word of sympathy reached him from his foes, and from his bed he grimly directed and encouraged the counter-attacks with the spirit of the Jackson of New Orleans. In his final Message to Congress, he paid tribute to the fidelity and integrity of his subordinates, and in ordinary times this would have been permitted to pass unchallenged in view of his early relinquishment of power. But the times were not ordinary. The last short session was to be one of extraordinary bitterness, with personal altercations commonplace, and with statesmen of prominence toying all too lightly with their pistols.

Thus the tribute to the subordinates of the Executive departments was eagerly seized upon by Henry A. Wise, the brilliant and impassioned young Whig of Virginia, as a pretext for a bitter personal attack — one of the most severe, satiric, sarcastic philippics to be found in the records of Congress from the first session to the present hour. The way was paved for it through the presentation of a resolution providing for the appointment of a special committee to deal with that portion of the Message to which Wise took exception. He summoned to his purpose all the accumulated charges of eight years of rancorous party warfare, marched them with a militant swing before the House, and demanded an investigation to determine, on the eve of the stricken President's departure from public life, whether he had been falsely accused. Had Jackson actually made such claims for his subordinates? he asked. No, he had not even written the Message because physically unfit. "It comes to us and the country reeking with the fumes of the Kitchen Cabinet."

The excited Representatives gathered about the young orator were not kept long in doubt as to the particular object of his attack. Describing Jackson's electioneering activities in Tennessee, Wise dropped the veil: "I am told," he said, "that they carried him around like a lion for show, and made him roar like a lion. They had catechisms prepared for him, and the negotiations of the mission were conducted by preconcerted questions and answers. A crowd would collect on the highway, or in the bar-rooms, and some village politician of the party would inquire, 'What think you, General, of such a man?' In a loud tone, much too stentorian for those lungs which are now lacerated, the answer rang, 'He is a traitor, sir.' 'There, there,' repeated the demagogues in the crowd, 'did you not hear that?' 'What think you of another, General?' 'He is a liar, sir.' 'What of another?' 'He made a speech for which he paid a stenographer five dollars.' And another was 'on the fence sir, on the fence.' 'But, General, what think you of Mr. [the first time that Reuben was ever called 'Mister'] Reuben M. Whitney?' 'There is no just cause of complaint against Mr. Whitney, sir; he is as true a patriot as ever was; they are all liars who accuse him of aught of wrong.'"[1] Thus it was evident from the speech of Wise that the attack was aimed at Whitney, erroneously described by some historians as a member of the Kitchen Cabinet,[2]

[1] Appendix, *Cong. Globe*, 2d Session, 24th Congress, 274–77.
[2] Schouler, IV, 133.

but nevertheless entrusted with the public money. Little can be said in defense of Jackson's confidence in this man, who had been ferociously assailed in the House in the preceding spring by Wise and Balie Peyton, a hot-headed Whig from Tennessee. With the clever support of the Democrats, the resolution was adopted and Wise was made chairman of the investigating committee. This investigation, probably intended merely as a peg on which to hang partisan harangues against the stricken President, to whose physical condition Wise had made sneering reference, accomplished nothing.

Before the committee had got fairly started, it struck a snag in a personal altercation in the committee room between Peyton and Wise on one side, and Whitney on the other, resulting in the refusal of the latter to appear again unless assured that members of the committee would attend unarmed! The balking witness was thereupon cited for contempt and dragged to the bar of the House; and the clever Administration leaders quickly grasped the opportunity to divert attention from the main question to the arrogant, violent methods of the hot-headed young Whigs in charge. Thus Whitney set himself to the task of proving that he could not appear before the committee without serious danger of assassination. Witnesses to the altercation, on which he based his conclusion, were summoned, and a week was consumed in the hearing of evidence and the cross-examination of witnesses.

The incident on which Whitney based his fears is graphically described in the testimony of John Fairfield, a Representative from Maine.[1] The picture painted of the committee room scene is not inspiring. Whitney had declined to answer a question because of reflections on his integrity by Peyton, and it seems that he had gone so far as to scowl at the Tennessee Hotspur in explaining his refusal. It was a day when honor was a sensitive plant, and Peyton sprang to his

[1] Afterward Senator.

feet with a promise to "take his life upon the spot." The equally fiery Wise, ever ready for a combat, rose to the occasion, and took his position beside his irate colleague with the comment that "this damned insolence is intolerable." Encouraged by the open sympathy of Wise, the Tennesseean began to meditate aloud, as on the stage, on the enormity of the insult, and to mutter that he would not be insulted "by a damned thief and robber." His passion, feeding on his hot meditations, and his excitement growing greater, he wheeled upon Whitney, who, alarmed, sprang to his feet and claimed the protection of the committee. "Damn you — damn you!" shouted the white-faced Peyton, "you shan't say a word while in this room — if you do I will put you to death." With these words he put his hand to his bosom and moved toward the object of his fury, and Wise and other members of the committee tried to calm the infuriated statesman. "Don't, Peyton," cried Wise, "damn him, he is not worth your notice." Somewhat mollified by this assurance, the insulted Representative sank into his chair — but his blood still boiled. "Damn him, his eyes are upon me!" he cried as in a melodrama. "Damn him, he is looking at me — he shan't do it!" By this time it was thought possible to calm the nerves of the jumpy Peyton if the witness, whose eyes were so offensive, could be removed from the room; and as he passed out, Wise requested the committee to remain seated to prevent an encounter in the corridor.[1] Thus far the impulsive Virginian appeared in the favorable light of a peacemaker, but, finding pleasure in the narration of the manner in which the hated minion of the Administration had been frightened out of his wits, he began to boast that his purpose in getting close to Whitney had been to shoot him at the slightest provocation, and he was thus drawn into the controversy along with Peyton.

Nothing could have been more pleasing to the political

[1] Fairfield's testimony, *Cong. Globe*, 2d Session, 24th Congress.

managers of the Administration. Before the galleries, packed to hear the eye-witnesses, the two Whigs began to appear more and more as quarrelsome, pistol-toting bullies taking advantage of their position to browbeat and intimidate an unprotected witness. The Democratic press, under the inspiration of Blair and Kendall, devoted columns to the evidence, and sentiment was turned against the Whig leaders until they began to complain that they, and not Whitney, were apparently at the bar. "Sir," Wise declared, "it is I who am on trial and not Reuben M. Whitney. I have no doubt of the contrivance to make this issue before the country. . . . I wish to know, sir, if there are not other officers of the Government who have issued the order that the power of this House, and the Executive power of the country, are both to be brought to bear upon two humble and inexperienced members of the House. Sir, I have felt it."

The affair had now worked around to the distinct advantage of the Administration, and Wise and Peyton, and not Jackson, were in distress. The psychological hour had struck to end the farce. The motion to dismiss Whitney was made and carried, and when the name of Wise was called, he solemnly rose:

"Mr. Speaker," he said, "I shall not vote until I ascertain whether I am discharged from prosecution or not."

As the smiling House offered no information, his name is not recorded among those voting. Thus the one offensive against Jackson, launched by his enemies on the eve of his relinquishment of power, ended in a riproaring farce.

II

In the Senate the offensive was taken by Jackson's supporters when Benton served notice that he would demand a vote on his motion to expunge the vote of censure from the records. Much water had passed over the dam since the persistent Missourian had first offered his resolution. With the aid of the Kitchen Cabinet, he had made it a national issue. The fight had been carried into the States of the Senators who had voted for the censure, and, in numerous instances, the offending member had either been defeated for reëlection, or the legislature had been prevailed upon to instruct him to vote to expunge. One of the opponents of the Benton resolution had died and been succeeded by a Jackson sympathizer. Through defeat, or resignations forced by instructions from legislatures, enemies had given place to friends from Connecticut, New Jersey, North Carolina, Illinois, Mississippi, and Virginia. New Senators, friends of Jackson, had entered from the new States of Arkansas and Michigan. A private poll convinced Benton that the triumph was at hand, all the sweeter because coming on the eve of Jackson's retirement. The day after Christmas he reintroduced his original resolution, and on January 12th supported it in a speech laudatory of Jackson — a pæan of anticipated triumph. The old man, always a trifle pompous and stilted in his style, was never more so, but in his most extravagant praise he unquestionably spoke the language of his heart. Beginning by recalling the discouraging circumstances under which he first offered his resolution, he gloatingly declared that the Opposition had become "more and more odious to the public mind and musters now but a slender phalanx of friends." The people had been passing on the censure; had passed upon it in the triumph of Van Buren, who had publicly proclaimed his adherence to the plans of Benton. He would not rehash the constitutional arguments. The debate had ended and the verdict had been rendered, but the occasion called for some reference to the achievements and triumphs of the Administration. Then he hastily sketched its battles, claiming in the aftermath of each the vindication of events — the destruction of the Bank, the removal of the deposits, the triumphant termination of the controversy with the French.

"And now, sir," he concluded, as we may imagine with his chest thrown out, "I finish the task which, three years ago, I imposed upon myself. Solitary and alone, and amidst the taunts and jeers of my opponents, I put this ball in motion. The people have taken it up and rolled it forward, and I am no longer anything but a unit in the vast mass which now propels it. In the name of that mass, I speak. I demand the execution of the edict of the people; I demand the expurgation of that sentence which the voice of a few Senators and the power of their confederate, the Bank of the United States, has caused to be placed upon the journal of the Senate, and which the voice of millions of freemen has ordered to be expunged from it."

Thus spoke the champion of Jackson in the tones and manner of a conqueror. As he resumed his seat, John J. Crittenden of Kentucky rose to protest against the "party desecration" of the record, and after a few words from Senator Dana, who favored the expunging record, the Senate adjourned. On the following day some of the great orators of the Opposition were put forward to oppose the resolution.

We are told by an eye-witness that the eloquent Preston "spoke in a strain of eloquence inspired by his feelings of great aversion."[1] If Benton was theatrical, as has been justly charged by historians, the Whigs were even more so, as we shall see. Beginning with great solemnity, and describing his shock and sorrow, Preston proceeded:

"Execution is demanded — aye, sir, the executioners are here with ready hands. Exercise your function, gentlemen. . . . The axe is in your hand — perform that which is so loudly called for. Execution, sir, of what, of whom? Is the axe aimed at men who voted for the resolution you are about to expunge? Is it us you strike at? If so, . . . in God's name let the blow come, and as the fatal edge fell upon my neck, I would declare with honest sincerity that I would rather be

[1] Sargent's *Public Men and Events*, I, 334.

the criminal of 1834 than the executioner of 1837." More: the names of the Senators refusing to expunge would in the future "be familiar as household words" and be "taught to children as the names of Washington and Adams and Hancock and Lee and Lafayette are now taught to our children."

A moment later the orator's pensive melancholy had turned to rage.

"Why not expunge those who made the record?" he thundered, forgetting how many had been "expunged." "If the proceedings had a guilt so monstrous as to render necessary this novel and extraordinary course, the men themselves who perpetrated the deed — it is they who should be expunged. Men who entered so foul a page upon the journal cannot be worthy of a seat here. Remove us! Turn us out! Expel us from the Senate! Would to God you could! Call in the pretorian guard! Take us — apprehend us — march us off!" [1]

After Rives and Niles had spoken in support of the resolution, Calhoun mournfully rose, and with funereal sadness, not unmixed with scorn, pointed out the resemblance of the proceedings to the degenerate days of Rome. "But why do I waste my breath?" he asked, in conclusion. "I know it is all utterly vain. The day is gone; night approaches, and night is suitable to the dark deed we meditate. There is a sort of destiny in this thing. The act must be performed; and it is an act that will tell on the political history of this country forever. . . . It is a melancholy evidence of a broken spirit, ready to bow at the feet of power. The former act [2] was such a one as might have been perpetrated in the days of Pompey and Cæsar; but an act like this could never have been consummated by a Roman Senate until the times of Caligula and Nero."

After Calhoun concluded, unsuccessful efforts to adjourn

[1] Appendix, *Cong. Globe*, 2d Session, 24th Congress, 135.

[2] Removal of deposits.

were made, until Clay announced his intention to speak at length, and his request for delay was granted. Had his supporters realized how far from absolute certainty of success Benton felt, they would have favored, instead of fought, an adjournment. The following day was Saturday, and a careful poll disclosed the disconcerting diversity of opinion as to details which threatened the success of the project, and Benton gladly agreed to a postponement of the discussion until Monday. That night the then famous restaurant of Boulanger found all the Jacksonian Senators seated about the banquet board. The clever host had loaded the table with his choicest offerings, and as soon as the statesmen had reached the mellow, accommodating mood, they settled down to the real purpose of the feast. Realizing that he lacked the deftness and finesse required for ironing out all differences as to details, Benton had assigned the work of conciliation to Silas Wright, Allen of Ohio, and Linn of Missouri. Even so, it "required all the moderation, tact, and skill of the prime movers to obtain and maintain the union upon details, on the success of which the measure depended." [1] But when, at midnight, the Senators dispersed, all conflicting views had been reconciled, and for the first time an actual majority was pledged to a single programme. It was decided to call the resolution up on Monday, and to keep it constantly before the Senate, without adjournment, until the "deed" was done.

To prevent any of his flock from wandering afield in search of refreshments, Benton had made ample preparations, and a tourist, wandering into Benton's committee room at four o'clock on Monday afternoon, would have assumed, in view of the vast quantities of cold ham, turkey, rounds of beef, pickles, wines, and coffee, that he had stumbled into a senatorial café. That day, Clay appeared in the Senate ostentatiously garbed in black as though in mourning for the murdered Constitution. So ugly was his mood that he even

[1] *Thirty Years' View,* I, 727.

refused snuff offered by a Democratic Senator he knew was going to vote to expunge. The galleries were packed to witness the drama, or melodrama, and impatiently sat through the preliminary work of the Senate. At length the hour came for the consideration of the resolution, and all eyes turned to Clay, who thoroughly enjoyed his rôle in the play. As his tall form slowly rose, there was a rustling in the galleries as the spectators shifted their position to get a better view of the great enemy of Jackson. On his feet, he stood a moment in silence, as though weighed down by the importance of his task, if not by its hopelessness. Then he began in subdued tones, albeit his silvery voice was heard distinctly over the chamber. Such a hardened observer of historical incidents as Sargent describes the scene as "grand, impressive, and imposing," and "even solemn," as though "some terrible rite was to be performed, some bloody sacrifice to be made upon the altar of Moloch."[1]

"What object?" he demanded. Was it necessary because of the President? "In one hand," he continued, "he holds the purse, and in the other he brandishes the sword of the country. Myriads of dependents and partisans, scattered all over the land, are ever ready to sing hosannas to him, and to laud to the skies whatever he does. He has swept over the Government during the last eight years like a tropical tornado. Every department exhibits traces of the ravages of the storm. . . . What object of his ambition is unsatisfied? When, disabled from age any longer to hold the scepter of power, he designates his successor, and transmits it to his favorite, what more does he want? Must we blot, deface, and mutilate the records of the country, to punish the presumptuousness of expressing any opinion contrary to his own?

"What object?" demanded Clay. "Do you intend to thrust your hands into our hearts and pluck out the deeply rooted convictions which are there? Or is it your design merely to

[1] Sargent describes Clay's manner and the effect, *Public Men and Events*, I, 337–39.

stigmatize us? Standing securely upon our conscious rectitude, and bearing aloft the Constitution of our country, your puny efforts are impotent; and we defy all your power.

"What object?" reiterated the orator. "To please the President? He would reject, with scorn and contempt as unworthy of his fame, your black scratches and your baby lines in the fair records of his country. Black lines. Black lines. . . . And hereafter, when we shall lose the forms of our free institutions, all that now remain to us, some future American monarch, in gratitude to those by whose means he has been enabled, upon the ruins of civil liberty, to erect a throne, and to commemorate especially this expunging resolution, may institute a new order of knighthood, and confer on it the appropriate name of the 'Knights of the Black Lines.'"

But why continue, he inquired, as he closed his fierce philippic. "Proceed then with your noble work. . . . And when you have perpetrated it, go home to the people, and tell them what glorious honors you have achieved for our common country. Tell them that you have extinguished one of the brightest and purest lights that ever burned on the altar of civil liberty. Tell them that you have silenced one of the noblest batteries that ever thundered in defense of the Constitution, and bravely spiked the cannon. Tell them that henceforth, no matter what daring or outrageous act any President may perform, you have forever hermetically sealed the mouth of the Senate. Tell them that he may fearlessly assume what powers he pleases, snatch from its lawful custody the public purse, and command a military detachment to enter the halls of the Capitol, overawe Congress, trample down the Constitution, and raze every bulwark of freedom; but that the Senate must stand mute, in silent submission, and not dare to raise its opposing voice."

Such the theatrical strain of a speech which the schoolboys of well-regulated Whig families were to declaim for the delight of their elders for a generation, and to call forth a fulsome note from the sober-minded Kent.

As Clay sat down, James Buchanan rose to reply, admitting that it was the part of prudence to remain silent after the Whig orator had "enchanted the attention of his audience." Fluent, logical, if not eloquent, he followed Clay's speech point by point, rehashing with him the Bank controversy — leading up to the removal of the deposits and the vote of censure — defending Jackson at every step. If Jackson's act was one of tyranny, unconstitutional, aimed at civil liberty, why, he demanded, "had the Whigs merely censured him without giving him the opportunity to reply? Why had they not done their duty and instituted impeachment proceedings? True, they insisted that they had not imputed any criminal motive to the President —"

Clay was instantly on his feet, hotly insisting that "personally he had never acquitted the President of improper intentions." To which the courtly Buchanan replied with a compliment to the Kentuckian's "frank and manly nature," and passed on.

The Whigs now attempted to adjourn, but Benton's drilled forces were on hand to vote down Bayard's motion, and the debate proceeded. Other speakers followed, men of lesser light, while the Senators themselves, satiated with the arguments, began to pass out in twos and threes to regale and refresh themselves in Benton's room. Such of the Whigs as were not too bitter were cordially invited to partake of the feast, and some accepted. Clay sent some of his friends to the committee room to ascertain the nature of the attraction, and the emissaries lingered too long over the meat, and especially the drink, and he became furious. With the coming of night the curious packed the corridors and lobbies, and the great chandelier which lighted the little chamber shed its glow on the gay dresses of the ladies of fashion, many of whom had been admitted to the floor.

As the hour grew late, and there was a pause in the debate, the eyes of all were fixed on Webster, who sat gloomily in his seat. He glanced around to see if others proposed to speak, then rose to make the final protest. An eye-witness tells us that "his dark visage assumed a darker hue"; that "his deep-toned voice seemed almost sepulchral." [1] As was his custom, he spoke with more moderation than Clay, Calhoun, or Preston, and was all the more impressive on that account. He refrained from hysterical denunciations, and from comparisons with the degenerate days of Rome. "But," he said, "we make up our minds to behold the spectacle which is to ensue. We collect ourselves to look on in silence while a scene is exhibited which, if we do not regard it as a ruthless violation of a sacred instrument, would appear to us to be but little elevated above the character of a contemptible farce. This scene we shall behold, and hundreds of American citizens — as many as may crowd into these lobbies and galleries — will behold it also — with what feelings I do not undertake to say."

Reiterating, then, his protest, he concluded: "Having made this protest, our duty is performed. We rescue our own names, characters, and honor from all participation in this matter; and whatever the wayward character of the times, the headlong and plunging spirit of party devotion, or the fear or the love of power, may have been able to bring about elsewhere, we desire to thank God that we have not, as yet, overcome the love of liberty, fidelity to true republican principles, and a sacred regard for the Constitution, in that State whose soil was drenched to a mire by the first and best blood of the Revolution."

While Webster was speaking, two Whig Senators, realizing that the contest had degenerated into a trial of nerves and muscle, went to Benton with the suggestion that nothing could be gained by delaying the vote.[2] When no one rose to

[1] Sargent, *Public Men and Events* I, 341. [2] *Thirty Years' View*, I, 730.

continue the argument at the conclusion, there was a moment of silence and then the cry of "Question" rose. The roll was called, with forty-three Senators in their seats, five absent, and the resolution was passed by a vote of 24 to 19.

Benton instantly demanded the execution of the order of the Senate. While the clerk was out to get the original journal, Benton, in perfect ecstasy, ostentatiously congratulated persons in the lower gallery, until the glowering countenance of Balie Peyton warned him of a possible explosion.[1] But the Tennessee firebrand was not the only person in the gallery, or, for that matter, on the floor, with a deadly hate of Benton in the heart. The galleries remained true to the Bank and Biddle, and some of the Senators, having freely indulged themselves, were in a quarrelsome mood. Fear was entertained for Benton's life by some of his friends, including his wife. Just previous to the vote, Senator Linn had brought in pistols for the defense, if required, and Mrs. Benton, seriously alarmed, took her place by her husband's side on the floor. As the clerk returned with the record, the defeated statesmen, pretending to a patriotism that could not look upon the "deed," filed out of the chamber — all but Hugh Lawson White who never deserted his post. As the President *pro tem* announced that the "deed" was done, the hitherto sullen and silent gallery broke into groans, hisses, imprecations. Enraged and excited, Benton sprang to his feet with the demand that the "ruffians" that caused the disturbance be apprehended and brought to the bar. "I hope the sergeant-at-arms will be directed to enter the gallery, and seize the ruffians. . . . Let him seize the Bank ruffians. I hope they will not be suffered to insult the Senate as they did when it was under the power of the Bank of the United States when ruffians, with arms upon them, insulted us with impunity. . . . Here is one just above me that may easily be identified — the Bank ruffians!"

[1] Wise, *Seven Decades of the Union*, 143.

Thus the ringleader was dragged to the bar. But here was a diversion that had not entered into the agreement as to details at Boulanger's on Saturday night, and the wrangle that followed ended in the discharge of the culprit from custody. As the vote to discharge was announced, the person in custody demanded to be heard. "Begone!" cried King, in the chair — and the incident was closed. But Benton's blood was hot, and on leaving the Capitol he encountered Clay, whom he suspected of having instigated the gallery disturbance, and a bitter altercation resulted. But after the two men, personally not unfriendly and related by marriage, had exercised their vituperative vocabulary, Benton insisted on seeing Clay home, and did not leave until three in the morning when Clay had sought his couch. Thus ended a dramatic episode — so dramatic and historic that on the following morning Webster requested Henry A. Wise to prepare a description which was afterwards given in an address at Norfolk.[1]

The triumph, we may be sure, was sweet to the stricken veteran in the White House. Within a week he invited all his senatorial friends and their wives to an elaborate dinner. Hovering on the verge of the grave, he dragged himself from his bed to greet his guests, accompanied them to the dining-room, seated Benton in his place at the head of the table, and retired to his couch, while the celebration below continued until a late hour.

III

THE last days of Jackson in the White House could not have been other than days of joyous thanksgiving. Entering the White House the most popular of all Americans, eight years of the most bitter controversies in the Nation's history had only tended to strengthen the affections of the people. Through the greater part of his Presidency he had been con-

[1] Wise, *Seven Decades of the Union*, 144.

stantly harassed by a hostile Senate, and his enemies had been defeated or otherwise retired, until now both branches of the Congress were devoted to his policies. His most powerful enemies had been humiliated. The prize of the Presidency dangling before Calhoun in the beginning was now forever beyond his reach. Clay had been defeated in his ambition and shamefully set aside by his ungrateful party. The man of his own choice had been elected to succeed him, and the hated censure of the Senate had been expunged by the order of the people. Few Presidents have ever departed from the scene of their power with more for which to be grateful and less to regret.

But the old man had run his race and been surfeited with the sweets of personal triumphs, and was eager to return to the calm of his beloved Hermitage, among his old and cherished friends and faithful slaves, and near to the tomb of his idolized Rachel. By sheer will power he had fought back the specter which had hovered by his sick-bed, to this end. Confined to his room most of the time, debilitated by age and disease, the old man's mind was not free from anxieties for the future of his country. He knew too well the temper of public men, and comprehended too keenly the delicate problems pressing for solution, not to know that there were dangers ahead. It was his desire to give some parting advice to the people in his final Message, but he was persuaded to convey his last word in the form of a "Farewell," like Washington. To the preparation of this paper he devoted much time and thought during the last two months, and, while he had the assistance of Roger B. Taney in the phrasing of his thoughts, all the ideas, and much of the language, originated with him. Strangely enough, the "Farewell" of Jackson is scarcely known, and some historians are prone to smile upon it as an unworthy imitation of the Washington paper. It was nothing of the sort. It smacks, in large part, of prophecy. The man who wrote it saw, in fancy, the swaying columns of the blue and gray, and he strove to avert the clash. The old hero of the Nullification fight, feeble and sick, bending over his desk in the White House of 1837, was writing and pleading in the spirit of the Lincoln of 1861 as he wrote his touching inaugural appeal for peace.[1] Having finished his "Farewell," to be given out on the day of leaving office, the old man impatiently awaited his release. His friends, he knew, would not suffer by the change. The Jackson Cabinet was to be continued, with the exception of Cass, who was to be sent to France, thus making way for Joel Poinsett, who had been Jackson's right hand in the Nullification struggle.

On Washington's birthday he received the public in a farewell reception, famous because of the mammoth cheese donated by admirers, greater in circumference than a hogshead. Two men with knives made from saw blades cut into the enormous mass, giving each guest a piece weighing from two to three pounds. Some, who had provided themselves with paper, wrapped their portion and bore it away as a souvenir; others, not so thoughtful, carried theirs in their hands. Much of it crumbled in the hands of the bearers and was trampled on the floor. It was Jackson's farewell, and thousands pushed their way into the White House, and, after getting their portion of the cheese, pressed on into the Blue Room, where the President, much too feeble to stand, received and greeted his visitors from his chair. Beside him stood the cordial Mrs. Donelson, while just behind him Martin Van Buren greeted all with a smile and a courtly bow.[2]

IV

THE Jackson of the White House would have commanded attention in any assembly, even to the last. More than six feet in height and slender to attenuation, his limbs long and

[1] Richardson, *Messages and Papers.*

[2] Wilson, *Washington the Capital City*, I, 328.

straight, and his shoulders slightly stooped, he carried himself proudly, and not without grace. His white hair stood erect, giving a full view of a forehead that indicated intellectual power. His eyes, deep-set, clear but small, were blue in color and noticeably penetrating, and the great spectacles he wore accentuated their boring quality. These eyes, flashing with the fierceness of the fight, could easily melt, in tenderness, to tears. His strong cheek-bones and lantern jaws denoted the warrior. His strongly chiseled chin and firm mouth told of his inflexibility. His chest was flat, and indicated his most pronounced physical weakness. Seen upon his walks about Washington, wearing his high white beaver hat, with his widower's weed, and carrying a stout cane adorned with a silken tassel, he looked the part of the patriarch who could either bestow a benediction or a blow. Throughout his two terms his health was wretched, and time and again, stricken with disease, his death had seemed only a matter of days, but the iron will prevailed over the failing flesh. His hair grew whiter. The lines in his face deepened. His step lost some of its spring. He was forced to abandon his long walks and the pleasures of the saddle, and remain more and more in the White House. But the eye retained its fire, his voice its fervor, and his spirit never flagged. In moments of relaxation, toward the close, there was a softened expression, but in his fighting moments he differed little from the grim old man who entered the mansion of the Presidents as Adams took his departure.

The libels of his enemies of the Whig aristocracy notwithstanding, he had not been unworthy, socially, of the stately traditions of his environment, and had impressed all visitors with his fine courtesy, courtliness, ability, and graciousness.[1] Never before or afterwards were there such incongruous

[1] Mrs. Wharton, *Social Life of the Republic*, 261; Wise, *Seven Decades of the Union*, 81; Seward, *Autobiography*, I, 278; Frederick Seward, *Reminiscences of a War-Time Statesman and Diplomat*, 17; Quincy, *Figures of the Past*; Powers, *Impressions of America*.

crowds at the receptions, but this disclosed less the taste of the master of the Mansion than his political principles; and his dinners in tone and taste commanded the admiration of his enemies.[1] These receptions and dinners had drawn heavily on his resources, and toward the close left him seriously embarrassed. He himself could have lived on monastic fare. A weak stomach forced him to eat sparingly, and he often dined on bread, milk, and vegetables; but there were always guests at the table, which was invariably ladened as for a feast.[2]

Perhaps it was not without regret that he passed through the rooms of the historic house in those last days, for he had converted the White House into a home, and it was rich in memories of the sort that tug at the heart. Fond of his family, and especially of the young women members, this "home" had been the scene of several marriages and christenings. The beautiful Emily Donelson, the wife of his secretary and niece, the mistress of the mansion, had presided with grace and dignity and brightened the days and nights. In a physical sense she was an exquisite woman, of medium height, her figure slender and symmetrical, her hands and feet as tiny as a child's. Her hair and eyes were a dark brown, her lips beautifully moulded, her complexion fair. Many found in her a striking resemblance to Mary, Queen of Scots, as she appears in her pictures. Her taste in dress was beyond reproach, and soon after entering the White House her toilette was "the envy and admiration of the fashionable circles."[3] Her judgment in social matters was infallible, and Jackson depended upon her advice. "You know best, my dear, do as you please," was his only suggestion when delicate problems were submitted to him. Fond of society, vivacious, dignified, and always gracious, she not only com-

[1] Hone's *Diary*, March 15, 1832; *Life and Letters of Story*, II, 117.

[2] Letter of John Fairfield, quoted from manuscript by Professor Bassett in his *Life of Jackson*.

[3] Holloway, *Ladies of the White House*.

manded admiration, but affection. An excellent conversationalist, she possessed the art, so seldom found in good talkers, of being an ingratiating listener. In contact with the brightest minds of the capital, she lost nothing by the comparison. "Madame, you dance with the grace of a Parisian," remarked a condescending foreign minister. "I can hardly realize that you were born in Tennessee." "Count," she retorted, "you forget that grace is a cosmopolite, and, like a wild flower, is much oftener found in the woods than in the streets of a city." During her days in the White House her four children were born, and Jackson, who was delighted to have childhood about him, took a keen interest in their christenings. He was godfather for two, Van Buren for one, and Polk — all Presidents — for the other.

• Another of the White House women was Sarah Yorke Jackson, daughter of Peter Yorke, of Philadelphia, and wife of another nephew. She was much younger than Mrs. Donelson, having been married but a short time before the inauguration, but Jackson, fearing some misunderstanding as to precedence, called them together and announced his will. "You, my dear," he said to Mrs. Jackson, "are mistress of the Hermitage, and Emily is hostess of the White House." The arrangement was satisfactory to both, and no misunderstandings marred their relations. Mrs. Jackson was happily indifferent to social prestige, but in the spirit of helpfulness did her part. Highly accomplished and beautiful, graceful, and possessed of wonderful poise in one so young, she was intensely devoted to Jackson, and the old man reciprocated the affection in full measure.

Usually, in the evening, Jackson gathered his family about him, and if Senators, diplomats, or Cabinet Ministers appeared, they were drawn into the family circle. If the business which brought them happened to be of importance, he would, perhaps, draw them into a distant part of the simply furnished parlor which was lighted from above by a chandelier. In the winter the fire blazed in the grate, and, arranging their chairs about the fireplace, the women applied themselves to their sewing while gossiping of the events of the day. Here would be found Mrs. Jackson and Mrs. Donelson, perhaps Mrs. Livingston, possibly Mrs. McLane, or some other woman of the White House circle. Playing about the room would be five or six children in irreverent disregard of the old man in the long loose coat, seated in an armchair, smoking his long reed-stem pipe with a red clay bowl. Mayhap Livingston or Van Buren or Forsyth would be reading him an important dispatch from a foreign minister, while the children, with their shouts and screams, would all but drown the voice of the visitor. Nothing disturbed by the clamor, the old man would bend forward and listen more intently. Perhaps he would wave his long-stemmed pipe toward the rowdies, with an apologetic smile. But never a cross word.

The hour for retirement would come. The children would withdraw and be tucked in their beds. The President would go to his room. There he would sit awhile at the table, and, by the light of a single candle, would read a chapter from the Bible that had belonged to Rachel, and then gaze awhile at her picture propped up before him. The light would be snuffed. The old man would retire, and the negro bodyguard would lie down on the floor and join his master in sleep. Suddenly a child's cry would penetrate the President's chamber, and he would awaken — and listen. Then he would get up, go to the room of the little one, and, brushing objections aside, take it in his arms and walk the floor with it until it slept. This was not an unusual occurrence.[1]

After breakfasting in the morning, Jackson would go to his office, on the second floor, and, lighting his pipe, would settle down to the routine work of the day. Bookshelves lined the room. Busts of the President, the work of various sculptors,

[1] Holloway, *Ladies of the White House*, and Mary Crawford, *Romantic Days of the Young Republic*, 22–23.

and a number of portraits, all by Earle, looked upon the original from shelves and tables. There flocked the politicians, Lewis with a report, Blair with a leader, Kendall with a programme. There he planned and fought his battles with the politicians, but when evening came he looked forward to the joys of domesticity, or the diversions of the company of women upon whom he looked "with the most romantic, pure, and poetic devotion.[1] The accomplished Mrs. Livingston would enliven him with her vivacious conversation on all manner of topics, her daughter Cora would delight him with her animation and wit, and his eyes would fill when Mrs. Philip Hamilton, daughter of McLane, responded to his never-failing invitation to play and sing his favorite song from Burns. Mrs. McLane, an attractive and entertaining chatterbox, with interested motives for attempting to fascinate the old warrior, was always a welcome diversion, and Mrs. Rives, the stately wife of the Virginia Senator; Mrs. Macomb, wife of the General; and Sallie Coles Stevenson, who resembled Mrs. Livingston in intelligence and tact, were frequent guests. These had given to the White House something of the charm of the Hermitage; but at times, in the bitterness of the continual struggle, when the old man grew weary of the bauble of power, and felt his faith in mankind slipping, and homesickness for the Hermitage possessing him, he had often laid aside the cares of state, turned his back upon the scene of his struggle and the house of his triumphs, and walked across the Avenue to the home of the Blairs, where he knew he could find a haven of rest. There he knew he could appear, not as the head of the State, but as Andrew Jackson of the Hermitage. It became his second home. There he could forget his enemies, and, in the homey atmosphere of a house pervaded by the personality of a sincere and unaffected woman, he could revive his fainting spirits.

But he was surfeited with triumphs, and the Hermitage

[1] Wise, *Seven Decades of the Union.*

called him home to the tomb of Rachel. The twilight was closing in upon him. He knew it was time to go.

V

THE dawn of inauguration day found him so ill and debilitated that he should have remained in bed, but the soldier spirit of the man refused to yield to the promptings of the flesh. He was up early, doing his full part. The day was ideal — as Van Buren had promised Clay. The clear sky, the bright, cheery sunshine, the balmy air could not have been better ordered for the distinguished invalid. A great throng stretched back from the east front of the Capitol to witness the historic scene, and the eastern windows were packed with the more favored spectators. It was plainly to be seen from the attitude of the multitude that the real reverence and enthusiasm was for the leader whose race was run, rather than for his successor. "For once," observed Benton, "the rising was eclipsed by the setting sun." The old man, feeble and bowed, sat listening to the inaugural address of the man he had elevated to the highest office in the world. Van Buren concluded. Jackson rose and began slowly to descend the steps of the portico to his carriage which was waiting to convey him back to the White House. At that moment, the pent-up feelings of the crowd burst forth in cheers and acclamations. "It was the acclaim of posterity breaking from the bosom of contemporaries," wrote Benton. The old man, deeply touched to tenderness and humility, acknowledged his appreciation by mute signs. From one of the upper windows a rough fighting man witnessed the scene with an emotion he had never felt before. From thence, Benton looked down upon the close of a memorable "reign," of which he was to become the historian as he had been its defender.

That night Jackson slept as usual in the White House as the guest of President Van Buren, who insisted that he remain in his old quarters until in May or June the trip back to the Hermitage could be made in greater comfort, but the journey held no terrors for the homesick statesman. The following afternoon he walked across the Avenue to the home of Frank Blair for a final visit with the family within whose bosom he had passed many joyous hours during the eight years of storm and stress. A little later, Benton called with William Allen, then Senator from Ohio, and for many years the world knew nothing of the nature of that final conference. Benton himself was mysteriously silent, nor did he furnish any enlightenment in his great history of the "Thirty Years." But long after most of the participants in the politics of that day were mouldering in the grave, Blair and Allen told the story to one of the President's biographers. Jackson talked, and the others listened. He told them of his two principal regrets — that he had never had an opportunity to shoot Clay or to hang Calhoun. He had no regrets because of his crushing of the Bank, nor because of his encouragement of the spoils system. But he left office feeling that his work would have been more nearly completed if Texas had been annexed and the Oregon boundary dispute had been settled at fifty-four-forty. To his loyal supporters he left one admonition that afternoon:

"Of all things, never once take your eyes off Texas, and never let go of fifty-four-forty."

The following day witnessed his departure. He took with him the picture of Rachel which had been upon his desk through his eight years of trial, her Bible, to which he had been devoted, her protégé Earle, the artist, who was to remain with him at the Hermitage, and to be buried in its peaceful shade.

Thus ended the reign of Andrew Jackson.

THE END

BOOKS, PAPERS, AND MANUSCRIPTS CITED AND CONSULTED

BOOKS, PAPERS, AND MANUSCRIPTS CITED AND CONSULTED

ABDY, EDWARD S., *Journal of a Tour of the United States.* 3 vols. London, 1835.

ADAMS, JOHN QUINCY, *Memoirs* of, ed. by C. F. Adams. 12 vols. Philadelphia, 1876.

AMBLER, CHARLES HENRY, *Thomas Ritchie: A Study of Virginia Politics.* Richmond, 1913.

Anonymous, *Life of Lewis Cass.* Detroit, 1848.

BABER, GEORGE, *The Blairs of Kentucky. Register Kentucky Historical Society,* XIV.

BASSETT, JOHN SPENCER, *Life of Andrew Jackson.* 2 vols. New York, 1911.

BENNETT, JAMES GORDON. *See* Isaac C. Pray.

BENTON, THOMAS H., *Thirty Years' View, or a History of the Working of the American Government from 1820 to 1850.* New York, 1861. *See* Theodore Roosevelt.

BEVERIDGE, ALBERT J., *Life of John Marshall.* 4 vols. Boston, 1916–19.

BIDDLE, NICHOLAS. *See* Reginald C. McGrane.

BINNEY, C. N., *Life of Horace Binney.* Philadelphia, 1903.

BINNEY, HORACE. *See* C. N. Binney.

BLAIR, GIST, *The Annals of Silver Springs. Columbian Historical Society,* XXI.

BRADLEY, CYRUS P., *Life of Isaac Hill.* Concord, 1835.

BRANCH, JOHN. *See* Marshall de Lancey Haywood.

BUCHANAN, JAMES. *See* John Bassett Moore.

BUELL, AUGUSTUS C., *Life of Andrew Jackson.* 2 vols. New York, 1904.

BUTLER, WILLIAM ALLEN, *A Retrospect of Forty Years.* New York, 1911.

CALHOUN, JOHN. *See* John Stilwell Jenkins, H. von Holst, Richard K. Cralle.

CASS, LEWIS. *See* Andrew C. McLaughlin, W. L. G. Smith, William T. Young, Anonymous.

CATTERALL, RALPH C. H., *The Second Bank of the United States.* University of Chicago, 1903.

CLAY, HENRY. *See* Calvin Colton, Carl Schurz, Joseph M. Rogers.

CLAYTON, JOHN M. *See* Joseph P. Comegys.

COLTON, CALVIN, editor, *Works of Henry Clay.* 10 vols. New York, 1904.

COMEGYS, JOSEPH P., *Memoir of John M. Clayton.* Wilmington, 1882. *Papers, Historical Society of Delaware,* vol. 4.

CRALLE, RICHARD K., editor, *Works of John C. Calhoun.* 6 vols. New York, 1883.

CRAWFORD, MARY C., *Romantic Days of the Early Republic.* Boston, 1912.

CRAWFORD, WILLIAM H. *See* J. E. D. Shipp.

CROCKETT, DAVY, *Life of Martin Van Buren.* Philadelphia, 1835.

CURTIS, GEORGE TICKNOR, *Life of Daniel Webster.* 2 vols. New York, 1870.

DAVIS, JEFFERSON, *The Rise and Fall of the Confederate Government.* 2 vols. New York, 1881.

ELLET, E. F., *Court Circles of the Republic.* Hartford, 1869.

FISHER, SIDNEY GEORGE, *The Real Daniel Webster.* Philadelphia, 1911.

FISKE, JOHN, *Historical and Political Essays.* 2 vols. New York, 1902.

FOOTE, HENRY S., *A Casket of Reminiscences.* Washington, 1874.

FORSYTH, JOHN, manuscript letters.

FOSTER, JOHN W., *A Century of American Diplomacy.* Boston, 1901.

HALE, EDWARD EVERETT, *Memories of a Hundred Years.* 2 vols. New York, 1902.

HAMILTON, JAMES, *Reminiscences of Hamilton, or Men and Events at Home and Abroad During Three Quarters of a Century.* New York, 1869.

HAMILTON, THOMAS, *Men and Manners in America.* 2 vols. Philadelphia, 1833.

HAMMOND, JABEZ D., *Life of Silas Wright.* New York, 1848.

HARRISON, W. H. *See* H. Montgomery.

HART, ALBERT BUSHNELL, *American History Told by Contemporaries.* New York, 1902.

HARVEY, PETER, *Reminiscences of Daniel Webster.* Boston, 1877.

HAYNE, ROBERT Y. *See* Theodore Dehon Jervey.

HAYWOOD, MARSHALL DE LANCEY, *John Branch* (pamphlet). Raleigh, 1915.

HILL, Isaac. *See* Cyrus P. Bradley.

HOLLAND, W. H., *Life of Martin Van Buren.* Hartford, 1835.

HONE, PHILIP. *Diary.* New York, 1889.

HOUSTON, DAVID F., *A Study of Nullification in South Carolina.* New York, 1896.

HUNT, CHARLES HAVENS, *Life of Edward Livingston.* New York. 1902.

HUNT, GAILLARD, *First Forty Years of Washington Society* (Letters of Mrs. Samuel Harrison Smith). New York, 1906.

HUNT, LOUISE LIVINGSTON, *Life of Mrs. Edward Livingston.* New York, 1902.

JACKSON, ANDREW. *See* James Parton, Augustus C. Buell, John Spencer Bassett, William Graham Sumner, William MacDonald, Charles H. Peck, Francis Newton Thorp, Frederic Austin Ogg.

JACKSON, R. P., *The Chronicles of Georgetown*, Washington, 1878.
JENKINS, JOHN STILWELL, *Life of John C. Calhoun* (Arlington edition). *Life of James K. Polk*. Buffalo, 1850.
JERVEY, THEODORE DEHON, *Robert Y. Hayne and His Times*. New York, 1909.
JOHNSTON, ALEXANDER, *American Political History*. 2 vols. N. Y., 1905.

KEMBLE, FRANCES A., *Records of a Girlhood*. New York, 1884.
KENDALL, AMOS, *Autobiography*. Boston, 1902.
KENNEDY, JOHN P., *Life of William Wirt*, 2 vols., Philadelphia, 1849.
KNIGHT, LUCIAN LAMAR, *Reminiscences of Famous Georgians*. Los Angeles, 1907.

LABORDE, MAXIMILIAN, *History of South Carolina College*. Columbia, 1859.
LEGARÉ, HUGH SWINTON, *Works*. 2 vols., ed. by sister. Charleston, 1846.
LINDER, USHER F., *Reminiscences of the Early Bench and Bar of Illinois*. Chicago, 1879.
LIVINGSTON, EDWARD. *See* Charles Havens Hunt.
LIVINGSTON, MRS. EDWARD. *See* Louise Livingston Hunt.
LODGE, HENRY CABOT, *Life of Daniel Webster*. Boston, 1883 (American Statesmen).

MACDONALD, WILLIAM, *Jacksonian Democracy*. New York, 1906 (The American Nation).
MCGRANE, REGINALD C., *Correspondence of Nicholas Biddle*. Boston, 1919.
MCKEE, THOMAS H., *National Conventions and Platforms*. Baltimore, 1906.
MACKENZIE, WILLIAM L., *Life of Martin Van Buren*. Boston, 1846.
MCKINNEY, THOMAS LORRAINE, *The Office-Holder's Sword of Damocles*. *See* Albert Bushnell Hart.
MCLAUGHLIN, ANDREW C., *Life of Lewis Cass*. Boston, 1899 (American Statesmen).
MCMASTER, JOHN BACH, *History of the People of the United States*. 8 vols. New York (Library edition), 1914.
MARCH, CHARLES W., *Reminiscences of Congress*. New York, 1853.
MARRYAT, CAPT. FREDERICK, *A Diary in America*. 2 vols. Philadelphia, 1839.
MARTINEAU, HARRIET, *A Retrospect of Western Travel*. 2 vols. London, 1838.
MILLER, S. F., *The Bench and Bar of Georgia*. 2 vols. Philadelphia.
MONTGOMERY, H., *Life of William Henry Harrison*. Cleveland, 1852.
MOORE, JOHN BASSETT, *Works of Buchanan*. 12 vols. Philadelphia, 1908.

NORTHERN, WILLIAM JONATHAN, *Men of Mark in Georgia*. Atlanta, 1907.

OGG, FREDERIC AUSTIN, *The Reign of Andrew Jackson* (*Chronicles of America*, vol. x.) Yale University Press, 1919.

O'NEALL, JAMES BELTON, *Bench and Bar of South Carolina.* 2 vols. Charleston, 1859.

PARTON, JAMES, *Life of Andrew Jackson.* 3 vols. New York, 1860.

PAYNE, GEORGE HENRY, *A Short History of Journalism in the United States.* New York.

PECK, CHARLES H., *The Jacksonian Epoch.* New York, 1899.

POINSETT, JOEL R. *See* Charles J. Stille.

POLK, JAMES K. *See* John Stilwell Jenkins.

POORE, BENJAMIN PERLEY, *Reminiscences of Sixty Years in the National Metropolis.* 2 vols. Philadelphia, 1886.

PRAY, ISAAC C., *Memoirs of James Gordon Bennett.* New York, 1855.

QUINCY, JOSIAH, *Figures of the Past from Leaves of Old Journals.* Boston, 1883.

RICHARDSON, JAMES DANIEL, *Messages and Papers of the Presidents.* 10 vols. Washington, 1900.

ROGERS, JOSEPH M., *The Real Henry Clay.* Philadelphia, 1905.

Life of Thomas H. Benton. Philadelphia, 1905 (American Crisis).

ROOSEVELT, THEODORE, *Life of Thomas H. Benton.* Boston, 1890 (American Statesmen).

SARGENT, NATHAN, *Public Men and Events.* 2 vols. Philadelphia, 1875.

SATO, SHOSUKE, *History of the Land Question in the United States. Johns Hopkins University Studies*, IV, 259–441.

SCHOULER, JAMES, *History of the United States of America under the Constitution.* 5 vols. New York, 1889–91.

SCHURZ, CARL, *Life of Henry Clay.* 2 vols. Boston, 1887 (American Statesmen).

SCOTT, NANCY N., *Memoir of Hugh Lawson White.* Philadelphia, 1856.

SEWARD, FREDERICK, *Reminiscences of a War-Time Statesman and Diplomat.* New York, 1916.

SEWARD, WILLIAM H., *Autobiography.* 3 vols. New York, 1891.

SHEPARD, EDWARD M., *Life of Martin Van Buren.* Boston, 1899 (American Statesmen).

SHIPP, J. E. D., *Life of William H. Crawford.* Americus, Georgia, 1908.

SMITH, OLIVER H., *Early Indiana Trials and Sketches.* Cincinnati, 1858.

SMITH, MRS. SAMUEL HARRISON. *See* Gaillard Hunt.

SMITH, W. L. G., *Life of Lewis Cass.* New York, 1856

SPARKS, W. H., *Memories of Fifty Years.* Philadelphia, 1882.

STANWOOD, EDWARD, *History of Presidential Elections in the United States.* Boston, 1912.

American Tariff Controversies of the Nineteenth Century. Boston, 1903.

STILLÉ, CHARLES J., *Life and Services of Joel R. Poinsett* (pamphlet). Philadelphia, 1888.

STORY, JOSEPH. *See* W. W. Story.

STORY, W. W., *Life and Letters of Joseph Story.* 2 vols. Boston, 1851.

SUMNER, WILLIAM GRAHAM, *Life of Andrew Jackson.* Boston, 1882 (American Statesmen).

TANEY, ROGER B. *See* Samuel Tyler.

TAUSSIG, F. W., *A Tariff History of the United States.* New York, 1888.

THORP, FRANCIS NEWTON, *The Statesmanship of Andrew Jackson.* New York, 1909.

TYLER, LYON GARDINER, *Letters and Times of the Tylers.* 2 vols. Richmond, 1884.

TYLER, SAMUEL, *Memoir of Roger Brooke Taney.* Baltimore, 1872.

VAN BUREN, MARTIN, *Autobiography*, edited by John C. Fitzpatrick. *American Historical Association Report*, 1918, vol. II.

VIGNE, GODFREY T., *Six Months in America.* Philadelphia, 1833.

VON HOLST, H., *The Constitutional and Political History of the United States.* 6 vols. Chicago, 1889.

Life of John C. Calhoun. Boston, 1886 (American Statesmen).

WEBSTER, DANIEL. *See* Henry Cabot Lodge, Peter Harvey, George Ticknor Curtis, Sidney George Fisher, and Fletcher Webster.

WEBSTER, FLETCHER, *Private Correspondence of Daniel Webster.* 2 vols. Boston, 1857.

WEED, THURLOW, *Autobiography.* 2 vols. Boston, 1884.

WHARTON, ANNE HOLLINGSWORTH, *Social Life of the Early Republic.* Philadelphia, 1902.

WHITE, HUGH LAWSON. *See* Nancy N. Scott.

WILLIS, N. P., *American Scenery.* 3 vols. London, 1840.

WILSON, RUFUS R., *Washington the Capital City.* Philadelphia, 1901.

WILSON, WOODROW, *History of the United States.* 5 vols. New York, 1902.

WIRT, WILLIAM. *See* John P. Kennedy.

WISE, BARTON, *Life of Henry A. Wise.* New York, 1899.

WISE, HENRY A., *Seven Decades of the Union.* Philadelphia, 1872. *See* Barton Wise.

WRIGHT, SILAS. *See* Jabez D. Hammond.

Congressional Debates and *Congressional Globe*, 1830–37.

The National Intelligencer, 1829–37.

The Washington Globe, 1831–37.

Documentary History of the U.S. Capitol Buildings and Grounds. House Doc. 646, 58th Congress, 1st Session.

Biographical Congressional Directory. Senate Doc. 654, 61st Congress, 2d Session.

John Forsyth MSS., in possession of Waddy Wood, Washington, D.C.

INDEX

INDEX